The Practice of Special Education

A Reader edited by WILL SWANN
for the *Special Needs in Education* Course Team
at the Open University

BASIL BLACKWELL
in association with
THE OPEN UNIVERSITY PRESS

First published 1981
Reprinted 1983, 1985, 1986

Basil Blackwell Ltd
108 Cowley Road, Oxford OX4 1JF, UK

Basil Blackwell Inc.
432 Park Avenue South, Suite 1503
New York, NY 10016, USA

British Library Cataloguing in Publication Data

The practice of special education
    1. Exceptional children — Education
    I. Swann, Will
    371.9   LC3955
    ISBN 0-631-12879-4
    ISBN 0-631-12885-9 Pbk

Typeset by Cambrian Typesetters, Aldershot, Hants
Printed in Great Britain by
Page Bros (Norwich) Ltd

Contents

Preface   viii

General introduction   ix

Part One   Handicap: the Individual and the Environment

1.1   How children cope   2
       Monika Jamieson, Malcolm Parlett and
       Keith Pocklington
1.2   Sociological perspectives on mild mental retardation   13
       Jane R. Mercer
1.3   Physical handicap in children: sources of variation   25
       Jean Golding
1.4   The effects of lead pollution on children's development   41
       The Lawther Report and The Conservation Society
       Report
1.5   Early influences on development: fact or fancy?   64
       Arnold J. Sameroff

Part Two   The History of Special Education

2.1   Mental handicap: the historical background   80
       Joanna Ryan and Frank Thomas
2.2   The origins of special education   93
       Gillian Sutherland
2.3   Maladjustment: a history of the category   102
       Irene Bowman

Part Three   Varieties of Special Provision

3.1   Young children with special needs in ordinary schools   122
       Maurice Chazan, Alice Laing, Michael Shackleton
       Bailey and Glenys Jones

3.2   A junior school resource area for the visually impaired   136
       Seamus Hegarty and Keith Pocklington
3.3   Special provision for PH pupils in secondary schools   153
       Christine Cope and Elizabeth Anderson
3.4   Whose remedies, whose ills? A critical review of
       remedial education   173
       Michael Golby and John R. Gulliver
3.5   Intermediate treatment, special education and the
       personalization of urban problems   187
       Peter Beresford and Suzy Croft
3.6   Special provision in post-school education   208
       John Panckhurst

Part Four   Parents, Children and Professionals

4.1   Parents and professionals   226
       John Gliedman and William Roth
4.2   From normal baby to handicapped child: unravelling
       the idea of subnormality in families of mentally   242
       handicapped children
       Timothy A. Booth
4.3   Professionals and ESN(M) education   260
       Sally Tomlinson
4.4   The provision of health services to handicapped
       children and their families   278
       The Court Report

Part Five   Power and Policy in Special Education

5.1   Demystifying integration   288
       Tony Booth
5.2   Finance and policy-making in special education   314
       J.R. Lukes
5.3   Handicap in Northern Ireland: a special case?   335
       Fiona Stephen
5.4   Education can compensate   353
       A.H. Halsey
5.5   The end of a quiet revolution: the United States
       Education for All Handicapped Children Act, 1975   359
       Alan Abeson and Jeffrey Zettel
5.6   Street level bureaucrats and institutional innovation:
       implementing special education reform   378
       Richard Weatherley and Michael Lipsky

Part Six   Research, Theory and Practice

6.1   The role of psychological research in special education   400
       Chris Sinha
6.2   Theory and research in classrooms: lessons from deaf
       education   417
       David Wood
6.3   Principles of curriculum and methods development in
       special education   435
       D.J. Power

Index   448

Preface

This collection forms part of the Open University course E241: Special Needs in Education. Many people have contributed to the selection, revision and preparation of papers. Material was selected by Tony Booth, Keith Pocklington, Patricia Potts, Will Swann, David Thomas and Richard Tomlinson. Early assistance was given by Carolyn Baxter and a very considerable amount of work in the preparation of the manuscript was done by Sue Sheldon.

Twelve of the twenty-eight papers comprising this book are published here for the first time; the remainder has been selected and edited from many different sources. This diversity produced some editorial problems. In edited material omissions are indicated by the sign: [. . .], editorial insertions necessary for coherence have been placed in square brackets, and some editorial notes, marked as such, have been prepared to aid the reader. Complete consistency of referencing style has not been possible, thus some papers use footnotes, others in-text references. Obvious misprints and mistakes in previously published material have been corrected, but idiosyncratic style and non-standard English spellings have not been altered.

General Introduction

Representing the whole of special education in one book is a formidable task, and comprehensive coverage is simply not possible. The contributions that make up this book have been chosen to illuminate key issues in the field. We have made no attempt to cover the full range of handicaps, of settings, or of approaches to their analysis. However the brief is general and is not tied to the special school system or even to the education service. Papers describe provision in special schools, ordinary schools and outside schools. And although we had no intention to deal systematically with categories of special need, most are represented. Where groups, such as children with epilepsy, are omitted, we hope that the issues discussed will prove pertinent and will stimulate further investigation.

The notion of practice is often narrowly defined to mean classroom practice. But in choosing a title for this book we have tried to give the word a much wider meaning, for the practices that affect children's lives are carried on by people at all levels of the education system. The practices of policy-makers and LEA-based professionals are as significant to the experience of children with special needs and their families as are the practices of teachers. We have set out to provide critical analyses of this full range of practices in special education.

The contributions have been arranged into six sections. In Part One, five papers are assembled which put forward the view that handicap is not simply a feature of individuals nor the result of individual defects. The causes and nature of handicap involve individual and social factors, and these interact in many complex ways to determine the lifestyle of children. This is of course equally true of all children. It is in a sense highly artificial to leave out of this section many contributions later on which show the vital role education plays in this process, for if we take seriously the idea that handicap is the result of, and a property of, interactions between children and settings, then the implications for education are profound.

Part Two turns to the origins and growth of special education in the UK. Historical studies in the past have often tended to be restricted to the development of small specialist provision, often established by voluntary agencies or philanthropists, and they have frequently had a feeling of steady progress towards meeting special needs. The papers in this section look at the origins of provision for the much larger groups of slow and difficult children whose education is closely tied to the emergence of mass education, and provision for mentally handicapped people, whose right to an education at all was established only ten years ago.

In Part Three, we have compiled six papers which reflect current practices and illuminate the possibilities for change in special schooling. They illustrate how educators attempt to meet needs in various settings, and the problems and limitations they face in doing so. These papers provide many examples of the way education can both ameliorate and exacerbate children's problems. Sometimes special education is a useful response to individual needs that enables a child to function within the settings we all live in; on other occasions, and for other children, special provision reflects fundamental, structural problems in ordinary education and in our society. It can be said that some children fail in school, but it can also be said with equal force that schools fail some children. Special provision may be an attempt to repair or prevent the former, but it is difficult to justify it for the latter.

Part Four is about one very prominent aspect of most handicapped children's and their parents' lives – the professionals they encounter. All of them are ostensibly in business to help children and their families, yet it would take little time to discover that many parents see matters very differently. Often professionals appear to act not in the interests of parents and children, but for 'the system', themselves or their masters. The four contributions in this section focus on different aspects of the frequently uneasy relationship between professionals, their employers and their clients.

Contributions in Part Five take a wider view of the context of special education. It is a serious criticism of the field to date that writers have been too prepared to look no further than the classroom door. Yet the lives of children in and out of school depend upon social, political, ideological and economic forces. Enhancing the quality of their lives may require changes in these more pervasive and powerful factors, rather than only piecemeal innovations in classroom practice that may be thwarted by the very forces they are intended to overcome.

Finally, Part Six returns to the classroom to look at the contribution that theory and research, particularly in child development, can make to special education. Despite much effort being devoted to the investigation of the development of handicapped and normal children, the impact of this research has been notably small. Where psychological thinking, in particular, has been introduced into classrooms it is not always obvious that it has had a beneficial effect on the children's experience. The three contributions in this section look at recent developments in this area; they provide some insights into why applications of research have not always been successful and they offer some models for a more effective strategy.

In sum, this is a book about how our education system copes with children with special needs. It is as much a book about the successes and failures of education as it is about the abilities and disabilities of children. We often think of special education in a positive manner, for the persuasive force of the term is considerable. Children receiving special education, we think, must be getting something extra, something worthwhile and they must have special needs that have been clearly determined. But this image on its own is highly misleading, and thorough analysis requires that we are not persuaded by the emotive force of 'special' to believe automatically that it *is* special. This book or any other cannot on its own provide anything near to a full analysis of the actual practice of special education, but analysis is desperately needed if all children are eventually to receive an education appropriate to their interests, needs and desires. Understanding what happens at the moment is a necessary part of trying to change it.

PART 1

Handicap: the Individual and the Environment

1.1 How children cope

MONIKA JAMIESON, MALCOLM PARLETT AND KEITH POCKLINGTON

It is very easy to fall into the trap of basing educational decisions on the nature of a disability and not on the nature of the child who has that disability. But to understand handicapped children, as much as any child, is to know them as people with personal identities in particular social milieux. In the study from which this extract comes, the authors investigated the lives of visually handicapped children in ordinary schools using this approach. Here, they show how a child's physical defect is only one component in a constellation of individual and social factors that determine his or her success and happiness at school. Handicap is not a characteristic of individuals, but of individuals in social settings, and it may change as rapidly as the individual or the setting changes. No more or less is true of everyone.

What is 'coping'?

Persistently, throughout our study, the question was raised about whether or not visually impaired pupils could 'cope' in ordinary school settings, especially when they received little or no support. We discovered, too, that a major component in decisions about retaining children in integrated settings was an evaluation of how well the child was 'coping'. The term 'coping' seems to have become an important if not crucial one in the lexicon of discussions about integration. Virtually a 'catch-phrase', it is used to describe, question and shed doubt or light upon a visually impaired pupil's ability to relate to the many different facets of his or her life at school.

As researchers new to this field of study, we were surprised by how often the term was used and by the variety of meanings it seemed to have acquired. People used the term 'coping' in arguments, they talked about it, were concerned about it — as if it meant something precise and specific, clearly understood by all involved. In reality, however, the term means different things to different people; it is a convenient 'umbrella

Source: Jamieson, M., Parlett, M. and Pocklington, K. (1977) *Towards Integration: a study of blind and partially sighted children in ordinary schools*, Windsor, NFER–Nelson Publishing Company Ltd

word' embracing a whole host of personal and educational adaptations. Coping may mean no more than 'keeping your head above water', a response very different from 'full achievement of academic and social potential'. It may denote 'distinct progress' or merely 'survival'. Our research has shown that 'successful integration' was frequently defined by both teachers and parents as a situation in which a pupil 'coped'. For them, coping and success had become synonymous.

In order to gain a better understanding of the concept, it is necessary to bear in mind several points. *First*, every visually impaired child's condition, circumstances, personality, strength, and adaptation are different. We have been constantly reminded of the importance of considering 'the individual needs of the child'. Coping, ultimately, relates to individual response. *Second*, in assessing the demands made upon a visually impaired child, the sighted cannot fully transpose themselves into the shoes of the blind or partially sighted and may not understand how difficult or easy particular concepts or demands are for them. Factors that facilitate or undermine adequate coping may be difficult to fathom. *Third*, as soon as a visually impaired child enters an ordinary school, he or she faces the demands of a dominant 'culture' where dependence upon sight is the norm – that child is immediately at a disadvantage, called upon to 'prove' him or herself before being granted a licence to continue. Coping, in this milieu, is defined quite differently from the way it would be in, say, a school for the blind. Definitions of coping vary with different social expectations. *Fourth*, there are two realms of activity in which integrated pupils are expected to cope if they are to be judged successful; 'achieving academic potential' and 'deriving social benefit' are the coveted goals. In practice, a pupil may be held to be coping in one sphere and not in the other without being labelled a 'failure'. Coping is divisible.

In unravelling the widescale use of 'coping', let us consider in more detail what the integrated pupil is required to deal with at school. First, some teacher-governed and formal tasks or demands: that the child follow lessons on the blackboard (a possible visual problem); that the child read, write and possibly draw to a certain standard, with limited allowance perhaps made for speed, legibility and clarity; that the child join in the majority of curriculum activities and participate in most class projects (be 'of' the class, not just 'in' it). Second, there are other implicit rather than explicit adaptations called for: being expected to form reciprocal relationships with peers; making friends, being accepted, participating with peers in classroom and extracurricular activities; not becoming too dependent upon peers; gaining their respect; and putting up with the teasing inevitably encountered. Integrated pupils also need to be able to handle the 'singling out' which they may experience as a result of sitting at the front of the class in order to see; to accept 'missing out' on activities which fall beyond their scope of vision; and finally they may periodically have to put up with the natural expectation that they can see when they cannot and, when they cannot, to make some explicit and public acknowledgement of this.

To meet the formal requirements, a number of physical resources are available, including low vision aids, and technical aids such as tape recorders, large print books, typewriters and magnifiers. There are also certain widely understood and accepted procedural modifications to teaching practices. These include greater verbalization on the part of the teacher, less reliance on blackboard work, permitting the child to have lesson notes, and making concessions for his or her slowness. There are other related allowances that can be made: for instance, the child may be given extra attention, either by being withdrawn from the class, or within the class itself by a supply teacher or the class teacher if he or she has time. There are additional 'resources' available to help the child handle the less explicit adaptations required: peers may be (indeed often are) sympathetic; the child's condition may be carefully explained so that its severity is properly understood; peers may make allowances both in the playground and the classroom; and singling the child out for particular activities or constantly placing him at the front of the class can be deliberately played down.

We can identify, therefore, a number of 'adaptations demanded' and 'supports proffered', some of which are spelled out and others that are known about by the parties concerned but are not always widely acknowledged. Some children will need more of the supports than others to make the adaptations; some will use the supports with more fluency or public visibility than others. Certain teachers or particular circumstances may call for a greater degree of adjustment by the child, and the child's degree of adaptation will be affected by the rigour of the demands made, the accessibility of useful supports, and by the child's own capacity to deploy supports to meet demands.

Judgments about a child's ability to cope in the ordinary school draw in other factors —particularly the child's 'personality', 'the influence of home' and 'the allowances made by the school'.

[Here we] will concentrate on the child's personality — particularly those aspects that may be influential in determining how well a child with a vision loss contends with an integrated school life.

The critical role of 'confidence'
Some of the most influential 'personal characteristics' thought to be

significant in contributing to 'successful integration' are intelligence, confidence, independence, sociability and an ability to come to terms with impaired vision. Some of these characteristics are more basic than others and have a more general effect upon a child's total adaptation. In particular, we can single out 'confidence'.

Confidence – however difficult for psychologists to define, operationalize, or adequately measure – seems to affect every facet of a child's life. Pupils in our study, who were consistently identified as lacking confidence, were those held to be coping less well than others. Often their future in integrated education was in doubt.

It is clearly artificial to isolate personal characteristics from home attitudes, school concessions, the severity of vision loss, and the external constraints and demands. Nevertheless, for purposes of the present discussion, let us examine the central factor of confidence by looking at one or two case histories.

Susan was an 11-year-old suffering from congenital cataracts on both eyes. She attended her local junior school. She was registered as partially sighted, had a visual acuity of 6/24[1] with correcting glasses and a severely contracted field of vision. Although Susan continued in integrated education, her future there was questionable. She was thought to have 'little confidence'. Here are some extracts from case notes written up at the time of our visit.

On transferring to infants school at the age of five, the nursery teacher told Susan's infant teacher that she was 'nearly blind'. Susan was not a 'particularly active child', and these two problems combined resulted in her being left by herself, largely ignored, since she was little trouble to the staff. Her mother clearly felt that she had been 'held back' by not being allowed to play under the same conditions as non-handicapped children. She claimed that the infants head had made fun of Susan because of her visual difficulties and her 'reticent personality'.[2]

Susan appeared to have been ignored, teased, and defined as 'a clinging child' during her first school experience. At junior school, 'much of the first year seems to have been spent in undoing the harm that the negative approach of the infants school had resulted in'.[3] She joined an ordinary class but also received individual attention from a home tutor. But educational progress was slow. Since a psychologist had once assured Susan's mother that she was a 'very bright child', she blamed the schools for Susan's lack of confidence. Her teachers described Susan as 'sluggish . . . totally lacking any initiative': her mother, on the other hand, saw her as 'very active, never still'. Her mother was confident that 'it is just a question of gaining her interest', yet her class teacher described Susan as 'in her class, but not *of* it. It may seem that I'm ignoring her, but there's not much she can do with the rest.' She claimed that Susan had an 'inflated view of herself' and attributed this to 'too much help' in the past. Her reticence and 'sluggishness', it was agreed, were the result of a total 'lack of independence' rather than of vision loss *per se*.

Peer relations were also affected by Susan's personality: she was described as 'withdrawn' and 'immature', she had 'done nothing' to gain respect or admiration from her classmates. Not surprisingly, she was excluded from many informal activities. That she was an 'outsider', an 'isolate', was not perhaps helped by her physical appearance, (she was overweight and wore thick glasses). Of her classmates, her class teacher commented, 'some have got used to her, but some still regard her as a freak'. She had no 'real friends' and 'the ones (children) on her table (are those who) tolerate her the most'. She was the victim of considerable teasing.

In short, Susan's case demonstrates how easily children with an added educational handicap may come to have a 'dented morale'. Susan was not particularly gifted academically and she certainly lacked confidence – manifested in her questionable independence, her reticence to capitalise upon special help, and her social immaturity.

Our second example is Karen, a 10-year-old girl, with dislocated lenses.[4] She was described as 'a happy youngster'. Until recently she attended an ordinary school and was thought perfectly able 'to cope' by both her parents and teachers. The latter felt that academically she had 'kept her head above water quite well'. No one felt that she was being unduly teased nor that she was unhappy. She was, however, variously described as a 'very quiet girl . . . timid . . . wary . . . afraid . . . reserved . . . does not mix well'. Her friends often tended to be other 'isolates' in the school and friendship was thought often to be based on 'friendly consideration'. While both her parents and teachers acknowledged Karen's visual impairment, they made every attempt to treat her 'normally'.

It was, in fact, Karen who recently decided that she did not want to remain in the ordinary school. She did not feel she was achieving as well as she might academically and would prefer to be in a school where those around her would 'know' of her situation and where there would be no need to 'explain it'. Her mother finally agreed that a special school 'would encourage Karen to go out more and gain greater confidence'. There would be 'activities designed to boost confidence, for example, doing the shopping for old people'. At present, she only went out with her brother, too afraid to be 'caught out' by giving the wrong money or by mis-identifying the article she wanted to buy.

At the time of transfer it was found that there was in fact considerable teasing by her peer group and that she was over-dependent upon friends to shield and protect her from it: 'She cannot always stand up for herself completely on her own . . . Karen still lacks confidence . . . We (her parents) did not realize how dependent she was upon Dick (her brother) until he went to school . . . She is only confident with friends.'

A number of the individual case histories reflect the same emphasis on the fundamental need for confidence. Confidence so often forms the basis of further adaptations, in particular, a realistic acceptance of visual impairment and adjusting to its limitations. Consider Robert's success. He was 15, partially sighted[5] and attended a local comprehensive. His teachers enumerated a number of factors that had helped him: in all of them one sees evidence of (and further reinforcement for) a sense of personal confidence.

He is conscientious, determined, hard-working . . . he tries all the time . . . his disability has forced him to think in original ways . . . he is as bright, if not brighter than those in his class . . . he likes to please . . . he is determined to do well . . . he is prepared to accept his handicap and to soldier on . . . he is in a good class, with sympathetic classmates – half the battle is being in a class with a good atmosphere . . . if he were unaware of his limitations, more withdrawn or less intelligent, he would not integrate – he would be a partially sighted delinquent . . . he gets a tremendous drive from home.

Robert himself felt that integration was not the panacea for everyone. In order to succeed he felt it was necessary to be intelligent and, also, confident – 'have a nerve, be determined, not frightened, not shy, and not imagine that I couldn't do all the things that others do'.

Understanding coping

We have focused on coping for several reasons. There was our swift discovery of its frequent use, already mentioned. Second, in advocating more integrated provision, one argument is that children with vision loss should 'learn to cope' with an environment that is as normal – i.e. sighted – as possible; yet here again, 'learning to cope' is rarely examined with any precision. Third, many of those holding a middle-ground position advocate a modest increase of integrated provision for 'suitable children who can cope', with special schools held in reserve for children who cannot. Lastly, the topic seems a general one, certainly applicable throughout special education and to a lesser extent in perhaps all spheres of schooling. Moreover, coping — as tolerably successful self-management — is not even confined to the domain of education but recurs, as an idea, throughout the helping professions.[6] Arguably, if coping is so predominant an idea in currency, it should be better understood than it is.

What we have done so far is to point out a number of different concomitants or contributory resources that favour successful coping for children with a vision loss in local schools. Some of these resources are personal: the child's intellectual capability and self-confidence being pre-eminent, along with the degree of functional vision. Some of the resources derive from the family, from a child's pre-school experience, early assessment, diagnosis and guidance. Parents and siblings may give practical assistance, encouragement, and can inject positive attitudes. (Some parents may, however, be over-protective, neglectful, uninformed. Failure to encourage independence, activity and self-reliance may have far-reaching effects on a child's personal resources.) Other resources are institutional: the school or itinerant advisory teacher can provide assistance — e.g. aids, concessions, timetable modifications, special tutoring, as well as encouragement and a high level of acceptance.

Although we appear to have picked upon a single factor, confidence, and to have elevated it into first place, all the evidence points towards a complicated interaction of many different factors. On the one side are all the resources, the pluses; on the other, all the demands to be met and difficulties to be overcome, the minuses.

A boy with reasonable functional vision, who has academic interests, is able and confident; who comes from a supportive, relaxed, and interested home, who is personable and physically good looking; who has a teacher who is interested in him but does not draw attention to his poor sight, is sensitive to his special requirements and explains why, on a particular occasion, these requirements cannot be met; who is in a class that is supportive but that does not fuss or pamper him, is — almost by definition — successfully coping with the classroom reality of integration: the pluses clearly outweigh the minuses.

Another boy, however, more retiring and without marked ability; with less functional vision and perhaps a slight physical handicap as well; coming from a home, say, where the parents have separated and there are several siblings; and attending a school where the teacher does not appreciate how little he can see but draws attention to his unusual status or lets him drift along behind the rest of the class, is — in terms of integration — a child 'at risk': the pluses are fewer and the minuses may easily come to outweigh them.

This kind of simple 'cost accounting' exercise can be useful, (and is applicable to decisions both about special and ordinary education). When it is said 'that attention is given to the total needs of the child' (in placement or school transfer decisions), the professional is more than likely to be running through some similar kind of mental checklist and drawing up a balance sheet of pluses and minuses. If a child comes from 'a supportive home', has 'the right kind of personality', 'has a good school history', and 'does not read too slowly', then the prognosis for a successful integrated experience seems good: the child will cope. However, if the child has had a previously poor school experience, is lacking in confidence, reads slowly, and has, say, a slight impairment of hearing as well, the prognosis is less favourable and special schooling may be indicated.

The 'cost accounting' and 'checklist' approaches to predicting a child's coping capacity (or to explaining present coping or non-coping) have much to commend them. They embody a straightforward and easily understood principle; they recognize the multiplicity of potentially relevant influences, and the dangers of generalizing from one case to another. There is also the recognition of 'trade-off': a child with a severe vision loss but with supportive parents and school, a determined personality, and so forth, may do better than another child with a comparatively minor defect of vision but with other 'minus' factors strongly evident. However, there are also limitations to the cost accounting model and these need to be understood.

The first caution is that it is difficult to draw up the accounts. Even with a one or two day study of the school and family circumstances, such as we were able to conduct, it was not always easy to delineate all the possible pluses and minuses. There is a pronounced danger that busy professionals, called upon to make a recommendation about placement, will have at their fingertips only a small part of the relevant information. Systemizing procedures of evaluation might offset this somewhat, and the present day trend is towards more far-ranging and detailed review of the child's total circumstances.[7]

A second point to consider is that though two independent cost accounting kinds of evaluation might reveal similar patterns of plus and minus factors, two independent evaluators might well differ in their decision criteria: one may require evidence of many plus factors before recommending that a child attend a local school for the sighted; the other may be willing to take more of a risk and 'give the child the benefit of the doubt'. It appears that there is a general, slow shift in the decision criteria being applied in such evaluations. Now, fewer partially sighted children are thought to require placement in a special residential school.

Different countries and regions have different prevailing norms: almost every partially sighted child in Massachusetts and in Denmark, for instance, attends an ordinary school.

A third reservation about the cost accounting model is that it is simplistic. Although it acknowledges that there are many different influences, it treats them as separate and distinct from one another, and this is false. Manifestly, they do not act in isolation but together. They interlock and interweave: academic performance cannot be divorced from confidence, confidence from personality, expression of personality from the quality of peer relations, the kind of relations with classmates from the prevailing attitudes of the school. Not only do all the various resources complement and reinforce each other, but the demands and difficulties can also combine together, so that the child has little chance. As well as tending to ignore how much the various factors interact, the cost accounting model is also basically a static one, an interpretation fixed in time: it describes the various influential forces acting upon the individual (in this instance, in an integrated school setting) at one point in time. This again, violates common sense. The various resources do not remain constant: teachers move, confidence wanes, a crucial friend moves abroad. The cost accounting kind of thinking is no longer so applicable: a new audit is necessary.

We wish to suggest here a variant of the above way of thinking about coping – one that accepts the inter-relatedness of the various influences and is dynamic rather than static.

What characterized Robert, our last example, was that he had many plus factors: we heard that he was conscientious, determined, bright, accepted handicap and soldiered on, had sympathetic classmates, got tremendous drive from home, and so on. These clearly interacted and enhanced each other: they formed a constellation of relevant influences. In a preceding example, Susan, one found a different constellation, a diminishing rather than enhancing one: thus, we were told, she was withdrawn, immature, had no real friends, was a victim of teasing, reticent, lacked independence, and so on. In both cases it is easy to see how the existence of a constellation can become a fixed fact of every-day existence – Robert has a great deal going for him, Susan has very little; Robert's upsets, if any, may be dismissed as uncharacteristic whereas Susan's may be seen as further evidence of her inadequacy; Robert's lot, if anything, may improve as increased confidence leads to even greater independence which in turn may prompt even better academic work, whereas Susan's chances could easily deteriorate, each setback reducing her confidence and making the next setback more likely.

Cycles such as these are often referred to as vicious circles or 'positive feedback loops'. They rarely exist in such pronounced form. Doubtless, Robert, if he became over-confident, would over-reach himself or be 'taken down a peg or two'; Susan, if she seemed to be noticeably unhappy or academically unsuccessful, would hopefully be given extra support and help. The systems, in cybernetic jargon, are 'error-correcting'. Most of the time, for the children we studied, there were both 'enhancing' connections (e.g. the presence of a friend made for greater academic effort and more success) and 'diminishing' connections (e.g. necessary exclusion from certain activities leading to a sense of feeling 'odd') that were affecting individuals simultaneously. Robert and Susan were unusual in our sample in that their cases were extreme.

The main practical implication of the foregoing is that instead of straightforwardly tabulating pluses and minuses, the assessment of present or future degrees of coping might include a simple analysis to see how the various influences may be interacting. It might be possible to look more systematically at 'enhancing' and 'diminishing' connections. More specifically, we found in the histories of individual children, examples of both 'the setback' and 'the leap forward'. These were instances of where a sudden and noticeable change had occurred in how well the child was coping at school. Customarily, such changes followed a shift of class or school, the arrival of a new teacher, a sudden change in the extent of vision, a long school absence, the making of a close friend or the departure of an old one. In our terms, each of these represents a major shift in the constellation of influences acting upon the child. It means that what might have once been an enhancing connection (e.g. a teacher offering encouragement that fostered independence) may have become a diminishing one (e.g. a teacher being indifferent and thereby discouraging initiatives) – or vice versa. A shift of school (a massive change in the constellation) can be the beginning of a successful new phase or may be a severe setback.

Attention to enhancing and diminishing connections, to setbacks and leaps forward, suggests somewhat different priorities when assessing the degree of coping. It may be useful to bear in mind that sometimes all that pupils may need is some shift in the constellation of influences surrounding them to release an enhancing cycle in place of one that diminishes. These ideas are speculative and deserve more extended elaboration. But at least they demonstrate that behind even a commonly voiced and little thought about term, coping, there lie several highly significant issues.

Notes

1 Distance vision acuity is measured using the familiar Senellen letter charts. The fraction indicates that Susan can see at 6 metres what people with normal vision can see at 24 metres. (Ed.)

2 Fieldnotes, 18/6/75.

3 Fieldnotes, *ibid*.

4 Karen had a visual acuity of 60/60 for distance, but could see well at a distance of 8".

5 Robert suffered from congenital cataracts and aphakia. He had a visual acuity of 6/36 for distance and N6 for near vision. His vision was improved with the help of low vision aids.

6 A social worker, met during the writing of this report, was heard remarking that 'being able to cope' was critical. Asked to define what she meant, she replied — saying how difficult it was to be precise — that to cope was 'to recognize your limitations and not go under'.

7 Such a development has its own dangers — i.e. of making the procedure rigid and bureaucratic, so that a child who might bring some strong personal qualities to offset his or her handicaps might in fact be denied opportunities because the 'situation profile' revealed a high minus score.

1.2 Sociological perspectives on mild mental retardation

JANE R. MERCER

In the early 1970s Jane Mercer was one of a number of writers who investigated the over-representation of ethnic minority children in special education in the USA. She found that part of the phenomenon was due to the processing of these children through a social system in which they achieved a particular, and lowly, status. Their presence in special education could not be fully explained by their individual deficiencies. Thus, understanding the causes of handicap involves understanding the social system of which handicapped children are a marginal component. Here, Jane Mercer explores this approach.

[. . .] The perspective taken toward the phenomenon of mental retardation is a fundamental issue in mental retardation today. The clinical tradition, which most of us share, conceptualizes mental retardation within a clinical perspective. The clinical perspective is essentially a pathological model borrowed from medicine. This medical or 'disease' model has been a very powerful intellectual tool in directing research and treatment of conditions resulting from disease processes and biological damage. Because it has proven so productive a tool in medicine, the medical model has been extended to related but not identical kinds of human problems. The mentally deranged, the alcoholic, the drug addict, and the mental retardate are examples of categories of persons who are now defined as 'sick' rather than depraved, immoral, or 'possessed of devils', as they were in earlier ages. Defining such persons as 'ill' changes their status in society, the roles they are expected to play, the social institutions which will treat them, and the professional persons who will be responsible for their care. It is more than coincidence that, with the rise of the medical perspective in the field of mental retardation, many institutions for the care of mentally retarded persons are now designated as 'hospitals' rather than as homes, colonies, or schools; and are staffed by nurses, medical doctors, and psychiatric

Source: Jane R. Mercer, Sociological Perspectives on Mild Mental Retardation, in *Sociocultural Aspects of Mental Retardation* edited by H. Carl Haywood, ©1970, pp. 379–391. Reprinted by permission of Prentice-Hall, Inc., Englewood Cliffs, NJ

technicians, rather than by house mothers, matrons, and other persons playing surrogate parent roles.

It is significant that Tizard (1970) referred to the persons in the hospitals he studied as 'patients' and 'inmates' — roles very different from the role of the 'child' or 'pupil' played by persons who lived in the homes and hostels. Although the individuals studied were similar in their physical and intellectual characteristics, they were located in different social systems which were composed of very different status and role configurations. When a condition is defined as essentially medical in nature, the traditional medical relationships are elicited. The disabled person holds the status of 'patient' and plays the 'sick' role, while the caretaker holds the status of 'doctor' or 'nurse' and plays the role of the medically trained professional. The set of mutual obligations and privileges which govern the relationship between 'doctor' and 'patient' have evolved within the context of physical illness and disease. The doctor is the actor and the patient is the one acted upon. The focus of concern is the biological organism of the patient. His characteristics as a social being are secondary to the essential basis upon which the relationship has been established.

When a person defined as mentally retarded is placed in the social system called a hospital, he must play the role of 'patient' or 'inmate' and the staff must play the reciprocal roles of disinterested medical professionals concerned primarily with the patient's physical well-being. That is the nature of the social system and the definition of the roles and the statuses which occur in that kind of social system. [. . .]

The size of the institution, the size of the subgroup in the institution, and the staff ratio are essentially irrelevant. The two social systems differ in a much more fundamental fashion — they are composed of entirely different sets of statuses and roles. Here, in my opinion, is the critical dimension; here is the critical issue for social policy and for perspectives toward the mildly mentally retarded.

The significance of the medical perspective on mental retardation, however, transcends its impact in institutional functioning. In our epidemiology of mental retardation in Riverside, California, we found that the clinical perspective has become so pervasive in conceptualizing mental retardation that it virtually permeates all community institutions and programmes. The characteristics of this medical model are familiar. The model views mental retardation primarily as a physical condition, a handicap characterizing the person being observed. We say that a person *is* mentally retarded with the clear implication that mental retardation is a condition that exists *in* that person. Implicit in this viewpoint is the assumption that mental retardation can be present in a person although undetected – that it is a condition which can exist independent of its being identified and labelled, just as a case of rheumatic fever can exist undiagnosed.

The clinical perspective regards mental retardation as a complex phenomenon composed of various syndromes. These syndromes are patterns of symptoms by which it is possible to identify the presence of mental retardation. Although it is recognized that these characteristic syndromes vary somewhat from culture to culture, cross-societal studies of prevalence and incidence rates are made, and differences in the rates secured are treated as 'real' differences in the characteristics of the individuals who make up the various populations studied.

In the clinical framework, 'normal' is essentially a statistical notion. Those people who are close to the statistical average for the population –usually defined as plus or minus one standard deviation from the mean –are the 'normals'. Persons at either of the two extremes of the distribution are 'abnormal'. Frequently, being in the 'normal range' is equated with health, although, for some socially valued characteristics such as intelligence, being abnormal at the positive end of the normal curve is socially valued.

The impact of the disease model is evident in the vocabulary used by professionals in the field of mental retardation. Ideas of prevalence and incidence, for example, are basically medical, epidemiological notions. A case of mental retardation is 'diagnosed' by a professional who then may make a 'prognosis' about the probable course of the condition. The clinical perspective has produced a remarkable elaboration of the diagnostic nomenclature, well illustrated by the American Association on Mental Deficiency manual on the subject (Heber, 1961).

Because proper diagnosis is a central issue in a medical perspective, the disease model promotes the development of more precise diagnostic instruments. It is significant that the intelligence test – the most highly developed and elaborated of the psychometric measures – was conceived as a tool to identify the intellectually subnormal and is the primary diagnostic instrument used in the field of mental retardation. [. . .]

Diagnostic precision requires properly trained and certified diagnosticians. It is significant that pressures for governmental regulation and certification of psychological practitioners in the public schools and community has increased as the medical model has become more pervasive. With the medical perspective comes the professionalization of the diagnostic function.

The research for etiological, i.e., causal, relations is a preeminent characteristic of the medical perspective, for this model assumes that a phenomenon can best be explained through 'cause and effect' reasoning.

The mental retardation literature abounds with attempts to differentiate between endogenous and exogenous causes; primary and secondary causes; hereditary versus environmental causes; biological versus social causes of mental retardation. Research and theorizing about 'causal' sequences is based on the implicit assumption that mental retardation is a condition in the individual, 'caused' by the action of identifiable factors, either external or internal, and that social policy toward mental retardation should first discover the 'causes' and seek to remove them in order to 'prevent' mental retardation. The clinical perspective has also envisioned mental retardation as basically a 'chronic' condition which cannot be 'cured' but may be ameliorated. [. . .]

If all persons who are now defined as mentally retarded in the United States continue to be regarded from a medical perspective, we will continue to search for essentially biological 'causes' for their behaviour. Even when environmental factors are clearly influential, we will continue to look for changes in the biological organism which have resulted from these environmental factors. The focus is on the individual.

For persons who are severely and profoundly retarded and for persons who show clear evidence of organic damage or pathology, the medical model provides a very adequate frame of reference and basis for action. The pathological perspective has proven to be immensely fruitful in the study of phenylketonuria (PKU), of Down's Syndrome, and other clearly organic and/or genetic conditions. However, in the area of mild retardation, the clinical model has been relatively unproductive in providing illuminating insights. Therefore, I should like to propose an alternative model — a social system perspective — for your consideration in thinking about the mildly retarded.

One of the more useful conceptual tools of the sociologist is the notion of the social system. A social system consists of a set of statuses or positions which are bound together by mutual privileges, obligations, and expectations. For example, in a classroom social system, there are two basic statuses — that of teacher and that of student. A person occupying a status plays the role associated with that status. That is, he behaves like a 'teacher' or a 'student', as the case may be. Within a social system, there are shared expectations as to how a person occupying a particular status ought to play his role. These shared expectations are the norms of the system. For example, there are certain expectations as to how a person holding the status of teacher ought to play his role, and also expectations as to how a child occupying the status of student ought to behave if he is a 'normal' student. These role expectations are one of the most important aspects of the normative structure of any social system.

An equally important aspect of the normative structure of a social system consists of the sanctions which are used to enforce the norms and to assure that persons perform their roles in an acceptable fashion. Positive sanctions are the rewards which other members of the system give to the person who performs his role satisfactorily. These rewards may be physical, material rewards, such as money or prizes, or they may be symbolic rewards, such as an 'A' on a report card or praise from the teacher or peers. Among the most prized of the symbolic rewards is assignment to special valued statuses within the system. [. . .]

Social systems also use negative sanctions to enforce adequate role performance. These may take the form of physical punishment, such as a spanking or may be primarily symbolic, such as an 'F' on the report card or a frown from the teacher. Parallel to its repertoire of valued statuses, most social systems have a series of devalued statuses reserved for those whose role performance is inadequate. A sanction even more powerful than assignment to a disesteemed status is removal from the social system itself. When the offending person has been stripped of his status and deprived of his role, the social system has used its ultimate sanction – it has made him an 'outsider'.

It is this aspect of a social system's normative structure which is of primary interest in a social system analysis of mental retardation – the fact that the social system has the ability to create deviant, disesteemed statuses for persons who do not fulfill role expectations and has the ability to punish persons who deviate from system norms by assigning them to a devalued status or by removing them entirely from the group.

For example, the school system has numerous deviant statuses available for students who do not meet expectations. Such students may be assigned position in the low reading group [or the remedial group]. Or, the system may remove the student from his regular status altogether, place him in a 'special education' class, and thus assign him to a very special and very disesteemed status, that of a mental retardate.

From a social system perspective, mental retardation is not viewed as individual pathology but as a status which an individual holds in a particular social system and a role which he plays as an occupant of that status. In this context, mental retardation is not a characteristic of the individual, but rather, a description of an individual's location in a social system, the role he is expected to play in the system, and the expectations which others in the system will have for his behaviour. Mental retardation is an achieved status. It is a position in the group that is contingent upon the performance or, in this case, the lack of performance, of the individual. Thus, mental retardation is specific to a particular social system. A person may hold the status of a mental retardate in one social system and may play the role of a mental retardate in that system, yet may also participate in other social systems in which he is not regarded as mentally retarded and does not hold that status. If a social system does not place a person in the status or role of mental retardate then he is not retarded in that system, although he might qualify for the status of mental retardate if he were participating in some other system. Consequently, the 'prevalence' rate for mental retardation is relative to the level of the norms of specific social systems and will vary with the expectations of the definer.

'Normal' behaviour, from a social system perspective, is that behaviour which conforms to the norms of the system. Since each social system has a normative structure which defines the reciprocal privileges and obligations of persons occupying various statuses and playing various roles in that system, what is 'normal' in one system may be deviant in another. This is quite different from the statistical concept of normal which typifies the clinical perspective. Behaviour which conforms to the system norms is 'normal', regardless of how it may be viewed by outsiders from other social systems with different norms. We can learn much about the norms of a social system by observing the characteristics of persons defined as deviant.

The social system view of mental retardation is quite different from the pathological perspective. It focuses attention on the 'definer' as well as the 'defined', and permits us to move away from the search for causes, cures, treatments, and true 'prevalence rates' in order to restructure the phenomenon of mental retardation from a different vantage point. It leads us not only to see the world differently, but to pose new and different kinds of research questions.

In our community epidemiology, we conducted a traditional epidemiological analysis of mental retardation using a clinical, medical perspective. In addition, we are analysing community data from a social system perspective. A system model that we have developed to describe the process by which a person achieves the status of mental retardate in the public schools will serve to illustrate the application of a social system perspective to the study of mild mental retardation. Some of the primary research questions in a social system study of mental retardation are: Does the social system have a mental retardate status? How do the persons who occupy this status differ from those who occupy other statuses in the system? What are the role expectations for persons holding this status? By what process does an individual acquire the status of retardate? How does he relinquish this status?

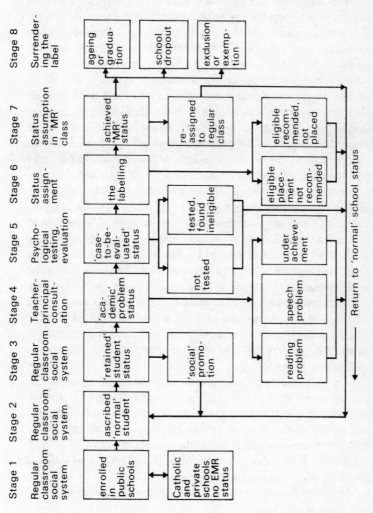

Figure 1 Achieving the status of mental retardate in the public schools

We have found that the mildly mentally retarded child (the EMR)[1] typically progresses through several rather clearly differentiated stages as he moves from the status of 'normal' student to the status of 'EMR' student. Figure 1 depicts these stages schematically.

The first step toward acquiring the status of EMR in the public school system is to enrol in the public schools. This statement is not so trivial as it may appear. There are 2500 elementary school students in the community we studied who attend Catholic parochial schools. These schools do not have special classes for mentally retarded children. Therefore. there is no status position for a mental retardate in that school system. We discovered several dozen children attending these Catholic schools who would have been eligible − by intelligence test scores − for the EMR status if they had attended public schools. However, they were not exposed to the risk of assignment to that status because it did not exist in the schools they were attending. Although perceived as 'slow learners', they did not occupy the status of a mental retardate.

Once enrolled in public school, each student, except those who are visibly disabled, is automatically assigned to the status of normal student in the regular classroom and given an opportunity to play the role of normal student. Should he fail to meet the role expectations of the teacher, he may be assigned a deviant status by being asked to repeat a grade and thus become a 'retained' student. However, he is still in the regular classroom and the stigma of failure may be forgotten in time. We found that the deviant status of retained students is one through which most children pass in the process of acquiring the status of EMR in the public schools. Seventy-two per cent of the EMR children in the school system studied had repeated one or more grades at some time during their educational careers.

At Stage 3, the child may meet role expectations and continue in the status of a 'normal' student who has been retained. However, if the role performance continues to be unsatisfactory, the teacher has two options: to give him an 'unearned social promotion' or to refer his case to the principal for special consideration. If she decides in favour of a social promotion, the child will escape the EMR status and retain his status as a regular student. If not, he moves to Stage 4. He is now an 'academic problem' to be evaluated by teacher and principal for possible referral for psychological assessment.

There are several alternatives at this critical juncture − the child may be defined as a 'reading problem', a 'speech problem', an 'underachiever', or some other label that keeps him in his status as student in a regular class but gives him access to special educational resources such as remedial reading teachers and speech therapists. The other alternative is to send him through the doorway to the psychologist's office and Stage 5, a 'case-to-be-evaluated'.

The school psychologist typically does not have time to administer intelligence tests to all children who are referred to him by teachers and principals. Using his clinical judgement, he may decide that a particular child is 'emotionally disturbed', 'situationally distressed', or, for other reasons, does not need to be tested individually. Because no child can acquire the status of an EMR in the state of California unless he has been given an individual intelligence test, an untested child automatically returns to his regular class status, possibly with a psychological recommendation for psychotherapy or counselling. On the other hand, the psychologist may decide that an intelligence test is indicated, may test the child, and may find that he scores too high for placement in an EMR class. He is ineligible and also returns to his regular class status. Those who fail the IQ test move on to Stage 6 – the labelling.

California law requires that parents be notified before a child is placed in special education. The parental conference may find the parents adamant about placement and this resistance may dissuade the professional diagnostician from assigning a child to an EMR status, especially if the IQ is borderline. The staff planning session may conclude that, although the test score is low, the child is not really 'retarded'. He may be labelled 'emotionally disturbed'. In this case it is assumed that the test score does not reveal his 'real' potential. Although eligible, he is not recommended for placement and returns to his regular class status.

Even if the child is found eligible by reason of low IQ and recommended for placement, he may still slip through the labelling process and return to a regular student status if his parents decide to move to another school district. In that case, the process must begin over again in the new district and may never be initiated at all. Similarly, his parents may send him to a Catholic school or other nonpublic schools which do not have classes for the mentally retarded. If he remains outside the public school system through the elementary school years when most of the labelling is done, he may escape the status of mental retardation altogether.

Those children who survive this strenuous screening enter Stage 7 and become mental retardates. They assume the status of an EMR child, attend special education classes with their own special curriculum and play area, and probably will remain in this status throughout the remainder of their school career. Very few are reassigned to regular classes after once being labelled as a mental retardate. The limited nature of the special education curriculum makes reassignment to the regular class virtually impossible after a period of time. Escape from the EMR (Stage

8) status for most children occurs when they age out of the programme, drop out of school, or are expelled or exempted. A few middle class children 'graduate'.

This model, like any 'ideal type' construct, does not describe every detail of every public school system. However, it can still serve as an analytic tool for investigating the process of achieving a mental retardate status in a particular social system. If the investigator can determine the inputs to the system and monitor the characteristics of individuals who escape the label at various stages in the process, he can determine the 'exposure to risk' of mental retardation of various population groups exposed to system processes. Not only can he assess the relevance of characteristics of individuals to the probability of being labelled mentally retarded – characteristics such as ethnic group membership, sex, and IQ score – but he can also assess the interplay between individual and system characteristics. He can study the outputs from the system, i.e., the characteristics of those who are labelled. From this he can make inferences about system properties.

Within this model, the critical research questions centre on calculating the probabilities of various types of children being labelled as mentally retarded at various stages in the labelling process. An analysis of those who escape the label is quite as important in understanding the process as is an analysis of those who eventually play the EMR role.

[. . .] We have found [in our community epidemiological study] that, at every stage in the labelling process, a child of Spanish surname is exposed to a higher probability of going on to the next stage in the process than is an English-speaking Caucasian child or a Negro child. Those children most likely to complete the sequence are those who have many academic problems, who come from homes where little English is spoken, and who have difficulty communicating in English. The English-speaking Caucasian children who are most likely to escape the label after initial referral are those with mental health problems, with many interpersonal problems, and with poor social adjustments. Those with physical handicaps, neurologic involvements, and poor speech facility complete the course. These factors did not differentiate labelled from nonlabelled children of Spanish surname. Negro children who were eventually placed in EMR classes tended to have significantly more interpersonal problems than did English-speaking Caucasian children who were placed. [. . .] In almost every county we investigated in Riverside, California, there are two to three times more Negro children and children of Spanish surname holding the status of retardate in the public schools than their proportion in the total school population.

Epidemiological studies conducted from a clinical perspective have interpreted similar differentials as 'real' differences in rates of pathology in the three ethnic groups. However, closer inspection reveals that the situation is much too complex to be described adequately within a simple clinical model. As part of the study of desegregation[2] in the schools of the southern California community, we administered the Wechsler Intelligence Scale for Children (WISC) to all Spanish-surname and Negro children in three segregated elementary schools and to a random sample of English-speaking Caucasian children in the predominately Caucasian schools of the district. While 1.2 per cent of the English-speaking Caucasian children, 8 through 14 years of age, who were tested had IQs below 80, 15.3 per cent of the Spanish-surname children, and 12.4 per cent of the Negro children, had IQs in this range. All of these children were holding the status of the 'normal' student in the regular classroom. Although they would be eligible for placement in an EMR status by reason of their low intelligence-test scores, none had achieved that status in the school system at the time of our study. Further investigation revealed that there was no significant difference between the average total WISC scores of those children with a total intelligence score of 79 or below who were holding a 'normal' student status and children of the same ethnic group in the same schools who were in special educational classes. Why were some labelled mentally retarded while others were not? An analysis from the social system perspective is likely to be more illuminating than is one using a pathological model.

The social system perspective may be used as an analytic tool in studying mental retardation in other social systems of the community — the family, the neighbourhood, law enforcement, welfare, churches, and public institutions for the retarded.

There are several values in redefining mental retardation as a 'social status' rather than a 'handicap'; as a social category rather than a clinical diagnosis; as a role rather than a disability.

Because this perspective focuses attention on the 'definer' rather than the 'defined', it reverses the traditional emphasis on the characteristics of the professional labellers — those who have the legitimate societal function of labelling, categorizing, and placing the mentally retarded. The social system perspective highlights the extent to which the medical perspective in mild mental retardation may be implicated in creating and perpetuating the very condition it seeks to prevent. Once assigned the status of a mental retardate, an individual soon becomes socialized to play the role and to meet the lesser expectations of his retarded status. When being mildly retarded is viewed as a social process in which a person moves from one status to another, new approaches to prevention and intervention are revealed. There are many alternative labels and programmes available. By what rationale should some children be placed in an EMR status in the public schools when 121 other children of equivalent intellectual attainment remain unstigmatized?

The pathological model tends to be pessimistic and permeated with associations related to the severely and profoundly retarded – notions of chronicity, genetic deficiency, and biological impairment. Many mildly retarded persons escape their mental retardate status and stigma once they leave the public schools, and play relatively normal adult roles. They hold jobs, marry, and have children (Mercer, 1965). Was their assignment to the deviant status of mental retardate during the school years necessary or desirable?

The medical model projects the deficiency into the individual. He is the one who lacks the necessary intelligence to pass the test, who cannot think abstractly, who is presumed to suffer from lack of the g factor. The assessment of the characteristics of those who are thus categorized leads to the conclusion that it is the culturally different and the disinherited of the American society who bear the major burden of this deviant status. Does the pathological model, applied to mild mental retardation, divert attention from the norms and assumptions of the instruments and procedures used to diagnose 'the deviant'? Has special education and mild retardation become a sophisticated rationalization for maintaining the present status relationships in our society? These are hard questions. They demand our thoughtful consideration.

Notes

1 Educable Mentally Retarded. This is the approximate equivalent of the UK category ESN(M). (Ed.)
2 Desegregation here means racial desegregation. (Ed.)

References

Heber, R.A. (1961) Manual on Terminology and Classification in Mental Retardation (2nd ed.), *American Journal of Mental Deficiency* (Monograph Supplement).

Mercer, J.R. (1965) Social system perspective and clinical perspective: Frames of reference for understanding career patterns of persons labelled as mentally retarded, *Social Problems*, 13, 18–34.

Tizard, J. (1970) The role of social institutions in the causation, prevention, and alleviation of mental retardation, in H.C. Haywood (Ed.), *Socio-cultural Aspects of Mental Retardation*, New York, Appleton-Century-Crofts.

1.3 Physical handicap in children: sources of variation

JEAN GOLDING

The causes of some biological impairments continue to evade discovery, whilst for others, such as Down's Syndrome, the causes are partially understood but subject to only limited control. Many congenital defects whose causes are still obscure show considerable variation in incidence according to social class, region, diet and drug usage. Investigation of these variations aims at providing both the key to understanding and prevention. However, as Jean Golding shows, the degree of prevention possible at the moment is limited.

In this article the term 'physical handicap' is used to define a variety of different defects which produce a loss of function to the limbs or senses. In the United Kingdom the majority of such defects are congenital; they have been present since birth. But children may also acquire defects as a result of infection or injury; polio in a non-immunized child may result in the loss of the use of limbs; meningitis can cause deafness or blindness; accidents in the home or street or child battering may produce physical or sensory defects or even cerebral palsy. In the Third World now, as was true for the United Kingdom in previous eras, acquired defects, particularly as a result of infections, account for by far the majority of physical handicaps.

Although much is known about the nature of congenital defects their precise cause is often shrouded in mystery. Part of the aetiology has been unravelled for certain defects, such as Down's Syndrome (mongolism) which results when there is a specific extra chromosome present from conception, or shortly thereafter, but that does not explain how or why that extra chromosome was present. Other fairly rare defects are known to result from the presence of a single dominant gene. One example of such a defect is achondroplasia (the form of dwarf with almost normal size trunk but very short limbs). Half of any offspring of a parent with such a gene will also be affected. Other defects are associated with a recessive gene on an X-chromosome, resulting in disorders in boys rather than girls. Such disorders will be passed through

Specially commissioned for this volume
©The Open University, 1981

apparently normal women (carriers) to affect half their sons. Queen Victoria was a carrier for the haemophilia gene which then affected a large proportion of the European royal families and was thought to have an effect on the course of European history in the first half of this century. Other examples of such X-linked genetic disorders are muscular dystrophy with its distressing pattern of progressive paralysis culminating in death in adolescence or soon thereafter.

In most instances, however, there are no easily identifiable direct causes of defects in a child. In the past explanations were sought in the occurrence of a magical or religious event and the birth of a malformed child was sometimes imbued with divine significance. Among tablets found in Nineveh were examples of such prophecies. One states that when a woman gave birth to an infant without the right ear, it meant that the king would live to a ripe old age. Another that if a woman gave birth to an infant with no fingers, there would be no births in the town; if a hermaphrodite was born calamity and affliction would seize the land. In ancient Egypt malformed infants have been found mummified with sacred animals. They must have been looked upon as objects of wonder and worship. Far different was the attitude in Europe in the Middle Ages and in early Puritan America when such a birth would probably be regarded as evidence of the mother's witchcraft (Warkany, 1959). Nowadays, although no overt blame is attached to the mother, nor many references made to divine intervention, there are feelings of mystery, unease and often guilt.

The problem of discovering ways in which defects can be prevented from occurring is difficult and has to rely on the epidemiological approach. This involves studying the ways in which the incidence or prevalence of each lesion varies with different factors. After defining the concepts of incidence and prevalence, the rest of this article will discuss variation of different lesions with environmental, social and biological factors, and discuss possible ways in which defects may be prevented in the future.

Incidence and prevalence of defects

Incidence is used to mean the proportion of births in the total population which have a particular disorder. Thus 'the incidence of Down's Syndrome is about 1.1 per 1,000' and this can be written as 'about 1 in every 900 births has Down's Syndrome'.

Prevalence refers to the proportion of the population with a particular lesion at a given time. Thus prevalence at birth is the same as the incidence, but prevalence among five year olds might be quite different. For example, infants with Down's Syndrome have a high mortality rate in their early years due to their increased susceptibility to respiratory infection, as well as their increased risk of having a malformed heart. Although the prevalence at birth is around 1.1 per 1,000, among seven year olds it is of the order of 0.5 (or 1 in 2,000).

A similar pattern is seen with congenital heart disease. Table 1 shows data concerning a cohort of children born in England, Scotland and Wales in one week in March 1958. It can be seen that the prevalence just at delivery is almost double that found among seven year olds. The majority of the deaths have occurred within the first weeks of delivery, and are due to the fact that either the malformations are incompatible with life, or the newborn infant has not sufficient reserves to withstand corrective surgery, or respiratory infections.

Table 1 Prevalence of congenital heart disease (CHD) at various points in time; the 1958 cohort study (Butler and Alberman, 1969)

Population	No. at risk	No. with CHD	Prevalence CHD per 1,000
At birth	17,406	112	6.4
Alive at delivery	17,018	101	5.9
Alive at end of 28th day	16,740	76	4.5
Alive at end of 7th year	16,597	57	3.4

A different pattern has been presented by the malformation known as spina bifida. This is a defect of the spinal column, and is usually accompanied by paralysis of the lower limbs and double incontinence. The infants are often born with, or later develop, hydrocephalus which if left untreated will frequently result in mental retardation, fits and possible sensory defects. Until some twenty years ago the process was allowed to run its natural course, and most such children would die within days or weeks of delivery. Children who had mild forms of the disease would survive, but few would be without some sort of handicap.

Then in the 1960s a more aggressive approach was adopted for children born with this lesion. It became accepted that early surgery to a large proportion of children with spina bifida would result in improved survival with little loss of function. Doubt was later expressed by Lorber (1971) as to the effects of this policy. He showed that although the survival of such infants greatly improved under such a regime, the proportion of survivors with *severe* physical handicap was a constant

80 per cent. On publication of his findings there was an attempt to revert to a more conservative approach to treatment.

This chopping and changing of policies had a marked effect on the prevalence of the lesion in the community. Table 2 shows that although the *incidence* of spina bifida and/or hydrocephalus remained constant over the years 1960–72, the prevalence of the lesion among one year olds rose strikingly, so that for infants born in 1970 it was three times that for infants born in 1960. A drop in prevalence can be seen in 1972: presumably the result of the change in surgical practice.

Table 2 Births with spina bifida and/or hydrocephalus 1960–72.
Incidence at birth compared with prevalence at 1 year
(adapted from Weatherall and White, 1976)

Year of birth	No. of births with spina bifida	No. of infants with spina bifida alive at one year	Incidence at birth[a]	Prevalence at one year[b]
1960	2,444	420	3.1	0.5
1962	2,607	607	3.1	0.7
1964	2,718	933	3.1	1.0
1966	2,634	1,053	3.1	1.2
1968	2,537	1,124	3.1	1.3
1970	2,426	1,191	3.1	1.5
1972	2,241	926	3.1	1.2

[a] per 1,000 total births.
[b] per 1,000 infants alive at one year.

Sex differences

Genetically the difference between males and females lies in only one of the forty-six chromosomes possessed by each cell of a normal individual. The female has a much larger forty-sixth chromosome (an X) than has the male (Y chromosome), to be held in balance with its partner (an X in both cases). Any deleterious recessive gene held on the X chromosome would act as a dominant gene in the male, and accounts for the very marked excess of males in conditions such as Duchenne muscular dystrophy, haemophilia and red–green colour blindness.

Shortly after conception it seems that there are about 120 male embryos to every 100 females. The rate of spontaneous abortion is higher in males though, and by the start of the seventh month of pregnancy the ratio of males to females has dropped to about 108:100. Throughout their lives males have a higher mortality rate than females of the same age, resulting in an increasing excess of females over males in populations of age 65+.

Among most common congenital malformations recognized at birth, there are usually more boys than girls, but there are notable exceptions to this (spina bifida, anencephalus and congenital dislocation of the hip). Anencephalus is a fatal defect, where much of the child's brain is missing. It is incompatible with life outside the uterus. Congenital dislocation of the hip is totally compatible with life, however, but is potentially handicapping. Providing the lesion is identified soon after birth, it can be treated successfully, but when it has been missed the result can be severe physical disability.

A recent survey has shown that by the age of five the differences between the sexes are very marked (Table 3); the boys in general having a medical history considerably more detailed than that of the girls. Part of this could be linked to the fact that females generally appear to be able to produce higher levels of antibodies to common viruses (Michaels and Rogers, 1971) and partly to the males' excessive ability to have accidents of all types. Boys are also far more likely than girls to have hearing and speech defects as well as behaviour and emotional problems.

Table 3 The numbers of children of each sex aged 5 with different problems (Child Health and Education Study)

Problem	Boys	Girls	Ratio boys:girls
Asthma	174	96	1.8:1
Bronchitis	1,241	924	1.3:1
Stammers or stutters	525	268	2.0:1
Hearing difficulty	603	452	1.3:1
Frequent temper tantrums	981	607	1.6:1
Wets bed	1,691	1,139	1.5:1
Bites nails	1,635	2,104	0.7:1
All children in study	6,808	6,327	1.1:1

Social class differences

Although the concept of 'social class' based on the occupation of the head of the household has been used in Britain as a useful parameter in the study of the population, it has only relatively recently been considered in regard to the aetiology of physical handicap. Using this classification we have shown that the incidence of several congenital defects varies with social class, the most extreme variation being apparent for cases of anencephalus and spina bifida (Table 4).

Other lesions such as hare lip and cleft palate, congenital dislocation of the hip and Down's Syndrome show no associations with social class.

Table 4 Incidence per 1,000 births of anencephalus and
spina bifida by social class

Social class	Incidence of anencephalus	Incidence of spina bifida
I and II	1.4	1.3
III	2.4	2.6
IV	2.6	2.8
V	3.9	3.2

In contrast, defects which have resulted from trauma show a very marked social class variation. This is interesting in that although there is little difference between the social classes in the proportion of young children having accidents, the death and handicap rates from accidents are much higher in the lower social groups.

But what aspect of social class is responsible for the trends we have described? There are wide variations in parental attitudes to their children, as well as in their basic wealth and standards of living. Women in the 'lower' social classes are more likely to smoke heavily and have different diets than those in the upper social groups. It is unlikely that the actual job in which the husband is employed, and on which the classification is based, is the crucial factor.

Geographical variation

Little is known of the way in which physical defects vary across the world, because few details are available. Studies have, however, been made of lesions easily identified at birth. Hare lip, for example, has been shown to have a higher incidence in those parts of the world where the mongoloid races are found (China and Japan, the American Indians). Populations of Negro origin have a much lower rate, and Caucasians have an incidence midway between the two (Leck, 1978).

Incidence of spina bifida and anencephalus also show a striking variation with area of the world, but the pattern is quite different. Highest rates are found in Great Britain, north-west India and the Arab countries of the Middle East. Lowest rates are found in countries as disparate as those of South and Central America, France, Italy and Uganda (Table 5). It is difficult to invoke a wholly racial explanation since in Canada the French Canadians now have an incidence almost identical to that found among the Canadians of British origin.

Within Britain even, the incidence also varies quite dramatically; Ireland, Scotland, Wales and the north-west of England having highest rates, and East Anglia, London and the south-east having the lowest values. Such local variation has been found in several countries and

Table 5 International variation in the incidence of anencephalus:
summary of data currently available

Magnitude of incidence	Areas	
Very high (3 per 1,000 or more)	North-west India Ulster Scotland	Eire South Wales
High (2.0–2.9 per 1,000)	Middle East (including Israel) England	New Zealand
Medium (1.0–1.9 per 1,000)	Canada Taiwan Netherlands Hungary	North-east USA Rest of India Denmark
Low (0.6–0.9 per 1,000)	Most of USA South Africa Israel Austria W.Germany	Australia Nigeria Sweden E.Germany Spain
Very low (less than 0.6 per 1,000)	Central America South America Japan Finland Yugoslavia	Uganda Czechoslovakia Italy France Switzerland

shown to be correlated with the softness of the local water supplies, not only in Britain, but also in Canada, the United States and Holland.

Age of Parents

Certain lesions have a very marked association with the age of the mother. The most striking is that found for the incidence of Down's Syndrome, where the risk varies by a factor of 30 according to whether the mother is a teenager, or in her late 40s (Table 6).

Table 6 Incidence of Down's Syndrome by age of
mother (from Lilienfeld and Benesch, 1969)

Maternal age	Incidence of Down's Syndrome per 1,000 births
under 20	0.6
20–4	0.7
25–9	0.7
30–4	1.1
35–9	3.6
40–4	10.3
45+	17.8

Because of the greatly increased risk to older women, amniocentesis is now often offered to those over thirty-eight. This procedure involves puncturing the membranes and withdrawing a small amount of the fluid. By culturing this it is possible to identify the chromosome constitution of the foetus. If Down's Syndrome is diagnosed, a termination of pregnancy is offered to the mother.

The number of women becoming pregnant at such ages has, however, become smaller and smaller over the past twenty years, and the vast majority of affected infants are born undetected to younger mothers.

Other malformations are found to vary with the age of the mother, but in a different way. Anencephalus and spina bifida, for example, follow a U-shaped pattern in incidence which is difficult to explain (Table 7).

Table 7 Incidence of anencephalus and spina bifida (and/or hydrocephalus) by maternal age (from Rogers and Weatherall, 1976)

Maternal age	Incidence of anencephalus	Incidence of spina bifida and/or hydrocephalus
under 20	2.2	3.0
20—4	1.9	2.5
25—9	1.6	2.0
30—4	1.6	2.2
35—9	2.0	2.6
40+	2.1	3.2

Raised father's age has been found in only a small number of specific defects such as achondroplasia. It is thought that such a finding is the result of gene mutation more likely to occur the more often the sperms have been replicated (and hence the higher the paternal age). In most of the common lesions, however, it is the mother's age that has the predominant effect.

Birth order

It has been well established that the more elder siblings a child has, the lower will be his educational attainment, and his IQ score (Davie, Butler and Goldstein, 1972). This is thought to be not so much a consequence of diminished potential at birth, but rather the result of parents having to share their attention between a large number of children. As a result, the younger children of a large family suffer from lack of intellectual stimulation and encouragement.

A different mechanism has, however, to be invoked for those physical defects whose incidence increases with increasing birth order. Some of such associations are more apparent than real though. For example, crude analysis would suggest that the incidence of Down's Syndrome increases with birth order, but this is because the older the mother, the more likely she is to have had previous children. In other defects the incidence certainly increases with birth order, independent of the mother's age or any other factor.

One of the very odd findings in studies of anencephalus and spina bifida is a J-shaped effect, with the highest incidence found among first pregnancies, the lowest in second pregnancies and a progressive rise in risk thereafter (Table 8). This cannot be wholly explained by the U-shaped maternal age pattern already described, but a curious pattern emerges when both factors are analysed simultaneously (Figure 1) in

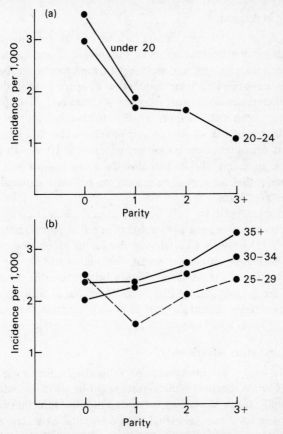

Figure 1 Estimated incidence of anencephalus by parity for different maternal age groups: 1958 British Perinatal Mortality Survey

that the incidence in young mothers falls with increasing birth order, whereas the incidence in older mothers rises with increasing birth order.

Table 8 Incidence of anencephalus and spina bifida by
birth order (from Wilson, 1971)

Birth order	Incidence of anencephalus	Incidence of spina bifida
1	2.8	3.0
2	2.2	2.3
3	2.4	2.5
4	3.0	2.1
5+	4.6	4.2

Smoking in pregnancy

The smoking of cigarettes results in a variety of potentially harmful chemicals getting into the serum of the smoker. These include carbon monoxide, thiocyanates and nicotine. In the case of the father, this might conceivably affect the production of sperm, and in the case of the mother the products will cross the placenta and affect the foetus. It has now been well documented that the mother who smokes is at greatly increased risk of having a spontaneous abortion (miscarriage), an infant who dies in the period before and just after birth (perinatal death) or an infant who though alive has a low birthweight. Evidence is also mounting for a positive association between maternal smoking and later 'cot' death.

In contrast, there are only isolated suggestions that congenital malformations are associated with smoking in either parent, but the possibility is far from resolved. Certainly in Britain the proportion of smoking parents increases with lower social class, but curiously perhaps, the reverse is true on the continent. Within Britain too, the proportion of women who smoke during their pregnancies varies with region — not surprisingly being highest in those areas with the greatest proportion of families of lower social classes.

Rubella and other infections

In 1941, Gregg, a doctor practising in Australia, first suggested that rubella (German measles) in the mother might be associated with defects in the child. It has become apparent that the virus infection contracted during pregnancy was associated with congenital cataracts, and other eye defects, congenital heart lesions, mental retardation, cerebral palsy and deafness (Dudgeon, 1976).

Once the pregnant woman has contracted the illness, there are three factors which determine whether the foetus be affected: firstly, it must be the first time the mother has had rubella, secondly the virus must be present in the blood stream, and thirdly the infection must occur within the first half of pregnancy. Indeed the earlier in pregnancy, the more likely is the foetus to be damaged. As many as a third of infants infected in the first month of pregnancy will have the syndrome of defects, whereas only about 5 per cent will have such defects if the infection does not occur until the fourth month.

There is only one other viral infection that is known to have a major effect on the foetus, and that is cytomegalovirus. Again this causes only a very mild infection in the mother, often unnoticed by her, but it can result in deafness, mental retardation, cerebral palsy and other defects.

Compared with these two viruses, with well substantiated and striking effects, the evidence for other viruses or bacterial infections in pregnancy having an association with physical defects in the unborn child is largely circumstantial. There is a certain basis for suggesting that the influenza virus might be responsible for a small proportion of cases of anencephalus.

In 1937, de Lee had remarked that during the 1918 epidemic a number of 'monstrosities' had been delivered to women in his practice, and that these women had all had influenza in the early part of pregnancy. The virus responsible for the 1918 pandemic bears, of course, little resemblance to the influenza A viruses that were responsible for the major epidemics in most parts of the world in 1957 and 1958. This prompted a large number of studies to be set up to examine the possibility of harmful effect, with conflicting results.

Retrospective enquiry of the mothers of anencephalics as to whether they had had influenza during pregnancy is prone to reporting bias. In the collaborative project, however, Elizan and his co-workers (1969) were able to retrieve paired specimens of sera collected during twenty-three pregnancies which were subsequently found to be anencephalic. None of these provided evidence of influenza or any other of several virus infections during the first three months of pregnancy.

Drugs consumed in pregnancy

Surprisingly perhaps, it was not until the thalidomide tragedy in the early 1960s that the possibility was considered that drugs taken in pregnancy could harm the foetus. The results of thalidomide ingestion in certain critical weeks of pregnancy, were striking. A high proportion of children were born with absent limbs and other defects. These abnormalities were normally very rare, so it was relatively easy to spot the sudden increase and link it to the new drug that had appeared on the scene. It has been admitted, however, that it will be very difficult to spot drugs that produce more common types of defect.

Using a variety of methods it is now well established that epileptic women taking anticonvulsant drugs during pregnancy double the risk of many types of malformation in their offspring, especially hare lip and cleft palate (Sullivan, 1976). This knowledge has had little effect on the prescribing of anti-convulsants, since in most cases the treatment is necessary to control the epilepsy.

Other drugs that are known to affect the foetus include the antibiotics tetracycline, which results in discolouration and deformity of the child's teeth, and streptomycin, which is associated with deafness. Certain sex hormones given to the mother may have an effect on the genitalia of the foetus: progestogens may result in virilization of the female infant, but oestrogens can produce feminization of male infants. One oestrogen compound (stilboestrol) administered to pregnant women has been found to be responsible for a rare cancer of the vagina appearing some twenty years later in some of the female offspring. Although little is certain of adverse effects of other drugs consumed during pregnancy, it is reasonable to limit prescriptions to those drugs that are absolutely necessary.

We have talked only of the effect on the foetus when the mother has consumed a particular drug, but it is quite conceivable that paternal drug ingestion might have an effect if it occurred during the crucial period of sperm production (i.e. 36–49 days before conception).

Dietary factors

Not only may drugs have an effect on the unborn foetus, it is perhaps even more likely that constituents of the diet are at fault. Various hypotheses have been put forward, but perhaps the most appealing was that of Renwick (1972). He stated that the geographical variation of potato blight closely correlated with that for the incidence of anencephalus and spina bifida; that the lower social classes eat more potatoes (the lower social class housewife being more likely to peel a large number of potatoes, such potatoes being anyway more likely to be blighted); that the association with large quantities of potatoes to be peeled, and that the increase in risk with maternal age was due to the fact that as she got older the woman took longer to peel potatoes. The association with young women giving birth to a first child was taken to indicate that these girls were still living at the parental home and also had a large number of potatoes to peel.

The hypothesis is difficult to test because the author is continually changing his ground. After initially appearing to state that the cause was the fungus itself, he later went on to suggest that the blight was not involved but rather some unknown substance within the potato, possibly one that reacts as an antibody to the blight. Nor could he anticipate whether the substance was inhaled as a spray, absorbed through the skin during peeling, or ingested.

Renwick's original paper provoked a number of epidemiological and animal studies, most of which failed to confirm his hypothesis. In addition, a trial was carried out with women who had had a previous infant with anencephaly or spina bifida. These women are known to be at increased risk of having another affected infant. They were advised to avoid potatoes prior to conception of the next pregnancy. Of eight such women who had avoided potatoes during pregnancy two had children with one of the malformations (Lorber, 1974; Lorber, Stewart and Ward, 1973). Similarly in Belfast eighty-eight women who had had a previous infant with anencephalus or spina bifida were advised to avoid potatoes prior to conceiving. Of the twenty-three who complied with this advice, two (9 per cent) had a further infant with a defect, whereas this happened to only two of the fifty-six (4 per cent) who did not avoid potatoes.

In 1972, Knox published the results of a comparison of rates of anencephalus in England and Wales with the average quarterly consumption of various foodstuffs as published by the National Food Survey between five and nine months earlier. The period covered was from 1961 to 1967, and of the 385 correlation coefficients computed, 133 (35 per cent) were significant at the 5 per cent level.

Knox felt that those items with chemical additives would be most likely to be damaging, and stressed the associations with canned peas (with magnesium salts added to retain the colour) and cooked and cured meats (with sodium nitrate added as a preservative). The possibility of canned peas being the culprit is given added impetus by the fact that the regions of Wales, the north, north-west, Yorkshire and Humberside have the highest consumption of tinned peas in England and Wales as well as high rates of anencephalus. Knox did not mention, however, that in Scotland there is a very low consumption – whereas, of course, the anencephalic rate is high.

That addition of nitrates and nitrites to meat may produce nitrosamines, among other cancer-causing agents, has long been recognized although no correlation between cancer in man and the consumption of cooked or cured meats has ever been substantiated.

A further hypothesis was created from consideration of the world-wide variation in incidence of anencephalus. Fedrick (1974) showed that the areas with high incidences were also those areas of the world where the tea consumption was high. She found too that within Britain the tea-drinking habit increased dramatically with social class, in exactly the same way as did the incidence of anencephaly. She then carried out a survey and demonstrated that women who had borne anencephalics were indeed more likely to be tea drinkers than controls of the same age, number of pregnancies and social class. It also appeared that the effect was confined to areas of soft water.

Other hypotheses have suggested that it is poor diets that are largely responsible for the defect, and intervention studies with either dietary advice or a cocktail pill containing a mixture of vitamins and trace elements taken before conception do appear to have reduced the incidence of anencephalus and spina bifida.

Alcohol is a further candidate for censure. It is now well established that women who are chronic alcoholics are likely to bear children with a variety of defects including mental subnormality, growth retardation and congenital heart disease. This is known as the foetal alcohol syndrome. There is, as yet, little information as to what effect mild or moderate alcohol consumption may have on the foetus.

Discussion

With the highly developed technical skills of the obstetrician and paediatrician the survival of infants with congenital defects is gradually increasing. Prevention rather than amelioration is obviously the most economic and humane aim, but the reason for the development of the majority of these defects is still very much shrouded in mystery. True, in a very small proportion of cases a viral infection such as rubella can be implicated, or some dominant or recessive gene, or the maternal consumption of a drug, such as thalidomide, but in the vast majority of cases no such mechanism has been demonstrated.

What then is the way ahead? As we have described, there is some indication that a balanced diet, giving up smoking, and drinking only small amounts of alcohol may improve the chances that the infant will be born fit and healthy. The woman who has already borne a defective child will be likely to seek advice on further pregnancies. In cases where the risk is high of a similar outcome in a subsequent pregnancy, it is important that she see a genetic counsellor. In certain cases it is possible to detect early in pregnancy whether the next child is affected. In these cases, termination of the pregnancy would be offered.

A very interesting controversy has arisen recently in regard to cerebral palsy. It has been suggested by various fund-raising and political authorities that the incidence would be reduced if the standard of obstetric and neonatal care were improved. While this is intellectually appealing, the evidence for such a statement is lacking. This is due to the fact that incidence figures for cerebral palsy are infrequently obtained, and there are consequently no data to either support or refute the suggestion.

Other methods of decreasing handicap include the screening of children in early infancy. Congenital dislocation of the hip can be identified and successfully treated, metabolic disorders such as phenylketonuria can be found and the infant put on a diet before severe mental retardation develops, hearing defects can be identified and a hearing aid fitted early, so that speech development is not delayed.

Finally, a small number of major defects would be prevented if every girl was immunized against rubella in early adolescence. In spite of all these preventive measures, however, the majority of lesions will occur apparently out of the blue. One of the major needs is for new ideas and good research methods to attempt to identify further causes of these lesions.

References

Butler, N.R. and Alberman, E.D. (1969) *Perinatal Problems: The Second Report of the 1958 British Perinatal Mortality Survey,* London, E. & S. Livingstone.

Davie, R., Butler, N.R. and Goldstein, H. (1972) *From Birth to Seven: A Report of the National Child Development Study,* London, Longman.

Dudgeon, J.A. (1976) Infective causes of human malformations, *British Medical Bulletin,* 32, 77–83.

Elizan, T.S., Ajero-Froehlich, L., Fabiyi, A., Ley, A. and Sever, J.L. (1969) Viral infection in pregnancy and congenital CNS malformations in man, *Archives of Neurology,* 20, 115–19.

Fedrick, J. (1974) Anencephalus and maternal tea drinking: evidence for a possible association, *Proceedings of the Royal Society of Medicine,* 67, 356–60.

Knox, E.G. (1972) Anencephalus and dietary intakes, *British Journal of Preventive and Social Medicine,* 26, 219–23.

Leck, I. (1978) Correlations of malformation frequency with environmental and genetic attributes in man, in J.G. Wilson and F. Clarke-Fraser (Eds), *Handbook of Teratology,* vol. 3, New York, Plenum Press.

Lilienfeld, A.M. and Benesch, C.H. (1969) *Epidemiology of Mongolism,* Baltimore, Johns Hopkins Press.

Lorber, J. (1971) Results of treatment of myelomeningocele, *Developmental Medicine and Child Neurology,* 13, 279–303.

Lorber, J. (1974) The potato trial, *Link,* 30, 7.

Lorber, J., Stewart, C.R. and Ward, A.M. (1973) Alpha-fetoprotein in antenatal diagnosis of anencephaly and spina bifida, *Lancet,* 1, 1187.

Michaels, R.H. and Rogers, K.D. (1971) A sex difference in immunologic responsiveness, *Pediatrics,* 47, 120.

Renwick, J.H. (1972) Hypothesis: anencephaly and spina bifida are usually preventable by avoidance of a specific but unidentified substance present in certain potato tubers, *British Journal of Preventive and Social Medicine*, 26, 67–88.

Rogers, S.C. and Weatherall, J.A.C. (1976) Anencephalus, spina bifida and congenital hydrocephalus, *Studies on Medical and Population Subjects*, no. 32, London, HMSO.

Smith, G.K. and Smith, E.D. (1973) Selection for treatment in spina bifida, *British Medical Journal*, 3, 189–97.

Sullivan, F.M. (1976) Effect of drugs on fetal development, in R.W. Beard and P.W. Nathaniels (Eds), *Fetal Physiology and Medicine: The Basis of Perinatology*, London, R.W. Saunders.

Warkany, J. (1959) Congenital malformations in the past, *Journal of Chronic Diseases*, 10, 84–96.

Weatherall, J.A.C. and White, G.C. (1976) A study of survival of children with spina bifida, *Studies on Medical and Population Subjects*, no. 31, London, HMSO.

Wilson, T.S. (1971) A study of congenital malformations of the central nervous system among Glasgow births, *Health Bulletin*, 29, 1–9.

1.4 The effects of lead pollution on children's development

THE LAWTHER REPORT
THE CONSERVATION SOCIETY REPORT:

The power of the social environment to determine children's abilities has never been in question, even if the implications of this have never been taken seriously enough. Now, as a result of ever-increasing environmental pollution, the physical environment has come under scrutiny as a possible source of impairment.

The single most debated pollutant in this context has been lead. 1980 saw the publication of a DHSS Working Party Report on the subject, closely followed by a highly critical counter-attack by the Conservation Society. Many basic issues divided the two reports, particularly the extent of the contribution of airborne lead, largely from petrol exhausts, to man's lead intake, which the Conservation Society maintained that the DHSS Report had seriously underestimated.

Reprinted here are extracts from both reports, contrasting the extent of neurobehavioural damage caused to children by lead pollution.

1 THE LAWTHER REPORT: LEAD AND HEALTH

Introduction

There is no doubt that lead is a toxic substance which in sufficient amounts can cause an encephalopathy[1] which could result in permanent brain damage to babies and children. The response of a particular child exposed to lead from any source depends upon so intricate a network of inter-related factors that a simple relationship between dosage and degree of injury which would allow the relative risks to be calculated

Sources:
1   DHSS (1980) *Lead and Health*, The Report of a DHSS Working Party on Lead in the Environment (Lawther Report), London, HMSO
2   Conservation Society (1980) *Lead or Health*, A review of contemporary lead pollution and a commentary on the H.M. Government Working Party Report 'Lead and Health'. Prepared by D. Bryce-Smith and R. Stephens, London, Conservation Society

has not and possibly cannot be established. As with all biological phenomena, the sensitivity of any individual child to lead exposure will vary; nevertheless it is recognized that once a child shows signs of lead encephalopathy there is a danger that permanent damage may result.

A large proportion of the Working Party's time was devoted to the consideration of the effect of lead on the intelligence, behaviour, attainment and performance of children. Particular attention was given, therefore, to the possibility that exposure to lead at levels below those producing symptoms of poisoning can result in impaired intellectual functioning and related problems. [. . .]

Effect of social conditions on the measurements

One of the major problems in both analysing and interpreting studies of this type is that of confounding variables. Exposure to lead tends to be associated with poor environmental conditions, e.g. old houses with lead-containing paintwork, houses close to sources of lead emission, such as smelter or battery works, or to roads with high traffic density. In general, children with lower than average intelligence tend to come from families living in areas where the standard of nutrition and schooling may be low and where their companions are affected by the same depressed environment. Often such cases are in the inner part of a city where the exposure to lead is also greatest. [. . .]

Effect of medical conditions on the measurements

As well as the confounding variables due to social conditions there are many medical conditions which can have a depressing effect, both permanent and transitory, on the child's response to an IQ test. Babies who have suffered various forms of birth injury and anoxia, as well as children who have brain damage from an infection or an accident may well have a permanent IQ deficit ranging from slight to gross. Although it is normal practice to exclude these children from the analysis, it is not always done. Minor degrees of ill-health, such as an infection, anaemia or poor nutrition, may cause a temporary lack of responsiveness. While motivation is usually included as part of the general psychological assessment of the child, most studies rely on a single IQ measurement so that no allowance is made for any temporary upset in the child. Children who are mentally retarded may take longer to learn to walk and may therefore be exposed to lead-containing dust and dirt for a longer period than those who are mobile earlier, as well as being more likely to have abnormal habits, such as eating paint, plaster and dirt. Thus, they run the risk of having a higher than average intake of lead. [. . .]

Effects of lead on intellectual function

[. . .]

Clinic-type studies of children with high lead levels

[. . .] Some of these studies report on patients who have received treatment with chelating agents to reduce the blood lead concentration. All these studies were carried out over a period of seven years during which time there has been a considerable accumulation of knowledge. The findings tend to be contradictory; some studies claim that persistently raised lead levels above 60 μg/dl [2] can be associated with a reduction in performance in intelligence tests among even asymptomatic children;[3] on the other hand, other studies do not claim to show this relationship. Greater decrements and associated behavioural disorders are evident in children who have suffered from lead encephalopathy. [. . .]

Smelter studies

[. . .] Studies of children living nearby compared with those far away from an extrinsic source of lead should constitute a good test of the hypothesis that raised lead levels cause intellectual deficits or behavioural deviance. In fact this has not proved to be the case, in part because very large samples are needed to test for small differences and in part because of incomplete reporting and inadequate analyses of some of the studies undertaken. Some of the studies report a mean IQ deficit of up to 5 points associated with raised lead concentrations in an approximate range of 40–80 μg/dl. However, other studies with equally high blood levels do not show this relationship.

General population studies of dental lead

Several general population studies of dental lead published in the last few years have suggested that modest exposure to environmental lead may be causally related to intellectual deficits in children.

Needleman and Shapiro (1974) reported that dentine[4] lead levels are higher in children with lead poisoning than in asymptomatic children; similar results have been obtained by De la Burde and Choate (1975). It is also known that dentine lead is higher in a school district in Philadelphia in which there was a high concentration of smelters, foundries and lead processing plants than in a district without these industrial activities (Needleman et al., 1974) and this difference has been attributed to airborne lead.

A more recent study (Needleman et al., 1979) has investigated the neuropsychological functioning of children in the general population with 'high' and 'low' levels as assessed by dentine analysis using shed deciduous teeth from first and second grade children in two towns in Massachusetts between 1975 and 1978. Of 3,329 children, 2,235 donated one or more teeth and the teachers completed a behavioural assessment questionnaire on 2,146 of these children. [...] If the samples gave a mean level of greater than 20 $\mu g/g$ or lower than 10 $\mu g/g$ they were classified as 'high' and 'low' lead respectively. [. . .] The final sample for statistical analysis was 158, i.e. 100 'low' and 58 'high' lead.

Detailed neuropsychological testing was then carried out in the children of both groups while the mothers completed social and medical questionnaires and tests to assess attitude and vocabulary. In addition, the teachers completed an 11-item forced-choice behavioural rating on each child. The choice of the tests was generally sound. The high and low lead groups were broadly similar on background variables but the high lead group was slightly older, slightly more socially disadvantaged and the parental IQs were slightly lower. [. . .]

The corrected mean full scale WISC-R[5] IQ of the low dentine group was 106.6 compared with 102.1 for the high lead children. Examination of the individual subtest scores and of the various additional tests showed a general tendency for the high lead children to perform less well. The authors state that verbal performance and auditory processing was particularly impaired but the variations between different types of test functions were quite small. The findings are highly suggestive but some caution is needed in their interpretation. [. . .]

A further limitation in the published paper is the fact that [the effects of] pica[6] [were not controlled] although the high lead children had a much higher frequency of this condition (29 per cent cf. 11 per cent). Although pica was not associated with the behavioural ratings it was associated with performance IQ in both the low and the high tooth lead group and with verbal IQ in the low lead but not the high lead group. The possibility remains that both pica and raised lead levels are independently associated with lower IQ. Another question concerns the effect of omitting the middle group of children with dentine lead levels between 8.5 and 20. It seems important to know whether the intermediate lead group was also psychologically intermediate; if it were not it would weaken the argument that the association represents a causal influence of lead. Furthermore, it is not known how much bias has been created by the very high non-cooperation rate. [. . .]

It must be emphasized that many of the queries raised here apply even more strongly to most other investigations but the Needleman study has been discussed in detail because it is one of the most comprehensive so far undertaken. The implication of the findings is that children in roughly the top 10 per cent of the dentine lead distribution as defined in this study differ from those in the bottom 10 per cent in intelligence and the mean difference in the intelligence quotient is of the order of 4 points after correcting for differences in family background. It is suggested that the 4 point mean difference in the two groups is associated with a difference in mean blood lead concentrations between 23 and 35 µg/dl although this is based on blood lead determinations performed some 4–5 years previously on approximately half of the children involved in the study. [. . .]

Together these studies (Needleman *et al.*, 1979: Hrdina and Winneke, 1978) provide some evidence of an association between raised tooth dentine lead levels and a slight lowering of measured intelligence. There are a number of reservations about these studies and the inferences to be drawn from them which in our view weakens their conclusions.

Effects of lead on educational attainment and behaviour

In an earlier study on children with lead poisoning (Byers and Lord, 1943) most of the children showed poor school performance after lead intoxication but the absence of either controls or pre-poisoning measurements makes it impossible to determine how far the psychological deficits were directly due to the lead intoxication. Following these findings concern has been expressed that exposure to lead has adverse effects on children's psychological development. However it should be noted that methods of treatment have now improved considerably. In recent years the hypothesis has been proposed that lower levels of lead absorption than those leading to lead intoxication may be associated with an increase in learning difficulties and behavioural problems. In particular, it has been claimed that increased blood lead concentrations are associated with hyperactivity. [. . .]

(i)   *Educational attainment*

[. . .] Albert *et al.* (1974) reported an increase in special class placements in schools in children with symptoms of lead poisoning other than encephalopathy (19 per cent) and in children with blood levels above 60 µg/dl (9 per cent) compared with a control group (3 per cent). However, the children's attainment was not measured and the groups were not matched for socio-economic variables, Pihl and Parkes (1977) attempted to examine the association the other way round. They compared the hair lead levels of 31 'learning disabled' children with 22 controls. Unfortunately, their definition of 'learning disability' is unacceptable psychometrically, so that their findings of higher levels of many elements, including lead, is of doubtful validity. Lansdown *et al.*

(1974) gathered data on children's intelligence and reading levels, but did not publish the latter results. However, they found no relationship between blood lead levels and scores on a word reading test. (Lansdown, personal communication.)

Hebel *et al.* (1976) report a tendency, although not statistically significant, for children living closer to a battery factory in Birmingham to score about 1 or 2 points lower on verbal reasoning, mathematics and English than those living further away. The differences remained after adjusting for social class, birth rank and maternal age. However, since the children's blood lead levels were not taken it is difficult to relate these findings to actual, as opposed to assumed, lead exposure. Needleman *et al.* (1979) assessed the children's educational attainment but do not report their results.

(ii) *Hyperactivity*

Although it appears to be widely held that an association has been demonstrated between high body lead levels and hyperactivity in children, there is no satisfactory evidence which confirms this view. It is clear that American writers use the terms 'hyperactivity' and 'hyperkinesis' much more loosely than clinicians in Britain (Sandberg *et al.*, 1978). Recent evidence suggests that children's levels of activity must be monitored in at least two different settings before a diagnosis of hyperactivity can be considered. Moreover, few of the existing rating scales stand close psychometric scrutiny.

The main papers which relate to this question are summarized below. Baloh *et al.* (1975) compared 27 high lead children with a similar number of low lead children. While the two groups did not differ on a number of indices such as IQ scores and did not differ on their level of activity during testing, nevertheless, 44 per cent of the high lead children compared with 15 per cent of the controls were regarded as 'hyperactive' by either parents or teachers. It is unfortunate that standardized questionnaires were not used since this markedly reduces the weight that can be given to this isolated finding. Landrigan *et al.* (1975a and b) found no differences between high lead groups and controls on hyperactivity whether measured by parental questionnaire or as observed by a physician. McNeil *et al.* (1975) used the Werry—Weiss—Peters hyperactivity scale and found no difference between high lead children and controls. Needleman *et al.* (1979) asked teachers of over 2,000 children to complete an unstandardized, crude rating scale of 11 simple yes—no items. Nine of the items showed increasing 'pathology' with increasing tooth lead levels. One of the items which failed to show such a relationship was 'hyperactive'. David *et al.* (1972, 1976b) studied hyperactive children and claimed that they had higher levels of lead in their blood. However, his definition of hyperactivity in this study is dubious and the methodology is such that no firm conclusions can be drawn from his work. [. . .]

Epidemiological aspects of the papers on the effect of exposure to lead on the mental development of children

The object of this section has been to devise a framework which would enable the results from several studies on the effect of exposure to lead on the mental development of children to be compared with each other. Sixteen published papers were found which would allow such a comparison. The studies were of three types:

(a) *Effect of pollution from smelters or lead battery works.* There were [four] in all. [One] compared the children with blood levels of over 40 µg/dl with matched controls who had levels of less than 40 µg/dl (Landrigan *et al.*, 1975b). One had a complicated sample comparing children with different blood lead levels (Ratcliffe, 1977). The remaining two compared populations living at varying distances from the smelter (Lansdown *et al.*, 1974; McNeil *et al.*, 1975).

(b) *Population studies.* In two studies, the children had been followed up since birth and, from information already gathered, groups were defined and compared with matched controls.[7] (De la Burde and Choate, 1972, 1975). There were three studies where the children had been selected from a school population who had donated teeth. Those whose teeth had a high lead content were matched with others with a low lead content (Hrdina and Winneke, 1978) or the group with the highest tooth lead was compared with another group with the lowest tooth lead, but they were not matched (Needleman *et al.*, 1978, 1979).

(c) *Hospital studies.* In these five studies, selected hospital patients with a history of exposure to lead were compared with a control group. In the first patients were matched with their siblings (Sachs *et al.*, 1978). In three studies patients with varying degrees of lead intoxication were matched with controls (Albert *et al.*, 1974; Kotok *et al.*, 1977; Rummo *et al.*, 1979). In the fifth, patients with blood lead levels greater than 50 µg/dl were matched with patients with a level of less than 30 µg/dl (Baloh *et al.*, 1975).

Measurements

To compare the results it was assumed that the deficit between two IQ means using the same standardized scale[8] could be compared with the deficit between two IQ means using another standardized scale, regardless of the age of the children. While it is possible that these differences are not strictly comparable, it is unlikely to have any appreciable effect upon the results and the conclusions drawn from this analysis. Unfortunately, the lead levels were not so easy to compare, as different methods were used to identify the high and low lead groups. In some cases the blood analysis had been carried out several years before the IQ tests. Where the blood tests had been repeated when the IQ tests were carried out, those nearest in time were used in the analysis. Sometimes mean levels were not given, merely the cut-off points, e.g. above and below 30 μg/dl blood lead. In some the mean related to a wide range of observations, while in others the distribution was curtailed. Therefore, the differences between the mean IQs and the mean blood levels could not be compared in all the studies. A major difficulty which is inherent in any combination of studies is that the results of investigations of a very different quality have to be pooled.

Effect of ordering the mean IQ differences

The studies were first ordered according to the differences in the mean IQs between the high and low lead groups and according to the type of study. Two of the hospital studies included different groups of patients compared with a single control and these were separated so that each group could be compared with the control. There were, therefore, 20 items among the 16 studies.

The comparison is presented in Figure 1. Along the base of the figure are the number of studies according to the differences in mean IQ and above each study is the highest and lowest mean blood lead level (where known). It can be seen that there is little relationship between the size of the difference between the mean blood lead concentrations and the mean IQ differences. However, there is an ordering of the studies. The results from the hospitals spread from no effect to a large deficit in IQ. Those from the smelter studies range from no loss to a deficit of 5 points and those from the population studies a deficit of 4 up to 10 points. All three types overlap around the 5 point mark resulting in a clustering of the observations. [. . .]

This review has shown that the deficits in IQs noted in the various studies show little relationship with the size of the difference in the mean blood lead levels. It suggests that the selection of the control group is of crucial importance and it may be that factors other than the exposure to lead may have a more direct bearing on the IQ differences. In addition, several of the studies suffer seriously from a large loss of cases, which could introduce serious bias and from inadequate matching. It should also be noted that in most of the studies there is inadequate

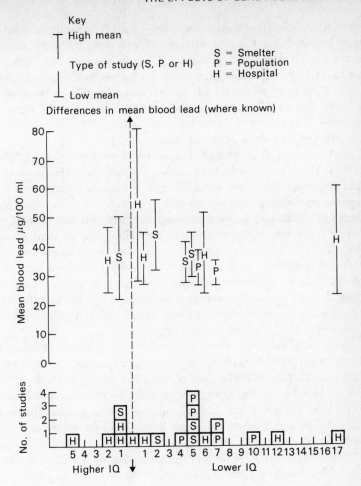

Figure 1 Differences in mean IQ and mean blood lead in high and low
lead groups

description of the main source of lead, its chemical and physical form,
the length of exposure or the dosage. [. . .]

Conclusions

The problem of measuring the total lead intake received by a child over
a long period has not been solved. The concentration of lead in the blood
is generally considered to be the most reliable index of recent exposure
to lead. At a blood lead concentration of 15 μg/dl the results will be
accurate within ±10 per cent, providing that the quality control is

meticulous. Tooth lead is increasingly being used as an indicator of long-term exposure but the concentration of lead varies according to the tooth examined and the part analysed. Again accuracy and precision are exceedingly important. Most of the studies we have seen have relied upon a single measurement of the lead concentration in the blood, without making allowance for the intensity, duration and time of exposure. The source of the lead is rarely determined and the physical condition of the child is often not assessed. [. . .]

In two ranges of blood lead concentrations we have no doubt about effects. There is no convincing evidence of deleterious effects at blood lead concentrations below about 35 μg/dl. It might be thought that the dentine lead studies provide a *possible* exception to this statement but there are difficulties in their interpretation and it is not possible to translate dentine lead concentrations into blood lead concentrations. We also have no doubt about the neuropsychological consequences of high concentrations of blood lead. Symptoms of lead poisoning and encephalopathy occur with levels in excess of, say, 80 μg/dl. Permanent brain damage may follow encephalopathy, although prompt effective measures to reduce exposure and also blood lead concentration may reduce the risk of permanent consequences.

It is therefore in the range of blood lead concentrations between 35–80 μg/dl that doubt remains. In the published studies it is customary either to compare the difference between two groups of children, the average blood lead levels being higher in one group than in the other, or to consider blood lead concentrations in several broad groups. There are some studies which report that mean blood lead concentrations in this range are associated with deficits in intellectual functioning of the order of 5 points on the IQ scale, while other studies do not show such an effect. In considering the relative weight to be given to apparently conflicting reports, we note that contrary to usual dose-effect principles there appears to be no consistent relationship between the concentration of blood or tooth lead and the degree of reported intellectual impairment. If there were a causally linked association one would expect to see such a relationship and its absence lends some support to those reports which have noted no deficit in IQ within the 35–80 μg/dl range of blood lead. At present no single blood concentration of lead within this range can be defined above which an individual child is liable to be harmed. Nevertheless, where a child is found to have a blood lead concentration over 35 μg/dl we would recommend that he or she should be carefully followed up to ascertain the source of the lead and to reduce the exposure of the child and of other persons who might be affected.

Notes

1 Structural damage to the brain.
2 Micrograms per 100 millilitres. (Ed.)
3 Children who do not show overt signs of lead poisoning. (Ed.)
4 The inner hard dense tissue of the teeth. (Ed.)
5 Wechsler Intelligence Scale for Children. A commonly used intelligence test. (Ed.)
6 Substances picked up and ingested by children such as paint and dirt. The term derives from the Latin name for the jackdaw. (Ed.)
7 Matching refers to the comparison of groups of children selected to be equivalent on certain dimensions that might affect the results of the comparison. In this way high and low lead groups might be matched for social class. (Ed.)
8 Standardization is the process of establishing the average score and spread of scores for an IQ test for a population. The average is usually transformed to a score of 100. It cannot be automatically assumed that the same sample would score the same average score on two IQ tests. (Ed.)

References

Albert, R.E., Shore, R.E., Sayers, A.J., Strehlow, C., Kneip, T.J., Pasternack, B.S., Friedhoff, A.J., Covan, F. and Cimino, J.A. (1974) Follow-up of children over-exposed to lead, *Environmental Health Perspectives*, 7, 33–9.

Baloh, R., Sturm, R., Green, B. and Gleser, G. (1975) Neuropsychological effects of chronic asymptomatic increased lead absorption: a controlled study, *Archives of Neurology*, 32, 326–30.

Byers, R.K. and Lord, E.E. (1943) Late effects of lead poisoning on mental development, *American Journal of Diseases of Children*, 66, 471–94.

David, O.J., Clark, J. and Voeller, K. (1972) Lead and hyperactivity, *The Lancet*, 2, 900.

David, O.J., Hoffman, S. and Kagey, B. (1978) In Proceedings of the Symposium on Lead Pollution – Health Effects, London Conservation Society.

David, O.J., Hoffman, S., McGann, B., Sverd, J. and Clark, J. (1976a) Low lead levels and mental retardation, *The Lancet*, 2, 1376–8.

David, O.J., Hoffman, S., Sverd, J., Clark, J. and Voeller, K. (1976b) Lead and hyperactivity: behavioural response to chelation pilot-study, *American Journal of Psychiatry*, 133, 115–8.

De la Burde, B. and Choate, M.S. (1972) Does asymptomatic lead exposure in children have latent sequelae? *Journal of Pediatrics*, 81, 1088.

De la Burde, B. and Choate, M.S. (1975) Early asymptomatic lead exposure and development at school age, *Journal of Pediatrics*, 87, 638–42.

Hebel, J.R., Kinch, D. and Armstrong, E. (1976) Mental capability of children exposed to lead pollution, *British Journal of Preventive and Social Medicine*, 30, 170–4.

Hrdina, K. and Winneke, G. (1978) Paper delivered at the working conference of the German Association of Hygiene and Microbiology, 2–3 October, Mainz: Proceedings of the symposium, *Lead Pollution – Health Effects*, London, Conservation Society.

Kotok, D., Kotok, R. and Heriot, J.T. (1977) Cognitive evaluation of children with elevated blood lead levels, *American Journal of Diseases of Children*, 131, 791–3.

Landrigan, P.J., Gelbach, S.H., Rosenblum, B.F., Schoults, J.M., Candelaria, R.M., Barthel, W.F., Little, J.A., Smrek, A.L., Staehling, N.W. and Sanders, J.F. (1975a) Epidemic lead absorption near a smelter: the role of particulate lead, *New England Journal of Medicine*, 292, 123.

Landrigan, P.J., Whitworth, R.H., Baloh, R.W., Staehling, N.W., Barthel, W.F. and Rosenblum, B.F. (1975b) Neuropsychological dysfunction in children with chronic low-level lead absorption, *The Lancet*, 1, 708–12.

Lansdown, R.G., Shepherd, J., Clayton, B.E., Delves, H.T., Graham, P.J. and Turner, W.C. (1974) Blood-lead levels, behaviour and intelligence: a population study, *The Lancet*, 1, 538.

McNeil, J.L., Ptasnik, J.A. and Croft, D.B. (1975) Evaluation of long-term effects of elevated blood lead concentrations, *Archives of Industrial Hygiene and Toxicology*, 26, 97–118.

Needleman, H.L., Davidson, I., Sewell, E.M. and Shapiro, I.M. (1974) Subclinical lead exposure in Philadelphia schoolchildren: identification in dentine lead analysis, *New England Journal of Medicine*, 290, 245–8.

Needleman, H.L., Gunnoe, C., Leviton, A. and Peresie, H. (1978) Neuropsychological dysfunction in children with silent lead-exposure, *Pediatric Research*, 12, 374.

Needleman, H.L., Gunnoe, C., Leviton, A., Reed, R., Peresie, H., Maher, C. and Barnett, P. (1979) Deficits in psychologic and classroom performance of children with elevated dentin lead levels, *New England Journal of Medicine*, 300, 689–95.

Needleman, H.L. and Shapiro, I.M. (1974) Dentin lead levels in asymptomatic Philadelphia school children: sub clinical exposure in high and low risk groups, *Environmental Health Perspectives*, 7, 27–31.

Pihl, R.O. and Parkes, M. (1977) Hair element content in learning disabled children, *Science*, 198, 204–6.

Ratcliffe, J.M. (1977) Developmental and behavioural functions in young children with elevated blood lead levels, *British Journal of Preventive and Social Medicine*, 31, 258–64.

Rummo, J.H., Routh, D.K., Rummo, N.J. and Brown, J.F. (1979) Behavioural and neurological effects of symptomatic and asymptomatic lead-exposure in children, *Archives of Environmental Health*, 34, 120–4.

Sachs, H.K., Krall, V., McCaughran, D.A., Rozenfeld, I.H., Yongsmith, N., Growe, G., Lazar, B.S., Novar, L., O'Connell, L. and Rayson, B.

(1978) IQ following treatment of lead-poisoning: patient-sibling comparison, *Journal of Pediatrics*, 93, 428–31.

Sandberg, S.T., Rutter, M. and Taylor, E. (1978) Hyperkinetic disorder in psychiatric clinic attenders, *Developmental Medicine and Child Neurology*, 20, 279–99.

2 THE CONSERVATION SOCIETY REPORT: LEAD OR HEALTH

Neurobehavioural effects of lead

Lead is a neurotoxin. And it is a general property of neurotoxins, to which we know of no exceptions, that the earliest manifestations of their neurotoxicity are disturbances of behaviour and/or intelligence: these effects may appear at exposure levels about one-tenth to one-hundredth of those which produce overt symptoms of 'clinical' illness. Alcohol provides the most familiar example of this more general phenomenon (though exposure to alcohol is of course voluntary, unlike breathing leaded air). The study of such chemically induced effects on behaviour and intelligence forms the subject of *behavioural toxicology*.

This relatively new subject constitutes a bridge between the physical and social sciences, though it is not yet sufficiently well known in either. Thus the phenomena studied in behavioural toxicology are complementary to those conventionally recognized in the social sciences, adding a new dimension to existing social concepts rather than rendering them obsolete. Stress, for example, can have both social and biochemical components, as those who seek to assuage its effects by alcohol, nicotine, or tranquillizers are implicitly recognizing.

To those familiar with the field of behavioural toxicology, the finding that lead disturbs behaviour long before it produces clinical illness is to be expected *a priori*, for all known neurotoxins act thus. Moreover, since it is non-controversial that some children can exhibit overt symptoms of *clinical* lead poisoning (e.g. vomiting, excessive lethargy, anorexia) at blood-lead levels above about 40 μg/dl (Conservation Society, 1978; Bryce-Smith *et al.*, 1978), it is fully to be expected that intelligence and behaviour are liable to be disturbed at blood-lead levels well below that. [. . .]

We have been surprised therefore to discover the Lawther Working Party in their Report making the tacit assumption that the reported effects of lead on behaviour, intelligence, etc. are so intrinsically improbable as to merit the most hypercritical form of scrutiny – such as might be applied, for example, to reports of ghosts, flying saucers, and similar phenomena which appear to violate existing physical laws. Moreover, their scepticism is selective: we can find no word of criticism of the few apparently negative reports, even of those which have already received strong technical criticism in the medical literature. It is interesting that Professor Rutter, a member of the Working Party, published almost simultaneously a more detailed and scholarly review of the neurobehavioural effects of lead which while failing to cover the effects on adults and experimental animals, and not perhaps entirely escaping a charge of unconstructive hypercriticality, did at least distribute its criticism more even-handedly, and clearly indicated a higher level of concern for the implications of the effects of 'low level' lead on mental function in children (Rutter, 1980). We have had difficulty in reconciling certain aspects of Rutter's review with his apparent endorsement of the Lawther Report.

The Working Party confess themselves unable to reach clear conclusions on the key question of adverse behavioural effects induced by lead in nominally asymptomatic children. They say, however, they have 'no doubt' that such effects have not been established in children at blood-levels below about 35 μg/dl. Rutter on the other hand clearly indicated that he does take very seriously at least some of the evidence for 'low level' lead effects on children's mental functioning, particularly that of Needleman and his co-workers.

Thus he expresses himself as much more certain that persistently raised blood-lead levels above 40 μg/dl can cause an average mental impairment of 1–5 IQ points and goes on to state that 'less (than 40 μg/dl) *certainly* may increase the risk of behavioural difficulties' (our emphasis). He does not specify just how far below 40 μg/dl this risk extends, though studies with rats (which he does not cite) show behavioural effects of lead at dose levels down to those which give a blood-lead level of as little as 5 μg/dl (Cory-Slechta and Thompson, 1979). [. . .]

David *et al.* (whose pioneering work is cited but then curtly dismissed, partly for lack of information which could easily have been obtained by writing to the author, as we have done, also found significant lead-related educational and behavioural disorders in a large group of New York children having blood-lead levels upwards from 5 μg/dl (David *et al.*, 1978).

Thus we agreed with Rutter that aspects of mental function and/or behaviour in children are certainly liable to be damaged at blood-lead levels below 40 μg/dl. But we go further, and draw attention to recent evidence that such damage can be expected to occur down to 5 μg/dl, a level exceeded in the great majority of children in the UK (see Figure 1) and the USA.

There are other instructive differences between the Rutter review

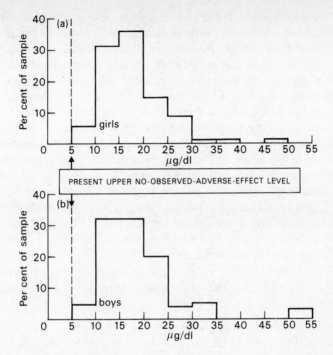

Figure 1 Frequency distribution of blood-lead concentrations in randomly selected Birmingham pre-school children (mean 18.8 μg/dl, N = 243)

and the Lawther Report. Thus Rutter concludes a lengthy assessment of Needleman's important findings (Needleman *et al.*, 1979) on dentine lead levels in relation to mental function as follows: 'There are a number of important questions and reservations about the study and the inferences to be drawn from it, *but none of these are sufficient to invalidate the findings*' (our emphasis). In comparison with this, the Lawther Report states: 'There are a number of reservations about these studies and the inferences to be drawn from them which in our view weaken their conclusions.'

Needleman *et al.* found that carefully matched groups of children having high- and low-dentine lead levels differed significantly in intelligence, behaviour, and measures of reaction time and auditory or speech processing. All these differences favoured the low-lead children. Closely similar lead-related behavioural differences were found within the whole study population of 2,146 children. Moreover, the frequency of all measures of disturbed classroom behaviour increased with increasing dentine lead levels in a *dose-related* fashion. The results are shown in Figure 2. No complex statistical analyses are needed to reveal the progressive increase in the frequency of all the problems with increasing lead level. It is clear that no 'no-effect' threshold exists throughout the whole range of lead burdens now regarded as normal in children, upwards from at least 5 ppm [parts per million] dentine lead. Needleman's findings based on dentine lead are supported by Winneke's independent but closely related smaller-scale study based on 'whole tooth' lead (Hrdina and Winneke, 1979). They accord well with the above-cited work of David *et al*. (1978) which showed that adverse lead-related behavioural and educational effects appear upwards from the lowest blood-lead levels which can now be found among children in the UK (see Figure 1) and USA. [. . .]

Both the Rutter review and the Lawther Report place great stress on social factors, and both for example dismiss various pieces of work on the ground that insufficient attention had been paid to possible social differences. For example, Rutter chose to regard the findings of David *et al*. as unreliable for this major reason. David has in fact written as follows:

In all my studies with the exception of the hyperactivity study in *Lancet* (1972) social class was accounted for. We found a lead effect after social class was controlled. In the hyperactivity study there was a slight (very slight) social class bias. However the bias was in the wrong direction — that is, if there was a difference in social class it was the hyperactive group not the control group that had more upper-class subjects within it. (David, private communication)

Sociologists, educationalists, and psychiatrists may care to reflect that most if not all the existing studies of social factors in relation to behaviour could be deemed invalid because no account was taken of differences in lead burdens between groups.

Be that as it may, we do feel it rather naive to treat social factors and neurobehavioural effects as if they were independent alternatives. Neurobehavioural effects induced in individuals by lead, alcohol, or whatever, must inevitably produce effects on social interactions. Such effects are an everyday experience in the case of alcohol, some individuals becoming less aggressive for example, and others more aggressive. Similar *social* changes have been induced by administration of lead to laboratory animals (Schonmann and Greuner, 1975; Cutler, 1977; Bushnell and Bowman, 1979; Allen *et al*., 1974; Sauerhoff and Michaelson, 1973), and lactating mice even tend to become cannibalistic under the influence of lead (Maker *et al*., 1975). In humans, the effects of lead

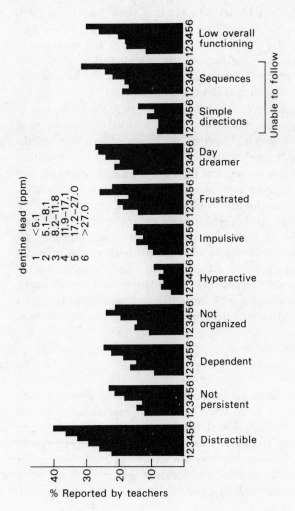

Figure 2 Classroom behaviour in relation to dentine lead concentration; results for 2,146 children (Needleman *et al.*, 1979)

are undoubtedly modulated by social factors. Thus the American Academy of Pediatrics has reported that behavioural abnormalities induced in a child by lead can be greatly intensified by an abnormal mother–child relationship (American Academy of Pediatrics, 1969). It would therefore be simplistic to claim that *either* lead *or* the social factor is the cause of the disturbed behaviour: they interact, and each exacerbates the effect of the other. The lack of any real awareness of these matters in the Lawther Report must raise doubts concerning the Working Party's criticism of the work of those others who have demonstrated such awareness, such as David and Needleman.

One of the most impressive features of Needleman's comparison of matched groups was the great attention given to a total of 39 sociological, medical, and other non-lead factors which might have affected the subject's development and behaviour (Needleman *et al.*, 1979). Statistical analysis of variance showed that none of these factors could account for the observed differences between the high- and low-lead children. A conclusion which appears to follow from this, though it was not drawn by Needleman, is that lead burdens are not to be seen as merely one among a host of social and other factors which influence the development of a normal child's brain and personality, but rather *the* most important single factor yet discovered. That, if true, carries far-reaching implications. Nevertheless, the relationship between neurochemistry and behaviour is a two-way affair: changed neurochemistry alters behaviour, and altered behaviour changes neurochemistry (Barchas, *et al.*, 1978).

Hyperactivity

Hyperactivity in children has been defined as a sustained and excessive level of motor activity which gives rise to significant complaints both at home and at school (Werry, 1968). Recent follow-up studies of children originally diagnosed as hyperactive have shown, in comparison with controls, a higher drop-out and expulsion rate from school, a higher rate of involvement in motor vehicle accidents, a greater tendency to be involved in drug abuse, and a greater risk of coming before the courts (David *et al.*, 1972). [. . .]

Hyperactivity is often found in children with cerebral palsy, temporal lobe epilepsy, and other mental defects, and may be found among the long-term consequences of meningitis and a difficult birth with anoxia. [. . .]

However, many hyperactive children seem to have none of the above predisposing causes for their condition, and it is these 'no obvious cause' children for whom there is growing evidence for lead as a toxic environmental factor which produces 'minimal brain dysfunction' (David *et al.*, 1972; 1976; 1978). Landrigan *et al.*, (1975) also found a higher level of hyperactivity, pica, colic, clumsiness, and irritability in high-lead children, though the differences did not reach statistical significance, but an industry-sponsored study in the same area (El Paso) produced negative findings (McNeil *et al.*, 1975).

Concerning Needleman's study, the Lawther Report incorrectly states that the proportion of children designated as hyperactive did not increase with increasing dentine lead levels: see Figure 2. The proportions of children specified to be hyperactive were comparatively small because the term now carries a certain social stigma in the USA, no doubt because of its association with delinquency, and teachers were therefore reluctant to apply it except to the most marked cases. But as Needleman and others (Ferguson and Pappas, 1979) have pointed out, hyperactivity is in some ways a rather poorly chosen term: the 'distractible', 'not organized', and 'impulsive' categories form part of the same syndrome, and Figure 2 clearly shows the same dependence of these on the lead dose.

The cause-and-effect nature of the relationship between lead and hyperactivity of otherwise unknown origin has been strongly indicated by animal studies and by the marked abatement of this condition achieved by detoxification of children with chelating agents which promote excretion of lead from the body (David *et al.*, 1977; Cohen *et al.*, 1976). [. . .]

Lead and delinquency

[. . .] The proposal that a connection between lead pollution and certain types of delinquent behaviour might exist was at first greeted with considerable scepticism. Although the authors of a Swiss prison study (Lob and Desbaumes, 1971) which appeared to support the proposition have since suggested that data they had given must have been inaccurate (Lob and Desbaumes, 1976), a major study since then has strengthened it. We refer to the important report 'Lead Burden of Sydney Schoolchildren', by Garnys, Freeman and Smythe (1979). These workers also found significant connections between raised lead levels and both blood-forming processes and behavioural abnormalities, in particular, 'current over-activity (and) classroom antisocial problems'. They reported that *'whenever antisocial or delinquent children were encountered they had raised blood-lead levels'* (our emphasis). Although they freely admitted that they had insufficient resources to make as full a study of effects on health and behaviour as they would have wished, and various criticisms have consequently been made of this side of their work, the findings show good though not perfect internal consistency, and are extremely important and provocative. [. . .]

Rutter did not mention the Sydney study at all, and the Lawther Report alludes only to those parts of it concerning the uptake of lead by children without revealing that lead-related behavioural effects were also found. [. . .]

Conclusions

Concerning effects on the mental development of children, the Lawther Report adopts an unconstructively hypercritical attitude, except towards the few 'negative' reports. Effects on the unborn child are scarcely mentioned, and the vast amount of highly relevant evidence from biochemical and animal studies is excluded. [. . .]

Concerning human over-exposure, the recommendations for follow-up and 'appropriate action' are unjustifiably restricted to those, including children, having blood-lead levels above 35 μg/dl. It cannot be emphasized too strongly that this figure has no real scientific or medical basis. Its adoption is likely to breed unwarranted complacency concerning the hazard to children. Likewise, we note with concern that the Report's gravely distorted underassessment of the hazard from airborne and fall-out lead appears to accord closely with long-standing Whitehall and commercial laissez-faire policy. For these reasons, we regret that the Lawther Report represents a wasted opportunity to bring Public Health up to date in a seriously neglected area. In the present Report, we have sought to redress the imbalance, repair the omissions, and correct the errors.

Our own main conclusions, based on a much wider range of evidence than that cited by the Lawther Working Party, are as follows:

(1)   Some 90 per cent of airborne lead comes from lead petrol additives. In this we agree with the Lawther Report.

(2)   Direct inhalation of airborne lead, plus indirect intake by ingestion of food, etc. contaminated by fall-out, provides a major source of lead burdens among the general population, and the main source for many, especially urban children. In addition to this universal source, the following may also be important in certain locations and in certain situations: industrial emissions, lead-rich soil in former lead mining regions and sewage dumping areas, lead paint and cosmetics, lead glazed earthenware, lead polluted tapwater (a major source in some areas), and lead from food cans and other containers for food and drink.

(3)   The sections of the population at greatest risk from present levels of exposure to all sources of lead are as follows:

(i)   Industrial workers with lead and its compounds, especially women of childbearing capacity and men who intend to father children.

(ii)   Populations living in the vicinity of lead smelters, battery factories, and some scrap-yards.

(iii) Populations who receive seriously lead-polluted tapwater.

(iv)   City dwellers and those living or working close to heavy traffic, and especially urban pre-school children.

(v)   Pregnant women. [. . .]

(4)   The concept of thresholds of toxic effect is probably untenable. In the light of present knowledge, the no-observed-adverse-effect levels of lead in children cannot be set any higher than 5 $\mu g/g$ in dentine, and 5 $\mu g/dl$ in blood. Above these levels, neurotoxic effects are liable to occur. These levels allow no safety margin. The blood level is now certainly exceeded in most UK children and the tooth level probably so.

(5)   The neurotoxic effects in children can be produced by post-natal exposure, and pre-natally by parental exposure. They are of types liable to be manifest as educational and/or conduct disorders, and these are now being revealed by careful studies. [. . .]

(6)   The risk of *clinical* lead poisoning increases as the body lead burden increases. This condition normally occurs at blood-lead levels above about 40 $\mu g/dl$ in children, though there are such great variations in individual susceptibility that this figure should not be regarded as a threshold of safety for either children or adults.

(7)   The hazard to the unborn child is not less than that to young children, and probably greater, for lead is readily translocated from the pregnant mother. This hazard may be variously manifest as stillbirth, premature birth, or as mental retardation in children born live and seemingly normal. It is not known what level of maternal lead could be regarded as safe for the unborn child. [. . .]

We conclude overall that most UK children, in common with those of many other countries, are now suffering an epidemic, even a pandemic, of low-grade lead intoxication for which the addition of lead to petrol is largely, though not wholly, to blame. The disease does not normally produce overt symptoms of illness, but is manifest as intelligence deficits ranging from a few IQ points to classifiable mental retardation, and/or socially important behavioural disturbances. The mildness of the symptoms for most individual children is more than offset by the strong evidence that most children are at risk of suffering them to some degree. All the known effects are adverse.

References

Allen, J.R., McWey, P.J. and Suomi, S.J. (1974) Pathobiological and behavioral effects of lead intoxication in the infant rhesus monkey, *Environmental Health Perspectives,* 239–46.

American Academy of Pediatrics (1969) Prevention, diagnosis, and treatment of lead poisoning in childhood, *Pediatrics,* 44, 291.

Barchas, J.D., Akil, H., Elliott, G.R., Holman, R.B. and Watson, S.J. (1978) Behavioral neurochemistry-neuroregulators and behavioral states, *Science,* 200, 964–73.

Bryce-Smith, D., Stephens, R. and Mathews, J. (1978) Mental health effects of lead on children, *Ambio,* 7, 192–203.

Bushnell, P.J. and Bowman, R.E. (1979) Reversal-learning deficits in young monkeys exposed to lead, *Pharmacology, Biochemistry and Behavior,* 10, 733–42.

Cohen, D.J., Johnson, W.T. and Caparulo, B.K. (1976) Management of life-threatening asthma and intravenous isoproterenol infusions, *American Journal of Diseases of Children,* 130, 47–8.

Conservation Society (1978) *The Health Effects of Lead on Children,* London, Conservation Society.

Cory-Slechta, D.A. and Thompson, T. (1979) Behavioral toxicity of chronic post-weaning lead-exposure in the rat, *Toxicology and Applied Pharmacology,* 47, 151–9.

Cutler, M.G. (1977) Effects of exposure to lead on social behavior in the laboratory mouse, *Psychopharmacology,* 52, 279–82.

David, O.J., Clark, J. and Voeller, K. (1972) Lead and hyperactivity, *The Lancet,* 2, 900.

David, O.J., Hoffman, S. and Kagey, B. (1978) *Proceedings of the symposium 'Lead Pollution–Health Effects',* London, Conservation Society.

David, O.J., Hoffman, S., Sverd, J., Clark, J. and Voeller, K. (1976) Lead and hyperactivity: behavioral response to chelation pilot-study, *American Journal of Psychiatry,* 133, 1155–8.

Ferguson, H.B. and Pappas, B.A. (1979) *Hyperactivity in children,* Baltimore, University Park Press.

Garnys, V.P., Freeman, R. and Smythe, L.E. (1979) *Lead Burdens of Sydney Schoolchildren,* Sydney, University of New South Wales.

Hrdina, K. and Winneke, G. (1979) Paper delivered at the working conference of the German Association of Hygiene and Microbiology, Mainz, October, 1978: Proceedings of the symposium *Lead Pollution – Health Effects,* London, Conservation Society.

Landrigan, P.J., Whitworth, R.H., Balsh, R.W., Staehling, N.W., Barthel, W.F. and Rosenblum, B.F. (1975) Neuropsychological dysfunction in children with chronic low-level lead absorption, *The Lancet,* 1, 708–12.

Lob, M. and Desbaumes, P. (1971) Fever from diphenylmethane diisocyanate, *Schweizerische Medizinische Wochenschrift,* 101, 357.

Lob, M. and Desbaumes, P. (1976) Lead and Criminality, *British Journal of Industrial Medicine,* 33, 125–7.

Maker, H.S., Lehrer, G.M. and Filides, D.J. (1975) Effect of lead on mouse-brain development, *Environmental Research*, 10, 76—91.

McNeil, J.L., Ptasnik, J.A. and Croft, D.B. (1975) Evaluation of long-term effects of elevated blood lead concentrations, *Archives of Industrial Hygiene and Toxicology,* 26, 97—118.

Needleman, H.L., Gunnoe, C., Leviton, A., Reed, R., Peresie, H., Maher, C. and Barrett, P. (1979) Deficits in psychologic and class-room performance of children with elevated dentin lead levels, *New England Journal of Medicine,* 300, 689—95.

Rutter, M. (1980) Raised lead levels and impaired cognitive/behavioural functioning: a review of the evidence, *Developmental Medicine and Child Neurology,* 22, supplement 42.

Schonmann, S. and Greuner, N. (1975) The effect of lead-acetate on isolation-induced aggression in mice, in Abstracts of International Conference on Heavy Metals in the Environment, Toronto, Ontario, Canada.

Sauerhoff, M.W. and Michaelson, I.A. (1973) Hyperactivity and brain catecholamines in lead-exposed developing rats, *Science*, 182, 1022—4.

Werry, J.S. (1968) Developmental hyperactivity, *Pediatric Clinics of North America,* 15, 568—81.

1.5 Early influences on development: fact or fancy?

ARNOLD J. SAMEROFF

In this seminal paper, Sameroff presents evidence from obstetrics and child development that challenges the theory that children's development can be predicted either from a knowledge of their characteristics in infancy alone or from a knowledge of the caretaking environment alone. He shows that deviant outcomes in the form of mental retardation or behavioural disturbance depend upon the continual and progressive interaction of the child and the environment. Understanding the causes of handicap thus means examining both the child as an individual, the environment and their interaction. The transactional model Sameroff presents has application far beyond the limited areas he analyses.

[. . .]

Continuum of reproductive casualty

In recent years increasing attention has been directed toward the study and early identification of various factors which place children at a greater than average risk to later disease or disorder. Although persons of all ages are menaced by a range of life hazards, most of the available research literature has focused on a variety of trauma that are suffered early in infancy and that are expected to play a principal role in the developmental outcome of the affected individual. The seriousness of such early hazards is underscored by the fact that the death rates during the perinatal period are four times greater than those of other ages (Niswander and Gordon, 1972). Of perhaps even greater significance is a broad *continuum of reproductive casualty*, hypothesized to include congenital malformations, cerebral palsy, mental retardation, deafness, blindness, and other neurosensory defects which are thought to result from early hazards and traumas (Lilienfeld and Parkhurst, 1951: Lilienfeld, Pasamanick and Rogers, 1955). It has been estimated that approximately 10% of the population in the United States has handi-

Reprinted from Early Influences on Development: fact or fancy?, *Merrill-Palmer Quarterly*, 21 (1975), 267–94 by Arnold J. Sameroff, by permission of the Wayne State University Press

caps or defects that are present at or soon after birth (Niswander and Gordon, 1972).

Of the 5–10 million conceptions occurring annually in the United States, 2–3 million result in spontaneous abortions due to genetic or chromosomal defects and pathogens, and another one million are terminated legally or illegally. Of the approximately 3.5 million foetuses that reach 20 weeks of gestational age, 1.5% die before delivery, 1.5% die in the first postnatal month, 1.5% have severe congenital malformations, and about 10% will have learning disorders that range from mild to severe retardation (Babson and Benson, 1971).

The large number of general learning disorders and specific deficits in behaviours such as reading are of great concern to clinicians. The lack of either a clear genetic basis or anatomical damage in many children with sensory and behavioural disorders was puzzling to investigators who adhered closely to a traditional 'medical model'. If, according to this point of view, a disorder existed, there should have been some clear aetiological factor, preferably biological, somewhere in the patient's history. If such a factor could not be located, it was presumably because diagnostic techniques were not yet sufficiently sophisticated to detect it. Gesell and Amatruda (1941), strong advocates of such a straight-forward cause-effect model, proposed the concept of 'minimal cerebral injury' as an explanation. The supposed reason for not being able to document the existence of such injury is because it is, by definition, minimal, i.e., undetectable. Current usage of terms like 'minimal brain damage' or 'special learning disabilities' are expressions of the continuing need for clinicians to be able to explain disorder on the basis of simple cause-effect relationships rather than complex developmental processes.

Pasamanick and Knobloch (1966) reviewed a series of retrospective studies which examined the delivery and birth complications of children with a variety of subsequent disorders. They found a number of such later disorders to be significantly associated with greater numbers of complications of pregnancy and prematurity. These included cerebral palsy, epilepsy, mental deficiency, behaviour disorders, and reading disabilities.

Almost all studies in this area have proceeded on the general assumption that it is possible to specify particular characteristics of either the child or his parents that will permit long range predictions regarding the ultimate course of growth and development.

These retrospective studies have implicated a number of factors in early development, such as (1) anoxia, (2) prematurity, (3) delivery complications, and (4) social conditions, as being related to later disorder.

After a lengthy review of studies exploring the later effects of perinatal factors Sameroff and Chandler (1975) were forced to conclude that 'even if one continues to believe that a continuum of reproductive casualty exists, its importance pales in comparison to the massive influences of socio-economic factors on both prenatal and postnatal development.' Space does not permit a lengthy survey of the evidence for this conclusion to be made here, but a brief survey of some typical findings will follow. For more detail the reviews of Gottfried (1973) and Sameroff and Chandler (1975) are recommended.

Anoxia

It appears logical to assume that cerebral oxygen deprivation early in development would produce later deficits in intellectual functioning. Animal studies seemed to indicate that oxygen deprivation at birth produced brain damage and learning deficits (Windle, 1944).

Gottfried (1973) reviewed twenty studies of the effects of perinatal anoxia on later intellectual functioning. His conclusions were quite similar to those arrived at by Sameroff and Chandler (1975) in their review of the same literature. These findings can be typified by the results of a large longitudinal study carried out in St. Louis. Several hundred infants were seen in the newborn period (Graham, Matarazzo and Caldwell, 1956), followed up at 3 years (Graham, Ernhart, Thurston and Craft, 1962), and again at 7 years (Corah, Anthony, Painter, Stern and Thurston, 1965). As expected, when examined during the first days of life anoxic infants were found to be 'impaired' on a series of five measures which included maturation level, visual responsiveness, irritability, muscle tension, and pain threshold (Graham, Pennoyer, Caldwell, Greenman and Hartman, 1957). When the performance on these measures was compared with scores based on the degree of prenatal anoxia, postnatal anoxia, and the clinical assessment of central nervous system disturbance, those infants with the poorest scores performed most poorly on the newborn assessments. These same infants were seen again at three years of age and tested with a battery of cognitive, perceptual-motor, personality and neurologic tests (Graham et al., 1962). The group of anoxic infants scored lower than controls on all tests of cognitive function, had more positive neurological findings, and showed some personality differences.

At seven years of age these children were again tested (Corah et al., 1965). Surprisingly, significant IQ differences had *disappeared* between the anoxic group and the control population. Of the twenty-one cognitive and perceptual measures, only two tasks still seemed to show these children deficient. It was concluded that anoxics showed minimal impairment of functioning at seven years and that efforts to predict current functioning on the basis of severity of anoxia were highly unreliable. To summarize, the St. Louis study showed that anoxic infants did poorly on newborn measures, still showed effects at three years of age, but by seven performed almost as well as non-anoxic controls. Gottfried (1973) concluded his review by noting that there were many methodological problems in the literature but that anoxic infants as a group do not appear to become retarded.

Prematurity

Prematurity is another of the classic perinatal hazards that has been related to later deviancy in behaviour. Since prematurity is an outcome of many complications in pregnancy and represents the most prevalent abnormality of birth, it may be considered as a modal problem for assessing the effects of the continuum of reproductive casualty (Birch and Gussow, 1970).

As in the studies of anoxia, the data on long term effects of prematurity do not lead to any clear cut conclusions. Although many studies of prematurity have found small IQ deficits later in development, it is by no means clear whether these adverse consequences associated with prematurity are a function of the prematurity itself, the accompanying low birth weight, an extended period of living in an incubator, accompanying perinatal trauma, or the social climate in which the child is raised (Parmelee and Haber, 1976). A gestationally premature infant who suffers no prenatal, perinatal, or postnatal traumas other than prematurity itself, and is raised in an optimal home environment may turn out to be no different from a normal full-term infant raised under the same circumstances.

It is interesting that the studies of the effects of prematurity have shown consistent, albeit small, IQ deficits, while studies of the effects of anoxia have not. A possible explanation is that the premature infant is more easily recognized and labelled by his parent than the anoxic infant. The parents may not even know if their infant had some form of asphyxia, while the premature, and especially the lower birth weight premature, is quite easily identified not only by its physical appearance but also by the initial separation from the parents, and the subsequent intense caretaking demands. It will be seen that the parents' perception of the child can play a major role in its deviant development exclusive of any actual deficit that may be present in the child.

Newborn status

The research literature offers little evidence to suggest a relationship between specific pregnancy and delivery complications and later abnormal behaviour. Another source for specific predictions of later deviancy has been aberrations in newborn behaviour. Parmelee and Michaelis (1971) have provided an excellent review of the relationship between newborn neurological status and later deviancy. Although the diagnostic search for neurological signs was a successful means of identifying infants with contemporary neurological problems, there was little evidence to suggest that such signs were of any utility as predictors of later adaptational problems.

Socio-economic influences

A recurrent theme that has run through much of the research in this area is that social status variables seem to play an important role in modulating the effects of perinatal factors. Birch and Gussow (1970) argued that high risk to infants is associated with depressed social status and ethnicity. The highest rates of infant loss were found among populations which are both poor and black. Pasamanick, Knobloch and Lilienfeld (1956) found that the proportion of infants having some complication increased from 5% in the white upper social class stratum, to 15% in the lowest white socio-economic group, to 51% among all non-whites. These data imply that the biological outcomes of pregnancy are worse for those in poorer environments.

One of the most ambitious and revealing of the longitudinal studies of the effects of early complications has recently been completed in Hawaii. Werner, Bierman and French (1971), reported on all 670 children born on the island of Kauai in 1955. Because of the multiracial nature of Hawaii and the variety of social classes sampled when the whole population was used, Werner et al. were able to provide ample controls for both variables.

Each infant was initially scored on a four-point scale for severity of perinatal complications. At twenty months and again at ten years of age, these perinatal scores were related to assessments of physical health, psychological status, and the environmental variables of socio-economic status, family stability, and the mother's intelligence.

At 20 months of age infants who had suffered severe perinatal stress were found to have lower scores on their assessments. In addition, however, there was a clear interaction between the impairing effect of perinatal complications and environmental variables, especially socio-economic status. For infants living in a high socio-economic environment, with a stable family, or with a mother of high intelligence, the IQ differences between children with and without complication scores was only 5–7 points. For infants living in a low socio-economic environment, with low family stability, or with a mother of low intelligence, the difference in mean Cattell IQs[1] between the high and low perinatal complications groups and between infants without perinatal complications ranged from 19 to 37 points.

The results of the Kauai study seem to indicate that perinatal complications were consistently related to later physical and psychological development only when combined with and supported by persistently poor environmental circumstances. In addition, when good prenatal care is available, socio-economic differences in the initial distribution of perinatal complications were found to disappear.

The infants of the Kauai sample were again examined when they reached 10 years of age (Werner, Honzik and Smith, 1968). There was no correlation between the perinatal-stress score and the 10-year measures. Some correlation was, however, found between the 20-month and 10-year data, especially when social-economic status and parents' educational level were taken into consideration. Stability of intellectual functioning was much higher for those children who had IQs below 80 at the 10-year testing. All of these children had 20-month Cattell scores of 100 or less, with almost half below 80. The majority of these children had parents with little education and of low socio-economic status. The Kauai study seemed to suggest that risk factors operative during the perinatal period disappear during childhood as more potent familial and social factors exert their influence.

Werner and her associates (Werner *et al.*, 1971) noted that of every 1,000 live births in Kauai, by age 10 only 660 would be adequately functioning in school with no recognized physical, intellectual, or behaviour problems. Of the 34% who would have problems at the age of 10 only a minor proportion could be attributed to the effects of serious perinatal stress. The biologically vulnerable child represents only a small proportion of those children who will not function adequately. The authors concluded that in their study 'ten times more children had problems related to the effects of poor early environment than to the effects of perinatal stress.'

The data from these various longitudinal studies of prenatal and perinatal complications have yet to produce a single predictive variable more potent than the familial and socio-economic characteristics of the caretaking environment. The predictive efficiency of the variable of socio-economic class is especially pronounced for the low end of the IQ scale. Willerman, Broman and Fiedler (1970), compared Bayley[2] developmental scores obtained at 8 months with Stanford-Binet IQs[3] at age 4. For children with a high socio-economic status there was little relationship between their 8-month Bayley scores and their 4-year scores. For children with a low socio-economic status, however, those who did poorly at 8 months continued to do so at 4 years of age. In addition, there was a crossover effect, where the high socio-economic status children who were in the lowest quartile at the 8-month examination were performing better at 4 years than were the low socio-economic status children who scored in the highest quartile at 8 months. Willerman *et al*. (1970) see poverty as amplifying IQ deficits in poorly developed infants.

The preceding survey of early biological complications conceptualized in the continuum of reproductive casualty (Lilienfeld, Rogers and Pasamanick, 1955) has not found much support for direct long-range consequences. The hypothesized 'continuity' in development from early trauma to later deviancy does not appear to hold. There is a serious question as to whether a child who has suffered perinatal trauma, but shows no obvious physical damage, is at any greater risk for later deviancy, either neurological, perceptual, or intellectual, than a child who has not suffered perinatal trauma. In the studies reviewed, the effects of social status tended to reduce or amplify intellectual deficits. In advantaged families infants who had suffered perinatal complications generally showed minor residual effects, if any, at follow-up. Many infants from lower social class homes with identical histories of complications showed significant retardations in later functioning. Socio-economic status appears to have much stronger influence on the course of development than perinatal history.

Continuum of caretaking casualty

Sameroff and Chandler (1975) were led to propose a *continuum of caretaking casualty* to incorporate the environmental risk factors leading toward poor developmental outcomes. Although reproductive casualties may play an initiating role in the production of later problems, it is the caretaking environment that will determine the ultimate outcome. At one end of the caretaking continuum, supportive, compensatory and normalizing environments appear to be able to eliminate the effects of early complications. On the other end of the continuum, caretaking by deprived, stressed, or poorly educated parents tends to exacerbate early difficulties.

Where environmental factors have generally been ignored in research efforts aimed at finding linear chains of causality between early pregnancy and delivery complications and later deviancy, they have been the central focus for investigators exploring the role of caretaking practices in producing poor developmental outcomes. Unfortunately, environmentally oriented researchers have generally been equally one-sided in the way they ignore the child's individuality as a major influence on the caretaking to which he is exposed. Despite these limitations, research into the developmental implications of early caretaking practices has identified many circumstances that contribute to risk. Breakdowns in in the parent—child relationship may take a great variety of forms. The most heavily researched and carefully documented of these transactional failures relates to the inability of parents and their children to work out an interactional style which both guarantees the child a reasonable margin of safety and satisfies the child's basic biological and social needs. This is the issue of child abuse. Physical abuse is dramatic evidence of a disorder in the parent—child relationship.

Child abuse

The major focus of research on the battered child has been devoted to characterizing the personality of the abusive parent. Spinetta and Rigler (1972) in a summary of this research characterized these deviant parents as of lower intelligence and with higher levels of aggressiveness, impulsivity, immaturity, self-centredness, tenseness and self-criticism. However, knowing this constellation of personality characteristics does not greatly improve the probability of correctly predicting that child abuse will occur. Other parents with very similar characteristics do not abuse their children, while parents who are abusive will only batter one or two of their children. It appears that certain children are selected for abuse, or rather, that certain children tend to elicit, abusive behaviour from their parents.

Sameroff and Chandler (1975) were able to find support for the hypothesis that characteristics of the child may predispose the parents to battering or neglect. Klein and Stern (1971), for example, found an association between low birth weight and the battered-child syndrome. Whereas typically 10% of births are of low birth weights, among battered children the rate runs as high as 40%. Klaus and Kennell (1970) suggested that the birth of a premature child may function to overtax the limited resources of certain mothers and precipitate an acute emotional crisis. Many battered children whose birth weights were within normal limits had other significant medical illnesses which might also have served to deplete their mothers' emotional resources.

It has been suggested that these problems may be partly the result of separation in the newborn period (Klaus and Kennell, 1970). Because of prematurity or serious illness a high proportion of battered children had been separated earlier from their parents for prolonged periods. Early prolonged separation may permanently impair the affectional ties between parents and children and leave the children vulnerable to parental abuse and neglect.

Although it is not always possible to separate truth from rationalization, the parents of abused children frequently describe their offspring
as difficult and unmanageable. In one study (Morse, Sahler and Friedman, 1970), for example, 15 of the 25 children studied were considered
'difficult' by their parents. Other data collected tended to support the
impressions of the parents that many battered children were problem
children preceding the reported abuse or neglect.

Reciprocity in child–caretaker relations

In all of the risk categories of this survey (including prenatal and perinatal pathology, parental characteristics, and other intra- or extra-familial
environmental factors) it is possible to identify significant numbers of
children who, although subjected to these negative influences, nevertheless develop normally (Chess, 1971). Only some of the children subjected
to these presumed psychological pathogens do in fact develop disturbances, and only small quantitative relationships have been demonstrated
to exist between pathology in either the parents or the environment and
pathology in the child (Beiser, 1964).

The failure to predict adequately the cases of child abuse appears to
have been the result of a research strategy which has been almost exclusively concerned with environmental effects. Children labelled 'at risk'
have often been regarded as passive victims of external forces and as a
consequence are thought to be incapable of having in any way provoked
or participated in the difficulties in which they have found themselves
(Galdston, 1971). As a consequence the victims have often been purpose-
fully excluded from study because their roles have been presumed to be
irrelevant. Because much of the research on child abuse has been prompted by concerns with prevention and remediation, attention has been
focused on those aspects of the problem which have been thought to be
more easily changed. The evident importance of the parents and their
child-rearing practices pushes characteristics of the children themselves
into an incidental role.

Bell (1968) took a fresh view of the literature on direction of effects
in the caretaking interaction. He pointed out that while viewing infants
as helpless victims fits a one-sided model of parental determination of
behaviour, many studies have shown that the infant is more involved in
determining the nature of the interpersonal relationship than was once
supposed. Many parent behaviours are not spontaneously emitted in the
service of educating the child, but rather are elicited by many of the
child's own characteristics and behaviours.

The infant's appearance of helplessness and dependency appears to
be a strong contributor to the parents' desire to provide care (Rheingold,

1966). However, the response of all caretakers is not necessarily the same. The helplessness of a child can arouse negative as well as positive parental response. To the extent that the helplessness and dependency are accompanied by aggravating factors such as restlessness, colic, and digestive difficulties, the chance of eliciting negative caretaking responses is increased (Bell, 1968).

The frequent assumption that the newborn is too ineffectual to carry any legitimate burden of responsibility for the quality of his or her relationship with various caretakers is contradicted by much current research. Constitutional variability in children strongly affects the parents' attitudes and caretaking styles. The systematic investigation of such idiosyncracies in the child's behavioural organization is, however, of fairly recent origin. In research at New York University, Thomas, Chess and Birch (1968) studied the changes that occur in the child's temperament as a function of the transactions with his family environment. These investigators have described a temperamental constellation which they have labelled 'the difficult child'. Difficult infants were found to have low thresholds for arousal, intense reactions when aroused, poor adaptability and irregularity in biological functioning. Although only 10% of their sample were categorized as difficult, 25% of the children who later had behavioural disturbances fell in this group. Without the benefit of longitudinal studies one could easily misinterpret these difficulties of temperament as constitutional weaknesses that predisposed the child to later emotional difficulties. Such static predictions would not, however, prove to be very accurate. In fact, when Thomas *et al.* examined the relationship between behaviour in the first and fifth year of life few significant correlations were found. What made the difference in outcome for these children appeared to be the behaviour of their parents. If the parents were able to adjust to the child's difficult temperament, a good behavioural outcome was likely. If not, the difficulties were exacerbated and behavioural disturbance often resulted.

The transaction was not simply the unidirectional influence of the parents on the child, but also the reciprocal influence of the child on his parents. The impact of these difficult children was such as to disrupt the normal caretaking abilities of their parents. The New York group reported that there were no marked differences in child-rearing attitudes expressed among the various parents in the sample. Whatever differences eventually characterized the parental attitudes of the deviant children apparently arose as a consequence of experience in the parent–child interaction.

The range of findings cited in the preceding section tends to support the hypothesis that knowing *only* the temperament of the child or knowing *only* the child-rearing attitudes and practices of the parents would not allow one to predict the developmental outcome for the child. It would appear, rather, that it is the character of the *specific transactions* that occurred between a given child and his parents which determined the course of his subsequent development. If the continuum of caretaking casualty is to be useful in elucidating developmental consequences, it must be related to the individual characteristics of the child in question. Neither the constitutionally oriented 'continuum of reproductive casualty' nor the environmentally oriented 'continuum of caretaking casualty' is predictive when taken alone. It is the combination of these dimensions which would make an understanding of development possible. [. . .]

A transactional model of development

Any truly transactional model must stress the plastic character of both the environment and the organisation as it actively participates in its own growth. In this model the child's behaviour is more than a simple reaction to his environment. Instead, he is actively engaged in attempts to organize and structure his world. The child is in a perpetual state of active re-organization and cannot properly be regarded as maintaining inborn characteristics as static qualities. In this view, the constants in development are not some set of traits but rather the *processes* by which these traits are maintained in the transactions between organism and environment.

Exceptional outcomes from this organismic or transactional point-of-view are not seen simply as a function of an inborn inability to respond appropriately, but rather as a function of some *continuous* malfunction in the organism—environment transaction across time which prevents the child from organizing his world adaptively. Forces preventing the child's normal integration with his environment act not just at one traumatic point, but must operate throughout his development. [. . .]

Evolution appears to have built into the human organism regulative mechanisms to produce normal developmental outcomes under all but the most adverse of circumstances (Waddington, 1966). Any understanding of deviancies in outcome must be interpreted in the light of this self-righting and self-organizing tendency, which appears to move children toward normality in the face of pressure toward deviation.

Two possibilities that defeat the self-righting tendencies of the organism and produce deviant development can be considered. The first possibility is that an insult to the organism's integrative mechanisms prevents the functioning of its self-righting ability, and the second possibility is that environmental forces present throughout development prevent the normal integrations that would occur in a more model environment. The former possibility can be seen in the pregnancy and delivery complications related to the *continuum of reproductive casualty*. The latter possibility can be seen in the familial and social abnormalities related to the *continuum of caretaking casualty*. These two sources of risk appear to be closely interrelated in the production of positive or negative developmental outcomes. Where the child's vulnerability is heightened through massive or recurrent trauma only an extremely supportive environment can help to restore the normal integrative growth process. A seriously brain-damaged child requiring institutional care would be an instance of such an extreme case of reproductive casualty. On the other extreme a highly disordered care-taking setting might convert the most sturdy and integrated of children into a caretaking casualty. [. . .]

To summarize, disorders in development have been retrospectively attributed to a variety of early constitutional or environmental factors. When these predisposing factors have been studied prospectively little support is given to their causal role or their predictive value for later deviancy. Evidence for qualitative continuities and stabilities in develop-ment appear to be artifacts of an incomplete analysis of the child in its environment. When the two are examined in combination, complex reciprocal transactions are found which reduce or amplify early prob-lems in behaviour.

Developmental outcomes must be interpreted as the products of a child's characteristics, his material environment and the cognitive levels and values of his social milieu. Where the social environment fosters rigidity, stereotyping, and concreteness in thought and behaviour, early deviancies can become resistant to the normal restructuring implicit in development. Where flexibility, openness, and adaptability are funda-mental characteristics of the environment, early problems are dissipated as the child advances in his construction and organization of both his cognitive and social world.

Notes

1 The Cattell Infant Intelligence Scale: an observational measure of early development. (Ed.)
2 The Bayley Scales: observational measures of infant development. (Ed.)
3 A commonly used intelligence test for children from three to sixteen.

References

Babson, S.G. and Benson, R.C. (1971) *Management of High-risk Preg-nancy and Intensive care of the Neonate*, St. Louis, Mosby.

Beiser, H.R. (1964) Discrepancies in the symptomatology of parents and children, *Journal of the American Academy of Child Psychiatry*, 3, 457–68.

Bell, R.Q., (1968) A reinterpretation of the direction of effects in studies of socialization, *Psychological Review*, 75, 81–95.

Birch, H. and Gussow, G.D. (1970) *Disadvantaged Children*, New York, Grune & Stratton.

Chess, S. (1971) Genesis of behaviour disorder, in J.G. Howells (Ed.), *Modern Perspectives in International Child Psychiatry*, New York, Brunner/Mazel.

Corah, N.L., Anthony, E.J., Painter, P., Stern, J.A. and Thurston, D.L. (1965) Effects of perinatal anoxia after seven years, *Psychological Monographs*, 79, (whole No. 596).

Galdston, R. (1971) Dysfunction of parenting: The battered child, the neglected child, the emotional child, in J.G. Howells (Ed.), *Modern Perspectives in International Child Psychiatry*, New York, Brunner/Mazel.

Gesell, A. and Amatruda, C. (1941) *Developmental Diagnosis*, New York, Hoeber.

Gottfried, A.W. (1973) Intellectual consequences of perinatal anoxia, *Psychological Bulletin*, 80, 231–42.

Graham, F.K., Ernhart, C.B., Thurston, D. and Craft, M. (1962) Development three years after perinatal anoxia and other potentially damaging newborn experiences, *Psychological Monographs*, Whole No. 522.

Graham, F.K., Matarazzo, R.G. and Caldwell, B.M. (1956) Behavioural differences between normal and traumatized newborns: II Standardization, reliability and validity, *Psychological Monographs*, Whole No. 428.

Graham, F.K., Pennoyer, M.M., Caldwell, B.M., Greenman, M. and Hartman, A.F. (1957) Relationship between clinical status and behaviour test performance in a newborn group with histories suggesting anoxia, *Journal of Pediatrics*, 50, 177–89.

Klaus, M.H. and Kennell, J.H. (1970) Mothers separated from their newborn infants, *Pediatric Clinics of North America*, 17, 1015–37.

Klein, M. and Stern, L. (1971) Low birth weight and the battered child syndrome, *American Journal of Diseases of Children*, 122, 15–18.

Lilienfeld, A.M. and Parkhurst, E. (1951) A study of the association of factors of pregnancy and parturition with the development of cerebral palsy: A preliminary report, *American Journal of Hygiene*, 53, 262–82.

Lilienfeld, A.M., Pasamanick, B. and Rogers, M. (1955) Relationships between pregnancy experience and the development of certain neuropsychiatric disorders in childhood, *American Journal of Public Health*, 45, 637–43.

Morse, C., Sahler, O. and Friedman, S. (1970) A three-year follow-up study of abused and neglected children, *American Journal of Diseases of Children*, 120, 439–46.

Niswander, K.R. and Gordon, M. (Eds.) (1972) *The Collaborative Perinatal Study of the National Institute of Neurological Diseases and Stroke: the women and their pregnancies*, Philadelphia, Saunders.

Parmelee, A.H. and Haber, A. (1976) Who is the 'risk infant'?, unpublished paper.

Parmelee, A.H. and Michaelis, R. (1971) Neurological examination of the newborn, in J. Hellmuth (Ed.), *Exceptional Infant: studies in abnormalities*, vol. 2, New York, Brunner/Mazel.

Pasamanick, B. and Knobloch, H. (1966) Retrospective studies on the epidemiology of reproductive casualty: old and new, *Merrill Palmer Quarterly*, 12, 7–26.

Pasamanick, B., Knobloch, H. and Lilienfeld, A.M. (1956) Socio-economic status and some precursors of neuropsychiatric disorders, *American Journal of Orthopsychiatry*, 26, 594–601.

Piaget, J. (1950) *Psychology of Intelligence,* New York, Harcourt, Brace & World.

Rheingold, H.L. (1966) The development of social behaviour in the human infant, in H.W. Stevenson (Ed.), The concept of development, *Monographs of the Society for Research in Child Development*, 31 (whole No. 107).

Sameroff, A.J. and Chandler, M.J. (1975) Reproductive risk and the continuum of caretaking casualty, in F.D. Horowitz, M. Hetherington, S. Scarr-Salapatek and G. Siegel (Eds.), *Review of Child Development Research*, vol. 4, Chicago, University of Chicago Press.

Spinetta, J.J. and Rigler, D. (1972) The child abusing parent: A psychological review, *Psychological Bulletin*, 77, 296–304.

Thomas, A., Chess, S. and Birch, H. (1968) *Temperament and Behavior Disorders in Children,* New York, New York University Press.

Tinbergen, N. (1974) Ethology and stress diseases, *Science*, 185, 20--7.

Waddington, C.H. (1966) *Principles of Development and Differentiation*, New York, Macmillan.

Werner, E.E., Bierman, J.M. and French, F.E. (1971) *The Children of Kauai*, Honolulu, University of Hawaii Press.

Werner, E., Honzik, M. and Smith, R. (1968) Prediction of intelligence and achievement at ten years from twenty months pediatric and psychologic examinations, *Child Development*, 39, 1063–75.

Willerman, L., Broman, S.H. and Fiedler, M. (1970) Infant development, preschool IQ and social class, *Child Development*, 41, 69–77.

Windle, W.F. (1944) Structural and functional changes in the brain following neonatal asphyxia, *Psychosomatic Medicine*, 6, 155–6.

PART 2

The History of Special Education

2.1 Mental handicap: the historical background

JOANNA RYAN AND FRANK THOMAS

The history of attitudes to mental handicap is not one of increasing care and understanding. On the contrary, Ryan and Thomas give an account that shows the complex nature of religious, medical and moral beliefs that sometimes resulted in sympathy, but more often in censure and abuse. Nor is there much evidence of progress through history, as nineteenth-century theorists came increasingly to believe that sub-normality was the result of moral turpitude and racial and social inadequacy. In the twentieth century, these hereditarian views have continued to exert a considerable influence, as has the medical pro-fession. The predominance of medical ideas has led to a neglect of the social experience and meaning of mental handicap.

Early writings

Before the late eighteenth century discussions of idiocy are scattered and fragmentary; those that do remain show clearly a preoccupation with the human status of idiots and with their origins. One of the more extended treatises is that of Paracelsus, a Swiss physician of the early sixteenth century. His account of fools is detailed and searching.[1] Wishing to establish the full humanity of fools, he proposes a funda-mental Christian argument: '. . . his (man's) wisdom is nothing before God, but rather that all of us in our wisdom are like the fools . . . There-fore the fools, our brethren, stand before us . . . And he who redeemed the intelligent one, also redeemed the fool, as the fool, thus the intelli-gent one.' And further: '. . . death drives away from them the folly, the fantasy and so on, and it is the man within who perceives himself . . . even if the nature went wrong, yet nothing has been wrong with the soul and the spirit.' Paracelsus states that fools are not only equal to other people in God's eyes but even superior, being nearer to God. They differ from 'wise men' because the 'animal body they inhabit has been marred . . . the wisdom that is also in fools, like light in a fog, can shine through more clearly.' The wise man sometimes resists the 'true man' in his

Source: Ryan, J. and Thomas, F. (1980) *The Politics of Mental Handicap*, Harmondsworth, Penguin, pp. 86–91, 102–5, 112–15, © Joanna Ryan and Frank Thomas, 1980. Reprinted by permission of Penguin Books Ltd

animal body, the fool does not. Just as God made prophets with a crazy 'animal body' so people should listen to fools, especially those not pushed around by other people. Instead of which, Paracelsus notes, people mostly scorn them because they lack both understanding and control of their reason. Paracelsus's idea that idiots do not suffer from as many worldly corruptions as others and are nearer to some truer or more basic conception of human nature persists into the present.

On the other hand, the notion that idiots are a consequence of the evils of mankind is also a recurrent theme in the Christian world. St. Augustine states clearly that fools are a punishment for the fall of Adam and other sins.[2] Paracelsus does not blame individual parents for the birth of fools, as later writers did; for him, fools are simply one aspect of the way the whole of mankind has lost God's image. He favours kindly and respectful treatment of them, as an assertion of their rightful place in humanity.

What, however, causes wise parents to beget fools? Paracelsus maintains there is nothing defective in the material supplied by parents but something wrong in the subsequent processes that are beyond their control. Nature is a workshop inhabited by craftsmen, and children are made by carvers from the wood supplied by their parents. Fools are produced when inept apprentice carvers make mistakes and carve badly, as often happens. This picture has a similar logic to much later explanations of what was known as congenital idiocy, for example, the accounts of mongolism put forward before the discovery of chromosomal defects.[3] Combined accounts of fools, in terms both of their religious meaning and of defective causal mechanisms, were commonplace and continued to be so until the end of the nineteenth century.

It is not clear what the context of Paracelsus's treatise was, who he was arguing against, or whether any of his ideas were accepted. However, in the Middle Ages and before, there were many myths about changelings, children who were born deformed, handicapped or in some way peculiar: 'Fairies stole a mother's child from its cradle, and in its place laid a changeling with a big head and staring eyes who wanted to do nothing but eat and drink.'[4]

This is a story that has been embellished in all kinds of folklore and beliefs which have been handed down through centuries. Changelings were seen as sub-human, not born of a human mother. They came from the non-human underworld of envious demons, elves, fairies, etc. in exchange for the stolen human child. Their non-human status did not necessarily mean they were treated badly — indeed they were sometimes treated particularly well in the belief that this would ensure the good treatment of the stolen human child.

In these accounts, blame is attributed neither to the individual parents nor to mankind as a whole. All parents were exposed to the danger of having their child stolen even if they took every precaution. Blame and responsibility were directed outwards, on to the non-human underworld, beyond the control of ordinary people.

The Christian form of the idea of the handicapped child as an exchange can be seen in Luther's belief that it is the devil who has stolen the human child and then substituted himself for it. 'The devil sits in such changelings where the soul should have been.'[5] Changelings, 'more obnoxious than ten children with their crapping, eating and screaming', were just lumps of flesh with no soul; Luther even recommended killing them.[6] This is an early example of the common association of idiots with animality — no soul and over-dominant bodily functions — which was to become a familiar theme by the end of the nineteenth century.

The idea of handicapped children being a punishment for the sins of individual parents, rather than for those of mankind in general, is seen clearly in Luther. He explains the presence of abnormal children as stemming from the misdeeds of their parents — those who did not fear God enough, who bore illegitimate children, thought bad thoughts or cursed their offspring.[7]

The idea that abnormal children were the result of sexual intercourse between a woman and the devil was also common at the time. And for a long time giving birth to a handicapped child was grounds, in Europe, for considering a woman to be a witch. There are instances of blaming the mother specifically — a theme that was also to recur with much emphasis in the nineteenth and early twentieth centuries.

From the sixteenth century onwards there are scattered references to cretins.[8] These were particularly numerous in certain valleys of the Swiss Alps, due to deficiencies in the drinking water. Their deformed appearance — they suffered from large goitres — and odd behaviour made them seem hardly human to astonished travellers and other observers. An account written in 1574 notes that '. . . many fatuous people are found . . . who hardly deserve to be named people, since they use no human food; . . . one who used horse-droppings, another one who used hay, others who walked naked the whole winter and various monstrosities of this sort.'[9] Their ugliness was sometimes grounds for considering them as only semi-human: 'They have a hardly human face, a large mouth and spittle flowing down.'[10]

Their appearance and behaviour also gave rise to spectres of sensuality and immorality: 'They are deaf, dumb, imbecile, almost insensitive to blows, and carry goitres hanging down to the waist; rather good people otherwise, they are incapable of ideas, and have only a sort of violent attraction for their wants. They abandon themselves to the pleasures of the senses of all kinds and their imbecility prevents them seeing any crime in this.'[11] The idea that idiots enjoyed their animal nature is yet another one which occurs again later. In the same account cretins were also seen as a separate sub-species of man, comparable to albino Negroes and other alleged curiosities — foreshadowing again the nineteenth century and its ethnic comparisons of idiots with so-called primitive people.

On the other hand the cretins, it seems, were regarded by the Swiss valley inhabitants themselves as angels from heaven, a blessing to their families and incapable of sin. A family without one regarded itself as being on bad terms with heaven.[12] They were well looked after, if contemporary accounts are to be believed, often with special hospices for their care. This super-human status accorded to Swiss cretins by the people they lived among is unique in European history. It contrasts especially strongly with the more negative sub-human descriptions of them given by outside observers.

We do not know even now what it was about the life of the valley inhabitants that allowed them to see their idiots so favourably. But it is clear than an understanding of the social basis of these attitudes is vitally important to any overall understanding of idiocy. It is possible that the obviously endemic and environmental nature of cretinism lessened the tendency to blame and stigmatize. Cretinism could have been perceived simply as an unalterable fact of nature, part of the divine order of the world, rather than of the misdeeds of mankind.

By the sixteenth century, too, the link between cretinism, goitre and the drinking water of certain valleys was known and discussed in contemporary medical literature. Cretinism shows a particularly close association between mental and physical abnormalities and it may have been this which influenced later writers to believe that all forms of idiocy had a definite organic basis. Idiocy in general has often been confused with cretinism: the name 'cretin' has sometimes been used to refer to all kinds of idiots and is occasionally used in everyday speech now.

The general assumption of the organic cause of idiocy was not much questioned before the twentieth century, when 'social' categories of defectives were devised. As cretinism is also such a clear example of the environmental causation of idiocy, it is interesting that, in contrast to the organic views, this knowledge does not appear to have modified subsequent theories on the hereditary basis of idiocy, nor to have encouraged much investigation of other possible environmental or endemic causes. This is but one example of the general bias in the whole field towards any kind of hereditary explanation.[13]

It was a seventeenth-century English physician, Willis, who was the first to propose what was later to become a very common view of degeneration. Trying to answer the question of how fools could be born to intelligent, as opposed to foolish parents, he supposed that, apart from accidents at birth, there was something defective in the material supplied by parents for reproduction.[14] Willis argued that the defects arose from their behaviour. Parents (to paraphrase Willis) might do too much studying and reading, causing them to be 'weakly prolific', too much energy being directed to the mind as opposed to the body. Or there may be 'somatic insults' to the bodies of parents through intemperance, drunkennes, effeminacy, luxury or excessive youth or age.

Willis also suggested that sometimes the size and texture of the brain was abnormal, apparently one of the earliest ideas about this. In seeing stupidity as sometimes the result of brain impairment, Willis likened it to other diseases which do not reduce the human character of the sufferer. Like Paracelsus, he also recognized that stupidity could not be cured, but he did emphasize the importance of both physicians and teachers in alleviating it.

One of the earliest appeals for some kind of public provision for idiots was made by Daniel Defoe at the end of the seventeenth century. It did not, however, materialize. He argued for the creation of a 'public fool house' to be paid for by a tax on learning, levied on the authors of books, on the grounds of a kind of natural justice.[15] At the same time he attempted to wrestle with the problem of how to fit 'born fools or naturals' into humanity. 'Perhaps,' he wrote, 'they are a particular Rent-Charge on the Great Family of Mankind left by the Maker of us all — like a younger Brother, who tho' the Estate be given from him, yet his Father expected the Heir should take some care of him.' Care should be taken of fools, said Defoe, as a tribute to God's bounty to mankind, a tribute to be paid to all those who lacked this bounty. Defoe also likened fools to animals, for the apparent 'deadness of their souls'. [. . .]

The dehumanization of idiots

In the ideas that subsequently developed about idiots and the practices that these ideas led to, it is possible to observe the emergence of increasing dehumanization. No longer seen as a personal misfortune, idiocy came to be regarded as a widespread social evil.

One of the earliest writers to see idiocy as a social threat was Howe, usually regarded as one of American's leading humanitarian reformers. In 1848 he wrote *On the Causes of Idiocy* as part of his campaign to persuade the Massachusetts legislature to provide funds for a residential training school for idiots, and his ideas were subsequently very influential in England.

Seeing idiocy as 'part of the host of social evils which society is in vain trying to hold off by jails, almhouses etc.', Howe laid the blame squarely at the feet of parents; their drunkenness, masturbation, inter-marriage, attempts at abortion, fright and ill health were all violations of 'natural laws'. Such violations, in combination rather than singly, could result in an idiot child.

It was Howe who introduced the concept of a general predisposition or hereditary tendency to idiocy in certain families which subsequently dominated the history of ideas about idiocy. As evidence, he claimed 359 cases of idiocy, in all but 4 of which he could find deviations from healthy living on the part of the parents:

> The moral to be drawn from the existence of the individual idiot is this – he, or his parents, have so far violated the natural laws, so far marred the beautiful organism of the body, that it is an unfit mani-festation of the powers of the soul. The moral to be drawn from the prevalent existence of idiocy in society is that a very large class of persons ignore the conditions upon which alone health and reason are given to men, and consequently they sin in various ways.[16]

Howe's speculation on the origins of idiocy thus situates supposedly biological fact – organic damage to the bodies of parents, leading to reduced bodily and mental vigour in the child – within a religious and moral framework. Such evil is punishment for sins that have to be atoned for. This admixture of the moral and the biological was to persist throughout the nineteenth and twentieth century.

Séguin saw idiots somewhat differently, although still in a religious and social framework. At the opening of a school for idiots in Syracuse in 1854, he criticised those who considered idiots to be an evil and a punishment from God, preferring to see their potential benefit to man-kind: 'God has scattered among us, rare as the possessors of talent or genius, the idiot, the blind, the deaf-mute, in order to bind the talented to the incapable, the rich to the needy, all men to each other, by a tie of indissoluble solidarity.'[17]

Later, however, with the growing realization that idiot schools and asylums were not escaping the adverse consequences of increasing numbers, even Séguin turned to blame, though never to the extent of other nineteenth-century writers. Remarking, as they all do, on the apparent increase in idiocy, he asks what new causes there might be and identifies the changing status of women as a likely source: 'As soon as women assumed the anxieties pertaining to both sexes they gave birth to children whose like had hardly been met with thirty years ago.'[18] The changing aspirations of women 'has not taught them anything of womanhood'; other women 'are over-anxious about being a good wife' and altogether 'the foetus has no place to grow in peace'.

Séguin's radicalism clearly did not extend to the situation of women, nor to the aspirations of nineteenth-century feminists. Despite his general concern for the oppressed, even Séguin did not have a sufficiently deep understanding of the social changes that were affecting the position of all dependent people and their families and apparently causing an increase in the number of idiots. This failure led him, like others, to scapegoat one particular group of people as being to blame.

From the 1860s onwards, the collecting together of idiots in asylums made more possible the systematic study of different types and causes of idiocy. Interest grew in developmental causes and hereditary influences, and new conceptualizations of the differences between idiots (or mental defectives as they became known) and the rest of mankind were proposed.

Writers of the new medical textbooks tended to follow Howe's view that idiots represented the evils of society in the form of their parents' transgressions. Ireland, superintendent of a Scottish asylum, wrote in 1877: 'There can be no doubt of the great part played by heredity in the genesis of idiocy. Idiots frequently are born in families in which there is a decided neurotic tendency, as manifested by the appearance of insanity, imbecility, or epilepsy among the members.'[19] Seeing idiocy as particularly prevalent in a society 'struggling under unhealthy and disquieting influences' he follows Séguin in singling out the changing status of women and their nervous exhaustion as leading to children 'conceived in antagonism'. On the other hand he disagrees with Howe's indictment of alcoholism as a major factor.

Shuttleworth, superintendent of the Royal Albert Asylum, in a survey of more than 2,000 cases concluded that idiocy is caused not by a single factor but by many contributory ones, what he calls 'repeated transgressions' of the parents: 'Not every drunken parent procreates an idiot, but when inherited nervous instability from this or other causes is intensified in the next generation by injudicious marriage or by unfavourable environment, instances of mental degeneracy are apt to occur.'[20]

Bateman, physician at the Eastern Counties Asylum, views idiocy as '. . . an expression of parental defects and vices . . . a result of the violation of natural laws over several generations . . . people ignore conditions of health and reason, pervert their natural appetites . . .'[21] He claims that a large proportion of idiots have alcoholic parents or insane relatives. And once again women who step outside their customary role are blamed: '. . . a female mathematical athlete is unsuited for the duties and responsibilities of maternity . . . the mental endowments of her children are likely to be below the average.'

Tredgold takes the emphasis on heredity even further, claiming in 1908 that 90 per cent of all mental defectives were the result of 'inherent defects in germinal plasm'.[22] And a later textbook describes most forms of mental deficiency as being due to 'intrinsic causes' or 'morbid heredity'.[23]

Some medical textbooks included descriptions of idiots in which they were likened to allegedly more primitive non-European people. The most famous and most persistent racist classification is that of Langdon-Down, who identified one distinct sub-group of idiots as Mongolian: it was 'difficult to realize he [the idiot] is the child of Europeans'; there was 'no doubt that these ethnic features are the result of degeneration'.[24]

Other classifications were even more fanciful. Tredgold, for example, thought he could distinguish Negroid, Grecian, Egyptian and American-Indian types of mental defective. This ethnic form of classiciation was not some quirk of the writers concerned, but was put forward at a time of great interest in the biological evolution of mankind and of the increasing British colonization of hitherto 'uncivilized' parts of the world. Idiots were seen as unfinished and primitive forms of man, like savages in their nearness to nature and their distance from the heights of European civilization. Anthropology of the period is full of attempts to place the various tribes and races in evolutionary order, according to how primitive and ape-like they appeared. This classification system was applied also to the medical study of mental deficiency. [. . .]

Social and biological categories

An important development in the biological sciences was also to have its effect on ideas about the causes of mental subnormality. In the nineteenth and early twentieth century the phrase 'hereditary tendency' was used to describe almost any trait that could be related to the supposed defects of parents or other relatives and that was present from childhood. But the discoveries of Mendelian genetics and the increasing knowledge of embryonic development made such an over-inclusive notion less and less tenable. At least this was the case among people who claimed to be scientific and objective; as late as 1935 Burt was still attempting to combine together the vast range of genetic, congenital, developmental and familial disorders in one category of 'innate' deficiency as 'inherited'.

The Wood Committee report of 1929 did, however, reflect to some extent the changing views on the causation of mental deficiency. It introduced a distinction between two kinds of defective, those whose defects could be regarded as purely biological and those who were considered to be part of a sub-cultural social group without any clear organic pathology. This distinction was based on an IQ conception of intelligence. The sub-cultural group represented the bottom end of the 'normal' distribution of IQ scores, due to the ordinary variation that would be expected among any group of people. The biological or pathological group was seen as a consequence of various exceptional biological accidents, superimposed on the normal curve of IQ scores.

The pathological group supposedly formed the excess number of mental defectives with very low IQ scores, i.e. the excess over the numbers predicted by the normal distribution of IQ scores. This excess was simply assumed, never really verified; indeed many studies have reported dramatically fewer mentally handicapped people than predicted by IQ statistics.[25] The pathological group had a social-class composition that was representative of the whole population in contrast to the sub-cultural group which came exclusively from working-class backgrounds and which tended to have many relatives with low IQ scores as well.

The effect of this distinction was to separate those mental defectives of clear medical interest from those about whom medicine had little to say diagnostically, but who were regarded as a social problem. As such the distinction does at least reflect the real growth of more precise scientific knowledge: former generalized views about 'hereditary tendencies' could no longer be applied to the whole range of mental defectives, especially not to those 'biological accidents', with specific pathological syndromes and intelligent parents. It also signifies the removal of a section of the mentally defective population from indiscriminate association with other social problems, a suspension of blame from some (often middle-class) parents. Yet although the generalized blaming of parents had to be modified in the face of increasing scientific knowledge, it did reappear in the indictment of families of higher grade working-class defectives. These were the ones whose 'diagnosis' had been particularly facilitated by the invention of IQ tests and whose 'discovery' gave rise to such panic and repression. Their low intelligence was ascribed to their poor 'inheritance' from their parents.

Attempts to distinguish between two groups of mentally handicapped people, based on either class differences or the presence or absence of organic pathology, are still with us. In its American form the distinction 'organic' versus 'cultural-familial' (instead of pathological versus subcultural) is frequently found in textbooks on mental handicap, postulated as though soundly based. The 'cultural-familial' are even called 'garden variety' defectives.

Jensen particularly makes use of the distinction, both to back up his arguments for the high heritability of IQ, and to attempt to prove a genetically based difference between the learning processes of retarded children with different IQ scores and different racial and class backgrounds. 'Cultural-familial retardation', he claims, 'is predominantly concentrated in the lower social classes.'[26]

Not only the evidence on which this distinction is based, but also the attribution of high heritability to 'cultural-familial' retardation are both extremely dubious. To begin with, the supposed absence of any organic pathology is very much a question of the present state of scientific knowledge and investigations made in any particular case. Moreover, the data that purport to prove differences in family incidence of low IQ scores according to the grade of mental deficiency have been hotly disputed. The main study on which Jensen relies to prove these differences has fundamental flaws in the ways in which information was selected and computed.[27] Finally, there has been a large amount of empirical research which fails to find any actual differences between these two groups and thus throws serious doubt on the reality of the distinction at all.[28] Whilst claiming always to be more scientific and objective than his opponents. Jensen, in fact, is using some of the most socially biased and unsound categorizations that science has thrown up.

One of the significant effects of scientific interest in mentally handicapped people is a tendency to evaluate them in terms of clinical and behavioural symptoms and a consequent relative neglect of either their subjective experience or social existence. Since World War II, the identification of mentally deficient people as a widespread social threat has given way to an ideology that characterized them as sick and useless. This redefinition is reflected in the legislation passed in the Mental Health Act of 1959, which distinguished 'subnormality' from 'psychopathy', thereby dividing off those who were regarded as social threats (whatever their intelligence level) from those who simply suffered from low intelligence. Definitions became increasingly medical, as the Act reflects: 'Subnormality means a state of arrested and incomplete development of mind . . . of a nature and degree which is susceptible to medical treatment or other special care or training of the patient.'[29] In this definition the mentally handicapped are referred to without question as patients and medical rather than educational treatment is given priority.

The increasing medical domination of the field is also reflected in the post-war incorporation of asylums into the National Health Service, as subnormality hospitals — without any public debate as to whether they should be or not. This move served to create a split between the centrally financed administration of the hospitals and the locally financed community and education services. It is a split which has heightened the isolation of the hospitals from the communities they are supposed to serve and which has left them stagnating with insufficient staff, resources or finance.

That scientific theories rather than moral or religious explanations of mental handicap have come to dominate the field does not therefore mean that other perspectives have disappeared. Medical and psychological knowledge all too frequently fails to provide what many parents and many handicapped people need to make sense of their lives, even supposing they, like medical staff, were to have access to such information. They ask the question, 'Why should this happen to me?', even when there is a clear medical diagnosis. Some parents may still see their handicapped child as the consequence of a misdeed or misfortune of their own or even as a blessing in disguise from God, sent to test their faith and fortitude.

Notes

1   All the following quotations are taken from Paracelsus, *De Generatione Stultorum*, translated by Cranefield P. and Federn W. (1967) as The begetting of fools, *Bulletin of the History of Medicine*, 41, with an annotated discussion. Paracelsus's treatise was written around 1530 and published in 1567.
2   St Augustine, Migne, *Patrologia Latina*.
3   A congenital condition is one which is present from and caused before birth, but which is not inherited, in the sense that the parents do not have or carry the same condition.
4   Grimm, quoted in Haffter, C. (1968) The changeling: history and psychodynamics of attitudes to handicapped children in European folklore, *Journal of the History of Behavioural Sciences*, 4.
5   ibid.
6   ibid.
7   ibid.
8   See Cranefield, P. (1961) The discovery of cretinism, *Bulletin of the History of Medicine*, 35.
9   J. Simler, quoted in Cranefield, as note 8.
10   Haller, a Swiss physician, in 1793, quoted in Cranefield, as note 8.
11   Coxe, W., (1779) *Annual Register*; a traveller's account of Swiss cretins that excited much interest and speculation.
12   ibid.
13   Even now there is relatively very little ecological research into the

prevalence of specific forms of mental handicap – research that could possibly reveal the presence of important toxic agents in the environment. And even when such agents are known (for example, lead and mercury poisoning), the caution of scientists in drawing conclusions from such findings and of governments in putting into practice relevant action, is in marked contrast to the readiness with which vague hereditary theories and policies of segregation and sterilization have been adopted.

14 See Cranefield, P. (1971) A seventeenth-century view of mental deficiency and schizophrenia – Thomas Willis on stupidity or foolishness, *Bulletin of the History of Medicine*, 35.

15 Defoe, D. (1697) A hospital for natural fools, in *An Essay upon Projects*, excerpted in R. Hunter and I. Macalpine (Eds.) (1963), *Three Hundred Years of Psychiatry*, Oxford University Press.

16 Howe, S. (1848) *The Causes of Idiocy*, Maclachlan and Stewart.

17 Séguin, E. (1866) *Idiocy and its Treatment by the Physiological Method*, New Jersey, Kelley.

18 Séguin, E. (1870) *New Facts and Remarks concerning Idiocy*, W. Woods and Co.

19 Ireland, W. (1877) *On Idiocy and Imbecility*, J. & A. Churchill.

20 Shuttleworth, G. (1895) *Mentally Deficient Children: Their Treatment and Training*, H.K. Lewis.

21 Bateman, F. (1897) *The Idiot: His Place in Creation and His Claims on Society*, Norwich, Jarrold and Sons.

22 Tredgold, A. (1908) *Mental Deficiency – Amentia*, Bailliere Tindall.

23 Shuttleworth, G. and Potts, W. (1904) *Mentally Deficient Children*, H.K. Lewis.

24 Langdon-Down, J., lecture at London Hospital, 1866, quoted in Kanner, L. (1964) *A History of the Cure and Study of the Mentally Retarded*, Illinois, C.C. Thomas.

25 A more detailed account of this fundamental categorization is to be found in Ryan, J. (1977) The production and management of stupidity: the involvement of medicine and psychology, in Robinson, D. and Wadsworth, M. (Eds.), *Studies in Everyday Medical Life*, Oxford, Martin Robertson. The conclusion of Clarke, A.D.B. and Clarke, A.M. (Eds.) in *Mental Deficiency: The Changing Outlook*, London, Methuen, is that less than one-third of the numbers of mental defectives predicted by IQ test statistics, extrapolated downwards, are actually ascertained. Their conclusion is that most of the remaining number are functioning happily in the community rather than that there is something amiss with the basis of the prediction.

26 Jensen, A. (1970) A theory of primary and secondary familial mental retardation, in N.R. Ellis (Ed.), *International Review of Research in Mental Retardation*, vol. 4, New York, Academic Press.

27 See Kamin, L. (1974) *The Science and Politics of IQ*, New York,

Halsted Press, for a critique of Burt's original twin data, and the subsequent use of it by Jensen and others.

28   For a review of this, see Ryan, J. (1970) Classification and behaviour in mental subnormality, in D. Primrose (Ed.), *Proceedings of the 2nd Congress of the International Association for the Scientific Study of Mental Deficiency.*

29   Mental Health Act, 1959.

2.2 The origins of special education

GILLIAN SUTHERLAND

Gillian Sutherland traces the growth of special provision in England and Wales from the middle of the eighteenth century to the Second World War. This period saw the intertwining of voluntary initiatives, permissive and mandatory legislation and the technology of intelligence testing, but it was the development of mass schooling that suddenly brought the full range of children into public view. However, in the climate of local autonomy, permissive central government and economic recession that followed the Great War, special education developed patchily.

The essential precondition for both a policy and any systematic provision for special education is compulsory mass education. Only when you attempt to bring all or most of the children of a country together in distinct institutions called schools, does the full variety of their needs begin to emerge. And the necessity to plan a curriculum for a group entails certain assumptions about normal ranges of performance. Mass compulsory education came later in England than in France, Germany and the USA — in the last quarter of the nineteenth century rather than the first half — and the beginnings of policy and system in special education were correspondingly later.

To say this is not, of course, to say that earlier generations had had no concern at all with the problems and educational needs of children with particular disabilities. Variety of needs can be perceived as soon as even a small number of children are grouped together for part of the process of socialization and such a concern can be traced in most experiments in formal schooling. But the centrality of school in the educational process, that is to say, a view of the upbringing and socialization of children which considers that a substantial part of it is best carried out in a distinct institution in company with their peers, is a relatively recent development, emerging decisively in Western society only by the end of the eighteenth century.

Lines of experiment with various kinds of special education can be traced unbroken from this time. In England the characteristic, indeed

Specially commissioned for this volume
©The Open University, 1981

the dominant form and vehicle for such experiments was the lay voluntary association, usually dependent for its funds upon charitable appeal. Typical was the London Society for Teaching the Blind to Read, which in 1838 opened a school in London and subsequently schools also in Nottingham and Exeter. Provision for mentally handicapped children was slower to develop than provision for children with more immediately identifiable physical handicaps; and for much of the nineteenth century English law made no distinction between mental defect and mental disorder. Thus children with severe mental handicaps were often confined in lunatic asylums. In 1847, however, the first separate institution was opened: the Asylum for Idiots at Park House, Highgate.

The Education Act of 1870, Forster's Act, contained a commitment to provide schools for the mass of the population, but somewhat illogically, no universal mechanism to compel them to attend. This followed only in the Education Act of 1880, when the problems generated by partial compulsion both for employers of child labour and for school administrators had become plain. Even then, the gap between provision on the statute book and enforcement in the locality could be a considerable one. As Flora Thompson commented, remembering school in rural Oxfordshire, 'It was only the second generation to be forcibly fed with the fruit of the tree of knowledge: what wonder if it did not always agree with it.'[1] Parents and children might connive to evade the officers of the education authority: those officers might be slack or over-worked; magistrates, both urban and rural, frequently refused to convict or imposed derisory fines. Regular school attendance was a habit gradually learnt over several generations and consolidated, perhaps, only with the collapse of much of the child labour market in the inter-war depression.

Among the most energetic education authorities were some of the great urban school boards and it soon became clear to them that actually getting the children into school raised as many problems as it solved. Mary Tabor, one of the investigators for Charles Booth's survey of *London Life and Labour*, wrote at the end of the 1880s of London slum children:

> Puny, pale-faced, scantily clad and badly shod, these small and feeble folk may be found sitting limp and chill on the school benches in all the poorer parts of London. They swell the bills of mortality as want and sickness thin them off, or survive to be needy and enfeebled adults whose burden of helplessness the next generation will have to bear.[2]

A London School Board Committee of 1889 estimated that one in eight of the children in their schools was habitually underfed. Chronic malnutrition and the diseases and disabilities associated with this were but the most easily identifiable aspects of a complex and intractable problem.

The difficulties of trying to teach undernourished, sick and handicapped children were dramatized at a very early stage because the school curriculum embodied what was simultaneously a very crude and a very elaborate and rigid notion of normality. From 1863 to the mid-1890s the bulk of the government grant to a school, roughly half its income, depended upon the performance of each child, each year in examinations in the three Rs, conducted by Her Majesty's Inspectors. The examinations were arranged in a series of 'Standards' and the child was expected to move up a Standard each year. This was the Procrustean framework known as payment by results.

The mechanistic rigidity of this combined with large classes to depress the status of the teacher almost to that of machine-minder, a role underlined by those school managers who made part of the teacher's salary dependent upon the rate of examination passes in his class. The teachers were therefore well to the fore in what became known as the 'over-pressure' row of the early 1880s. Discussion was initially triggered off by some rather speculative discussion among neurophysiologists about the ways in which overwork among children and adolescents might lead to brain strain and damage. Comments of this kind were at first used as a stick with which to beat the enthusiasts for girls' education; but in the hands of the National Union of Elementary School Teachers, they also became a useful weapon with which to attack payment by results. Detailed investigations of particular cases of alleged over-pressure served chiefly to raise questions about the scientific standards and standing of some of the neurophysiologists; but they did focus public attention on the health of school children and the one point on which there was no real disagreement: 'to educate a half-starved child at all is to over-press him'.[3]

In these same years the various voluntary organizations concerned with the education of the blind and the deaf had been lobbying independently for state aid. Eventually, in 1885–6 the Conservative administration bought time by setting up a Royal Commission, chaired by Lord Egerton of Tatton, with the following catch-all terms of reference:

to report upon the condition of the Blind in Our United Kingdom, the various systems of education of the blind, elementary, technical and professional, at home and abroad, and the existing institutions for that purpose, the employment open to and suitable for the blind, and the means by which education may be extended so as to increase the number of blind persons qualified for such employment . . . to investigate and report similarly upon the condition and education of the Deaf and Dumb, as well as such other cases as from special circumstances would seem to require exceptional methods of education.[4]

The Egerton Commission reported in 1889, their recommendations at times bearing the marks of conflicting opinions and interests. They recommended compulsory education for blind children from the ages of five to sixteen, and deaf children from seven to sixteen, to be provided in both cases by the local education authority. As far as methods of teaching were concerned, a majority favoured braille as the principal medium for teaching the blind to read, though a minority secured a recommendation for the use of embossed Roman type as well. Likewise, they recommended the use of both sign-and-manual and oralism in the teaching of the deaf.

The fundamental problem in dealing with mental handicap, as the Commission recognized, was the difficulty of precise diagnosis. Many doctors still relied almost wholly on external, physical signs, such as fits, vacantly staring eyes, over-large heads and other peculiarities of anthropometric measurement, as evidences of the existence of mental handicap. Eventually the Commissioners identified three categories of mentally handicapped children: idiots, imbeciles and the feeble-minded, arguing that children in the two latter categories were educable and should be provided for in special schools by the local education authority.

Even before the Egerton Commission had been established, some education authorities, notably London, had begun to establish special classes, if not special schools, for various kinds of handicap and this process snowballed during the 1880s, although the eligibility for government grant of such classes remained unclear. The lobbying of the local education authorities combined with the recommendations of the Egerton Commission to bring the first legislation for special education in the 1890s. An Act of 1893 required education authorities to make special provision for blind and deaf children and authorized some additional grant. Defining and identifying mental handicap continued to raise problems. Eventually, in 1899, legislation *allowed* local education authorities, if they chose, to create special classes and schools, eligible for grant at a special rate, for children 'who, not being imbecile and not being merely backward or dull children are, by reason of mental defect, incapable of receiving proper benefit from the instruction in ordinary schools'.[5]

The impact of permissive legislation like this was obviously more patchy and variable than that of mandatory legislation like the 1893 Act. Nevertheless, by 1903, London and fifty other authorities were making some provision for mentally handicapped children. Meanwhile concern for the physical and mental health of school children had ceased to be merely either the preoccupation of a handful of interested pressure groups or one of the battle grounds on which the NUT conducted their fight for professional status, and had become a central preoccupation for political and social commentators and reformers. In the 1890s it became increasingly common to use the language of Darwin's theory of evolution to describe human affairs. It became positively fashionable to talk of the struggle for the survival of the fittest both within society, with particular reference to the conditions of city life, and between nation states and empires. Allegations began to be made about the deterioration of the race. Comments like that of Mary Tabor quoted above, about the slum children who survived to be the needy and enfeebled adults whose burden of helplessness the next generation will have to bear, achieved an increasingly wide currency. The early disasters of the Boer War gave added impetus to this and to more general discussions of national efficiency, all of which helped fuel the inquiries of the Inter-Departmental Committee on Physical Deterioration, 1902–4, and the Royal Commission on the Care and Control of the Feeble-Minded, 1904–8.

For once, legislative action followed hard on the heels of such inquiries; and the decade before 1914 was a period of intensive activity to improve the health of a school child, in which, for the first time, the state took a leading role. In 1907 legislation allowed local authorities to spend rate money on school meals. In 1908 medical inspection of all school children became compulsory. Various local authorities, notably Manchester and London, began to experiment with special classes and schools for physically handicapped and delicate children. In this they were able to draw on the pioneering voluntary work for the care of crippled children led by Mrs Humphry Ward at the Passmore Edwards Settlement in London, by Sir Robert Jones and Dame Agnes Hunt at the West Kirby Convalescent Home and the Shropshire Surgical Home, and Dame Grace Kimmins at Chailey in Sussex.

At this very same time, the first sophisticated diagnostic tools for the identification of mental abnormality were being developed. In France the psychologists Alfred Binet and Théophile Simon had been pursuing their conviction that the higher mental processes could only be tested and measured by a complex battery of direct tests. In 1905, after trials on hundreds of Parisian school children, they published a first series of tests of vocabulary, spatial perception, memory, inductive and deductive reasoning and even 'judgement' and 'moral sense', with an age-related scale for scoring the results. A second series followed in 1908 and a third in 1911. The impact of this was immediate and world-wide. The German psychologist William Stern made it dramatically easier for the layman to appropriate and use – or abuse – Binet and Simon's calculations of mental ages with the device of the intelligence quotient or IQ. He divided mental age by chronological age, multiplied by 100 to eliminate the fractions and came up with a single number which could be used to describe the potential of one individual and contrast him with any other. In California Lewis Terman and in Liverpool Cyril Burt began work on the standardization of Binet and Simon's tests on American and English school children respectively. They began also to experiment with the possibility of a group test, that is, one that could be administered in written form to a number of people simultaneously and the results scored by an unskilled individual or even a machine. Already in 1910, the Board of Education's Chief Medical Officer, George Newman, was recommending Binet and Simon's tests for use in English schools. In 1913 the London County Council Education Committee made the first-ever appointment of a psychologist – Cyril Burt – to advise on the selection of children for special classes and schools. When the Mental Deficiency Acts of 1913 and 1914 at last laid upon local education authorities the *duty* of ascertaining the mental competence of all children between seven and sixteen and *required* them to provide appropriate education for all those deemed defective but educable, they had a diagnostic apparatus of some sophistication at their disposal.

The outbreak of war in August 1914 brought most things to a grinding halt. When in the years 1919–22 the committed – like George Newman at the Board of Education – sought to pick up the threads again, the world looked very different. Already by the end of 1920 the post-war economic boom had collapsed and as the economy slid deeper into depression, so governments retreated from initiatives in education. The failure to implement much of the 1918 Education Act is well known. There were similar retreats in the field of special education.

The history of the Wood Committee amply illustrates this. In 1923 Newman, in his capacity as Chief Medical Officer both to the Board of Education and the Ministry of Health, set up a specialist committee to investigate the variations in local authorities' estimates of the incidence of mental deficiency. The Committee, named after its chairman, spent four years at work and sponsored probably the most comprehensive investigation ever of the incidence of mental defect over the country as a whole. They looked in depth at six carefully chosen sample areas, each with a population of approximately 100,000. The class teachers in the elementary schools in each area were asked to select the 15 per cent of their class who were the most backward. These children were then examined by a group intelligence test and those with the lowest scores were given further individual Binet tests and in extreme cases a physical examination also. The chief investigator, Dr Lewis, concluded that besides the 33,000 defective children already identified by local authorities, only half of whom were actually in special schools, there were another 18,000 unascertained.

Following this, the Committee engaged in a discussion of mental defect far more elaborate than any in the pre-war period, their language showing the impress of developments in both medicine and psychology in the interim. When they got down to practical recommendations, they wanted to make a number of changes. Conventionally, local education authorities had come to regard children with IQs of below 70 as certifiable either for segregation in special schools or for referral to the local mental deficiency authority as ineducable. The Committee wanted only children with IQs of 50 or under to be referred to the care of the local mental deficiency authority. Children with IQs between 50 and 70 should now be grouped with those of IQs between 70 and 80, hitherto labelled 'dull and backward'; and this new group, the 'retarded', should be given special care within the framework of the ordinary school, not in a special school.

There was no challenge either to the Committee's methods or its findings. But nothing happened. The Board of Education had taken no steps, other than pious exhortations to local authorities, to implement the requirements of the 1913 and 1914 Acts. The Wood Committee's recommendations would, like these, cost money and probably need fresh legislation; so they were ignored. Only when the Board of Education attempted to resume the initiative in policy-making, in drafting what was to become the 1944 Education Act and its supplementary regulations, did the Wood recommendations begin to have an impact.

In rather similar fashion, three government committees conducted investigations of the teaching of blind and deaf children, drawing in particular on the very considerable advances made in the diagnosis of degrees of deafness. They concluded that both partially deaf and partially sighted children needed different treatment from that provided for the wholly deaf and the wholly blind and they felt this could best be given within the normal school system, not in special schools. Again, nothing was done by central government to implement these recommendations until after the Second World War.

The retreat of central government did not, however, mean complete inactivity. The 1902 Education Act had abolished school boards and county and county borough councils had replaced them as local education authorities. They had a considerable degree of autonomy, which most of them exploited. In some cases, of course, this could mean doing absolutely nothing, statutory obligations notwithstanding. But it could also mean that they engaged in experiment, were prepared to innovate; and the energy and initiative shown by school boards like those of London, Manchester and Leicester seemed to have been inherited by their successors in the inter-war years. A number of authorities worked hard to maintain their services and special schools for handicapped children. A handful even managed to add to these. In 1932 the Birmingham education authority helped set up a child guidance clinic, in connection with its special schools service. The funds came at first from private sources; but by 1935 the authority had persuaded the Board of Education to sanction the expenditure of some public money on this. By 1939 there were seventeen clinics wholly maintained and five partly maintained by local education authorities and the Board of Education had begun to give a grudging sanction to the expenditure of public funds on the boarding fees of a handful of particularly disturbed children.

But the very first child guidance clinic in the UK had been set up in East London in 1927 by the Jewish Health Organization. This – like the initial funding of the Birmingham clinic – serves to underline once more the importance of voluntary and charitable organizations in setting an example, providing a lead for even the most creative of local authorities. Voluntary enterprise and the variety of local authority practice were the major sources of ideas and examples when, after the Second World War, the central government sought once more to formulate a national policy on special education.

Notes

1 Flora Thompson, *Lark Rise*, first published in 1939, chapter 11.
2 Charles Booth *et al.* (1902) *Life and Labour of the People in London, 1st series: Poverty: London Children*, Collected edition, London, Macmillan, p. 207.
3 Parliamentary Papers, 1884, 1xi, *Report of Dr. Crichton-Browne upon the alleged overpressure*, f.268.
4 Parliamentary Papers, 1889, xix, *Report and Minutes of Evidence of the Royal Commission on the Blind, Deaf and Dumb etc. of the United Kingdom*, f.7.
5 Elementary Education (Defective and Epileptic Children) Act, 1899, 62 and 62 Vict. c.32.

Sources

Report and Minutes of Evidence of the Royal Commission on the Blind,

Deaf and Dumb etc. of the United Kingdom (Egerton Commission), Parliamentary Papers 1889 xix, xx.

Report and Minutes of Evidence of the Inter-Departmental Committee on Physical Deterioration, Parliamentary Papers, 1904 xxxii, Cd. 2175, 2210 and 2186.

Report and Minutes of Evidence of the Royal Commission on the Care and Control of the Feeble-Minded, Parliamentary Papers, 1908 xxxv–xxxix, Cd. 4202, 4215–4221.

Report of the Mental Deficiency Committee (Wood Committee), London, HMSO, 3 vols, 1929.

Ministry of Education, Statutory Rules and Orders no. 1076, *The Handicapped Pupils and School Health Service Regulations*, 1945.

Report of the Committee on Maladjusted Children (Underwood Committee), London, HMSO, 1955.

The School Health Service 1908–1974, London, HMSO, 1975.

Andrews, L. (1976) *The Education Act, 1918*, London, Routledge and Kegan Paul.

Gosden, P.H.J.H. (1966) *The Development of Educational Administration in England and Wales*, Oxford, Blackwell.

Gosden, P.H.J.H. (1976) *Education in the Second World War: a study in policy and administration*, London, Methuen.

Hearnshaw, L.S. (1979) *Cyril Burt, Psychologist*, London, Hodder and Stoughton.

Jones, K. (1972) *A History of the Mental Health Services*, London, Routledge and Kegan Paul.

Pritchard, D.G. (1963) *Education and the Handicapped 1760–1960*, London, Routledge and Kegan Paul.

Searle, G.R. (1971) *The Quest for National Efficiency: a study in British politics and political thought, 1899–1914*, Oxford, Blackwell.

Searle, G.R. (1976) *Eugenics and Politics in Britain 1900–1914*, Alphen an den Rijn, Sijthoff and Noordhoff International Publishers.

Sutherland, G. (1971) *Elementary Education in the Nineteenth Century*, London, Historical Association pamphlet.

Sutherland, G. (1973) *Policy-Making in Elementary Education 1870–1895*, London, Oxford University Press.

Sutherland, G. (1977) The magic of measurement: mental testing and English education 1900–1940, *Transactions of the Royal Historical Society*, 5th series, 27, 135–53.

Sutherland, G. and Sharp, S. (1980) 'The Fust Official Psychologist in the Wurrld': aspects of the professionalization of psychology in early twentieth century Britain, *History of Science*, 18, 181–208.

Trevelyan, J. (1923) *The Life of Mrs. Humphry Ward*, London, Constable.

Wolf, T.H. (1973) *Alfred Binet*, Chicago, University of Chicago Press.

2.3 Maladjustment: a history of the category

IRENE BOWMAN

Irene Bowman challenges the general assumption that special education for children called maladjusted has grown as a philanthropic response to severe individual emotional problems. She traces the development of professional groups whose early moral, and later psychological, explanations were differently applied to socially selected groups of pupils despite professional claims of the universal applicability of scientific theories. Since the early nineteenth century there has been continual conflict between professional preferences for working with children who respond in desired ways to ordinary schooling, child guidance or special schooling, and administrative demands to place children whose responses and social background have excluded them from such provisions. Throughout this paper, she argues that both pupils' problems and professionals' perceptions are shaped through political and economic constraints on family life, educational policy and professional theories and practices.

It is significant that histories of maladjustment have been written by psychologists, such as Cyril Burt, who made a substantial contribution to the historical section of the Underwood Report in 1955, and Maurice Bridgeland, the historian of 'pioneer' work in independent schools and communities (Bridgeland, 1971). These authors are part of an historical trend in which psychology has become taken for granted as a means of understanding certain pupils' problems. There has also been a tendency to believe that special education is an essentially philanthropic enterprise, and to treat schooling as a natural event rather than a social and political phenomenon.

So that we can look differently at the origins of the idea of maladjustment and of special schools for the maladjusted, I shall first point out some striking features in present school provision for difficult, unhappy and sometimes dangerous pupils. Then I shall ask some questions about those features and go on to reconsider historical events in the light of issues raised by them.

Specially commissioned for this volume

The present: the problems of professional preferences and real pupils

Traditionally, child guidance and special school staff have been trained in psychodynamic psychologies, treating what the child does and says as symbolic of stunted or distorted inner emotional states. The child steals, raises fires, destroys property, physically attacks himself and others or withdraws into a world of fantasy as an involuntary expression of unconscious problems. Difficulties in establishing and developing relationships in adolescence and adulthood are traced back to the emotional difficulties of early childhood. Here we see the influence of Freud's idea of neurotic conflict. Frequently a child's behaviour has had to be capable of being understood in this way, to gain him admission to a special school and himself and his mother to clinic treatment. An ideal maladjusted pupil has evolved.

'The maladjusted child' is defined as emotionally disturbed, ill, sick and said to require a certain kind of psychological treatment, whether psychotherapy or environmental therapy, to effect a cure. There are numerous examples of this, ranging from Robert Shields's classic description of his work as a psychotherapist in a local authority residential school in the 1950s (1962), through descriptions of their work by members of the Planned Environmental Therapy Trust (Barron, 1968), to Robert Laslett's recent (1977) textbook, *Educating Maladjusted Children*. [1] 'The maladjusted child' is presented as of average or above average intelligence, as in the Underwood Report (Ministry of Education, 1955). Especially in the independent sector, but also in the local authority residential schools, above-average intelligence has generally been a major criterion for placement. Professional assessment includes an inference that the child has the potential for certain mental and emotional changes: he has to be both 'treatment bright' and 'schooling bright'. He preferably has a mother with whom he lives, whose capacity for change is also assessed. The aspects of the child/mother relationship seem to be understood as natural attributes and adverse social circumstances are seen as separate and contaminating the professional work with what is assumed to have 'naturally gone wrong'. Maladjustment has thus come to mean natural pathology rather than a social or administrative status, and underlying this way of seeing pupils' problems is the creation of professional preferences for working in certain ways with certain pupils. The strength of professional beliefs expressed in those preferences only begins to be seen when we consider what has actually happened in the handicap category in the local authority sector, during the past fifteen years. [2]

The characterization of 'the maladjusted child' set out above has increasingly come under attack by the actual pupils coming forward for placement, especially in local authority day schools. Mary Wilson and Mary Evans comment: 'From the beginning many of the children causing concern showed excessively aggressive, angry and unsettled patterns of behaviour . . . but . . . this was associated with other clinical symptoms. Over the last decade . . . we have seen the referral of . . . an increasing number of conduct-disordered children some of whom are without such symptoms' (Wilson and Evans, 1980).

In one large urban authority during the past ten years I have found professional distress and continuing attempts to differentiate 'sick' children from those understood as socially hostile disciplinary problems, by calling the latter 'socially maladjusted'. The entry of large numbers of the 'socially maladjusted' to day special schools has been resisted by the staff but there have been administrators' attempts to renegotiate the meaning of the handicap category label to include a large proportion of such children.

This negotiation has coincided with the appearance of the term 'disruptive', together with provision outside both ordinary and special schools. Arguments have been made that 'disruptive' pupils are not 'maladjusted', that is, not emotionally disturbed (see Jones-Davies and Cave, 1976). So neither socially maladjusted nor disruptive pupils are among the preferred pupils of special schools. The DES (1977) survey of units and the Report of the Advisory Centre for Education (ACE, 1980), reveal that there are administrative uncertainties about distinguishing between 'maladjusted' and 'disruptive' pupils for placement purposes. However London shows greater clarity in differential placement, largely because psychiatric and teaching staff of special schools have shown greater resistance to admitting those pupils they define as not primarily emotionally disturbed. Such pupils are not 'schooling and treatment bright', they do not have co-operative mothers who are also 'treatment bright'. There seem to be class, cultural and ethnic factors in the exclusion of these pupils from the emotionally disturbed group.

Tony Kline, Principal Educational Psychologist to the ILEA argues that there has been a marked silence from child guidance staff with regard to helping others to manage or to treat such pupils (Kline, 1980). Psychoanalytically trained workers, including teachers in special schools, often place these pupils outside their treatment expertise and preference. Thus there is a struggle between professional and administrative groups as to what counts as maladjustment. There is a discrepancy between the apparently changing character of referred pupils and a strongly held professional view which does not, or perhaps cannot, allow for such changes. On the one hand maladjustment is presented as though it were a natural universally occurring problem of emotional development, on the other it is clearly a social artefact, involving social selection.

How, and why, might all this have come about? As a sociologist, I am interested in the social and ideological effects of material constraints which have arisen in the development of a particular political economy. I therefore want to concentrate on some economic and political origins of maladjustment, both as a statutory category and as a professional concept of emotional disturbance which excludes certain social groups, while including others. I am not setting out to argue that personal, emotional and physical suffering would not exist if psychologists and doctors had not 'discovered' them. Nor am I denying the care and concern of voluntary and professional groups. I am saying that a material analysis has something important to offer.

Nineteenth-century antecedents of 'social maladjustment'

How did professional groups come to understand certain problems of the social groups we call families as natural pathologies of individual behaviour and feelings? By referring to nineteenth-century developments in England, I shall indicate that crucial changes and stresses in family structure were both created — and then understood as due to personal pathologies — as a result of economic and political pressures. The production of problems and of professional groups and their explanations and practices were closely interrelated.

In early nineteenth-century England, what counted as family life for the purpose of craft and artisan production was destroyed by the introduction of mass manufacture, just as peasant lives had been destroyed by centuries of land enclosures (Thompson, 1968). Control of production, socialization, leisure and education was moved out of the family into the factory, into workers' own schools (McCann, 1977), into charity schools and onto the street. The nineteenth-century movement of child workers, segregated by a new division of skills and shift work into and out of workshops, factories and eventually into redundancy due to changes in the way goods were produced, led to problems of physical and social survival for them. In addition, families were further broken up by attempts to solve such problems through the Poor Laws: the scheme of unsupervised pauper apprenticeships resulted in thousands of young paupers being sent to factories and cities, from which many ran away, became vagrant or lived together in groups. This scheme was said to cause the rise in juvenile delinquency investigated in 1816 by the Committee for Investigating the Alarming Increase of Juvenile Delinquency in the Metropolis.

These problems, thrown up by *material factors*, were interpreted by professional groups as due to *moral defectiveness* requiring corrective action rather than imprisonment. The aim was to produce a reformed, controlled workforce, rather than a drain on national and parish funds. Further, the creation of a particular kind of childhood was a form of corrective action, involving the need to insure capital investment, rather than a philanthropic gesture. This is clearly seen in the correspondence between a noted charity figure Sir T. Phillips of Newport, and Chief HMI Kay, after the Chartist uprising of November 1839 in Newport. Phillips wrote to Kay requesting a grant towards establishing a school, and pointing out a connection between social unrest and lack of 'sound moral and religious training'. Offering a grant of only half the cost of the building, Kay called for local mining proprietors to liken the money contributed to the other half 'to the proportion of annual profits devoted to the insurance of capital'. Kay also comments that the proprietor's duty is like that of parents. (Minutes of the Committee of Council on Education, 1840–1.) The creation of a government grant system for charity schools, administered by professional HMIs (mostly clergy), was a response to the acute social unrest of the early part of the century. The earlier *ad hoc* arrangement of private charity, voluntary and workers' schools was to be controlled by state grants given if schools were judged to be efficient in moral training. School was to replace the family as the socializer of future adult workers.

From this period the perception of the 'normal' pupil of the workforce involved assumptions of a natural capacity for moral change. Training this natural attribute by discipline and religious instruction could ensure a child's conformity *despite* his material circumstances. Morally defective and badly brought up children required more training to strengthen weak will-power. In Mary Carpenter's discussions of the children of the 'dangerous and perishing classes' the main concern is to control behaviour by ensuring that the right rules and precepts were followed away from the undesirable opportunities and independence offered by workplaces, streets, public houses and 'gaffs' or gambling shops (Carpenter, 1851; 1861). The problems attributed to the whole workforce in the first half of the nineteenth-century sound very like those now attributed to 'disruptive' and 'socially maladjusted' pupils.

Social and political meanings of the term 'moral' in the nineteenth century

In the different meanings of 'moral' used in the nineteenth century we can see early signs of a definition of emotional disturbance which excludes certain social groups. The term 'moral' means different things, not only for adults and children, but for each of the social groupings popularly called at the time the upper classes and the lower orders. I shall discuss adults first, then children.

'Moral' meant evaluatory of behaviour when used with reference to the lower orders, whose behaviour was assessed according to the 'moral law' which was laid down *for them* in the rules of conduct set out by church, law and medicine. Moral training was the learning and practising of such rules. The emphasis upon moral sense, moral law, moral attributes, moral responsibility in professionals' writings, is to be found not only in schooling, but in medicine (Figlio, 1978), in charity (Stedman Jones, 1976) in eugenics (Lawler, 1978), and self-evidently, in the legal system. However, when referring to the adults of the upper classes the term moral meant two things (a) learning and practising rules of conduct laid down by *their own social group* and (b) *original thinking, imagination, feelings and sensitivities.* It is the latter meaning, applied only to upper class adults in the early nineteenth century, which is different from our own understanding of 'moral'.

In the writings of early physicians of the insane, three factors presage the eventual appearance of the idea of emotional disturbance. The first is the assumption that one social class inherits 'higher order' attributes – the emotions and a delicate mechanism of both mind and body – but also inherits the lifestyle which enforces its 'irritation' and disorder. The second is that they are not responsible for their condition. For example, in 1828 George Man Burrows wrote in a section of his *Commentaries on Insanity*:

> Habitual luxury and the vices of refinement are peculiar to the rich, and consequently a greater degree of susceptibility and irritability is superinduced. The lower orders, who ought more generally to be exempt from the concomitant of wealth and indolence, that is disease, unhappily provoke it by their excesses, and thus voluntarily ingraft on themselves the evils which, from their condition, they might otherwise escape.

The third is that they can be cured by 'moral treatment': a *relationship* with physician or keeper in a private asylum away from irritants such as urban society. However, when in mid nineteenth century concern was expressed for 'the spread of nervous disorders' to the lower orders, these were said to be due to inherited organic defect, not delicacy.[3] In addition, as the lower orders inherited a 'station in life' of hard labour and frugality both of which were good for the mental state, they were responsible for voluntarily indulging the excesses which caused derangement. Consequently, there may be no cure for the organic condition, but moral training and abstinence were likely to restore proper behaviour.

At the beginning of the century children of both social groups were considered by physicians to have unstable and easily overexcited mental mechanisms, rather than intellects and emotions. In 1828 George Man Burrows thought that insanity could not occur before the age of puberty and in 1812 Benjamin Rush, an American, thought that 'children's minds were too unstable for mental impressions to produce more than transient effects', but his contemporary, Amariah Brigham, argued that mental excitement during childhood predisposed to 'this terrible disease' of adult insanity (Walk, 1964). The clergy offered a moral explanation of children's behaviour problems, based on assumptions of an inherent moral weakness of children who were all born in a state of sin. Possession by the Devil or devils is given by Leo Kanner (1962) and Basil Clarke (1975) as another explanation of children's unacceptable behaviour. (Clarke points to the present continuation of such explanations in reports in *The Times* dated 7 March 1971 and 20 April 1972.) Thus the early nineteenth-century views of children's problems were not of emotional difficulties but of organic and moral weakness requiring control by limited access to learning. By mid nineteenth century, curricula suited to social class and sex were to perform this function. Moral, organic and social class factors were closely linked in professional explanations of juvenile delinquency, vagrancy, insanity and adult opposition to the material conditions of their real lives.

Thus we see that personal and social problems, closely related to material conditions, were understood by the professional groups on the basis of assumptions about a natural mental, emotional and social class hierarchy. How did these ideas affect the schooling of deviants?

Schooling as the moral transformation of deviants

At the beginning of the century the aim was to change the whole labouring population, which was totally deviant in comparison with the required worker. However, schooling the masses was constrained by two major factors. First, great economic and organizational problems occurred due to increases in the population which had quadrupled by the end of the nineteenth century (census returns quoted by Friedman, 1977). Second was the ideology of moral change – training minds to change social problems – linked with the idea of the God- and Nature-given differences between upper and lower social classes. The effects of these factors can be seen in the early part of the century when many charity schools were organized like factories on the monitorial system, in which one teacher and a few monitors (older pupils) managed more than a hundred pupils who were arranged in rows in one huge room. The aim was to 'train in' rules of conduct and simple skills by reducing the material to be learned to tiny steps and using mass recitation methods. Those who succeeded were moved row by row to the top row, in response to a system of bells, flags or whistles. This kind of mechanical learning was cheap, could deal with huge numbers and its adherents judged the 'good pupil' in terms of obedience and memory, not thinking or making social relationships.

However, by mid century both HMIs and progressive educators such as Carpenter recognized that many children stayed away or were otherwise unresponsive to mechanical schooling. Carpenter records other accounts of difficulties in pupils who were stealing lights, locking the teacher out, and putting 'crackers' on the floor so that the teacher stepped on them when moving to quell a fight (Carpenter, 1851). She argued that teachers lacked the ability to make a relationship with the pupils. HMIs began formally to train teachers, both to do this and to introduce a wider curriculum. Teachers were to relate to their pupils as benign patriarchs, to change by moral *persuasion* (see Johnson, 1976). In this movement we see the beginnings of the concept of moral *treatment* in schooling, together with the idea of the school as substitute family for children who had lacked the experience of the kind of childhood which professional groups recalled as being the foundation for their own success. Children should be dependent upon adults. The Factory Acts were already ensuring *economic dependency*, by gradually disbanding child labour, but moral treatment was based upon *emotional dependency*, created by enclosing the children for long periods of time with carefully chosen and trained adults. Thus in late nineteenth-century schools, the child's response to the teacher was used to assess character and moral strength or will-power to resist temptation, and was added to the basic skills and good work habits of the early nineteenth-century definition of the 'good pupil'. If moral training would not transform social problems then moral treatment might.

However, child vagrancy, unemployment, stealing, damage to property, gambling, alcoholism and misery continued. Carpenter (1875) argued that the Revised Code (1862) of standard achievements, attendance and appearance, *produced* delinquents since the Ragged Schools excluded 'children of the dangerous and perishing classes' who would lose them the grant. Twenty years previously HMI Watkins had argued for grants to Ragged Schools that *would* admit such children. These would act as 'filters through which the stream of the most polluted humanity should pass before it was poured into the broad reservoir of our national schools' (Minutes of the Committee of Council on Education, 1845). One could argue that prison, reformatory and industrial schools acted in this way too. Schools which received the grant were very selective. As in other professional and charity attempts at reform (for example rehousing in rule-bound, supervised model dwellings such as the Peabody Buildings in London), 'model standards' were devised which were so remote from the material constraints of the lives of large sections of the population, that further problems were created by them. These continued to be understood in the only way available, as problems of mental change appropriate to social class.[4]

After the 1876 Education Act, compulsory attendance at elementary schools meant that state schools could not turn away children. Gertrude Keir quotes Professor Francis Warner, surveyor of mental, moral and physical defect in the school population, who said in 1890: 'Almost from the first, both teachers and social workers predicted that "the co-existence of voluntary schools and of public elementary schools in the same district is likely to produce a congregation of *difficult children* in these schools which are no longer free to select their members" ' (Keir, 1952). A more practical intervention than benign patriarchal change and moral training was required, and a more compelling ideology to explain and remedy failures of, and opposition to, professional efforts to control and transform. This was found in the new sciences of biology and psychology and in child study (see also Sutherland, Chapter 2.2).

Psychology in state schooling, psychoanalysis in private practice, and 'the maladjusted child'

Cyril Burt was influenced by James Sully's argument that 'many cases of mental illness and mental defect were really cases of maladjustment' (Burt, 1953). Burt presented adjustment as a state of equilibrium between two forces: the child's genetic potential, including 'temperament and emotionality', and society, often called the environment and treated largely as school and home. Imbalance or maladjustment usually indicated a 'subnormal mind'. In *The Subnormal Mind* (1935) and *The Young Delinquent* (1925) this phrase clearly carries a moral evaluation. The humane management of maladjustment was thus to adjust the demands of schooling to the potential mental ability and 'social class' of the child: 'The whole school population [should be] broadly graded according to the education each child is fit to receive.' . . . 'A similar grading can be drawn up for adults according to their profession or trade ... [and] found in works on vocational psychology' (Burt, 1935). Thus, if the tasks of school and work were properly graded and children selected and trained appropriately, maladjustment would not occur. Adjustment problems stemming from the home could be modified by voluntary social workers: Burt commented that 'mental conditions are more potent than economic', and seemed to see these as unrelated.

For Burt, psychology was a biological 'science of the mind' (1953). He recognized disadvantage, exploitation and suffering but his understanding and his remedies revealed his naturalist assumptions. The facts of real lives affected by economics and politics were perceived and ordered by a biological theory. Like his nineteenth-century predecessors Burt was trying to achieve mental change suited to social class, but now also in accordance with measured potential. This strategy produced problems. In theory, high IQ pupils from 'good' homes, in 'good' schools, should be 'adjusted', but there were some who were not. Low attainment and 'bad' or 'nervous' behaviour occurred in bright middle-class children and more worrying, their low attainment could also be coupled with no apparent behaviour problems. Progressive educators such as A.S. Neill (1926) argued that the competitive ethos of standardized learning and testing produced anxiety, stealing, learning and sexual problems. Neurologists like Hector Cameron (1918) elaborated the concept of 'the nervous child' for such cases, of which there were increasing reports. Delinquency in pupils of high IQ and good family had always been hard to explain in eugenic terms and such families hid their problems in independent schools such as Mr Dodd's in Blackheath and George Lyward's in Kent which catered for pupils removed from other schools for stealing, bullying, sexual offences, and so on (see Bridgeland, 1971). Burt tried to take this into account by suggesting that 'supernormal minds' rarely repeated such acts but when they did it was due to 'deeper neuroses and to temperamental instability' (Burt, 1935). In so doing, he was influenced by his colleague Susan Isaacs and other members of the new psychoanalytic movement in child study. Like early physicians of the insane Burt drew on a notion of 'higher order' delicacies of mind, but in explaining these through the new Freudian theory of neuroses he did not seem to grasp the fundamental difference between Freud's concept of neurotic *conflict* and his own of imbalance. Neurotic conflict was said to be as demonstrable in normal child development as in serious problems of learning and of making adult relationships. Observable problems indicated invisible intrapsychic problems which could not be measured, nor readjusted by conscious effort. They were unconscious, repressed and derived from instinct, inevitably in conflict with social requirements which had been internalized. Reasonably resolved, by sublimation for example, neurosis was the normal person's gateway to a higher form of civilization. However, such a resolution required 'intellectual awakening' (Freud, 1927; 1961) and 'the masses' were therefore likely to remain miserable. The Freudian answer was psychoanalytic interviews, in which unresolved conflicts hampering emotional development might be resolved. Why did theories and practices originating with Freud, appeal to a small but later very influential professional group especially in post First World War London? In this period England was experiencing two changes in family life. The first was due to the creation of new managerial, technical and professional groups living in newly built suburbs, where mothers were often isolated with their young children. The second was due to the effect of the war on the new white collar and upper professional groups. Whereas the labouring population had always been subject to sudden changes in their lives from seasonal unemployment, shiftwork and wars, the 'middle classes' had been relatively protected until 'the war to end all wars' sent their daughters to work and killed their sons. Death, mutilation and 'shellshock', and a forced acceptance of women as workers outside the home, affected both parents and children. This newer social group was educated and often sent their children to nursery, preparatory and private day schools. Here were the clients for the new private and charity-funded treatment facilities of psychotherapy, for neurosis was a 'normal' abnormality, even reaching the pages of the *Nursery World* where Susan Isaacs gave mothers advice about their toddlers' problems, later attributing most of them to neurotic conflict (Isaacs, 1932).[5] To the progressive schools, regarding the child as emotionally disturbed was a respectable, humane alternative to thinking of him as evil or subnormal. Some became successful recipients of privately placed delinquent and retarded pupils refused by or sent down from other schools. A youth of good family did not have to be placed in a penal establishment by the court if entry to such a school could be arranged (see Burn's account of Lyward's work, 1956).

However, the recession also brought new members of the child psychiatry/psychotherapy professions to England, fleeing fascism. This group joined the 'child savers' (Platt, 1971) in voluntary organizations, who began to provide a service for state schools through privately funded child guidance clinics. Two organizations founded one clinic each. The Child Guidance Council (1926) obtained Commonwealth Fund money (from wealthy New Yorker, Mrs Harkness) to found the London Child Guidance Clinic in 1927 and to train staff in 'mental pathology', based on the theories of William Healy, an American influenced by Freud. This training of staff in clinical pathology marked out the new clinics from the work of Burt's teams in the London County Council which employed untrained volunteer workers. The Jewish Health Organization founded the East London Child Guidance Clinic and asked Emmanuel Miller, a neurologist interested in Freudian theories, to direct it. Olive

Sampson (1980) refers to the idealism of these workers who were looking for 'total understanding' of delinquency, learning problems, indeed *all* problems. Clinic provision spread in the 1930s, but ideas about universal helpfulness were undermined by the actual cases. Although the London County Council recognized that early referral could prevent court appearances, and made a small annual grant to the clinics which took its pupils, it reported in 1936 that only a few cases were suitable for the expenditure of time and money (Scott, 1959, Report of the Education Committee to the LCC, 1936). The beginnings of a formal separation between the pragmatic schools psychological service and the analytic child guidance clinics became visible in the Feversham Report's arguments in 1939 that training and discipline were the province of an educational psychologist and that child guidance tried to deal with too wide a variety of problems. Scott's (1959) historical review of child guidance in London, states that referrals from the LCC had changed from being mainly stealing and backwardness in 1931 to behaviour problems and nervousness in 1938.

This movement was connected with the classification and treatment of problems. In 1933 Miller published his findings about cases referred to the East London Child Guidance Clinic and divided them into two groups: mainly internally caused (pathologies or neuroses) and mainly externally caused (social conditions, poverty, overcrowding). Later in the 1930s this division was general and involved decisions to treat, to train or to pass to other agencies. Clinics *treated*. As child psychotherapy developed, children whose problems were thought to be internally caused became preferred clients, the rest, including most delinquents, created problems. Pragmatic psychologists favoured training and alteration of school and home regimes, but schools lacked psychologists. Clinics preferred treatment but pupils and parents, if there were any, often dropped out or refused to attend at all. In the social conditions of pre-war urban England, child guidance, like grant-aided early nineteenth-century schools, began to be socially selective, partly because they had to show that treatment worked, partly because of a preference for children and parents from reasonable living conditions whose problems included neuroses, and fitted the theory. Thus at the beginning of the 1939—45 war, local authority schools were without help for the majority of pupils who were maladjusted according to pragmatic psychologists.

Special schooling as treatment?

Four major factors affected the final formulation of the handicap category in 1944—5. First, there was the legal requirement to provide schooling for all those not ascertainable as severely mentally handicapped, and it was the socially democratic thing to do in the political movement towards the Welfare State. Second, child guidance clinic treatment was costly and lengthy, few children were suited to it and the schools often still had the child to deal with. Also, London and the home counties were the main source of trained personnel, but the problems were nationwide. Third, acute problems were encountered during the first two years of the war, with unbilletable evacuee children, children made homeless by the blitz, delinquency (again), and depressed evacuee mothers with young children. Fourth, there was some evidence from wartime hostels, residential schools, and from Leicester and Oxfordshire local authorities, that teachers working with clinic support could devise schooling to manage and to treat nervous and difficult children.

The concept of special educational treatment, written into the 1944 Education Act as 'education by special methods appropriate to the particular disability from which a child is suffering' had a special meaning when used in connection with maladjustment. In the nineteenth century Mary Carpenter had been concerned with social transformation by compensating for the privation of childhood. In the eighteenth century, Samuel Tuke seems to have been concerned to help his adult Quaker patients to work through 'childish' states of emotion and 'unreason' at an asylum funded by Quakers and called The Retreat. (Tuke referred to the patients and staff as 'The Family'.) Both of these themes were renewed in the twentieth-century work of George Lyward ('stern love') and David Wills ('shared responsibility') with delinquent and maladjusted youths (Burn, 1956; Wills, 1945). The special methods included dropping standardized learning and testing, and competition, and an emphasis on how life was lived together, community sharing of problems, rural and arts activities. Their practices were patriarchal, supporting the Freudian view of the natural family as the way to adjustment. The theories and practices of these beliefs were influential in pre-war day school provision where children who were said to be difficult but bright were helped in a more maternal, child-centred and relaxed school setting.

In 1944 special classes began in London for similar pupils, but with hospital or clinic psychiatric social work help for the mother. Parent and child were helped to change their feelings about each other and the school, often through psychotherapy for the child. When day and residential special schools were established in London for children coming into the new handicap category, psychiatric services were established within them. A child psychotherapist described to me his expectations on being appointed to one of the first day schools: there was to be child guidance treatment offered in the school with education on the premises designed to complement it. Immediate, persistent disillusionment was produced by the children actually encountered and their parents (where there were any). Few fitted treatment criteria, few were nervous, bright, difficult learning failures. In the late 1960s, possibly connected with the establishment of comprehensive schooling, the discrepancy was growing and by the mid-1970s it was severe. It seems to have been exacerbated by the national policy of moving into local authority social service departments the care and control of adolescents who would previously have been removed to Home Office approved schools, and thus selected out of local authority ordinary and special schools. Many of these pupils were not merely failing but opposing schooling and the substitute patriarchal family organization of the special methods. Often they were from an uncertain, insecure section of the job market, from overcrowded homes, from fluid family structures.

We see again the problem of social selection. IQ or potential schooling brightness and certain lifestyles reappear in attributions of emotional disturbance, and exclusions from it. The connection with other educational handicap categories becomes very clear here. Once social policy put all children together in maintained compulsory schools, legislation had to select out again on much the same basis as had happened before 1870: by mental and physical defect (see Sutherland, Chapter 2.2). Only those whose problems could not be attributed to mental or physical defect became possible cases of maladjustment. From those only the potentially schooling and treatment bright were and are likely to be understood as emotionally disturbed. We are reminded of Burt's comment that persistent deviance in 'super normal minds' indicated 'deeper neuroses' and Freud's suggestion that to deal satisfactorily with neuroses (and to 'achieve' them?) one had to be 'intellectually awake', or intelligent.

What might this mean? It is easy to say that psychoanalysis and psychometric psychology are simply élitist while professing social democracy. Ingleby (1976) reminds us that members of the 'people professions' practise a discipline which is essentially political. Psychologies are one expression of long-evolving politico-economic constraints upon everyone's understanding and behaviour. We know that the intelligence testing movement has been politically and culturally biased (Kamin, 1977). We know that testing has produced distributions of pupil intelligence closely related to the distribution of parental social class (here measured by the Registrar General's or Hall-Jones occupational index). My interpretation of the influence of IQ in originating and developing the handicap category of maladjustment is that it has been a means to select out those who are most likely to respond to whatever theories and practices are *preferred* by powerful professional groups. We have seen that at one point in the development of our economic system, the early twentieth century, a new social group in the workforce produced children whose problems were and still are responsive to old and new naturalist ideologies. At least since the eighteenth century, the underlying theme of these has been of support for the political and economic *status quo*, together with a genuine philanthropic intention to transform or to ameliorate the problems arising by the provision of temporary excursions into a different lifestyle. It seems to me that it is this very ideology which, often unintentionally, has been challenged by pupils in the state-maintained sector. In times of economic and political stress this challenge from the 'dangerous and perishing classes', 'the conduct disordered', the 'socially maladjusted' and 'the disruptive' becomes stronger. It reminds us that the origins of the handicap category of maladjustment lie not only in problems conceptualized by us in the twentieth century as individual and psychological but in the deeply entrenched social class relations of our political economy.

Notes

1   A new professional association came into being in November 1980 formed from the Association of Workers For Maladjusted Children and the Association For Therapeutic Education. In discussions about a new name for this association, the term 'maladjusted' has not been favoured, because members feel that the original term no longer means emotionally disturbed. Thus they have separated themselves from the handicap category.

2   The handicap category for those defined as 'pupils who suffer from emotional instability or psychological disturbance' has existed since 1944. However, in 1955 there were only thirty-two local authority boarding special schools and three day special schools. The expansion of day special school provision took place in the 1960s. In January 1979 there were eighty-six day special schools and ninety-six boarding special schools (Department of Education and Science Statistics of Education, vol. I, Schools, Table 26).

3   That 'nervous disorders . . . have taken root among the poorer as well as the middle orders of society' was attributed to too much intellectual education 'above what is suitable and adapted to their station in society', by Dr A. Maddock, a physician of the insane, who blamed the Ragged Schools' curriculum for this (Maddock, 1854).

4 Why did the professional groups understand the problems of social control and personal misery by reference to moral values and the 'right ideas'? There are several possibilities but I wish to point out only one here. They understood their own social group's position as individually achieved but within certain natural limits: their own jobs, superior social status and security were the results of hard, regular mental work, special knowledge fitted to their social status and obedience to religious precepts learned in childhood. They saw neither their security nor the insecurity of the workforce as a feature of the political economy of the period. Thus Samuel Smith, a noted philanthropist wrote in *The Contemporary Review* of January, 1885: 'The proletariat may strangle us unless we teach it the same virtues which have elevated the other classes of society.'

5 The London Society of Psychoanalysts was founded in 1913 by Ernest Jones, and later became the British Psychoanalytic Society. The Medico-Psychological Clinic of London, founded in 1913 and the Society for the Study of Orthopsychics in 1915, marked the beginning of the movement. The Tavistock Clinic founded by Crichton-Miller in 1920, started a children's department in 1926, and a department of child development led by Susan Isaacs in 1933 at the University of London Institute of Education.

References

Barron, A.T. (Ed.) (1968) *Studies in Environmental Therapy, Vol. 1*, Planned Environmental Therapy Trust.

Becker, H. (1971) Social class variations in the teacher-pupil relationship, in B.R. Cosin, I.R. Dale, G.M. Esland, D. Mackinnon and D.F. Swift (Eds.), *School and Society*, London, Routledge and Kegan Paul.

Bridgeland, M. (1971) *Pioneer Work With Maladjusted Children*, London, Staples Press.

Burn, M. (1956) *Mr Lyward's Answer*, London, Hamish Hamilton.

Burrows, G.M. (1828) *Commentaries on Insanity*, London, Underwood.

Burt, C. (1925, 4th edn 1944) *The Young Delinquent*, London, University of London Press.

Burt, C. (1935) *The Subnormal Mind*, London, University of London Press.

Burt, C. (1953) Conclusion to the symposium on psychologists and psychiatrists in the child guidance service, *British Journal of Educational Psychology*, 23, 8–28.

Cameron, H. (1918) *The Nervous Child*, London, Oxford University Press.

Carpenter, M. (1851) *Reformatory Schools For Children Of The Dangerous and Perishing Classes and For Juvenile Offenders*, London, Gilpin.

Carpenter, M. (1861) Letter to the editor of the *Bristol Daily Post* and *Western Daily Press*, September 1861.

Carpenter, M. (1875) Day industrial schools for children beyond the reach of school boards, a paper read before the Statistical Section of the British Society, Bristol.

Clarke, B. (1975) *Mental Disorder in Earlier Britain: Exploratory Studies*, Cardiff, University of Wales Press.

DES (1978) *Behavioural Units: A Survey of Special Units for Pupils with Behavioural Problems,* London, HMSO.

Feversham, Lord (1939) Report of the Committee on Voluntary Mental Health Services, London, Child Guidance Council and National Council for Mental Hygiene.

Figlio, K. (1978) Chlorosis and chronic disease in nineteenth century Britain: the social constitution of somatic illness in a capitalist society, *Social History*, 3, 167–97.

Freud, S. (1961) *The Future of An Illusion*, London, Hogarth Press.

Friedman, A.L. (1977) *Industry and Labour*, London, Macmillan.

Hearnshaw, L.S. (1980) *Cyril Burt: Psychologist*, London, Hodder and Stoughton.

Ingleby, D. (1976) The psychology of child psychology, in M.P.M. Richards (Ed.), *The Integration of the Child into a Social World*, London, Cambridge University Press.

Isaacs, S. (1932) Neurotic difficulties of young children, *British Journal of Educational Psychology*, 2, 71–90.

Johnson, R. (1976) Notes on the schooling of the English working class, 1780–1850, in R. Dale, G. Esland and M. MacDonald (Eds.), *Schooling and Capitalism*, London, Routledge and Kegan Paul.

Jones-Davies, C. and Cave, R. (1976) *The Disruptive Pupil in the Secondary School*, London, Ward Lock Educational.

Kamin, L.J. (1977) *The Science and Politics of IQ*, Harmondsworth, Penguin Education.

Kanner, L. (1962) Emotionally disturbed children: a historical review, *Child Development*, 33, 97–102.

Keir, G. (1952) A history of child guidance, *British Journal of Educational Psychology*, 22, 5–29.

Kline, T. (1980) More help for schools: A critical look at child guidance, *Therapeutic Education*, 8, 3–11.

Laslett, R. (1977) *Educating Maladjusted Children*, London, Crosby, Lockwood Staples.

Lawler, J.M. (1978) *IQ, Heritability and Racism*, London, Lawrence and Wishart.

McCann, P. (Ed.) (1977) *Popular Education and Socialisation in the Nineteenth Century*, London, Methuen.

Maddock, A.B. (1854) *Practical Observations On Mental and Nervous Disorders*, London, Simpkin and Marshall.

Miller, E. (1933) Temperamental difficulties in children, *British Journal of Educational Psychology*, 3, 222–35.

Ministry of Education (1955) *Report of the Committee on Maladjusted Children* (Underwood Report), London, HMSO.

Neill, A.S. (1926) *The Problem Child*, London, Herbert Jenkins.

Platt, A. (1971) The rise of the child saving movement: a study in social policy and correctional reform, in B.R. Cosin, I.R. Dale, G.M. Esland,

D. Mackinnon and D.F. Swift (Eds.), *School and Society*, London, Routledge and Kegan Paul.

Sampson, O. (1980) Child guidance: its history, provenance and future, *British Psychological Society Occasional Papers*, 3 (3).

Scott, J.A. (1959) Report of The County Medical Officer of Health and Principal School Medical Officer, London County Council.

Shields, R.W. (1962) *A Cure of Delinquents*, London, Heinemann.

Stedman Jones G. (1976) *Outcast London*, Harmondsworth, Penguin.

Thompson, E.P. (1968) *The Making of The English Working Class*, Harmondsworth, Penguin.

Walk, A. (1964) The prehistory of child psychiatry, *British Journal of Psychiatry*, 110, 754—67.

Wills, W.D. (1945) *The Barns Experiment*, London, Allen and Unwin.

Wilson, M. and Evans, M. (1980) *Education of Disturbed Pupils*, Schools Council Working Paper 65, London, Methuen Educational.

PART 3

Varieties of Special Provision

3.1 Young children with special needs in ordinary schools

MAURICE CHAZAN, ALICE LAING, MICHAEL SHACKLETON BAILEY AND GLENYS JONES

In a major study of early education for children with special needs, Maurice Chazan and his colleagues investigated the prevalence of and provision for pre-school aged handicapped children in two LEAs. Here, the authors describe the experiences of children and teachers in ordinary nursery schools and classes and reception classes in infant schools. They show the wide range of children and problems encountered and the equally wide range of responses by teachers. Physical disabilities presented only minor difficulties by comparison with the major upsets caused by mental handicap and deviant behaviour. But there were also a number of children who caused few problems but who needed extra and sensitive attention to benefit from their presence in school; in only some cases did they receive this.

It is not possible to make a list of the special needs which young children with problems have as these vary so much from child to child, even if the diagnosis of the difficulty is similar. It is also the case that a need which might be fairly easily satisfied in one classroom with a particular teacher might be almost impossible to deal with in another classroom with a different teacher. Sometimes the major consideration is the nature of the handicapping condition, sometimes the severity of the condition, but in many instances the provision of satisfactory early education depends on the teacher and the circumstances in which she is working. These are the reasons why 'blanket' decisions on integration are dangerous and separate consideration of each case is essential.

There were fifty-one children in the Child Study Sample[1] whose problems fell into the various categories indicated in Table 1. These children were given a grading from one to four to show the severity of their handicap. However, neither of these categorizations gave a good

Source: Chazan, M., Laing, A.F., Shackleton Bailey, M. and Jones, G. (1980) *Some of Our Children*, London, Open Books

picture of how far the school was able to cope effectively and so it was decided to re-group them into three broad bands:

A: children whose problems were of a kind or a degree of severity that they presented few serious difficulties to the teacher

B: children whose problems were such that they could *not* be coped with in the ordinary school or could be coped with only if outside support was given to the teacher and the child's family

C: children whose problems were considerable and where the teacher was crucial in whether or not they could be coped with.

Table 1 Classification of Child Study Sample by type and severity of handicap (N = 51)

	Mild	Moderate	Severe	Very severe	Total
1. Predominantly sensory	1	1	—	—	2
2. Predominantly physical	—	1	2	2	5
3. Speech defect	2	2	1	—	5
4. Mental handicap/developmental delay (aetiology known)	—	—	—	2	2
5. Developmental delay, especially language (aetiology not known)	1	3	5	—	9
6. Mental handicap/developmental delay (aetiology not known)	1	—	8	1	10
7. Multiple handicap	—	—	—	—	0
8. Emotional handicap (restless and/or aggressive)	1	1	3	—	5
9. Emotional handicap (withdrawn)	—	7	—	—	7
10. Emotional handicap (restless, aggressive and withdrawn)	—	2	—	—	2
11. Delicate/poor health	—	—	1	—	1
12. No significant problems	—	—	—	—	3
Total	6	17	20	5	51

Grouping the children in this way produced the classification in Table 2, where the category of handicap is given across the top and the severity of grading alongside each name.

Before looking at each grouping in detail, the following general points can be made:

(1) There were no children placed in ordinary schools who had severe multiple handicaps (i.e. mental handicap plus serious physical and/or sensory handicap). Category 7 children were all in special education if they were not at home [. . .]

(2) Most of the children placed in categories 5 and 6, which had

developmental delay in common, were placed in the C group, while children in categories 8 and 9 tended to be in the B group. Why such differences should have occurred may become clearer when these groups, and Group A, are looked at more closely.

Group A children (N = 12)

This grouping was of children with whom the teachers seemed well able to cope. They either had very mild problems (Judyth, Louise and Lewis) or their problems, although much more severe, were predominantly physical. Three of the children had spina bifida (Carole, Harold and Llewellyn), one had a leg deformity (Margaret), one was partially sighted (Dylan) and one (Tim) had a serious heart defect.

It may seem strange to say of these nine children, one of whom, Carole, was confined to a wheelchair, that they were doing as well as the rest of the children in the class, but they did not stand out noticeably from the group. The teachers accepted the handicaps and unobtrusively kept a watchful eye on them. Carole had sometimes to be restrained from 'using her chair as a battering ram'; Llewellyn had a lot of one-to-one support, especially with regard to toilet training, an additional hazard being that most of the classroom play area was covered with carpet which was difficult to clean; Harold managed leg braces and crutches but needed extra help in the toilet and would have been given more practice in hand/eye co-ordination if the staff could have found the time. Tim joined in when he could and knew that he had to take a spell out if he got puffed. Dylan had to peer very closely at small objects or print but was judged by the teacher to be 'by far the best of his friends at this level. His enquiring mind makes him a pleasure to teach'. The only child who was in difficulty was Margaret, who had a fairly long uphill walk to school during which she frequently tripped herself up, and had also to cope with a number of steps to get to the toilet. She was no problem to the teacher except that the teacher was distressed by the child's struggles to walk and felt that she should have been given free transport to school (Margaret's father was unemployed) and that her parents should have received detailed medical advice.

Dylan's teacher came nearest to revealing why this group of children can be coped with so well. None of them suffered from mental retardation or, as yet, from emotional upsets. When a teacher finds a child rewarding to teach, she is prepared to accept his physical difficulties, as are the other children at this age. Incontinence is not really a problem when accidents often occur anyway; a helping hand from an adult is part of normal routine; all children sometimes decide to join in group activities and sometimes prefer to watch.

Table 2 Teacher's ability to cope with children's special needs (Child Study Sample, N = 51)

	Category of handicap[a]										
	1	2	3	4	5	6	7	8	9	10	11
	Sensory	Physical	Speech	M.H./dev. delay	Dev. delay (esp. lang.)	M.H./dev. delay (n.k.)	Multiple	Emotional (rest. agg.)	Emotional (withdrawn)	Emotional rest. agg. and w'drawn	Delicate
A[b] Easy to cope with (N = 12)	Dylan 2	Margaret 2 Llewellyn 3 Carole 4 Harold 4	Judyth 1		Louise 1			Lewis 1			Tim 3
B Very difficult for teacher to cope with (N = 15)				Susan 4	Karen 3 Rosemary 3	Clare 3 Fergus 3 Jean 4		Garth 2 Emlyn 3 Clifford 3 David 3	Glyn 2 Nigel 2 Lucy 2 Gay 2 Kim 2		
C Outcome depends on the teacher (N = 24)	Jack 1	Paddy 1	Annabel 1 Stanley 2 Diane 2 Nicholas 3	Raymond 4	Alan 4 Gilbert 2 Sally 2 Neville 3 Miles 3 John 3	Terry 1 Thomas 3 Roger 3 Julie 3 Elizabeth 3 Ronald 3 Grahame 3			Geoffrey 2 Elaine 2	Ian 2 Trevor 3	

[a] For full description of category, see Table 1.
[b] Three children were judged to have no problems (George, Edward, Jim).
Degree of severity of handicap: 1. Mild. 2. Moderate. 3. Severe. 4. Very severe.

Group B children (N = 15)

These children had problems which the teachers seemed unable to cope with, mainly because of the nature of the problem itself. Two of the children had severe mental handicaps (Susan and Jean). Seven of them were very withdrawn and also, except for one case (Glyn), showed mental retardation. The remaining six children had problems which really needed to be dealt with outside the school. Co-operation with the home and/or help from other services were essential if any impression was to be made at all.

Susan was brain damaged and was epileptic as well as mentally handicapped. Despite regular drug treatment, she remained highly over-active and presented considerable handling problems to her teacher. She was aggressive towards other children, being disliked by many of them and feared by the timid ones. Her teacher, although having considerable classroom experience, was untrained and had problems of her own which added to the strain of coping with Susan. It is unlikely, however, that this child could have received the help she and her mother (single parent) needed in any ordinary school setting. Her teacher did feel that Susan's behaviour had become a little more con-trolled over the time she had been attending but this judgement was probably rather unrealistic. Indeed no one seemed to have understood the severity of Susan's problems. Hopes were simply being pinned on her transfer to special education.

Jean's case showed many similarities to Susan's. She too was restless, distractible and almost without speech. She did not attack other children so much, although she would bite them or her own fingers if thwarted. Jean was in a reception class along with thirty-four other children and there was no ancillary help. A single-handed teacher, no matter how competent or concerned, could scarcely be expected to provide the highly specialised programme this child needed and at the same time introduce formal skills to the rest of the class. The educational experiences available were simply inappropriate for Jean and no one was benefiting from the placement.

Teachers appear to find it difficult to respond effectively to with-drawn children. The problem can be identified readily enough but time to offer individual help is not found and opportunities to draw the children out of their isolation are missed. Withdrawn children need a great deal of help as their entire educational future is in jeopardy but, by the very nature of the problem, they are overlooked or neglected in favour of the more demanding children. It is not simply a question of availability of resources. Some of the Sample children were in groups where it would have been possible to organize help on a regular one-to-one basis. But teachers seem to prefer an optimistic approach to the problem of withdrawal believing that the attractiveness of the activities and the enjoyment of the rest of the children will bring the child out in the long run. In fact, these features may be pushing the child further back into even greater withdrawal, as he adjusts to non-participation and non-communication and accepts isolation.

Glyn is a typical example of an extremely withdrawn child. His teacher was aware of the problem — the child had addressed only one remark to her in eleven months — and had talked to his mother who agreed that he didn't speak to adults even in the family. Glyn was also considered listless, depressed and somewhat fearful. He had managed to work out a form of survival with the rest of the class, usually latching on to one other child and restraining himself from pushing and grabbing what he wanted. He was not totally indifferent to adults but the researcher who worked with him for the project found it hard work to get and keep a response ('I've rarely had to work so hard to maintain rapport with a child'). Glyn's problem, although severe, did not seem to attract anyone's attention. He was by no means a nuisance and could easily be overlooked.

In cases where withdrawal is compounded with other handicaps, for example mental handicap, teachers in ordinary schools are very unlikely to be able to cope effectively. Six of the Child Study Sample came into this classification, four showing some degree of mental retardation as well as withdrawal; one having poor gross and fine motor co-ordination and coming from a deprived home background; and one with exceptionally poor language usage. The mental retardation was not excessive, all four children having a general quotient on the Griffiths Scale[2] in the 70–80 band but it manifested itself in every case in a reluctance to speak in school. Their withdrawal also inhibited them from joining in the usual activities. These reactions left their teachers more than a little uncertain as to how much they could do and understand.

One of the children, Rosemary, had had a language programme worked out for her by the speech therapist but the teacher felt that she could not find the time to implement it. Karen had ten minutes of speech therapy per week but the teacher had not been advised on how she might help. The one boy of the four, Fergus, who came from a very poor home, was in a reception class with twenty-five other children, the teacher only having occasional help. She did, however, arrange for the helper to see Fergus on his own every week but very little progress was being made. The fourth child, Clare, was perhaps the most surprising child in the whole Sample. She was completely silent and unresponsive in school, limp, pale-looking and doll-like. She could not be tested at all in the school setting and so was seen at home where she proved to be full of vigour and laughter, willing to talk even to a comparative stranger. As far as Clare was concerned, school was a non-talking place and the lack of speech practice which followed this decision of hers had already retarded her language development fairly seriously.

Not only does social withdrawal affect children's cognitive and linguistic development, it also interferes with their patterns of play. Nigel, for example, who had poor co-ordination in addition to his inadequate socialization, would never play with other children and would only rarely paint or draw, seldom ventured into the Wendy House, certainly never sustaining any role there, and had been reluctant to be drawn into music and movement although this was improving slightly. Such a description helps to explain a teacher's bewilderment when faced with acute problems of withdrawal. In an educational setting organized around socialization, language extension and play, it is more than a little disconcerting to find a child who refuses on all counts.

Lucy was also placed in group B although she was within the average range of intelligence and in different circumstances might well have had no problems at all. Unfortunately, however, she was the youngest of four children and grossly over-mothered at home where she had neither the opportunity nor the need to speak. In addition, she attended a Welsh nursery school although the home was English-speaking. When she did speak, she used a jumble of English and Welsh monosyllables which made her difficult to understand. She herself seemed to follow quite well what was said to her in either language. The school was helping part of her problem by treating her as a person in her own right but at the same time it was adding to another part of it by making linguistic communication almost impossible for her.

Group B also contained six children whose problems were intractable within the school as their origins lay outside and required action which was other than strictly educational. All six showed emotional distur-bance, four of a restless, aggressive type and two (Gay and Kim) of a withdrawn type. The over-reacting children were all boys and it should be noted that this form of emotional disturbance, like withdrawal, appeared very difficult for schools to help in any way. Apart from Lewis who was placed in group A as his problem was very slight, all the other children who were identified as restless and aggressive were scarcely being contained within their schools, far less receiving specific help. Considering the problems they presented to their teachers, this is hardly surprising.

The four boys, Emlyn, Garth, Clifford and David, all had been badly and inconsistently handled at home. David was a 'battered' child who had had to be removed from his home and placed in a community foster home. The teacher's description of Emlyn will serve for all four boys: 'He shows frequent aggression towards other children; stubborn, self-willed, defiant; if he doesn't get his own way, he throws temper tantrums and screams and kicks'. Inconsistent handling was also at the root of the girls' problems, Kim not being toilet-trained and Gay being so spoilt that her mother spent three pounds a week on sweets to avoid scenes.

Counselling was essential for the parents of all six children, although only one set of parents, Emlyn's, was receiving any. Even in this case, the school was not included although it would have given the teacher considerably more confidence in her handling of the child had she been involved in the programme planned. The educational psychologist and the local advisory teacher were both working with the parents and combined support of this kind should also have been offered to the parents of Garth and Clifford. Whether David's own parents would have been helped by such counselling can also be considered. Kim's parents (although the mother was a nurse) could have been helped by counselling from a health visitor and Gay's parents, whose marriage was breaking down, needed prolonged marriage guidance counselling.

These six children were more sinned against than sinning. They were not being helped by their teachers because it was almost more than the teachers could do to contain them in the classroom. The boys disrupted the routine, threatened the other children and destroyed anything they could lay their hands on; one of the girls had such an unpleasant smell about her that the others were repelled, while Gay cried all the time and clung to the teacher, the effect on the rest of the children being just as off-putting. These cases exemplify the need for support from other professionals which should be given to teachers of young children with problems and which, at the moment, is not being offered.

Group C children (N = 24)

For these children, many of whom had considerable problems, integration with non-handicapped children had met with varying degrees of success. All of the children had special needs but the latter were not always dealt with as adequately as they might have been. Whether or not the placement was effective appeared to depend on a number of factors, including the resourcefulness of the teacher, the adult—child ratio, and the amount of support given to the teacher. The teacher, therefore, occupies a key position in dealing with these group C children. The nature and severity of the problems themselves, while not unimportant, did not constitute the critical factors as in the group A and group B children just discussed.

In four cases the children had speech defects. Their mental ability was well within the normal range and they could thus be distinguished from the group of children, placed in category 5, whose speech difficulties were linked to general retardation or developmental delay. Three of the children, Annabel, Stanley and Nicholas, had marked articulatory difficulties and one, Diane, had a stammer. All four required speech therapy but only three, Annabel, Nicholas and Diane, were receiving any. Nicholas went once a week to a central clinic for help, as did Annabel, only her visits were less frequent. Diane was seen in school for about a quarter of an hour each week. The teachers of Diane and Nicholas, who had not been advised as to how they could help, felt that daily sessions were necessary. Annabel's difficulties were much less severe than Nicholas's, so that while more help would not have come amiss, she could not be considered to have high priority and, indeed, her teacher was coping well by way of incidental encouragement and practice. Stanley, who had considerable difficulties, had not been referred for therapy and the school seemed to be making no provision at all. His parents, well-educated and articulate, were very worried about Stanley's speech but uncertain as to what should be done about it.

Children with speech defects, like children with physical handicaps, present no problems of identification to their teachers. Unlike with the physically handicapped, however, teachers seem to be reluctant to apply their ingenuity to helping children with speech defects. Perhaps they consider that such attempts would interfere with the interests of another profession; perhaps there is simply insufficient co-operation between teachers and therapists so that both sides overlook the possible contribution of the other. The severity of the problem is, of course, an important factor. It may be that Annabel's teacher was coping well with her because her speech difficulties were much less severe than those of the other three children. Yet of all handicaps, speech problems are surely an area where teachers, if given more advice from therapists and greater information on suitable materials and activities than is now the case, could fairly easily provide an effective and appropriate programme.

The mildness of his problem may also have been the reason why Jack was responding so well to his school experience. The teacher had worked with the mother to encourage speech, widen his interests and develop a good attitude to books and reading. Tonsillectomy had also helped. Although originally identified as having 'problems in language and understanding', Jack was perfectly normal in almost every way by the time the detailed assessment was made.

It was not only with the mild problems that teachers were successful. Paddy was brain-damaged and had poor locomotor ability. He also had a speech defect and, on entry to the reception class, was aggressive and over-active. As he was a big, sturdy boy, he soon drew attention to his difficulties. His teacher was not content merely to register these but set about deliberately planning activities, either in a small group or with Paddy alone, to help him. She saw, for example, that buttoning would help his poor co-ordination and used to the full the many opportunities that occur daily for dressing and undressing. She also gave him individual attention to develop his language skills to such good effect that, on assessment, he showed only slight deficits in comprehension (−4 months) and expressive language (−3 months). He was also reported to be on Book 2 of Ladybird, no small achievement at 4 years 7 months. His teacher was far from complacent. She felt that Paddy should be having speech therapy and far more training in hand/eye co-ordination than she could give. She felt very strongly and sincerely that she was not doing enough for Paddy but, in fact, considering his problems, he was doing very well and the credit to a large extent was the teacher's. She had contrived to find more time than might have been expected in order to give him the special help he needed.

In four other cases, differing in category of handicap and degree of severity, the teachers' organizational ability and their sensitivity to the children's needs enabled them to make very good provision in their ordinary nursery classes. Geoffrey was withdrawn, clumsy and timid; Raymond suffered epileptic fits and was also mentally retarded; Thomas was brain-damaged, poorly co-ordinated, aggressive and over-weight, going limp and floppy when reprimanded; Terry had limited intellectual ability and a poor home background. The teachers seemed to be able to select the most appropriate activities, to structure and modify other activities, to give the right amount of practice, and the necessary praise, to enable all four to benefit enormously. Their skill was not entirely a matter of experience (Terry's teacher was in her probationary year) or the result of good facilities (Geoffrey's school was poor in this respect). What these teachers had in common was the ability to find the time to give the child what he needed, a talent which is rather inadequately summed up by saying they were 'well organized'.

Six other children, Ian, Trevor, Roger, Elaine, Neville and Julie, were receiving a fair amount of help in school but could have been helped even more in a different setting or with a greater amount of individual attention or if the teacher had had more support from the headteacher or outside professionals. Ian's teacher was giving him a certain amount of special attention but unfortunately he was in a reception class of twenty-one children, small enough for no ancillary help to be provided. His problem was a social/emotional one. At home he was demanding and destructive but in school he usually showed withdrawn behaviour, wandering about in a dreamy fashion. He was not yet toilet-trained properly. Placement in a nursery class instead of a reception class would have helped Ian greatly, especially if the mother had also been given advice on handling him at home.

Trevor, on the other hand, was in a nursery school. He had very poor hand/eye co-ordination in addition to withdrawal. His teachers were trying to offer specific help for his problems of co-ordination, providing a lot of table top activities which Trevor disliked, perhaps because he found them difficult. His withdrawal would, they felt, be helped by encouragement to join in the normal nursery programme but such a view was probably over-optimistic. The setting did not help Trevor, any more than Ian's had, as he was in a highly active, open-plan nursery where there were constant interruptions and distractions. Trevor needed time to come to terms with his motor difficulties and sustained adult interest to develop his language and his confidence. He was really not getting very much of either, despite the fact that the staff were concerned and sensitive to the children's needs.

In Roger's case, the nursery staff had successfully toilet-trained him and developed his self-care skills. The wild, uncontrollable behaviour he had originally shown was moderating and he was beginning to join in with other children instead of knocking them over like skittles. What he desperately needed was for an adult to be with him for some continuous period of time, chatting and playing with him, showing him how to handle the difficulties he got himself into without simply lashing out. Individual contacts of this kind were not, however, part of his nursery regime. Elaine also had problems of adjustment, being withdrawn with other children and terrified of men. She was in a large nursery school with over one hundred children and, although it was fully staffed, she seldom surfaced for attention. Neville really required speech therapy, as teacher and mother agreed. Efforts to obtain it had not been successful. While the teacher was trying to do what she could to help Neville's speech and his motor co-ordination, which was markedly poor, she needed professional advice on both counts.

Julie was totally uncommunicative. As her teacher said, 'If she is distressed, we are often unable to find out why.' The teachers tried to engage her in conversation, talking with the children being important to them. She also saw the speech therapist fortnightly in school, and teachers and therapist had discussed Julie together. One of the main reasons why so little progress was being made was that Julie was also in a bustling open-plan nursery school with no areas for privacy or quiet activities. The teachers had asked for Julie to be referred to outside agencies and the headteacher had seen the social worker and the community medical officer about her. She did not, however, pass on any indication of what was said on these occasions to the other staff. It is particularly sad that in one of the few cases where a handicapped child was the focus of discussion by a number of professionals, no practical use was made of the opportunity.

Finally come the eight children who could have been helped in ordinary schools but who were not being given any special consideration at all. Five of them were placed in category 5 of the handicapping conditions and three in category 6, which could be thought of as a downward extension of category 5, the children having more limited general ability, which affected a wider range of their functional behaviour. Unless the problem is very mild, teachers have difficulty in coping with children who are placed in category 5. Two of these children, Susan and Jean, were so difficult to control in the ordinary school setting that they were placed in group B, being children the ordinary school could not really cope with. The five now under consideration, while some of their behaviour was similar to that of Susan and Jean, also showed sufficient differences to make it possible to say they could have benefited from placement in an ordinary school had they been given individual help specially designed for their needs. All five had poor expressive language skills. They said very little, often only answering an adult's direct questions in a whisper, and were difficult to understand. One of them, Sally, was receiving speech therapy at a central clinic but none of the teachers had had any discussion about the children's language difficulties with any professional. In fact, the teachers of these five children were doing almost nothing for their speech problems except trying to understand anything they might occasionally say.

All five children had some problem in their home background. Gilbert's mother was unmarried and the child was largely being brought up by his grandmother who also had a speech defect. Sally's mother was divorced and John's parents were separated, an experience which had left him with an aversion to men. Miles' father was unemployed and one of his siblings may also have had problems as he had been given speech therapy. Alan lived with both his parents but was brought to school by his father as his mother never left the house, only being seen peering through the curtains. No mention was made by the schools of any approach to or from the social services.

In two of the cases, Sally and Gilbert, the teacher said that the children presented no difficulties to the staff or to the other children. The same remark could certainly not be made about Alan, who took every opportunity to destroy other children's work or to strike them. The parents of the other children complained about him but the teachers used only negative control, apparently not realising that his aggression stemmed from frustration over his own inadequacies. When they did try to work with him on his own, they provided fine, table-top activities as for the other children, precisely the areas in which he was least able to cope. Motor co-ordination was poor in four of the children, encouragement of gross function being badly needed. The exception was John, whose performance skills were remarkable, by far the best developed of any child in the research sample, indeed in the highest bracket for any child of his age.

The teachers of these children appeared to hope that the normal programme would fulfil their special needs. They did not seem to realize the full extent of the children's handicaps. They provided good educational experiences for the majority of the children who could profit from them but they somehow failed to see what they could do about a child with special difficulties, even to the extent of claiming in two cases that there was no problem.

With the three children in category 6, it would have been very difficult for the teachers to overlook the problem. Two of them, Elizabeth and Ronald, were so poorly co-ordinated that they often fell over themselves. The other, Grahame, would settle to nothing and his most frequent remark was, 'not Grahame', whether appropriate or not. Their mental development was limited and their expressive language poor, but they were responsive to adults and aware of the classroom environment. Thomas who, it will be remembered, had benefited considerably from his school experience was just as seriously handicapped as Ronald or Grahame, so that failure to help the children was not the result of the handicapping condition. Elizabeth should not perhaps have been included with the two boys as she was about to receive help, a specially planned programme having just been worked out by the educational psychologist who hoped to implement it with the teacher's help. Without doubt, Ronald and Grahame required similar measures but no moves seemed to have been made to get outside professionals to draw up a programme, nor had the teachers tackled the task themselves.

Conclusions

To look at what happened to the Child Study Sample children in ordinary schools brings out six points.

(1) Very mild handicaps present no problems to most teachers. With just a little extra help, the children can join in the normal programme and benefit from it.

(2) Physical handicaps, if there is no mental retardation or emotional upset, are acceptable to teachers and other children, at least at this early stage.

(3) Professional advice for the teacher and the parents is essential in cases of speech problems, aggressive and restless behaviour, management difficulties and mental retardation.

(4) Teachers do not find it easy to help withdrawn children and children who show developmental lags, especially if expressive language is affected.

(5) Teachers who have ancillary help do not always use it to the advantage of the child with problems. But to be faced with such a child and have no help makes it impossible to cope adequately.

(6) Large, open-plan nursery schools seldom seem to help the child with special needs, especially if there is no provision for small group or individual quiet work. Placement in a reception class should also be very carefully considered as neither the staffing nor the programme may be suitable.

Notes

1 The 'Child Study Sample' consisted of eighty-two children selected by a two-stage screening process. At the first stage all teachers, health visitors and playgroup leaders completed a short schedule aimed at indicating whether a child definitely or possibly had a handicap in one or more of eight areas. At the second stage these children were given a more complete assessment and from these results the final sample, balanced for sex, type and severity of handicap, and type of provision was chosen. (Ed.)

2 The Griffiths Scale is a measurement of IQ in preschool aged children based on observational ratings. (Ed.)

3.2 A junior school resource area for the visually impaired

SEAMUS HEGARTY AND KEITH POCKLINGTON

Visual handicap is one of the most highly specialized areas of provision in special education, and the majority of blind and partially sighted children are educated in special schools, many of them residential. Although some other countries, notably Denmark, now provide for nearly all of these children in ordinary schools, schemes like the one described here are still uncommon in the United Kingdom. Yet this case study offers an illustration of how successful integration can be given adequate resources, sensitive staff and the necessary expertise. It also offers an interesting study of the growth of an integrated provision and the process by which the visually handicapped children became an integral part of this school.

Historical introduction

The particular authority we are concerned with, in common with many other small metropolitan boroughs, traditionally had very little in the way of specialist provision for pupils with special needs. As far as the visually impaired were concerned, those with mild loss of vision remained within the mainstream, while the special school provision of neighbouring LEAs was availed of in those cases where specialist provision was judged necessary. The shift toward developing provision locally came about for several reasons. Starting in the 1960s and running on into the '70s there was a shift within the broader society toward greater assimilation of the handicapped and other minority groups into the mainstream. The then assistant education officer (special education) was keen that his authority should be active on this front. Aided by a like-minded senior educational psychologist and the prevailing buoyancy of the economy, there was a positive explosion of special education provision, some of which had opportunities for integration built in.

Source: Unpublished report of the DES Project 'Education of Handicapped Children in Ordinary Schools', at the NFER.

Encouraged in particular by publication of the Report of the Vernon Committee (DES, 1972) which urged cautious experimentation with integrated provision for the visually handicapped, the authority pressed ahead with its plans. An 'embryonic unit', attached to a new school for the physically handicapped, opened with three children of primary age. It was envisaged that up to twenty-four blind and partially sighted pupils would eventually be educated together from nursery age through to the end of junior schooling. Each child's circumstances would be thoroughly reviewed at around age seven and, if it was considered to be in his or her best interests, he or she would then transfer to a special school. Along with this unit, the authority appointed its first peripatetic teacher of the visually handicapped early in 1977. Her responsibility was to support pupils with visual difficulties who were already attending ordinary school.

A new appointee at senior administrative level was strongly in favour of integrated provision, and one of his earliest actions was to seek to change the location of the planned provision for the visually impaired. He went in search of a suitable ordinary school, one that had the necessary resources and 'the right sort of staffing'. The school eventually alighted on was chosen because it was considered a good school, run by a head who was held in high regard within educational circles. It extended across the full primary age range – a nursery department was being planned at that particular time – and there was sufficient space to enable the nursery extension to be modified in order to incorporate a specialist resource for the visually impaired within a single new building. The head was happy to accept this as 'a new challenge', and thereafter her enthusiasm and commitment have always been to the fore. She immediately called a meeting of her staff at which she described what was proposed, expressed her own enthusiasm and enlisted their support.

The next consideration was the need to 'foresee problems that might arise and forestall them'. The head worked at fostering sound attitudes among staff toward pupils with special needs: allowing plenty of opportunities for anxieties and concerns to be talked out; obtaining relevant reading material; communicating information and insights she herself had gained, and so forth. Staff arranged visits to a range of special education establishments – schools for the visually impaired and for pupils with moderate and severe learning disorders, and provision within the authority for the hearing impaired. In addition, some attended a DES course on future developments within the education of the visually handicapped.

Advance preparation was not restricted to the teaching staff; the school's own pupils and their parents were also involved. The pupils were prepared mainly through assemblies — 'I told them stories about handicapped people, about the kind of problems they have, about the ways in which they will need help' (headteacher). With regard to their parents the head called a meeting where she and the principal educational psychologist spoke to parents about the planned development and showed them relevant slides. Time was put aside for answering parents' questions. The head considered this action had been particularly well rewarded: 'Parents can do a great deal of harm through ignorance . . . (the fear that handicapped) children will take up valuable teaching time and (our) children will suffer. . . . If you can answer their fears then they are always ready to support.'

The specialist facility — termed the Resource Area — opened at the beginning of 1978 with the transfer of three children plus their two members of staff from a temporary location in a special school. A gradual build-up of numbers was envisaged. This has perhaps been even more gradual than was anticipated. A week after opening four more children began. A period of sixteen months then elapsed before the next batch of four pupils arrived. Currently there are fourteen pupils on roll. Staff consider that the maximum number that could be catered for is about twenty.

Aims and organization

There was no existing provision within the authority that would provide a working model for the resource area. There were units for the hearing impaired that operated along traditional lines, and a visit was made to a unit for the visually impaired in another authority. These visits and other preparations had sensitized the head to possible problems that could arise with regard to integrating both special education staff *and* pupils with special needs into the mainstream. For the staff concerned however it was essentially a new venture and the early stages were exploratory — trying something out, appraising it, making any necessary modifications, and so forth.

There were certain broad principles that the headteacher was anxious to incorporate. The most outstanding of these was a determination that both pupils and their specialist teachers should be fully assimilated into the school. She did not 'want them to be isolated' and was quite prepared to force integration as much as possible. The head's initial emphasis was placed on building more normal modes of behaviour and developing social relations with sighted children. This was in marked contrast to the teacher in charge of the resource area whose attitude was that there would be plenty of time for social development later; what mattered most was developing sound educational foundations, especially for the educationally blind child who would be working within the medium of braille.

This is related to the differing perceptions of the headteacher and teacher in charge of how the specialist resource should operate. The latter envisaged a fairly independent unit. However, the headteacher intended that it should operate on a 'resource room' model, whereby pupils are withdrawn from the regular class for specialist assistance as and when necessary. Basic work in the '3Rs' was seen as the province of special education staff with integration for all creative and practical work, for blind and partially sighted children alike. It quickly became apparent that the partially sighted children were capable of remaining in regular classes for the bulk of the day. The resource room model appeared perfect for them. The educationally blind, by contrast, had need of a greater amount of specialist attention. This had to be provided within the resource area. (A further reason was that the teacher in charge was himself physically handicapped and became increasingly wheel-chair bound.)

A critical factor in the organization of the new resource area has been the team-teaching approach adopted by the school, based upon vertical grouping. Before the addition of the nursery and provision for the visually impaired, the school was divided into three departments: infants — five to seven years olds; lower school — seven to nine; and upper school — nine to eleven. In each department there were three teachers, one of whom held a Scale 2 post and acted as co-ordinator of the team. The co-ordinator was responsible for writing schemes of work, organizing the grouping of children (for mathematics, topic and reading), keeping records and monitoring the standard of display work. Each day the team met to discuss the following day's work and talk over any problems with individual children.

It was into this context that the resource area arrived. Little change was made in the existing organization of the school. A member of each team was given responsibility for liaising between immediate colleagues and staff in the resource area. Time was set aside for co-ordination to discuss 'what children are doing, how we can stretch them, problems encountered . . . whether (the educationally blind) can come in (to a lesson)', and so on. There were difficulties in the early days. The teacher in charge complained that the teachers with little or no specialist knowledge were deciding when he as the specialist could deliver special education: 'I don't agree that people who are non-specialists can assess whether a problem is there. . . . Ordinary teachers put forward the programme they wish and . . . I have to accept it.' The perception of main school staff was that 'the person with the know-how is not willing to pass this on', and they began to begrudge the extra effort that was demanded of them.

Some time later the teacher in charge retired. His replacement was a member of the school staff, a senior teacher who had been away on a year's secondment undertaking specialist training in visual handicap. On her return, the assistant in the resource area went on secondment, and was replaced by another teacher from the main school whose interest in the visually impaired had grown progressively. This led to considerable changes in working practice and an improvement in attitudes. Although the educationally blind children still spent some time withdrawn from main school they were now based in regular classes. In addition, both the resource area staff were in a position to work out in main school and felt at ease doing so.

The present level of operations was reached in September 1979 when two new members of staff were appointed, making a resource *team* for the first time. This has permitted the 'resource room' model of working to be fully embraced, with pupils being withdrawn only for specific training or in case of serious difficulty with work. A member of the resource team was placed in each department, becoming a full member of the departmental team but having the additional responsibility of teaching and preparing work for the visually impaired. The teacher in charge concentrates on the educationally blind as well as co-ordinating practice overall.

Pupils

Pupils provided for are those within the normal range of intelligence whose primary handicapping condition is visual. Pupils on roll suffer from a variety of visual disorders — nystagmus, glaucoma, retrolental fibroplasia, and so on. The pupil of markedly low ability who in addition has a vision problem is unlikely to be accepted on the grounds that the provision is intended for those whose primary handicapping condition is visual impairment. A visually impaired pupil with an additional physical problem is likely to be accepted as long as this does not necessitate constant nursing support. There is, in fact, a girl attending the school who has a severe arthritic condition.

The congenitally blind child is likely to be picked up at birth, or soon after; the partially sighted child, depending upon the severity of the vision loss, may be more difficult to spot. This is particularly the case where there is a very gradual deterioration in vision. Diagnosis and assessment in the more severe cases of vision loss is essentially a medical function whereas less severe visual deficits may well be first suspected by educators – a child's class teacher or the peripatetic teacher of the visually handicapped. It is this latter group who have given most cause for concern. Their more severely impaired peers are generally quickly recognized and the appropriate course of action taken. For the partially sighted there are two main areas of difficulty. First, the vision loss is often much harder to detect. Secondly, the peripatetic service has operated very fitfully since its inauguration in 1977. Only one teacher strong, the first appointee was off work for considerable periods of time. It is only since September 1979 that the service has operated consistently. It is now administered by the teacher in charge of the resource area in this school – officially designated 'co-ordinating teacher for the visually impaired'. One of the strengths of this arrangement is that the peripatetic teacher is no longer working alone – she has colleagues and a professional base that she can draw on.

It was originally conceived that the resource area would acquire the majority of its intake through individual headteachers querying particular children's vision. In fact, of the first seven entrants this seems to have applied in only one case, a partially sighted girl who had been 'coping quite well' in an ordinary infants school but who, it was felt, would experience mounting problems as school work became more difficult and print smaller. The visual impairment of the remaining six pupils was readily identifiable: one was suffering from leukaemia and his sight was deteriorating rapidly; a second was educationally blind, and a third had limited vision in one eye only; three others had significant vision loss.

Headteachers raising questions about individual pupils' capacity really came into play only with the third batch of entrants, four in all. It quickly became apparent that there were serious difficulties here. In one of the four the visual deterioration ought to have been noted – though the headteacher of the school containing the specialist resource remarked that she had only heard about the boy 'by accident'. All four pupils were six years or over. One, a boy of eight, was unable to read. In every case their educational development was significantly retarded through none was considered to be of below average intelligence. In the opinion of the resource area staff, their class teachers had either failed to pick up their visual problems or had wrongly diagnosed this, classifying them perhaps as 'less able', 'lazy' and so forth.

An alternative perception was that teachers were raising questions about certain children but educational psychologists were not acting quickly enough – 'Psychologists are just not prepared to get these forms through'. They were considered to be reluctant 'to take the child out of the home and (local) school environment'. Whatever the social and emotional gains, from an educational standpoint precious time was lost — 'We are getting them when (they) are getting frustrated; they can't cope, they are falling behind' (headteacher). In fact, all four pupils have shown considerable improvement since joining the resource area, but there is concern within the school about the possibility of other children missing out in this way. Not surprisingly, the psychologists' viewpoint was somewhat different. They felt too much emphasis was being placed on *potential* difficulties and were unwilling to make referrals based on prediction as opposed to demonstrated difficulties. The decision should be a pragmatic one: the child should not be removed from his own school just because difficulties can be anticipated for him but only when he or she had started meeting the difficulties.

Over the last six months of our study the headteacher and teacher in charge of the resource area have sought to tackle this problem. Their solution has been to develop what they call 'educational guidelines', practical guidelines to assist teachers in ordinary schools to determine for themselves whether a pupil has a visual deficit of sufficient severity to necessitate specialist *monitoring*, if not specialist assistance. Heads and teachers are being urged to call in the peripatetic teacher or even come direct to the resource centre if they have the slightest concern about a pupil's vision.

To date only one pupil has reached secondary stage, an educationally blind girl. She had been nearing the end of primary schooling when she transferred (from a special school) to the resource area. As she would have had only a few months there until the time of normal transfer, it had been decided that she would be retained for an additional year. Part way through this year the educational psychologist serving the school put forward two options, both residential special schools. After extensive debate, during which the educational issue was clouded by the girl's very sound social relationships within the home community, it was decided she should go to the more local of the two schools, even though academically she would probably not be 'stretched' there. However, the headteacher was still unhappy and proposed that the girl attend a comprehensive school close by. She visited the school and secured agreement for a two-week trial.

With intensive support from staff of the primary school the girl was fully integrated into the timetable over a two-week period. The only subject she was excused was French. At the end of this time the experiment was appraised, and there was unanimous agreement that it had been highly successful. It had worked 'extremely well' from an educational standpoint. In addition, the girl herself had enjoyed 'a very happy fortnight'. The head of the comprehensive was ready for her to transfer immediately but staff of the primary school urged caution in the belief that the girl's needs would be better met by a phased transfer. This was considered to be working quite well now after initial teething difficulties. However, all concerned are at pains to emphasize that this should not be regarded as an automatic transfer for all visually impaired pupils.

Staffing

This has increased as the number of pupils on roll has expanded. There were two members of staff — only one of whom had a specialist qualification — for the initial seven children. The present position is that three teachers — one of whom is qualified — form a resource *team*, attending in particular to the fourteen children on roll. In addition, the specialist peripatetic teacher is available for consultation — working out, as she does, from the resource area, and undertakes occasional teaching of pupils as necessary. However one cannot simply compute a simple staff–pupil ratio from this because of the school's team teaching approach. Members of the resource team also teach sighted pupils, while their main school colleagues will naturally deal with any visually impaired pupils in their teaching area. Because of the head-teacher's insistence that handicapped children should take part fully in the life of the school, no separate allocation of ancillaries was made to the resource area. The allocation of ancillaries to the school as a whole was increased by one.

Providing specialised training for the teachers involved has been accorded considerable importance. An unusual model of secondment operates: rather than advertise for teachers with an appropriate specialist qualification, the preference is to appoint someone — often from the existing school staff — with a good teaching record in ordinary education to work within one of the teaching teams, with a view to seconding them at a later date. This is a useful trial period, both for the school and the teacher concerned, prior to taking a decision on second-ment. Also, the value of the on-the-job training made possible by the team-teaching arrangement should not be overlooked. Advice and guidance can be given quite naturally as and when necessary with specialist expertise always close at hand.

There is considerable involvement of specialist agencies in this particular scheme. At its inception both the school medical officer and a senior medical colleague were particularly active. The latter — who was himself partially sighted — had visited the school and spoken to members of staff about the consequences of impaired vision for every-day living. The SMO has been extremely supportive throughout; as too has the educational psychologist. As the one outside specialist who makes a distinct educational contribution it is worth considering this latter person's involvement in more detail.

It is the preference of the individual concerned to play down the 'testing' role — 'there is not a lot of (traditional) psychology going on at the moment'. He visits roughly every three weeks during which time he seeks to question practitioners' assumptions and practices, feed in practical suggestions where a child is presenting particular difficulty, generally allowing and encouraging considerable teacher autonomy. For example, for several months a little girl in the school's nursery, suffering from 'a combination of handicap — retrolental fibroplasia, a general slow learner, language is particularly difficult', had presented tremendous management difficulties, and consequently with regard to appropriate educational programming. The psychologist had sought to 'sharpen up some of the programming and assessment they (teachers) might make in terms of criterion-referenced assessment'. In practical terms he stressed the need for more extensive and more focused individualized assistance, concentrating particularly upon attentional training and discrimination work.

A feature of the school's involvement with outside agencies is the assessment meetings held periodically (at first, half-termly, but now every six months). These were introduced by the headteacher because of concern at the poor working links with social services and with certain medical officials, notably, ophthalmologists. There has been improvement subsequently in both cases: specialist social workers have been regular attenders from the second meeting on; closer contact with ophthalmologists has come more recently, partly as a result of the senior medical officer persuading the consultants concerned to visit school and see how their clients were coping outside of the clinical setting. The value of these meetings is threefold. First, their primary purpose is to appraise both the general circumstances and the educational progress made by all the pupils over the six-month period. Secondly, it is a multi-disciplinary working group, with the majority of those present involved with the pupils in some way. Also, it is a forum within which the ordinary teacher has an active role when discussion turns to particular pupils that he or she teaches. Thirdly, these meetings have served as a means for disseminating information and concerns about a pupil across various professions and have led to various treatments and services being provided which would ordinarily have taken a great deal longer to organize, and possibly would not have materialized at all. An example of this was the senior medical officer arranging physiotherapy for a girl with severe arthritis. Hitherto she had not been receiving any therapy whatsoever. School staff made representations about this and as a result the SMO arranged first for intensive treatment in a hospital setting and then for twice-weekly visits by a physiotherapist to the school.

Accommodation and resources

The resource area is purpose-built and reflects the considerable thought that was given to the sort of facility needed at the planning stage. It comprises: a suite of four rooms, two quite large and well-equipped, and two others appropriate for individual or small group work; a pottery kiln which is extensively used by main school pupils; offices for the headteacher and secretary (originally intended for the teacher in charge but taken over by the head as a means of promoting integration — the existence of the resource area was kept at the forefront of people's minds in this way); and toileting provision. Given that pupils are now all based in regular classes and use the resource area only for withdrawal work, either individually or in small groups, the premises are highly satisfactory. They are quite open, colourful and have adequate lighting.

Over time an extensive stock of physical and material resources has been built up, not merely for the fourteen pupils on roll but for all pupils with visual problems within the authority. The original intention that it should serve as a resource centre for all schools is very much a reality. There is an extensive range of low vision aids which anyone can try out (under the supervision of the peripatetic teacher). Indeed, the local eye infirmary has referred children to the school in order that they may try out specialist aids. In addition, there are considerable large print resources, closed circuit television and video-recorder, and various large-scale play items. An additional allowance of £750 per year is made to finance classroom consumables (e.g., large print extracts of school texts), low vision aids, etc. Larger items of equipment (e.g., CCTV) have been financed out of the capital loan.

Two potential limitations are being increasingly realized however: the amount of time and effort required by having to braille out school texts and all school work set for some of the pupils; and the shortage of suitable large-print books for the partially sighted older juniors. Apart from the brailling that is done by the teacher in charge or the peripatetic teacher, staff receive considerable assistance from the RNIB and the Leeds Braille Book Club (subsequently renamed the Yorkshire Braille Service).

Curriculum

The curriculum followed by the visually impaired and the working philosophy on which it is based have evolved in the course of time. In the early days these pupils were taught largely by one teacher, joining regular classes only for the odd creative or practical activity. They were receiving a rather traditional education, in marked contrast to the informal, individualized approach based upon projects and workcards that the main school adopted. The then specialist teacher considered this totally inappropriate for his pupils, particularly the educationally blind: 'With this team-teaching, an individual research situation (i.e., topic-based) you can't ask a blind child to (do this) — they've got to use whatever braille material you have.' His reservations extended to the partially sighted. He pointed to numerous problems — print size, poorly designed and reproduced handouts and worksheets, and the difficulties they faced from a learning approach which placed such strong emphasis upon writing skills.

Above all, the disadvantage of being with teachers who had little real understanding of the educational consequences of vision impairment was stressed: 'The attitude is that the child can see, therefore we use formal methods. . . . How much they can see is not apparent to them.' Ordinary teachers were considered to be at a disadvantage in having very little specialized knowledge: 'In a way they don't think there is anything wrong with them . . . they (don't) fully understand what (partial sight) means.' In consequence pupils were considered to be missing out in certain respects; if they spent more time in the resource area, 'they would be getting a lot more care, social talking, language, sitting up straight . . . that would be brought out consciously'. However, as things stood, 'once they've done their educational bit (teachers) think they have done their task . . . there is a lot of this social training they are not getting here'.

As noted above, personnel changes and training have brought changes in philosophy and approach. All fourteen pupils are now based in the main school and receive individualized attention from the appropriate teaching team. The present working philosophy is one of sound infant and junior teaching, with close monitoring of individuals' progress — essentially by means of extensive working contact with the pupil — and delivering specific remediation and/or training in special skills (e.g., typing, brailling) as necessary. Wherever possible the visually impaired work on the same tasks and with the same materials as their sighted peers. The school seeks to provide 'a balanced curriculum of academic, creative and physical activities' for all its pupils. 'Each day is divided into four working sessions, one always catering for mathematics and another for topic. . . . The remaining times may be spent doing art and craft work, music, language or one of the following, physical education, games or swimming. Reading is done incidentally throughout the day.' The school's team-teaching approach relies upon extensive use of workcards and other individualized assignments, with teachers providing individual or small-group tuition — 'we work in small groups, each child . . . at his own level'. The individualized approach was considered most appropriate for all pupils but was particularly advantageous for the visually impaired.

The close working relationship between the resource team and the rest of the staff has been a critical factor. One member of main school staff described how colleagues had always been 'willing' but that they had not always been 'aware of how much extra attention the visually handicapped child required'. Liaison with the resource team had been necessary to overcome this problem. For example, whether working on the same tasks is feasible will have been discussed beforehand with the co-ordinator for the visually impaired. In many cases there is simply the need of closer supervision, a little extra attention. If the co-ordinator feels that a particular activity would not be to the pupil's benefit then she will arrange either for separate work or for the pupil to spend extra time on existing work where progress is perhaps slow or difficult.

Matters become considerably more complex when a pupil is working in the medium of braille. There are at present two braille users. In the past problems have arisen from the fact that there was only one member of staff with a knowledge of braille. If this person was already occupied or was otherwise not available, there was very little that main school staff could do except wait or send the child to the specialist teacher. There is in any case a time-consuming procedure of 'double-handling': the resource teacher brailles out a task set by the teacher for the pupil to do; when the pupil has completed it the specialist has to overwrite the brailled response for the ordinary teacher to mark. This, and other difficulties, while they have not disappeared entirely, have been eased with the advent of a second person versed in braille, and with the resource team being dispersed among departmental teams and working out within main school. For example, the co-ordinating teacher spends up to seventy-five minutes each day in main school. For much of this time she takes a mixed group of pupils for number work. Among its number the group contains an educationally blind girl and two partially sighted pupils. The various craft and practical activities, PE excluded, main school staff feel able to cope with. For PE, whenever apparatus is involved a teacher will be available to offer close supervision and assistance as necessary. In one girl's case, where vision loss was compounded by arthritis, a welfare assistant was detailed to work with the child, for the most part separately from the rest of the group.

Any pupil can be — and is — withdrawn whenever remediation is difficult within the classroom setting. Thus, in the case of the boy learning braille, he is sometimes withdrawn by the co-ordinator for specific training. Similarly, another child is being taught to use a jumbo typewriter by the school secretary. Again, should a pupil experience difficulty with some aspect of the curriculum then he is likely to be withdrawn at some stage and one of the resource team will work over the material or through the problem in detail.

Of particular note is the contribution made by one of the welfare assistants. This person spends a considerable part of her working week with the visually impaired pupils, and with the educationally blind in particular, helping out generally and undertaking specific activities where necessary. The physical education work referred to above is a case in point. Another concerns artwork. She had helped one educationally blind child to make a replica of a Viking ship from balsa wood. A considerable amount of carving was involved in this, some of which the girl had done for herself. The welfare assistant fully recognized the danger — it was a 'calculated risk . . . you blunt the edges' — but felt that it was justified in terms of the girl's sense of achievement.

Monitoring progress

Records are formally maintained on all pupils on a termly basis. Typically, the co-ordinating teacher comments on the specialized aspects of the pupil's education and the various members of the teaching team remark on the more general features. The following areas are addressed:
- social and emotional development
- physical development
- educational development; sub-divided into the following categories: reading, spelling, grammar, creative writing, mathematics, topic, art, PE, music, braille and typing (where appropriate)
- general observations.

Entries are, for the most part, descriptive, though reading ages are given. Any significant developments that occur within the term (e.g., a particular outcome of an assessment meeting — the two-week trial at the neighbouring comprehensive school for one pupil, for instance) are also formally recorded.

The major source of ongoing monitoring is the discussion that takes place on individual pupils at the termly assessment meetings which the headteacher inaugurated some fifteen months ago. Concerned about the apparent lack of working contact between different disciplines she set about bringing together representatives from different professions. These meetings are held, quite deliberately, at the school. This allows individual members of staff to attend, coming in on discussion about particular children within their area of the school. Although the educational psychologist functions as chairperson, the meetings are quite informal.

The social context

The concern at one stage in the past that some pupils, the partially sighted in particular, were missing out on the deliberate teaching of social skills has already been noted. The headteacher also was worried at that time by the mannerisms — 'baby voice, screaming, high pitched laughter' — that she noticed whenever the educationally blind children were in and around the resource area. 'You don't get this when they are in the main school.' However, as the working of the specialist resource has evolved, with both pupils and staff spending more and more time in the 'normal' environment of the main school, these negative aspects have been overcome. Various comments from teachers testified to this. 'Participates well in a group', was the remark on one infant child. 'She is talking about (being in) the juniors — socially it would be bad to keep her back', was said of a little girl in infants. 'You should see him eating his dinner . . . he doesn't like being helped — he's very independent', of a boy whose remaining sight is deteriorating. 'More independent than the other children', was said of a fourth child, a partially sighted girl in lower juniors.

The only cause for concern with regard to their development as independent individuals was a comment made with a particular boy in mind but considered by staff to apply to at least three others: 'Everybody loves him . . . (his good personal relations) work a bit too much in his favour' — in the sense that sighted pupils were a little too eager to assist, thereby depriving them of some opportunities for independence. This was reinforced in the case of one of the two educationally blind girls: 'Many of them (friends) are tending to spoil her . . . if you will do things for her she will let you.' However, school staff have taken steps to curb the excessive enthusiasm of sighted children to do things for the visually impaired. While not prohibiting this, teachers pointed out that it was not in the children's best interests: 'We're very grateful but if you carry on you're going to make Sarah very lazy.' It was felt that sighted children had modified their behaviour of their own accord once they had seen how their teachers responded.

The visually impaired pupils are an integral part of school life — registering with ordinary classes, attending and participating in assembly and school concerts, playing with sighted children at break times, taking dinner with friends from their respective classes, and spending time with them in the same lessons. This underlines how completely they have been accepted, and that the various opportunities open to other pupils are open to them also. All have friends in the school; some are part of quite extensive friendship circles. One particular action taken in the early days may well have influenced this — loosely teaming each visually impaired pupil with a 'buddy', a sighted pupil from main school recognized for his or her sympathetic qualities. The school never made a big issue of this, and in fact it quickly lapsed, but it may have helped in winning early acceptance. The present situation was succinctly expressed by an ancillary — 'We are even beginning to hear tales (about them)' — a sure sign of acceptance!

We conclude with an extract from our fieldnotes, an assembly which one of the research team sat in on:

> Clare, Sarah and Jane were all present with their respective classes. Sarah and Clare both gave the impression of being close to at least one child and in Clare's case there were three or four girls who stuck close by her. (It was later affirmed that she was very independent and preferred to do things for herself.) I was struck by the fact that all of them took a full part in assembly and did not stand out in any way. Even more noticeable was the general lack of concern that the non-handicapped children paid them. This is not to say that they were ignored . . . the point was that they just didn't stand out as anything exceptional . . . they were a normal part of things.

Pupils with impaired vision attend for the same length of day as any other pupil — something the headteacher had insisted on. Accordingly, they have every opportunity of taking part in the various clubs and activities that occur during school hours. When it comes to participating in extra-curricular activities they are at a disadvantage in living beyond the school's catchment area. This is particularly true of the out of county pupils. However, on various special occasions school staff have ferried children to and from school outside school hours when parents were unwilling or unable to do so.

Parental involvement

The school makes a point of having good relations with parents though, inevitably, the fact that some (about one third) live outside the authority means that the extent of contact is not always ideal. There is an open-house policy whereby if a parent is concerned about some matter he or she is encouraged to visit school and talk it out. The reverse applies too. The head and/or co-ordinator of the resource team quite regularly invite in certain mothers to talk about specific — mainly management — issues.

There are of course the customary occasions when school and home come together — open evenings, fetes, concerts, etc. There would appear to be many such occasions at this school. From discussion with two parents a high degree of parent–school involvement was evident — both parents, neither of whom we have any reason to believe was atypical, instancing six to eight contacts over a twelve-month period. These included open evening, school plays, the Christmas bazaar, and so on. More significantly, both were able to recollect at least one occasion when a visit to school had been for the express purpose of discussing some aspect of their child's schooling. In one case the mother spoke of two separate visits, one to discuss her daughter's progress generally, the other when she had been concerned about the development and quality of her daughter's handwriting.

However, we did become aware of several instances of management problems that parents were experiencing. To some extent these may stem from the fairly tight, hard-working regime which operates at the school so that children, when they arrive home, tend to unwind in a rather extreme way. The mother of one child remarked upon the very different behaviour exhibited by her daughter at home and in school and admitted that she felt unable to deal adequately with this. In another case a child's mother had on several occasions been 'dressed down' for neglecting her son. The two cases outlined above are quite contrasting, one a very motivated mother actively seeking to co-operate, the other careless perhaps, or possibly not taking in what she is told by teachers.

Where there have been extensive home visits this has tended to be where a child is presenting serious management problems at school and a marked discrepancy in handling between home and school is suspected as being at the root of this. This was certainly true of one little girl who began in the school's nursery and whose disturbed behaviour — screams and violent outbursts — used to frighten other children. She is now more balanced — although her parents had had difficulty in coming to terms with the likelihood that she would have considerable learning difficulties even if she was not visually impaired.

Summary

This is a good example of a school's existing academic organization, in this case team teaching, being extended to provide a highly effective example of resource model working. Visually impaired pupils have become an integral part of the school and their educational needs are met with very little separation from their peers. Key features have been the commitment and close involvement of the headteacher, and the seconding for specialist training of existing school staff who were teachers of proven quality and had developed an interest in teaching the visually impaired.

Reference

DES (1972) *The Education of the Visually Handicapped (Vernon Report)*, London, HMSO.

3.3 Special provision for PH pupils in secondary schools

CHRISTINE COPE AND ELIZABETH ANDERSON

Most physically handicapped (PH) children of secondary age are educated in special schools and many who have been in ordinary primary schools earlier in their careers transfer to a special school at or around eleven. In this review the authors examine schemes that exist in about half of the LEAs in England and Wales where secondary-aged PH children are educated in or near ordinary schools. They demonstrate the diversity of arrangements and the multiplicity of influences that combine to determine a disabled child's educational experiences: location can facilitate, but cannot determine the extent of integration. The actual degree of co-education depends upon the ordinary school's design and organization, the attitudes of staff and children, the degree of communication between unit and main school and the characteristics of the children. The variation in the extent and success of the schemes shows the degree to which problems may be controlled by careful planning and implementation.

The need for special provision

Special provision within selected ordinary schools at the secondary level may be needed by three main groups of PH pupils. Firstly, there are those *children who have coped in their local primary school*, but appear to be unlikely to manage in their local secondary school and so are often transferred to special schools. Reasons for such transfers vary greatly, but often physical problems predominate. Large areas of the local secondary school may be inaccessible to a child in a wheelchair or to a child who can only walk slowly and unsteadily; toileting facilities may be inadequate; the child may be unable to manage in a large crowded refectory; and so on. Sometimes LEAs who provide an extra helper for one or two children in a primary school may be unwilling to make similar provision at the secondary level, nor may the child wish to be the only one receiving such help. Heads may be reluctant to accept a

Source: Cope, C. and Anderson, E. (1977) *Special Units in Ordinary Schools: an exploratory study of special provision for disabled children*, London, University of London Institute of Education

PH child because of the greater risk of physical injury and the increased difficulty of keeping track of individual PH pupils in schools of over a thousand pupils.

Another common problem is the need of certain children for extra help. Children with brain disorders such as cerebral palsy or hydrocephalus may have been just able to cope in a primary school with some extra support from a sympathetic class teacher; but at the secondary school level, faced with a range of specialized subjects taught by different teachers, they may need more extra help than is normally available. Even if the school has a remedial department (in the DES 1971 survey only one-third of the 158 schools visited had one), the head may be reluctant to take on another child who will clearly need a great deal of extra help. Apart from academic problems, PH children may find it increasingly difficult to participate in the physical activities of their peers and may be unable to use the existing equipment in practical subjects. Another problem often raised is that children of secondary school age will accept PH and other handicapped children less readily than they did in primary school and that such children, even if not actively teased, may be left out of various peer-group social activities. All this will add to the normal emotional problems which adolescence brings, and the necessary support and advice may not be available in a large comprehensive.

Secondly, special provision within ordinary secondary schools will be needed for many *PH children who have attended special units at the primary level*. Thus, of the fifty-five sample children in the primary units,[1] there were twenty-six who teachers felt would quite definitely continue to require special help at the secondary level. Since special provision was available in an ordinary secondary school in only one of the study areas, it appears that many of these children may have to go on to residential special schools unless special day provision is set up before they reach secondary age.

Finally, there are many *children attending special schools at the primary level* who would benefit from the wider social contacts available in an ordinary secondary school and from the specialist teaching available there, since, as is noted in the recent Scottish Education Department Report (1975) on the secondary education of PH children in Scotland (p. 24), 'Special schools for the physically handicapped are all small and . . . it is difficult to provide a reasonable range of secondary education subjects.'

There are thus substantial numbers of PH children from three main sources, ordinary schools, special units in selected primary schools, and special schools, who would benefit greatly if special provision were made for them within selected ordinary secondary schools, and it is in response to their needs that a number of LEAs have begun to make such provision.

The secondary study: preliminary survey of LEAs making special provision in ordinary schools, and selection of schools to be visited

As part of the study of special provision at the secondary level, letters were sent in December 1975 to all 106 LEAs in England and Wales asking about the special educational provision which they made for PH pupils at the secondary level, and, in particular, whether they were making any special provision within selected ordinary schools for groups of PH pupils. Ninety LEAs (85 per cent) replied, about one-third of whom were making or planning some provision of this kind, and the information they provided is summarized in Table 1. There were three main ways (Types A–C) in which groups of PH pupils were being catered for in selected ordinary schools. In Type A, a secondary school would be selected, some physical adaptations made and in some cases, although not always, extra welfare assistance provided; the pupils

Table 1 LEAs making special arrangements for groups of PH pupils within selected ordinary schools at the secondary level

Nature of provision	No. of LEAs	
Type A		
Groups of PH children in selected schools. All in ordinary classes	14	
As above, planning stage only	5	19[a]
Type B		
Special classes/units for PH children in selected ordinary schools	4	
As above, planning stage only	9	13
Type C		
PH school sharing campus with ordinary school	11	
As above, planning stage only	6	17
Type D		
No existing or planned provision of Types A–C: reliance on special schools	52	
No information provided	16	
Total	117[b]	

[a] In seven cases this was in addition to special school provision and in twelve cases it was the main form of special provision in that area.
[b] This figure exceeds total number of LEAs since eleven LEAs were making or planning more than one type of special provision.

were then placed in the ordinary classes. In a few cases special provision had been incorporated in a new school at the planning stage. Type B was unit provision, and Type C was the placement of selected PH pupils in an ordinary secondary school on the same campus as the special school. LEAs making Type A and Type C provision were scattered throughout England and Wales, while those with Type B provision were all in the Midlands or North-East England.

Since little information is available about how provision for groups of PH children in ordinary secondary schools works in practice, it was decided that an exploratory survey would be made of provision in several schools from each of the three main Types, A–C. The number of schools which could be visited was limited by time and distance and in the end twenty-two were selected. Ten were schools making Type A provision, six were units of Type B (these included all the units then open), and six were schools sharing the same campus as a PH school.

Generally, a whole day was spent in each of these schools, during which data was collected by means of interviews with the heads, the teachers and/or nursing staff responsible for the PH pupils, other teachers, tutors and pastoral heads involved with PH pupils and the PH children themselves. The main areas covered in the interviews, and discussed in the sections which follow, included the way in which the provision had been set up, the nature of the children's handicaps, the quality of the special facilities available to them, the special teaching arrangements, the extent of academic integration and attitudes of the teachers, and finally the question of the social integration of the PH children.

Why had the special provision for PH pupils been made in the survey schools, and how much prior planning and consultation had there been?

Special provision in the twenty-two schools surveyed had been made for a variety of reasons. Of the ten schools with Type A provision (i.e. for groups of PH children who were then all placed in ordinary or remedial classes), four were in areas without day PH schools. These LEAs had been able to cater for most of the PH children within ordinary schools at the primary level, but it was felt that many would be unable to manage in ordinary secondary schools. Since the parents were reluctant to accept the only alternative, that of residential placement (also very costly for the LEA), special provision had been made in selected schools. In the other six Type A schools visited, special provision was already available in day PH schools. In three cases the LEA had felt that some of the special school children were 'missing out' on the normal secondary curriculum and so had made special arrangements for them in selected ordinary schools. In a fourth case the impetus had come from the special school head, who had initiated a link with a comprehensive which had been developed over a number of years; now this comprehensive takes sixteen PH children, and links with two other comprehensives are planned. Another LEA had made special provision in an ordinary secondary school for PH children who had previously attended a PH unit in a primary school, and in another the provision was to meet the needs of children who had coped in their local primary schools but needed more support at the secondary level.

In most cases there appeared to have been very little prior consultation on the part of the LEA with the heads and staff of the ordinary schools about taking PH children, and little discussion about organization and possible problems. One head, for example, said that he had been given very little information at the outset and knew of two other heads whose schools had been selected to take PH children in the near future who were in the same position (which proved to be the case when the heads were contacted). The only schools in which consultation was felt to have been adequate were the two schools designated to take groups of PH children from particular 'feeder' primary schools.

Even more worrying was the general lack of on-going support from LEAs, nor did the latter appear to be monitoring the adequacy of the provision in any systematic way. Heads commented on the lack of support, and remarks such as 'nobody comes to visit to see what's going on', or 'had to fight for facilities', or 'difficult to get extra help – we're coping on the bare minimum', were frequently made.

The six units in secondary schools (Type B provision) had been set up for two main reasons. Two units were purpose-built for PH children and had been set up because the LEAs felt the special schools were unable to offer a varied enough curriculum (and also, in one case, because of pressure for accommodation in the special school at the nursery level). The other units catered for children with various handicaps under the umbrella term 'delicate', and were intended as 'half-way houses' between ordinary and special schools in special educational treatment. Since most of the children in these units were in fact PH children they were included in the survey.

Much better supportive services were available to the purpose-built PH units than to the Type A schools, and the heads of the host schools had also been much more fully consulted and the setting up of the units more carefully planned. In one school with a purpose-built PH unit, for example, the head of the PH school which was to 'feed' the unit came to the comprehensive to talk about handicap, and a number of the ordinary teachers had visited the PH school at an early stage. The teacher in charge of the unit and another teacher from the PH school also taught full-time in the comprehensive before the arrival of the unit children.

The six special schools (Type C provision) on the same campus as comprehensives or high schools had been sited with some intention of liaison with the adjoining ordinary schools, although availability of land had also been a major factor in the choice of site. However, there had usually been little prior consultation between the ordinary heads and staff on the question of integrating PH pupils.

What criteria were used for selecting PH children for placement in the schools in the survey, and in what ways were the children handicapped?

LEAs varied in the criteria they used for placing PH children in the survey schools. Policy appeared to depend partly on the alternatives available (e.g. day PH schools), partly on accessibility and on other facilities available in the ordinary school, and partly on the general philosophy of the LEA regarding integration.

In most of the ten Type A schools, only those children who were thought to be able to benefit academically were accepted. Two of these schools also required that children be able to cope with their own toileting. However, three schools in areas without day PH schools admitted children with intellectual as well as severe physical handicaps. These children tended either to be placed full-time in remedial classes, or to spend a large proportion of their time in withdrawal classes. One-third of the PH children in the Type A schools came from ordinary primary schools and two-thirds from special schools, and just over one-third depended heavily on wheelchairs.

In the Type B schools with units for 'delicate' children, the main criterion for admission was mobility, since these schools were inaccessible to children in wheelchairs. In contrast, the two purpose-built PH units had initially admitted all PH pupils of secondary age. In one of the units policy had changed, and it was specified that the children admitted must be of a broadly similar intellectual level to the non-handicapped children so that they could spend a substantial proportion of their time in the ordinary classes. Overall, 81 per cent of the children in the six units had previously attended special schools (for PH or delicate children).

Where special and ordinary schools shared the same campus (Type C), the only children admitted to the ordinary schools were those who could fit in academically without requiring extra help. Further, since these schools were inaccessible to children in wheelchairs such children were generally excluded, even if of good ability.

In Table 2 the main handicaps of the children who had been placed in the twenty-two survey schools are shown. The children in the A and B types of provision were fairly evenly divided between those with and without brain disorders, contrasting with the same-campus schools, where very few children with brain disorders were being integrated. In Type A provision there were comparable numbers of spina bifida and cerebral-palsied children, whereas in the units there were more children with cerebral palsy or other brain disorders such as 'minimal cerebral dysfunction'. (This finding reflects the fact that only two of the six units had been purpose built for PH children; four were in schools which were inaccessible to wheelchair-bound children.) Most of the spina bifida children but only about one-third of the cerebral palsied children were severely physically handicapped.

What special facilities were available to PH pupils in the secondary schools visited and how adequate were these?

The actual physical suitability for PH pupils of the schools varied greatly. In those which integrated the PH children into ordinary classes (i.e. Type A and Type C schools), there was little in the way of special accommodation for them; in some Type A schools, for instance, the medical room was used as their base. Special toileting facilities were adequate in all schools but one. Accommodation in the purpose-built units, on the other hand, was good.

The main physical problems in the Type A schools and in those with units for 'delicate' children was one of access. Three multi-storey Type A schools, for example, had no lifts when the PH pupils were first admitted, so that children in wheelchairs had to be carried up and down flights of stairs. In two of these schools lifts were provided after about a year, but the third still had no lift after five years. In another school there was a lift to the first floor only, so that the remedial department and other specialist rooms which were on the top floor were inaccessible to some children. In the schools with purpose-built PH units there were no problems of access, but those with units for 'delicate' children could only take mobile children. The situation was least satisfactory in those secondary schools on the same campus as the PH schools. Although paths had been built to connect the schools (one with steps!), the distance between the schools — up to 200 yards — was a problem. The real difficulty was that none of the six schools had lifts nor (except for one with external ramps) any other modifications, to the toilets, etc. Full facilities in five out of these six schools were thus limited to mobile children.

It is often said that the amount and speed of movement between

Table 2 Main handicapping conditions of PH children attending selected ordinary secondary schools

Type of provision	No. of schools visited	Spina bifida N	%	Cerebral palsy N	%	Other N	%	Total N	%	Children without brain disorders N	%	B	G	Total
A Children fully integrated	10	14	24.6	11	19.3	2	3.5	27	47.4	30	52.6	28	29	57
B Units	6	7	8.0	25	28.7	16	18.4	48	55.2	39	44.8	57	30	87
C Same campus schools	6	6	24.0	3	12.0	0	0.0	9	36.0	16	64.0	16	9	25

classes in large comprehensives is something PH children will be unable to cope with. Teachers and pupils were asked about this and the general feeling was that, although this was confusing at first, the non-handicapped pupils were considerate and this was simply not a major problem. The only exception was a child with brittle bones who said that he was afraid of being knocked down.

What was a cause for concern among almost all the heads was the question of getting the PH children out safely and quickly in case of fire, although most had had discussions with local fire officers about the best way of tackling this problem. When making special provision in new schools close co-operation between the fire authority and the architects is essential. [. . .]

The next aspect of special provision looked at was special staffing arrangements. In all the Type A schools it had been recognized that someone must have overall responsibility for the PH children. In five schools a teacher (two with special training and experience with PH children) had this responsibility. Their workloads were adjusted so that they had time available for dealing with the various extra duties arising in connection with the PH group, such as counselling, making special arrangements with other teachers, visiting homes and visiting other schools. In two of the schools, welfare assistants had been appointed to help severely handicapped children, but in three the children looked after their own personal needs. In the case of the other five Type A schools a member of staff with nursing qualifications had responsibility for the PH children, including liaison with parents. In the three schools where the medical room was the children's base, this was a specially appointed assistant with nursing qualifications, while in the other two it was the school matron, with the help, in one case, of a welfare assistant.

While the appointment of a qualified nurse is valuable to schools with PH children (especially spina bifida children), the overall responsibility for the PH children should be in the hands of a teacher and, wherever possible, this should be a teacher with a qualification in the education of handicapped children. It may be argued that such a person will be under-employed in a school with only a handful of fully integrated children, but this will not be the case if her duties include giving extra tuition (if needed) to the PH children, liaising with their specialist teachers, liaising with schools which will provide the new intake of PH children, being available to parents, acting as a resource person to other children in the school with learning problems, and doing some teaching in the ordinary classes.

The only other extra member of staff who visited the Type A

schools was, in four cases, a physiotherapist. In fact all the schools would have benefited from contact with a physiotherapist. In four of the six schools not visited by a physiotherapist there was at least one child who needed physiotherapy and, quite apart from this, teachers in all the schools needed advice from someone with relevant special training on how to involve the PH children in physical activities and sports. Without this, it can easily happen – and was happening in three schools – that children in wheelchairs, as well as those with very limited mobility, get no form of exercise.

In the schools with units, special staffing arrangements were generally satisfactory. The two purpose-built units for PH children had excellent staffing ratios: both the teachers in charge had special qualifications as well as prior experience in PH schools, and the assistance of helpers. These units also had visiting physiotherapists; one had a full-time nurse who worked closely with the physiotherapist. Swimming was available for the children, one school having its own pool. Other special services from speech therapists, psychologists and social workers were also provided. In the units for 'delicate' children staffing ratios were also good. In two units teachers were satisfied with the availability of supportive services, while in two other contacts were limited.

Summing up, there was considerable variation in the adequacy of special provision in the survey schools, by far the most satisfactory provision being in those schools which incorporated purpose-built units for PH children. The quality of the provision was quite unrelated to the type of neighbourhood which the school served: good quality provision was as likely to be found in EPA[2] as in other schools. What did matter was whether the LEA had put into the school resources of the same quality as those available in PH schools. Thus, both purpose-built PH units had facilities that were, according to the unit teachers (who had previously worked in special schools), quite as good as those of special schools.

How were the teaching arrangements for the PH children organized, and how much integration was there?

Schools where children were fully integrated

For the fifty-seven children in this type of provision the normal curriculum was generally followed, any extra help needed being provided within the remedial department. In four of the ten schools none of the PH children used the remedial department while in the others children had varying amounts of extra help. In one school for example, two PH children were full-time in remedial classes and two more spent most of their time in remedial groups. In two other schools the teacher with responsibility for the PH children gave extra help to those who needed it and also to other children in the school. Overall, half of the children with cerebral palsy, one-third of those with spina bifida and 10 per cent of the children without brain disorders received some extra help. In these schools, and indeed in the same-campus schools and those with units, it was somewhat easier to place the PH children when mixed ability grouping rather than banding/streaming was used, since PH children with brain disorders are more likely to have an uneven patterning of intellectual abilities than are non-handicapped children.

Two in three of the PH children had come from special schools and a problem raised by teachers concerned the best age for making such a transfer. At eleven years old, PH children may be considerably less mature than their peers and many are behind in basic skills: should they then be kept on in the PH school till the age of thirteen? One school had tried this but had reached the conclusion through a number of years' experience (and this was endorsed by the children) that it was better for a child to start in a comprehensive at the same age as his peers.

A number of teachers commented on the rapid progress of some of the PH children on coming into the comprehensive and felt that they had not previously been 'stretched' enough. However, it was also the case that many PH children were still behind in basic skills and needed considerable extra help. Another problem was the lack of experience of PH children from special schools in certain specific subjects, such as science. Two comprehensives which were fed by PH schools had organized a scheme by which children who were to be transferred were given coaching in these areas while still at the PH school. In one case this was done by a specialist teacher in the PH school and in the other by a liaison teacher who worked in both the PH school and the comprehensive.

Practical work posed additional problems. In domestic science or workshops severely handicapped PH children were sometimes helped by a welfare assistant, and of course by other children, and in some cases special equipment had been provided. Adaptations to benches and to small pieces of equipment were often carried out by the schools themselves. Practical work in science had not been a major problem since children usually work in pairs. Only in exceptional cases had PH children been excluded from practical subjects.

On the academic side, a problem mentioned by several teachers was the rate at which the PH child worked, usually because of writing difficulties, while the general presentation of the work (quality of the writing, untidiness, etc.) also caused concern. Typewriters were used by children in two schools and one had begun a typing course for PH children. Apart from this, little in the way of special aids was available and a resource room run by a teacher with special qualifications would certainly have been needed had the proportion of cerebral-palsied and spina bifida children in these schools been greater.

Schools with units

Here, the situation was rather different. The special class was the child's base in five units, whilst in the sixth the children were based in ordinary or remedial classes and withdrawn to the unit for extra help, usually for a large proportion of their time.

Where the child was based in a special class the teacher in charge made the arrangements for part-time integration in the ordinary classes after consultation with colleagues there and, generally, with the head. First, the child's abilities in different areas — and also his emotional stability — were assessed by the unit staff, then the possibility of his joining an ordinary class was discussed. Much of the unit teacher's time was spent on public relations work, and whether or not integration succeeded depended heavily on her knowledge of the staff (some were more sensitive to the needs of PH children than others), and her relationships with them. Individual programming and flexibility in making arrangements were crucial, as this statement made by a teacher in charge of a two-class unit shows:

The number being taught in the unit fluctuates throughout the day as at any one time various children are joining in a variety of lessons in the main school. As these children progress, they begin to take part in more and more lessons in the main school. As far as possible these would be the classes which they might eventually be able to join completely, but this has to be kept flexible . . . In effect, each child has an individual timetable which gradually evolves and changes . . . Such timetabling needs a tremendous amount of good-will and co-operation on the part of all the staff involved . . . [it] can only be done on a personal basis, it takes time and has to be built up patiently and delicately. Sometimes a mistake involving personalities may be made, and it is important to sort it out whilst carefully trying to preserve goodwill. The unit has been particularly fortunate, as the staff of the main school have gone out of their way to co-operate and offer all kinds of assistance and opportunities . . . Once it is decided that a child is able to leave the unit completely we build up their timetables in the previous term so that they are very well settled with the particular class they are to join. In any one year we have averaged between fourteen and sixteen of our ex-unit children spread throughout the main school, and most of these have gone on to take CSE examinations . . . some have become school prefects.

The amount of integration varied greatly from school to school. In one unit all but one severely handicapped child were spending between 25 per cent and 100 per cent of their time in ordinary classes, whilst in another, two children were fully integrated and an additional one-third took CSE maths and geoscience in the main school. Also, every unit child was involved in creative studies in the ordinary classes. In two other units individual integration was gradually built up wherever possible, while those children unable to cope in a large group or of low ability remained with a special teacher. The other two units had only a small number of PH children. In one integration was very limited, while in the other unit children were in theory placed in ordinary classes and withdrawn for extra help, but in fact most spent the greatest proportion of their time in the unit or in a remedial class.

The PH children in two of the units had not entered the comprehensive until the age of thirteen. This made it more difficult for them to fit into the ordinary classes. However, in one unit a very successful tutorial system was being operated. The child could spend extra time on a subject, or go over work he did not understand, or work missed through absence, with the unit teacher who worked closely with the other members of staff. Many teachers will not place PH children in ordinary classes unless sure they will cope; this teacher was more optimistic and, if the child wanted it, would place him in an ordinary class for a particular subject even if she felt it would be a struggle for him to keep up. If he had continuing difficulty or found the number of subjects too many, it was understood that he could drop the subject without feeling a failure; this system appeared to be working very well.

Discussion with unit teachers indicated generally that, though successful academic integration depends partly on a child's ability, the relationship between a unit teacher and her colleagues is probably of even greater importance. Successful integration should not be dependent primarily upon the personality of the unit teacher: her job will be made much easier if integration is seen, *from the start*, by all members of staff, as something for everyone to aim at as a matter of policy. This is not nearly explicit enough, although in one of the schools with units new members of staff are told during interview that they will probably be asked to take PH children into their classes.

Same-campus schools

Communications regarding integration were usually between the heads or deputies of the two schools and generally integration was rather limited; but five of the six PH schools visited had not been in operation for long and hoped to build up the amount of integration gradually. In four of the schools a small number of children were integrating full-time (but remaining on the roll of the special school); in the other two a total of only five children attended the ordinary schools for one or two subjects.

In the same-campus schools the amount of integration was further limited by additional problems. These included the existence of two entirely separate organizations, the physical separation of the buildings, the inaccessibility of the ordinary schools to children in wheelchairs, and the lack of special toilet facilities in them. Often, too, the PH and ordinary schools operated different starting hours, lunch breaks and finishing times.

Good leadership (with a commitment to and belief in integration), coupled with very careful planning can, of course, overcome these problems to some extent, as was shown in one school (not included among the twenty-two survey schools as it had not been open at the beginning of the survey) which was visited right at the end of the study. This was a newly built PH school which had been physically attached to an existing comprehensive. It had been designed so that movement between the two schools (through swing doors to an open area with a lift giving access to all floors of the comprehensive) could be easy and rapid. In addition, the comprehensive had had special facilities installed in the domestic science area and the workshops to accommodate PH pupils. Most important, extensive consultation was going on between the two heads, and the staff and pupils of the PH school had also been fully consulted about the siting from the planning stage. The comprehensive head had previously had experience of integrating PH children and there were already a number of such children in the comprehensive.

In circumstances such as these there seem to be good possibilities for both academic and social integration of the PH pupils; however, in all those same-campus schools visited in the survey there was no doubt at all that integration was far more difficult to achieve than when the PH children were actually based in an ordinary school.

How well informed about the PH children were the teachers in the ordinary classes in secondary schools, and what were their feelings about accepting them?

It was not possible to talk to all of the teachers involved with the physically handicapped children, but information was obtained from as many of the staff as possible, including heads, year heads and tutors. Attitudes towards having PH children in ordinary schools were often very positive; for example, two members of staff were indignant because they believed that those planning the special provision had felt it necessary to 'sell' the idea to them.

However, both in the schools where the PH children were based in ordinary classes and in those with units, considerable apprehension was expressed by heads and teachers about taking PH children, especially by teachers who had had no prior contact with PH pupils. One of the unit teachers had carried out a careful study of attitudes (Cannon, 1975); this showed that teachers in three comprehensives with units had more favourable attitudes towards PH children than those in three very similar comprehensives which did not. Despite this, apprehensions did still exist, even in those schools which had been taking PH pupils for some time. The main anxiety expressed by ordinary teachers was whether they were doing the best thing for the PH child, the general assumption being that the quality of provision (and of the teaching in particular) would be better in a special school. Thus, remarks were made such as: 'I wonder whether they would be better off with other PH children?', or 'We don't know what's available to help them' or 'I feel that we're not doing enough'. Criticisms also arose when teachers felt overworked. One remedial teacher, for example, was unhappy about the PH child in her class: 'She hasn't progressed very much. I can't give enough individual attention . . . I don't feel qualified enough . . . She shouldn't be here.' This school did not have a teacher with special responsibility for the PH group, and in two other schools in the same situation, heads felt that their staff were overburdened.

In most of the schools ordinary teachers felt they needed more information about the PH pupils: in three cases, for example, a PH child suddenly appeared in a practical class without the teacher having any knowledge of his limitations. However, in a few schools real efforts had been made to keep ordinary teachers well-informed. The deputy head of one comprehensive on the same campus of a PH school had prepared with the help of staff in the PH school short outline sheets about different handicaps and about the problems the children might have. In five of the twenty-two survey schools some attempt had been made to provide the non-handicapped pupils with information about handicaps (e.g. by a unit teacher, a teacher from a PH school and a well-informed teacher in the ordinary school).

Teachers in ordinary classes need more than information; they need, especially, confirmation that they *are* doing the best for the child and this is something that the teacher responsible for the unit or the group of PH children can do, particularly if she has had special training. In the schools with a unit her role was usually well defined, but in Type A schools one teacher should be clearly recognized as having responsibility for the PH children. The arrangement which seemed to work best was that this teacher should belong to the remedial department and work there and in the ordinary classes, as well as giving extra tuition to the PH children where necessary. She, in turn, will need outside advice from back-up agencies, in particular the schools psychological service.

How well accepted socially were the physically handicapped pupils who attended ordinary secondary schools?

Although research findings show that physically handicapped children are usually well accepted by their peers in primary schools (as was found in this study, and, in the case of children placed mainly in their local schools, by Anderson, 1973, and Hicks, 1975), doubts are often expressed about what will happen at the secondary level. In all the survey schools the heads and the teachers responsible for the physically handicapped pupils were asked about this, and where possible the PH pupils themselves were interviewed about their friendships, social activities, and feelings about being in an ordinary school (nearly three-quarters of these pupils had previously been in special schools).

Schools where children were fully integrated

In the case of the fifty-seven pupils fully integrated into the ten comprehensive/high schools, there was general agreement among the heads and teachers involved that there were no major social problems. In one school only there was some disappointment that four out of the five PH children (all four of low ability) were not mixing with their peers as well as had been hoped. One of these children (placed in a remedial class) and three others out of the group of fifty-seven said that they had experienced some teasing, while several other children mentioned being stared at. However, all but one felt they could deal with teasing themselves. One girl said that she did not know of any teasing of PH children in her present school but that a great deal had gone on in her PH special school. It was noticeable in one comprehensive that most of the PH pupils kept together as a group at breaks and lunch, although they had been individually placed in different classes. When asked about this they said that they did have other friends but tended to stick together because they had known each other well in their previous PH school.

Altogether, nine of the fifty-seven children (four with spina bifida, three with cerebral palsy and two others) in this type of provision were reported by staff as apparently preferring their own company (or seeking that of adults) to that of their handicapped or non-handicapped peers and this was confirmed by interviews with the children. This proportion (16 per cent) is unlikely to differ much from the proportion showing solitary behaviour among teenagers attending PH schools, or, for that matter non-handicapped teenagers, but even so some of these children would certainly have benefited from counselling or other professional help.

As might be expected, although teasing and overt rejection was not a problem, there was considerable variation in the extent to which the PH children were fully accepted by their peers. While low ability was not necessarily a bar to acceptance, there was some indication that children were less likely to be well accepted if placed full-time in a remedial class than if based in ordinary classes and withdrawn for extra help; this is in line with Garnett's findings (1976) for ESN children in a comprehensive school. Children who joined the school during rather than at the beginning of the school year were also less likely to be accepted. Some of the older more successfully integrated children pointed out that making friends was dependent upon 'meeting people half-way'. Teachers felt that whether the child had the confidence to do this was closely related to the extent to which the parents had encouraged independence and, to a lesser extent, to the amount of support available to the child in the school.

Two very consistent findings emerged from discussion with the children of their feelings about being in an ordinary school. Firstly, most had been apprehensive about going to an ordinary school (65 per cent had previously been in special schools); secondly, all those interviewed said that they liked their present placement and none of those who had attended special schools wished to return. Many commented that they had found the special school 'boring' or 'too easy' and said that they were enjoying the greater range of subjects available and the chance to make friends with non-handicapped children.

Schools with units

For children in unit-type provision, the overall picture was also satisfactory. None of the unit teachers felt that the children were isolated within the school and opportunities for mixing were considerable, arising from contacts in the classroom and playground, from various social activities, educational visits, and so on. The siting of the unit was felt to affect integration. In one teacher's words: 'We are fortunate in that the unit . . . is in the heart of the school, from where the children can see the life of the school going on all round them from the security of their own base and . . . the ordinary children can see them.'

Friendship patterns varied considerably. In two of the units for 'delicate' children most of the PH children's friends were in the units, whereas in the other two units more of the children had friends in the ordinary classes. In the two purpose-built PH units the children had arrived as a group from PH schools and had known each other for some time. They said that they had retained their handicapped friends, but had also made new friendships outside the units, and teachers felt that this group support had helped to give them the confidence to do this. None of the unit children expressed a preference for special school placement and, again, a number reported that they had been bored or had 'not much to do' at special school. One handicapped sixth-former felt that mixing with non-handicapped teenagers had made him more mature; another that he certainly wouldn't have passed his examinations from the PH school, although he also commented that the unit definitely gave him a sense of security and that, although now fully integrated, he used it occasionally for private study or went there to chat with staff.

A general problem for children in the units and in the Type A schools was that very few were able to attend after-school clubs and other social activities held in the school, because they lacked special transport. For teenagers in particular this can be very frustrating, especially as many handicapped teenagers lead rather lonely and restricted lives at home. In two units the teachers were well aware of this problem and attempts were being made to provide transport.

All of the unit teachers said that some teasing had taken place, but that as far as they knew this was no longer a problem; this was again confirmed by the children themselves. One experienced unit teacher had this to say about teasing:

It would be unrealistic not to expect unkind comments or teasing from time to time but nearly always this results from thoughtlessness and ignorance. The remedy seems to be to try to discover the culprits and explain, for example, why someone is badly scarred, or perhaps, very simply, what 'spastic' means. These children are usually very penitent when they realise they have hurt someone's feelings. Nearly always they are themselves inadequate or unhappy children, who need help for their own problems . . . Children with a noticeable handicap have, sooner or later, to come to terms with this kind of thing, and it is surely easier for them to face up to it where they are in an environment where they can be given unobtrusive support . . . In any case, we must view these incidents in perspective, for they have been very few and far between.

Same-campus schools

Opportunities for social contacts with the non-handicapped children were fewest for the children in special schools sharing a campus with an ordinary school. Only a very small proportion of the PH children, including those who had all their lessons in the comprehensive (though remaining on the roll of the special school), had made friends with non-handicapped children, and in general the administrative arrangements did not facilitate this. Half of the PH children were in classes with children a year younger and they usually returned to the special school for lunch. In two schools a number of PH children felt that they 'missed out in both camps', and several were resentful about the arrangements, commenting, 'We miss out on social activities here and we're not allowed to join in everything in the "comp." ', or 'We come back over [to the PH school] when we're timetabled for games in the "comp." and we don't have any games'.

Other problems raised by children concerned their relationships with pupils and teachers in both schools. In one school the children who integrated said that the other PH children 'resent the comprehensive school children and the comprehensive school doesn't think much of us', while they had this to say about the comprehensive school staff: 'We're treated soft — too many allowances made for us. We would prefer to be treated like the others [ordinary class children].' There were problems, too, in their relationship with non-handicapped children. According to a girl with spina bifida 'it took a while to be accepted. There is some teasing but I shrug it off. The boys are worse than the girls.' A boy with spina bifida also mentioned that girls were more accepting: 'We get on all right with children in the other classes . . . better with the girls'. Some of the PH children were less positive. 'The others use us as skives: they get off early to get us downstairs!' Two children felt they were picked on: 'There's a boy in my class who seems to hate me; he takes it out on me; and the other (ordinary class) children are really bossy.' Another child said that 'we do get stared at and there is teasing . . .', but that they usually coped with it. Some teasing had occurred in all three comprehensives where PH children attended full-time while still based in the special school, and this appeared to be more of a problem than when children actually 'belonged' to an ordinary school. A problem for the integrated PH children from one special school was that they found it increasingly difficult to maintain friendships with the other PH children, while relations with special school staff had also become strained.

Of the eighteen PH children who had all their lessons in the comprehensives, nine said they would prefer to belong to the comprehensive school, eight liked both, and only one (a child with brittle bones) preferred the special school. The heads of two PH schools thought that probably five children in all really preferred the special school, but that pressure from parents and the fear of losing face kept them in the comprehensive. Whatever their actual preferences, the main finding was that from the social point of view the children in Type A and Type B provision were under less strain, and were better accepted than those whose time and loyalties were split between two different schools.

Notes

1 In the book from which this study is taken Cope and Anderson describe a very thorough study of the attainment, attitudes and social relationships of PH children in units attached to primary schools and a detailed description of the provision made. (Ed.)
2 Educational Priority Area. (Ed.)

References

Anderson, E. M. (1973) *The Disabled Schoolchild: a study of integration in primary schools*, London, Methuen.

Cannon, J. (1975) *Attitudes of Teachers and Fifth-Year Pupils in Comprehensive Schools Towards Pupils With Physical Disabilities*, unpublished dissertation for the Diploma in Special Education, University of Birmingham School of Education.

Department of Education and Science (1971) *Slow Learners in Secondary Schools, Education Survey 15*, London, HMSO.

Garnett, E. J. (1976) 'Special' children in a comprehensive, *Special Education: Forward Trends*, 3, 8–11.

Hicks, J. (1975) Personal communication.

Scottish Education Department (1975) *The Secondary Education of Physically Handicapped Children in Scotland*, Edinburgh, HMSO.

3.4 Whose remedies, whose ills? A critical review of remedial education

MICHAEL GOLBY AND JOHN R. GULLIVER

Remedial education is in transition in the early 1980s. The National Association for Remedial Education has pressed hard for a move away from traditional methods based on separate remedial classes that have often been isolated 'sinks' within schools. Golby and Gulliver trace the beliefs and policies upon which remedial education has been based. They argue that it has acted as an 'ambulance service' in an accident-prone system, but the system itself has never come under sufficient scrutiny. Changes in the organization and curriculum particularly of secondary education may in the future offer remedial teachers a chance to establish a role more supportive of children and subject teachers within the normal curriculum, and more preventive, in acting as an agent of institutional change aimed at developing schools' potential to cope with a wider range of ability.

Context

While there is an accelerating trend towards integration, most children in England and Wales who have gross physical or psychological handicaps are educated in special schools or units. A greater number, however, with less marked or even no clearly definable impediments, but for whom learning is for one reason or another difficult, disrupted, or delayed, are catered for in ordinary schools. The role of local rather than national authorities as the direct providers of education, and the delegation of much of the power of organization and direction to schools themselves, is reflected in a variety of provision for these children. This provision is commonly referred to as 'remedial education'.

No one who looks at remedial education systematically can fail to notice the diversity of organization, staffing and function which exists both between and within local authorities. Some authorities, for

Source: Golby, M. and Gulliver, J.R. (1979) Whose remedies, whose ills? A critical review of remedial education, *Journal of Curriculum Studies*, 11, 137–47

instance, have remedial advisory services, which guide and support the work of schools; others have none. Where they do exist, they may have a measure of autonomy, or they may be subservient to educational psychology services. Within schools, remedial education may be given in full- or part-time units, or to groups of children extracted regularly from normal classes. In full-time units, a whole curriculum package is normally offered; in extraction groups the focus is commonly on 'the basics', with reading in particular to the fore. Whether pupils receive remedial attention may depend upon attainments in basic skills alone, on assumed potential, or on a marked discrepancy between the two. Work content may stem directly from the rest of the curriculum, or bear no relationship to it whatever, except in so far as it is assumed that a general reading competence underlies other curricular activities. Children may cease to receive remedial education once they reach a certain level of proficiency in reading, or simply because there is no provision beyond a certain age. They may be taught by teachers who have recognized advanced qualifications in remedial education, or by others who have none.

The concept of remedial education

The range of practices suggested above should be more than enough to point up the diversity of conceptual assumptions at work under the label of remedial education. A question which now must be faced is whether such varied practices can meaningfully be included under one label.

It is suggested that there is a fundamental difference between the provision made in full-time special classes for pupils of low intellectual ability, and that made for other pupils whose difficulties are seen to lie in certain basic skills. Only 13 of the 158 schools investigated by Her Majesty's Inspectorate in 1971 referred to pupils being transferred frequently from full-time to ordinary classes.[1] If the aim of the special classes is to return pupils to the ordinary, then it would appear that they are singularly unsuccessful. What is more likely is that placement in such classes is seen to be a once-and-for-all measure. The intellectual condition of children thus placed is largely seen as permanent; even where it is not, the differences between the curricula of the special and the normal classes ensure that transfer is unlikely. In consequence, the question of remediation does not arise; the concern is to provide suitable long-term general education. Given this lack of transfer, it should be noted that the application of the term 'remedial' involves a departure from common usage, where it usually means 'putting things right, correcting, rectifying'. The use of the term to refer to such classes can therefore be regarded at best as euphemistic, and always as misleading. It might be better abandoned.

The exclusion of the term 'remedial' from special classes would leave it free for use in a way more consistent with everyday usage. We suggest that such usage is largely appropriate to remedial education as provided in withdrawal groups. For in common usage, rectifying implies firstly that there is a state of rightness, and secondly that something falls short of that state. Central to remedial education is a notion of discrepancy, for instance, between apparent mental ability and attainment. The implication is that the difficulties which many pupils have with basic skills stem from some kind of individual failure in their learning process.

Underlying this central concept, however, is an ideology, which, although never stated, is nevertheless implicit and is held by both remedial teachers and those who teach 'normal' children. It is that there is a level of functioning which may be regarded as 'normal'; and, distinct from this, there are others which are in different ways 'abnormal'. The condition ascribed to those children receiving remedial education is regarded essentially as pathological.

The ideology of pathology

The outward evidence for this 'ideology of pathology' is the use by teachers involved in remedial education of quasi-medical terms like 'diagnosis' and 'treatment'. But we would not regard such usage as crucial to the argument: 'Diagnosis', for instance, is now a term with wide usage – a Volkswagen, for example, is said to be designed for 'diagnostic maintenance'. And the Bullock Committee has suggested that all of us who work in primary schools should be diagnosticians now.

The clue to the underlying ideology of remedial education is to be found not so much in its terminology as in the forms of organization and methods it employs. A common type of remedial provision is some form of temporary withdrawal of the pupil from the 'normal' situation. The purpose of the withdrawal is to enable the pupil to undergo therapy; this almost always involves attention being directed towards weaknesses in basic skills. The object of the attention is to return the pupil as soon as possible to what is regarded as normal functioning. The remedial teacher's success is theoretically measured in terms of the number of pupils he returns to normal classes. As for the school counsellor, the ultimate accolade is to work himself out of a job, the improbability of which enables him to continue his struggle for professional status without fear that eventual victory will be Pyrrhic.

The effect of this pathological approach to remedial education has been two-fold. On the one hand, teachers directly engaged in remedial education have come to see themselves as therapists. There can be little doubt that many of them have acquired a considerable expertise in the application of diagnostic approaches to the teaching of reading, drawing in particular upon the discipline of psychology, and in some cases, too, upon neurology.[2] On the other hands, the far greater number of teachers who are not specifically involved in remedial work have come to assume that children with reading difficulties are not their concern. Their concept of normality involves, amongst other things, being able to meet the literacy demands of their fields of interest *as they stand at present*. That is to say, participation in a subject, such as history, requires a certain level of literacy, a level determined by the subject itself and the media through which it is taught. Neither content nor media are regarded as open to change. Those pupils who cannot meet this criterion are deemed in need of special help, and the improvement of their condition is to be achieved by remedial techniques which are not part of the normal teacher's function.

Criteria for selection

Here one finds a paradox. The subject teacher's exclusion of certain pupils on the grounds that they do not meet the entry criteria suggests that those criteria should play some part in the selection of pupils for remedial education. But generally they do not. Pupils are picked for remedial work on the basis of their intelligence, or their basic attainments, or by some notion which relates the one to the other. Few notions have achieved such respectability as the psychologist's assumption that intelligence tests measure educational potential, and that any shortfall between a child's mental age and his attainments in a particular area must be regarded as a remediable discrepancy. Certainly it is a respectability which has scarcely been shaken by the failure of remedial education to produce returns consistent with the discrepancies thus discovered.

The central feature of the selection criteria is that they are either psychometric or chronological, or both. No consistent attempt is made to define the standards of literacy and numeracy which are required for participation in the normal curriculum, and the provision and withdrawal of remedial education is not directly related to the attainment of such standards. If curricular rather than psychometric criteria were used, it is possible that far more pupils would be identified as in need of remedial education than at present. At secondary level, for instance, the reading demands posed by both printed texts and teacher-produced worksheets may effectively exclude from full participation in the curriculum far more pupils than are customarily picked out by psychometric measures. It is at least arguable that the continued emphasis on psychometrics, far from operating to the advantage of pupils who have difficulties, makes their situation worse by encouraging teachers to regard them as individual failures in an educational system which is basically sound.

Policy issues

Just as psychometric criteria for selection for remedial education focus on the individual and his failings, so the policies for remedial intervention are aimed at individual cures, a point which finds its most recent statement in Bullock: 'We see no advantage in mass testing and centrally stored data unless the outcome is special and individualised help directed precisely at the children who need it.'[3]

Here we have a call for positive discrimination, a policy remedial work shares with compensatory education, together with selectivity of focus, which it does not. At the same time, there is a failure to recognize that the data collected through such mass testing could be used to question at least one of the assumptions upon which mass education beyond the infant school rests.

The post-infant curriculum in British schools is based amongst other things on an assumption that most children have made at least a good start to reading by the time they enter the junior school. In consequence, there is little provision in schools beyond the infant stage for the initial teaching of reading except that which is provided through remedial education. Whereas the beginning reader in the infant school is surrounded by aids to the achievement of initial literacy, in the junior school and beyond he is commonly faced with reading matter most of which is quite beyond his capabilities. Unlike the able reader, he cannot use reading to learn. It may be argued that the exclusion of this possibility is a major factor in his common subsequent failure to learn to read. The props which were available to the more able child when he passed through the same stage some years earlier are denied to the pupil who comes to reading late. His condition is regarded as one of learning difficulty rather than mere lateness. The crucial point, though, is that the mass education approach confirms him in his abnormality. It is more than possible that the need for the remedial teacher as an ambulance-man is created and sustained by a system which by its design is accident-prone.

Historical and social genesis

That such a position has been reached calls for explanation. In order to understand what exists, we must see remedial education firstly in its historical context, and secondly as a manifestation of ideologies obtaining not only within education but also having co-relative applications within wider social policy.

What is striking about remedial provision, as it developed in the 1940s, is its congruence with other aspects of contemporary social policy. Education, like health, was primarily regarded as an individual and not a communal matter. Hawthorn and Carter's point that the structure of society and, thus, ecological conditions of health were not regarded as relevant either as causes or as cures was as applicable to the contemporary framework of education as it was to the early development of the National Health Service.[4] But this similarity should not be a cause for surprise, for the ideology which informed educational policy also informed social planning. Basically, society (including the educational system) was functioning properly; so long as care was taken of the less fortunate on an individual basis, there was no need to look to the system itself for the causes of their distress. It was only much later that one began to see the development of policies based on a recognition of 'the complex forces in school and community which determine the meaning and effectiveness of educational experience. . .'.[5] Given the reluctance of successive governments to implement to the full the measures for Educational Priority Areas recommended by Plowden, there is room for doubt that what Halsey regarded as the complementary nature of policies directed at individual needs and area approaches (ibid., p. 45) has achieved much more than academic recognition. In the meantime, we retain in education a policy towards children who for one reason or another find learning difficult which has its roots not in the latter 1970s but in the early years of the Second World War.

It is our contention that the 'ideology of pathology' outlined above has arisen largely because it was the psychologists who first showed an interest in individual differences. We are not trying to argue that the sole responsibility for this ideology can be laid at the psychologists' door. Neither do we seek to denigrate the very considerable benefits which have ensued from the work done on individual differences in the first half of this century. It is rather that, in the climate which prevailed at the time of the foundation of the first remedial services in the 1940s, psychological notions gave respectability and rationale to existing educational practices. Far from ensuring the development of a flexible system of education, the normative approach to psychological measurement had the effect of buttressing a mass education approach which had as its corollary a view of weakness as abnormality. Normality was represented by the abilities and attainments of the average child; abnormality by the statistically less common pupils whose achievements were markedly lower. It only needed the idea to be floated that weakness was not merely statistically rare, but also sometimes deviant, to ensure that abnormality would be seen as pathological. A hitherto unacknowledged achievement of early workers in the field of backwardness is that they supplied this idea.

Two books exercised a seminal influence — Burt's *The Backward Child*, and Schonell's *Backwardness in the Basic Subjects*. Burt distinguished between the innately dull and those whose backwardness was accidental or acquired. For the latter 'Individual attention . . . should result in progress being so speeded up that all who are not dull as well as backward should after one or two terms, be fit for retransference to the ordinary class'.[6] Thus the child was to be rehabilitated to fit a given curriculum rather than the curriculum altered to fit the child. Schonell accepted Burt's distinction, refining it to produce a notion of 'improvable scholastic deficiency (which) . . . may characterise dull, normal, or supernormal pupils'.[7] Typically such deficiency was confined to a single school subject, and treatment for the condition was through individual or small group short coaching sessions arranged at frequent intervals rather than in full-time backward classes.

Here then we have two notions central to the early tradition of remedial education: a distinction between the retarded and the innately dull, and a system of coaching in the basic subjects. The crucial point is that these two factors were identified by people whose concern was psychology, and who looked at schools and children from outside, and often from a clinical experience. Moreover, their ideas were offered to the world at the very time when those educational notions which culminated in the 1944 Act were being formed. An idea of retardation which was based on psychometrics fitted well with education which would be given in accordance with 'the age, ability, and aptitude of the pupil'. It buttressed the idea that ability was measurable, that children could therefore be grouped and taught in homogeneous units, and that the curriculum for each of these units was distinct. Moreover, even though the Primary section of the earlier Hadow Report had called for a curriculum conceived in terms of 'activity and experience rather than knowledge to be acquired or facts to be stored',[8] Burt and Schonell's focus upon reading and number confirmed teachers in the epistemic divisions which were still believed to be necessary by many educational practitioners.

Thus, when in the late 1940s the first remedial centres were set up, they were received with open arms by teachers, many of whom were newly trained, or had recently come back from the War to find the education system in relative disarray. At a time when reading standards were adversely affected by the aftermath of war, the establishment of remedial services by local authorities all over the country, and of remedial provision within individual schools, was seen to be a positive step towards the elimination of what were regarded as individual learning problems. The very fact that this development was seen to be a positive step, however, diverted attention from the 'normal' curriculum itself. So long as remedial provision was made – an ambulance service in a system which was prone to accident – the curriculum could remain a static entity.

We now want to argue that, even if wider social issues are disregarded, ideological and curricular changes in schools are forcing remedial education to adopt a new role.

A changing curriculum

A curriculum of the kind which existed when the first remedial services were set up needed an ambulance service. Literacy and numeracy were regarded as service skills which made participation in the whole curriculum possible. But the subject-oriented curriculum which was offered to pupils in rigorously streamed secondary schools (and many primary too), is now less prevalent than it was when the remedial movement developed in the 40s and 50s. One must therefore ask whether the perpetuation of a system which was partly the product of a particular education situation, and partly a determinant of its underlying ideology, is relevant in a changed educational world. We want in this section to look at some of the changes which have taken place, and at how they impinge on the work of the remedial teacher. Some of the changes are more of a hope than a reality, and we shall, in passing, try to distinguish them.

We think that the important changes relevant to remedial education are four in number: the gradual move away from grouping children by ability; the breaking down of subject boundaries; the move towards a common curriculum; and new ideas about the nature and acquisition of reading. We shall look at each in turn.

The move from grouping by ability

A major ideological shift in British education since the War has been the retreat from elitism and the espousal, first of equality of opportunity and then of equality of desert. The abolition of the 11+ selection test, which has been an outward sign, has been accompanied internally by the abandonment of streaming, first at primary level, and now at secondary. Special classes, which were part of the apparatus of streaming, have largely been abandoned; some schools have eschewed all forms of segregation, including the temporary kind involved in withdrawal systems.

It may be argued that the move from grouping by ability in schools is organizational rather than curricular. For two reasons we think this view is inadequate. Firstly, being selected for a particular ability grouping was part of the planned experience undergone by most pupils in schools until recently, and as such affected each pupil's image of himself and his relationship to society as a whole. It was thus part of his learning experience. Secondly, any form of grouping has pedagogical implications; alter the grouping principle and, in the long run, even if not in the short, you make it more likely that the teaching will change, if only because previous practices become unworkable.

The most frequent pedagogical response to the new situation has been the development of individualized approaches to teaching. Commonly this has meant presenting particular subjects at a variety of conceptual levels. But it has also entailed many teachers paying much greater attention to the demands they make on their pupils' literacy. Teachers increasingly accept that they must adapt the curriculum, not only for pupils of different cognitive levels, but also for pupils of varying degrees of literacy. The change represents a fundamental shift in their conception of normality.

In some schools structural change has been accompanied by curricular reform, but not in all. We would argue that where no attention has been paid to the curriculum, the retention of a conventional withdrawal remedial system has been essential. But where the curricular implications of the change have been thought through, the dependence on the 'ambulance service' has become much less marked.

The breaking-down of subject boundaries

In many schools where traditional subjects like history and geography have disappeared from the timetable, a particular notion of what it is to be a teacher has disappeared along with the subjects themselves. As Barnes has pointed out, part of teachers' conceptions of themselves and their subjects is bound up with the media through which they teach them.[9] Where they have relied heavily on textbooks, there has almost inevitably been an entry criterion involving a certain level of literacy. A feature of many of the new approaches, however, is their deliberate use of speech rather than writing as the main medium of communication. One could point to the Schools Council Humanities Curriculum Project as an example. Aimed at 'the average and below average' pupils, its emphasis is on small-group discussion. While pupils in need of remedial reading are supposed to be excluded (Introduction; p. 6), Gulliford and Widlake have noted that many schools are successfully using the materials with these children, either by concentrating on those parts which are not dependent upon reading, or by supplementing the published material with matter of their own choosing.[10] Thus they bypass the demand for literacy in some instances, and in others enable pupils to use reading as a medium for learning by tailoring the reading levels to their abilities. The important point here is that weakness in reading is not seen to be a disqualification; it is rather that the teachers are accepting the obligation to adapt their material to the pupils.

A common curriculum

In an increasingly pluralist society, calls for the development of curricular as well as organizational measures which aid social cohesion have become increasingly important. The implementation of common curricula in schools poses special problems for remedial education. Withdrawal is a temporal as well as a structural step, and time spent on the remediation of deficiencies in basic skills in the traditional way is time not spent on other aspects of the curriculum. Moreover, it is often time lost by pupils who can least cope with the attendant disruption.

The crucial problem is, what does the pupil drop in order to fit in enough remedial sessions? An essential feature of the notion of a common curriculum is that every pupil should reach a minimum level of understanding and experience in the areas it covers.[11] The implication here is clearly that there are certain parts of the curriculum from which the pupil ought not to be withdrawn. Much therefore depends upon whether one thinks that the whole or just a part of the curriculum should be compulsory.

Many writers have conceived of the curriculum in two parts, one obligatory, and the other optional. The existence of an optional element in the curriculum enables the planners to allocate time to remedial work without encroaching upon the pupil's exposure to the compulsory common part of the curriculum. Lawton, for instance, has envisaged a week made of ninety twenty-minute modules, a proportion of which could be used for compulsory studies, and the rest of which would be discretionary. Up to ten of the discretionary modules could be used for remedial work, to enable the child, for instance, to catch up on work missed through illness.[12]

We want to make several comments on Lawton's proposals. Firstly, the conception of remedial work is wide. Missing work, for instance, is not the sole prerogative of weak readers, even though they may be more prone than most to absence. The implication of Lawton's conception is that *all* pupils might need remedial work at some stage, and that their needs would not necessarily be confined to basic skills. Whether a single teacher could meet so varied a demand is open to doubt, and it might well be necessary to seek some other solution, such as setting some part of each day apart in which subject specialists would be free to fulfil this role. Given the breadth of this conception, we would prefer to find some other name for it, and retain the term 'remedial' in connection with problems of literacy and numeracy.

Secondly, the practice of remedial work (however defined) in the optional part of the curriculum does ensure that only those pupils who *ask* for help will get it. One feature of remedial provision at all levels is that it seldom works unless the customers want it to.

One worry, however, relates to the fact that there is any remedial provision at all. We argue later that there must be *some* provision, although on a smaller scale than is sometimes the case. Where the provision is lavish, however, there may be a tendency to institutionalize a situation in which teachers do not regard it as part of their function to adapt their material to the abilities of the weaker pupils. An impossible burden may be placed upon the remedial teachers, who may be required to produce a literacy competence in their pupils which might better be achieved by work within the subject areas themselves. In consequence remedial teaching gets a bad name, and a too-high literacy criterion effectively excludes many pupils from full participation in the common curriculum.

Changing assumptions about the nature and acquisition of literacy

A view of reading which has gained much ground in recent years, and which has been endorsed by Bullock, is that it is best acquired incrementally and in conjunction with writing, talking, and listening, and in the course of meaningful activities.[13] Alongside this view of how it is acquired has come the rejection of the idea of reading as a single skill (at least beyond the earliest levels) which can be applied to a range of different materials. Instead we have a conception of reading competence as a repertoire of linked processes which differ according to the purpose of the reader and the nature of the text.

If these views on reading are valid, then one must ask just how much can be expected of an approach to remedial provision which concentrates upon work away from the situation in which reading is to be

used. The consequence for the remedial teacher must be that the
location of much of his activity should be in the classrooms and work-
areas alongside the subject teachers, and the materials with which he
works must derive from the subjects themselves. A major part of his
work will entail helping the subject teachers to adapt their material to
the literacy and conceptual levels of their pupils. In this sense his
activity will be supportive rather than remedial. By making it possible
for pupils to use reading to learn, however, he may well help to develop
those conditions in which they will learn to read.

A role for the remedial teacher

It has been our contention in this essay that the traditional role of
remedial education has reflected particular notions of normality and
therefore abnormality. Curricular and organizational changes in schools
have pushed out the boundaries of what we mean by 'normal'. Teachers
at all levels increasingly accept an obligation to tailor their material to
children of very different abilities. In consequence many pupils now
have the opportunity to acquire through participation in the normal
curriculum skills which at one time they would only have attained
through some form of segregation. This raises the question of the role
of the remedial teacher in a much changed situation. We want to make
a number of points.

(a) For those who advocate that reading should be learned through
the normal curriculum, there are at least two pedagogical, as opposed to
ideological problems. Firstly, the amount by which the readability
demands of textual matter can be reduced is limited. Secondly, there
are a number of children, who for a variety of reasons reach even these
reduced levels only with the greatest difficulty. It would be unreasonable to expect every teacher to find the time or possess the necessary
knowledge to give these children the kind of help they need. It is for
them that the remedial teacher's traditional diagnostic and prescriptive
skills remain relevant. Thus, we would expect the remedial teacher to
retain his 'ambulance-man' role. But since many of the children who at
present depend upon remedial assistance would be helped by the
modification in the normal curriculum as described above, and the
accompanying changes in the ordinary teachers' conception of their
role, *the 'ambulance service' would be on a much reduced scale*.

(b) While in some schools teachers have already gone far towards
a change in outlook, in others they have hardly begun. In these more
traditional schools, we would expect an intensive 'ambulance service'
to be retained for some time. But a major obligation of the remedial
teacher would be to combine with other departments, of which English

would perhaps be the most important, to modify the prevailing climate. In these schools the remedial teacher would be an *agent of curricular and institutional change*.

(c) Modifying the media and the content of learning so that weaker pupils can profit from them is a task which requires both time and understanding. Given that neither would be abundantly at the disposal of many subject teachers, a major role for the remedial teacher would be to give support to the subject specialists in modifying their curricula to suit less able pupils. In order to fulfil this role adequately, it is likely that, in addition to his traditional concern with the psychology of teaching and learning, the remedial teacher would have to have a much greater understanding of linguistics and curriculum planning than he has at the moment. The role of the person providing this service would be *supportive to the subject teacher* rather than remedial in the 'putting things right' sense.

(d) The difficulties many pupils have in subject areas are both reading and cognitive problems. An extremely important aspect of the remedial teacher's work would be to help pupils cope with these aspects of their curriculum. The function of the remedial teacher here would be *supportive to the pupil*. Improvements to the pupil's literacy would be an accompanying but secondary concern.

(e) A variety of screening and monitoring techniques is now available which make it possible to identify those children who are likely to have difficulties with school work, and to watch their progress. The remedial teacher with his knowledge of psychometrics would have a vital role to play in using these techniques and making the information produced known to other members of staff. The role of the remedial teacher here would be *preventive*: he would ensure that appropriate measures were taken to help a pupil before he was put in a position in which he was bound to fail. He would thus maintain close links with compensatory education.

The role we envisage for the remedial teacher is therefore much altered from the traditional. It is one that cannot be adopted by the remedial teacher alone, for it depends on a different view of normality on the part of all teachers. The traditional remedial function would be much reduced, and alongside it a new emphasis on curricular change, support, and prevention developed. Whether the old name of 'remedial teacher' would still be appropriate is another matter. Certainly the ambulance-man would have in addition to become a consultant on road-safety.

Notes

1 Department of Education and Science (1971) *Education Survey 15, Slow Learners in Secondary Schools*, London, HMSO.

2 Tansley, A. (1967) *Reading and Remedial Reading*, London, Routledge and Kegan Paul.

3 Department of Education and Science (1975) *A Language for Life: Report of the Committee of Inquiry (Bullock Report)*, London, HMSO, para. 17.13.

4 Hawthorn, H. and Carter, G. The concept of deprivation (unpublished paper for DHSS/SSRC Working Party on Transmitted Deprivation, quoted in Open University course: *E361 Education and the Urban Environment*, Unit 14, p. 31).

5 Department of Education and Science (1972) *Educational Priority, Volume 1*, London, HMSO, p. 45.

6 Burt, C. (1937) *The Backward Child*, London, University of London Press, p. 606.

7 Schonell, F. (1942) *Backwardness in the Basic Subjects*, London, Oliver and Boyd, p. 61.

8 Board of Education (1931) *Report of the Consultative Committee on the Primary School (Hadow Report)*, London, HMSO.

9 Barnes, D., Britton, J. and Rosen, H. (1969) *Language, the Learner and the School*, London, Penguin Books.

10 Gulliford, R. and Widlake, P. (1975) *Teaching Materials for Disadvantaged Children*, Schools Council Curriculum Bulletin 5, London, Evans/Methuen Educational, p. 72.

11 Lawton, D. (1973) *Social Change, Educational Theory and Curriculum Planning*, London, University of London Press.

12 ibid., p. 151.

13 DES, *A Language for Life*, op. cit., para. 1.10.

3.5 Intermediate treatment, special education and the personalization of urban problems

PETER BERESFORD AND SUZY CROFT

Although all children now have a right in law to receive education, sizeable numbers of disruptive, troublesome and delinquent young people find themselves excluded from ordinary schools, often by virtue of their actions outside school. Community homes with education take some of these young people; others end up in detention centres. In either case, their chances of receiving an education that meets their needs are not high.

In the early 1970s, intermediate treatment emerged as an alternative for these young people, providing both care and education. Peter Beresford and Suzy Croft analyse the role played by one intermediate treatment centre in the lives of young people from a declining inner city area.

Introduction

Intermediate treatment, or IT as it has come to be known, is an expanding service ostensibly intended for young people who are perceived as delinquent or at risk of delinquency. It is advocated as a progressive alternative to institutionalization and criminalization for such young people. It was established under the 1969 Children and Young Persons Act as provision 'intermediate' between supervision on probation and removal to a residential institution. As well as a growing range and number of IT schemes, there has been a rapid development of IT centres. By 1980 there were over seventy of these, more than half of which had opened in the preceding two years, reflecting their increasing significance in the provision of IT (National Youth Bureau, 1980).

So far the discussion of IT has largely been confined to the context of juvenile justice. The aim here is to consider its role as a source of special education, relating it to broader social, economic, educational and social control issues. To do this we examined the workings, formal

Specially commissioned for this volume
©The Open University, 1981

aims, methods and philosophy of one IT centre in an inner city area of an inner London borough by means of structured interviews with the project leader and ILEA attached teacher, and related this to a cross-section of local young people's own accounts and perceptions of life and issues in the area.[1]

As a National Youth Bureau (1980) survey has shown, IT centres are a varied form of provision according to local circumstances and whether they are statutory or voluntary, community or residentially orientated. At the same time, a report on centres in the borough in question suggested a consistency in basic philosophy, aims and methods locally, and the educational and structural issues with which we are concerned here are ones which are likely to apply to IT generally. The IT centre which formed our case study offered day, evening and summer holiday programmes. It is the day programmes with which we were primarily concerned as a source of special education.

Although IT was not originally envisaged as a source of special education in the same way that ESN(M) schools or community homes with education were, for it to serve as an alternative to admission into care or custody it must provide an educational element – and it is primarily seen as an alternative to admission to care. According to the project leader:

> The most important aspects for us are not specifically the education, although we get a lot of referrals from educational welfare, a large number of them are in our grounds inappropriate because they are simply non-school attenders or in some way having school difficulties without any other at risk agent and therefore as far as we are concerned are more the responsibility of the education department of the schools. We're not an alternative education provision in that sense. We're an attempt to prevent the reception of kids into care.

A report by the local borough on IT showed up some of the contradictions inherent in this:

> A first question is whether day care should be an 'alternative school', a direct substitute for mainstream education. The study indicated that both participants and staff (of IT centres) tended to regard it as such to some degree. This was demonstrated by their adherence to school terms . . . and their attitude to school leaving age, which was normally regarded as a cut-off point, when participants would normally leave the programme to go out to find work. . . . It was understandable that day care should be seen as an alternative to school, as the education authority had recognized it as such and had

seconded teachers, whose holiday entitlement was the same as that of their colleagues in mainstream education.

The project leader saw the centre's role as less concerned with young people with school problems than with those known as the 'heavy end', that is those at additional risk because of offence and family problems. However as the borough report on day care in intermediate treatment observed: 'failure to attend school can lead to residential placement as surely as the commission of offences, so that possession of a criminal record does not need to be a prerequisite for entry to the (borough IT) programme, . . . no child (attending IT in the borough) could be described as satisfactorily settled at school at the time of referral to day care'. Mainstream schooling and young people's relationship with it clearly play a central role in the operation and role of intermediate treatment.

The centre we looked at provided day care in a three day a week programme, with a one day a week programme as well 'for kids who for social and other reasons – too disruptive', were not ready for the three-day group, 'or are not as high a risk'. According to the project leader: 'The majority of referrals are from social services, education welfare following and an increasing number from the juvenile bureau: few from schools, minimally few from probation and on the fringes, self-referrals.'

The young people were generally aged between thirteen and sixteen. Referral was not restricted to those subject to IT conditions of court orders or orders of any kind. The stated criteria for referral are imprecise: 'first kids most effectively worked with in a programme, and second (those who) are high priority'. Informally the criteria that seemed to crop up both in referrals and assessment were 'being out of school and in trouble'. Describing the young people who came to the centre, the project leader said that they were: 'usually at risk of going down for further offences or being received into care for non-school attendance plus offences, or in some way at risk because the family situation can't take care of him.'

Special education in the centre was very much one part of the overall programme to keep young people out of care. While this centre and IT more generally are now described as preventing young people at risk from going into care and custody, they were originally seen as provision 'within the community for those at risk of becoming, or those who have already become delinquent' (Paley and Thorpe, 1974). This is an important distinction, for it represents a clear shift from a criterion of individual behaviour to one of policy-making. Thus the borough report on day care in intermediate treatment reported of those placed in the programmes borough-wide that 'many had serious personal problems, some were delinquent', but the common denominator was that 'all were at some risk of removal from home'. The increasing body of evidence there is about admission to care and custody indicates that they are taking place arbitrarily and unnecessarily, and as one study has indicated, young people are much more likely to receive custodial sentences after they have had care orders made against them than before (Thorpe, Paley and Green, 1979a).

The number of children and young people in care and custody has grown rapidly during the 1970s, a trend that is likely to continue given the government's juvenile justice policies and ideological commitments. Furthermore, as Taylor, Lacey and Bracken (1979) have observed, most children and young people in care 'have played no part whatsoever in their eventual disposition'. Figures for 1977, for example, showed that less than one-fifth were in care for committing an offence. Instead most children were in care ostensibly in their own 'best interests' because of family circumstances, poverty, homelessness and a variety of other social and policy factors (Taylor, Lacey and Bracken, 1979). Their Lancaster sample of offenders in care in addition showed that most of the offences committed were non-serious (in all cases of theft, for example, the median figure of the value of the goods stolen was less than £10).

Children, their schools and the social setting

Talking about school and young people in IT, the project leader, while recognizing the interaction between the two, placed a major responsibility on the latter.

> If you look at the great majority of kids, they survive, grow and take their education from the comprehensive schools, so the kids we're dealing with are the kids who haven't made it in that system. It points up the faults and anomalies and inadequacies of the system and also unfortunately those of the kids. I would say that in large measure, it's an even balance between the kids' own inabilities to cope, social inadequacies, personality difficulties and behaviours and the lack of ability of those systems to cope with any difference.

This explanation, however neglects just how many young people are segregated out of mainstream education for a wide range of reasons and the growing trend there now is in this direction (Booth, chapter 5.1). The explanation here is that there is a subgroup of young people, different from others, delinquent and at risk of going into care, who can't deal with a less than perfect system. The IT centre teacher offered a similar interpretation: 'It is after all kids who can't exist in school, who act out more than schools can tolerate who find themselves in IT centres, so we are dealing with totally different students – the students the schools can't cope with and who can't cope with the schools.'

But is this an accurate analysis? All the evidence we have from young people in general in the area suggests that it is the majority of comprehensive school students rather than a deviant minority who 'don't make it in the system'.

A sample of thirty-one young people interviewed at school and youth club complained of schooling that was unrelated to their outside world. 'We can't get together in the school to do anything about outside. . . . Hardly any of the teachers come from round here. They should live locally and share some of the things we have to put up with'.

In another sample of sixteen fifth-form girls at the local single-sex comprehensive school a minority said they didn't like school, but more revealing were their answers to the question how they felt they were treated at school. Only five gave positive responses; the rest spoke of being treated 'unfairly', 'as objects', 'restricted all the time', according to 'how the teacher feels' about you, and 'as children'. Eight felt school wasn't relevant to the rest of their lives. Thirteen felt they had little or no say at school generally, or specifically in rules, punishment and other activities – and only in the choice of some subjects in the curriculum. Significantly while ten out of sixteen were looking forward to leaving school, even more (thirteen) intended to go on to further education, and eight already had places on educational or vocational courses. Thus their dissatisfaction was apparently not with education. If anything these girls seemed more conservative in their attitudes than other young people we encountered.

A similar picture emerged from the regular discussions with the two other groups of school students. Most felt they had little say in school and resented it; that teachers took little notice of what they had to say and that they had no control over their school lives, including even their free time. Generally they thought much of school was irrelevant to the rest of their lives; the subjects they were taught were often unrelated to the present or the jobs they would get. Careers advice kept them in their traditional place, particularly girls. They had to fit into school rather than school accommodate to them. In view of the resentment, hostility, resignation and boredom this led them to feel for school, it is not surprising that some truanted.

However under a provision of the 1969 Act, truanting itself puts children and young people at risk of reception into care. In 1977 4,300 children were in care as a result of this provision, largely on the grounds that they had persistently truanted. Yet an analysis by one of the authors of *In Whose Best Interests?* of an area in which such provision had been frequently invoked and persistent truancy perceived 'as evidence of a personal need for care', indicated that the regular truancy rate among school students over the age of thirteen in two schools was approximately 30 per cent (Taylor, Lacey and Bracken, 1979). Certainly the impression given by the many young people we encountered was that the actual number of truants in the area was far greater than the small minority of designated delinquents. Taylor, Lacey and Bracken (1979) also pointed to the court's unreadiness to hear any defence by the 'truant' which cited the inadequacy or inappropriateness of the education they received as grounds for their reluctance to attend. As they observed: 'This effectively insulates the education authority and its teaching staff from any blame for educational failure, and locates the dereliction within the personal characteristics of the truant — a further example of the transformation of a public issue into a private trouble.'

In an inner city area like that under discussion, the conditions associated with social deprivation are widespread; poverty, high unemployment, arbitrary redevelopment, bad housing, demographic change, poor environment and inadequate and worsening services and amenities. Almost half the households were living in unsatisfactory high rise blocks of council flats. At the same time there was a gross shortage of housing stock (Beresford and Beresford, 1978) and the housing situation is becoming worse because of local and central government policies. A 1979 research study by the local council for community relations showed that members of ethnic minorities were concentrated in the worst housing and estates.

The area has seen a massive decline in employment. Between 1968 and 1978 about 6,000 jobs were lost, most in manufacturing. In the last three months of 1980, the largest remaining private employers in the area closed with a loss of nearly 1,000 jobs. The local authority is now the largest employer and it is reducing its work force. The people worst affected by the decline in employment have been older workers, the unskilled, school leavers and ethnic minorities. The number of unemployed black young people and of young people who had not registered as unemployed was not known. It was thought almost certain that black unemployment in the borough was more than twice white unemployment. Recent research in Bristol has revealed that unemployed young people committed nine out of ten crimes in their age group (APEX, 1980).

Using educational priority area indices of deprivation, three of the area's six secondary schools were ranked the most deprived in the borough. The population has declined rapidly, by 20 per cent between 1961 and 1971. The traditional skilled workforce has left. There are now a disproportionate number of old people and single parent families, who together with the large local black ethnic minority population are groups with particular problems of low income and social disadvantage. In 1978 11.3 per cent of households qualified for rent or rate rebates (Beresford and Beresford, 1978). The arbitrary rehousing of people in large and isolating estates, and high private house prices, have undermined social relations and networks and weakened existing patterns of family support, friendship and neighbourhood, while compensatory state services which have always been inadequate are now sharply reduced by public expenditure cuts.

In a large-scale empirical study, local people rated the inadequacy of provision for adolescents the third major problem in the area, after the inadequacy of shopping and amenities for small children (Beresford and Beresford, 1978). The prevailing view from all those we spoke to in formal interviews, discussion groups and informal discussions was that there was little for them in the area: 'there's nothing for kids on my estate'; 'we had a good tenants' association representative who did a lot for kids, but when he went it was all forgot'. What amenities there were were often inappropriate, allowing young people little or no say. There were few discos and few if any good clubs. When something did start up, so many young people tried to use it that it tended to be closed as a source of trouble. As they said, 'there's no place of your own to go to to do as you like, to be out of the way of complaints from other people.' This had much to do with their visibility. The lack of places to meet as peers resulted in much of their behaviour and interaction being public, seen as threatening, provocative or a nuisance, and to come to anyone's attention, including the police. In the one place they could turn to – pubs – they were liable to exclusion for drinking under age. It was clear from the large-scale survey made of the area that many adults saw the lack of amenities for young people as a major reason for high rates of vandalism and juvenile crime (Beresford and Beresford, 1978).

Young people in the area recognized that it would be difficult and expensive to find somewhere to live when they wanted to leave home. Current housing policy is exacerbating discrimination against single people and increasing their dependence on the inadequate and unsatisfactory private rented sector. Single people in the borough are no longer being rehoused. While high rates of unemployment meant that

most of them certainly seemed to feel it was better to have a job than
to be on the dole, they were also afraid that the jobs they would get
would be poorly paid and dead-end.

The large-scale redevelopment the area has undergone, replacing
human-scale streets with concrete and tower block estates, has created
an alienating and unsympathetic environment which puts young people
further into conflict with others. Poor design and sound-proofing have
made their music a source of trouble. Lack of 'defensible space' has
transformed their presence 'hanging around' into a threat and a
nuisance. While old people seem to be subdued by what has been done
to them, many young people attack what they don't like. Significantly
the most unpopular estates in the area have the highest bills for
vandalism.

One group of local young people used to meet at the bottom of their
street, rain or shine, for want of anywhere else to go. But as they said:

The police kept coming and moving us on, night after night. They
kept checking the boys' [motor] bikes, looking at their papers,
taking them down to the station. The neighbours complained about
the noise and so did our parents, so we had to come to this estate,
by the car park here. It was OK at first. Now the police have started
coming again. They tell us to move on, so we have to. In the end
we'll have to find somewhere else.

But there's really nowhere else they *can* go without the whole
process being repeated. With such intense policing, only the narrowest
of lines separates these young people from being disposed of as delinquents — a wrong reaction, or a trivial act that could be construed as a
formal misdemeanour. These young people were not atypical. They
were ordinary working-class adolescent boys and girls. Their experience
of the police seemed to be shared by many young people in the area:
being stopped, questioned, picked up, told to move on, liable to arrest
for anything that could be perceived as an offence.

According to the teacher in the IT centre, the service often acted as
a haven:

I think very often all we do is provide somewhere where they can
come and hide . . . and long enough to allow everybody — people
can say — no, no, it's alright, they're coming to us — that gives the
kids a breathing space, gives them time to take some stock, sort
themselves out and they haven't got educational welfare, the police,
the courts, breathing down their necks.

This was something the research in the borough report seemed to confirm, noting, 'when a child was known to be contained in day care, pressure for residential placement tended to evaporate'.

The three samples of young people surveyed as well as the other young people whose views were obtained expressed a strong sense of powerlessness. Most (sixty-seven out of eighty-three) felt they had little or no say in decisions affecting them and their community; that the local authority took little or no notice of them and that their views did not count. As one said: 'They never ask us. We never hear anything about what young people want.'

All these indices of deprivation, difficulty and disadvantage are likely to have effects on the many children and young people experiencing them, although what they are for any individual cannot be said, and indeed the value of such a line of enquiry is questionable so long as such general conditions are allowed to continue. Emotional, social, educational and other problems are not confined to a particular group of young people identified as deviant.

Intermediate treatment as a response to urban problems

The IT centre project leader, when asked what he saw as the main problems facing the young people with whom he was concerned, framed them in terms of individual adaptation.

The origins of their problems might very well be social, political, family, whatever, but it's the way in which they've dealt with them. . . . For me I think they all face the same difficulties. It's the ones we get who develop the least effective coping strategies. That's the point of intervention.

. . . The strategies they've evolved and the behaviours they've evolved, whether creative or self-destructive or whatever are very individual and I would see a lot of our task in helping them learn to use for themselves more growthful effective strategies to get what they want in their lives because ultimately they've got to cope for themselves and grow up and if we're not successful that way then we're not likely to be any other, because certainly they're a small group, they're a very powerless group, a group that's mostly being pushed around by agencies and other people, where people are taking power over their lives, where courts and others are variously intervening in their lives and if we don't move them back towards taking their own power for their lives and growing to take responsibility for their own actions and behaviour, they will end up institutionalized. . . .

But it is difficult to see how these young people could effectively take power, any more than the more general run of young people with whom we were concerned, or how their predicament could be explained mainly in terms of their own maladaptation and inability to cope. Such emphasis on personal development and inadequacy underplays the structural and political issues bearing on them and the role of other institutions and agencies effectively denying them a say. IT by its focus on the individual, redefines severe and generalized problems for young people in such an area as confined to a small and delinquent group and this serves to defuse the problems and direct attention away from them. Advocating IT, Paley and Thorpe (1974) wrote:

A programme such as intermediate treatment, which is designed for particular children manifesting symptoms of deprivation, does not make sense independent of a wider programme – that of a general attack on the social, economic and educational problems of deprivation.

We are open to a charge of dishonesty if we attend to the problem only where it breaks out in the form of undesirable behaviour instead of attempting to combat it at source.

The development of IT however has not been accompanied by any such fundamental attack on poverty and deprivation. Instead it has coincided with a period of reduced public spending, increased social and economic problems and rising unemployment, especially in inner city areas – and now with a new commitment to law and order of which IT serves as part. In the inner city area under discussion, IT's expansion has coincided with severe cuts in major local services like housing, social services and recreation, with the loss of important rights, support and recreational services for young people. Children's homes have been closed, but arbitrarily, some to be sold off for private speculation. Significantly though in the council's latest and largest round of cuts, plans for extending IT are to be scrapped, in the same way that cuts are to be made in spending on childminding and adoption, which the council similarly had earlier advocated to justify its closure of day nurseries and children's homes. Thus there is scant security in relying on IT as a palliative for other services since it is susceptible to the same cuts. More generally as expenditure on IT has been increasing, the trend from the mid 1970s has been to reduce expenditure on the youth service, despite the preventive role seen for it (Smith, 1979).

The 1968 government report *Children in Trouble*, precursor of the

1969 Children and Young Persons Act (Home Office, 1968), emphasized that: 'The aim will be to bring the young person into contact with a new environment, and to secure his participation in some constructive activity.' As Paley and Thorpe (1974) remarked ' "new environment" ought to mean what it says if taken seriously', but if anything, the general environment facing young people in the area which we have described has got worse rather than better, and isolated oases like IT centres have little effect for most young people.

Both IT centre staff showed their understanding of the large issues and problems affecting the young people with whom they worked. But at the same time they acknowledged that there was little if anything they could do to change them or other major institutions and agencies affecting young people. The project leader felt they were able to have a positive influence on the local social services department and while not able to influence policing on the street, that they had a constructive relationship with the juvenile bureau, which they both believed could keep young people from being processed as delinquents as rapidly as they might otherwise, or at all, through the bureau's preparedness to use cautions rather than take young people to court.[2]

Both the IT staff members interviewed felt the centre could do virtually nothing to change schools. Thus the project leader said:

When I first came into intermediate treatment and when the section was still fairly new, it was seen as one of the aims and goals. But first of all just working with the kids takes that much energy and commitment that there's very little time left over to do any of the other stuff and second it's less rewarding because you can see dynamic change with kids whereas working with large immoveable systems like the schools is often a nightmare and takes so much energy for such little reward, it's not worth it and it's much better to put energy directly into kids. I would think that most people in section and certainly in this centre have begun to give up on any high flying aims of trying to change the schools or education system.

And the teacher[3] who had spent five years working in a neighbour-ing comprehensive school before coming to the IT centre: 'The pressures on schools come from different directions and are far greater than IT. . . . It would just be swimming against the stream – you haven't got that sort of clout.'

Both workers understood the deficiencies of schools as young people had described them. From his own experience, the teacher could see the school situation becoming worse:

Pressure for increased so-called academic standards, much greater pressure on examinations . . . (meant that) a lot of the flexibility disappeared . . . (and) led to increased tightening of authority as well which made the school a less pleasant place to be. . . . Pressure came well before the whole educational standards debate and [was] given a real cutting edge by falling rolls . . . [and] meant schools had to compete for intake. It was on the basis of academic standards that schools were going to sell themselves . . . and once you do that, then inevitably the concentration in terms of resources is on the most able kids and not on the intake as a whole.

Arguably, intermediate treatment may not only be unable to bring about reform in schools but may also serve to discourage it, by offering schools an alternative to reform, like the disruptive units described by the IT teacher:

I think they will allow schools and I think there's a sense in which their intention is to allow schools to become more authoritarian, more disciplined, by removing those kids who reject that increased discipline, and that certainly by the management of the schools.

The existence of IT similarly offers educational services the opportunity to wash their hands of unwanted obligations. Thus the teacher again:

It is my belief that the education authority is only too pleased that IT is fulfilling their legal responsibilities to kids they couldn't cope with in any other way . . . and that social services is providing the money for it. . . . Educational welfare are not concerned once they [their school students] are on the roll here.

Intermediate treatment as special education

The education offered by the IT centre could be said to be both broader and narrower than that conventionally provided in comprehensive schools. It was unquestionably different:

We operate a behaviour modification programme with a humanistic face. What I mean by that is that each kid is on a very clear behaviour modification contract about rewards and consequences for behaviour, reinforcing positive behaviour wherever possible, providing rewards or carrots on a stick wherever possible, as little as possible of any of the normal forms of punishment such as suspension, expulsion, caning, lines or whatever; for the most part a humanistic base and trying to work the relationship to what's the sense of respect or understanding between the people – what do I feel about what you've done? How do you feel? What gets you there? What are you trying to do to me? That kind of stuff, but with very clear consequences. If the whole group hasn't worked in the morning and sufficient work hasn't been done, there's no biscuits for tea at break. If the lunch rota was not prepared effectively and on time and not sufficient work was done in the morning, the ice cream doesn't come out for afters at lunch. If kids leave a mess when permission has been given to stay late in the building of an afternoon – the kind of thing they wouldn't get in schools where the school locks up and closes up – that's it – whereas here they have free run of the building; then the next afternoon, they lose that privilege until the building's cleared up. If a kid won't read but actually wants something from the centre like wants to go ice skating, then a month of fulfilling a contract of reading for fifteen minutes every day will earn the reward of being paid for and taken ice skating. So we use whatever the kid wants as earned rewards for the behaviour we want and then as much as possible begin to build in self-motivation, self-direction, self-assessment, and remove the external pressure and the carrot.

Both teacher and project leader referred to the grounding of the curriculum in the 3 Rs; 'basic numeracy and literacy are very important things for them, to control their lives . . . to survive . . . to express themselves'. It also included project work, according to the teacher 'one of the most enjoyable changes from formal education for me', as well as afternoon programmes of 'basic arts and crafts like woodwork, pottery and photography'. Both staff felt the centre had a number of advantages over ordinary schools. They determined what was taught, they were not tied to a subject or classroom approach to learning and could respond to students on a more individual basis:

We have the opportunity to be much more student centred than schools. The structure's much looser. I can work individually. The structure allows you to adapt yourself to where the kids are – with four staff and twelve kids. Each kid has an individualized work programme. There's a minimum of lesson type classroom learning. I'm not confined to the rigidities of presenting certain information in one particular period of time. We start from the level that the kids start from. [We have] very small specific goals for each kid from where they are to see and measure improvement. . . . We don't measure their education by exam criteria.

We don't teach subjects as such. We'll talk about birth control and end up doing a biology lesson on the human body or we'll start off with someone's breath smelling and do dental hygiene, or we'll start off with talking about how bad it is to live on one of the local estates and end up with environmental studies.

They felt the centre was able to be more flexible and available to young people than a mainstream school: 'they'll be in after the day care programme if they live locally. They pop in as they go by. They can come back after they leave and do. We're always available to them.' The centre catered for a wide range of abilities, from 'borderline ESN' to 'very able and bright kids'. The student—teacher relationship was seen as different to that generally found in schools. The teacher said:

Control in school — in most secondary schools at least, depends on a degree of separateness; so-called respect for authority and a degree of authority — even among the most radical teachers — a degree of separateness from students. They're not regarded as individuals with equal rights to staff whereas by and large here . . . we certainly relate to the kids as individuals — that is they have certain rights; the most basic thing is the individual 'contracts' they have and the only rules laid down are that they shouldn't bring in offensive weapons, shouldn't use violence to other kids or staff, should not bring in drugs or alcohol and shouldn't damage the property. Beyond that there is nothing that cannot be negotiated and their individual relationships with staff are entirely worked out between the kids and the staff and there's nothing laid down in advance.

The other major failing of the school (apart from its authoritarianism) . . . [is] . . children whose emotional needs are not being met outside the school who need something from the school (which they won't get). . . . Children who won't go to school because it's too alienating a place. . . . We seek to meet the kids' emotional needs as well as narrow educational needs.

The project leader saw 'social education' as a large part of the centre's role:

Everything we do is about education for life for these kids in a very broad sense . . . how to get along within a group, how to make friends, how to operate with other people . . . so you can be successful, have your needs met and not in any way exacerbate other people to the extent that they feel they've got to shut you out, scapegoat you. How to be a responsible animal and part of a group so that you don't just always grab for you first out of a sense of deprivation but learn that there will be enough, certainly in this place anyway, and that when you operate on that basis, there often is enough to go round and you share with others: a whole lot of changes from the self-centred street culture that some of them live with.

The project leader's and teacher's definition of 'social education' differed somewhat, reflecting differences in emphasis and orientation to IT more generally, but perhaps also reflecting its ambiguity. Thus the teacher said:

Some members of the team see the centre's philosophy as in some sense therapeutic. I would differ from that. I would see it as a tool for the kids which they could use to enable them to survive in the community . . . and not be put away and be able to make clear choices in their own lives. . . . This provides a place for them to come where they can learn to extend and sometimes regain . . . the control they have in their lives. Education plays only one part in that.

I don't see the role of the centre to teach kids to be good citizens. I see it to give the kids control over their own lives. They may see that as being good citizens − that's how they may want to run their lives. If they had the choice, they may want to become good crooks. If they want to, then we regard it as our role to ensure that that decision is taken rationally with as clear an understanding of what that might involve for their lives as possible and what pressures are on them leading them to make such a decision. I think . . . a lot of what we're doing here is patching up the damage that is done to kids by the unequal access that people have to resources in our society so I don't see it [the IT centre] as a structure [that] reinforces the authority of that society over individuals.

As well as the emphasis on 'social education', both staff members stressed 'the group' and 'group work' as the key method of working in the centre.

We don't just work individually. We use the group to educate . . . to get them to learn . . . to operate socially. [project leader]

Individuals feel able to go to the group for support. That is, if something is going on with a particular member of staff, they can look to
the group for support. That's good because it gives the kids more
power in relation to the staff and we will use the group to establish
norms of working. We won't lay them down from above. What we'll
do is negotiate them with the group and those individuals who find
those norms difficult to accept or don't want to accept them, we
will take that up with the group. Our method of work is not individual therapy — it's groupwork. I think it's the only reasonable way
to work with them. I think they don't have sufficient power to be
on anything like equal terms with staff members individually.
[teacher]

While this emphasis on co-operation rather than competition
between young people, giving them a source of strength in their dealings with staff, seems valuable, group work, like the education itself,
needs to be seen in the wider context of the centre's role of preventing
reception of children into care. The educational aims of the centre were
part of its larger change aim and there may be contradictions between
the two, for example between the commitment to education and self-
development and to behaviour modification. Education was part of
the centre's overall efforts to keep young people out of care, which
were concerned with discouraging further offending and court appearances. A further contradiction is that 'the group' which might serve as
an effective source of solidarity for young people, was also tied to the
purpose of passing on the centre's ruling norms, as we have seen, rather
than staff bearing the responsibility.

This raises the question of how much control young people actually
had in the centre. As the teacher acknowledged:

There's no denying staff have power in the building whereas kids
don't. . . . Ultimately we can exclude them but they can't exclude
us. However there's no restriction on their ability to make demands
. . . or to complain and very often they get some of those demands.

One of the key contradictions can be seen in microcosm in the case
of 'contracts'. Great emphasis was placed in this as in other IT projects
on contracts between staff and young people. They were negotiated
individually. As the project leader explained: 'if the kid does what the
staff want, they can have something they want.' The staff's part of the
contract was to be consistent, ensure the contract negotiated was
reasonable and attainable, be prepared to renegotiate where necessary

and meet the rewards when required. Such a contract hardly seems to be between equal parties or make equal demands, and while the young person was signing up to fulfil certain personal and behavioural obligations, staff responsibilities did not seem to involve the same psychic demands as might be placed on young people, and what the young people could earn by way of reward might be something to which they could feel entitled anyway, such as food or payment.

Like other examples of special education in separate institutions, the IT centre could not offer the range of resources, services and human and teaching skills that are available in mainstream comprehensive schools, as the teacher and project leader readily acknowledged. But at the same time these were not available for the many young people who rejected or were rejected by such schools, and in other ways they felt the education they offered was preferable to that in ordinary schools. 'I think in many ways kids get a better deal, have more freedom, more responsibility, are given more options on how to use the place, than anywhere else I know of.'

As the project leader pointed out, the limited opportunities available in the centre could mean that for some students it only had something to offer for a relatively short time. 'A year to a year and a half tends to get to be too long sometimes because they've gone through everything we can offer.'

Such a student coming to the centre at thirteen

> is one of our dilemmas. . . . Once we've made that commitment, we would never reject them, but they might end up rejecting the centre and then they would be back in the situation we took them from — back on the streets, a bit older, a bit wiser, having gone through a bit more than they would otherwise have gone through in normal school, but still then having nowhere else to go.

Intermediate treatment centres, while intended as a programme to prevent admission to care, are not intended to and cannot prevent students' loss of mainstream schooling. According to the two staff interviewed, most of their students had not been to school for on average, a year, before coming to them. Paradoxically some of the gains the centre offered students were also obstacles to their return to school. Thus the project leader observed:

> We've almost given up attempting to reintegrate kids from our programmes back into school . . . because we find that first of all our kind of culture and programme is totally unacceptable in any way to the school and once the kids have had that kind of relation-

ship, they won't tolerate being treated as objects or put down by the teachers or the school system, so they either won't go back or even when they're keen to go back for their education, the school in some way has labelled them — 'oh you're back again' — and of course the kid just doesn't make it. So we've recognized that we won't take kids who are too young or if we do, we know we've got them for the rest of their school career.

Whatever its advantages, the special education provided by the IT centre was only available for a tiny proportion of young people. Yet as the teacher said 'who wouldn't benefit from having more time from adults whose work really is to deal with [their] social, emotional and educational needs?' However there was only room for twelve on the three-day and eight on the one-day programme, with fifteen or sixteen young people a year passing through them and long waiting lists, even though the centre also tried where possible and appropriate to fit referrals they could not meet into their evening programmes. Furthermore because of its reliance on group work, the centre sought to have a balanced group in terms of sex, race and youth culture, and candidates had to fit in with this as well as be seen as those who can 'most effectively be worked with' and of high priority according to the 'at risk' criteria. Even if the education and approach offered by the centre were ideal for them, if they were not seen as sufficiently at risk, young people would not qualify.

As well as their own particular conditions, IT day programmes also face the problems that affect separate special education and its students more generally. Neither member of staff felt that the young people who came to the centre were stigmatized by it: 'IT's seen as a popular place to be — kids who get here are seen as being alright.' On the other hand, researchers at the Lancaster Centre of Youth, Crime and Community have suggested that such 'intermediate' measures instead of slowing down the development of a delinquent career, may instead promote and even accelerate it by making each consecutive official decision easier to make, and increasing the likelihood of children and young people being officially labelled delinquent (Thorpe, Paley and Green, 1979a, b).

The one case where the two centre staff members felt there might occasionally be some question of stigma was with employers. The teacher also acknowledged that some young people who came to the centre would not be as well equipped for the labour market in terms of formal qualifications as they might have been if they had been able to stay at school.

The teacher said he maintained good informal contact with a nearby comprehensive. 'It would be inconceivable for me to operate effectively without that close relationship.' But this followed from him having worked at that school for five years before joining the centre, and he still felt isolated from his peers in mainstream education.

Conclusion

The special education on offer in the IT centre was narrowly restricted to a small proportion of young people and while adding to their experience and opportunities, left those of most other young people in the area untouched, as well as being tied to a programme based on behaviour modification and social control. As has been said of other forms of separate special education, there is no reason why the advantages the centre's education offered could not equally be achieved and incorporated in ordinary schools by their reform (e.g. Beresford and Tuckwell, 1978).

But for the centre staff the issue was one of offering immediate help to young people for whom mainstream education has little if anything to offer as part of their efforts to prevent such young people being received into care and institutionalized. Their view is shared by many other people working in special education who see the reintegration of their students in inadequate and often inappropriate mainstream education as no solution at all, and cannot see it being reformed in such a way for it to offer a possible or realistic solution.

The IT centre teacher offered his own succinct analysis to reconcile the apparent contradiction between the centre's focus on individual young people and recognition of the structural origins of many of their problems.

There is a sense in which I believe that what we deal with are society's problems and not the problems of individuals. I don't think the kids are in any sense ill. I believe that school dissidents is the best way to describe them. . . . [Their delinquency] is behaviour that quite often in a different environment would find what was more likely to be a socially acceptable outcome. Because of the environment they live in, an inner city environment with very few facilities, often it's economically depressed, then it takes on a form that is supposedly anti-social, but I don't blame the kids for that. I think that's to do with the wider social aspects. . . .

However there is a sense in which capitalism has victims and it's all very well saying that we deal with kids, that we locate what's happening very much individually within students who we work with, but the alternative would be locking these kids up and for me there's no question that we actually contribute to the degree of freedom that they have. We allow them for the most part to continue their lives in the community which is very important and while they're here, we support them in looking at being effective in carrying out what they want.

However while such intervention may meet some visible needs, it also leaves the origins of the problems untouched and unopposed. It indeed may help divert attention from them, and does little or nothing for most young people who are also oppressed by them. This is true whether the institution in question is mainstream schooling, the juvenile justice system or government policy and the workings of the market more generally. Workers are caught in the conflict between the primacy of the immediate needs of young people who come their way and the need for fundamental reform. The same contradiction and dilemma confronts separate special education more generally which similarly seeks to resolve more general problems by hiving them off in separate institutions, when more radical educational, social or economic reform is indicated. Progress is likely to be achieved only when those concerned with separate special education combine their practice with critical discussion, action and campaigning on a broader front.

Notes

1 Data came from three main sources.
  (a) Questionnaire based interviews with four groups of young people in a comprehensive school and youth club (thirteen girls and eighteen boys; eighteen white and thirteen black), supported by interview data from a further thirty-six young people included in a representative sample of 581 households in the area.
  (b) Data from a small random sample (sixteen of a population of twenty-seven) of fifth-form school students from a local girls' single-sex comprehensive school, using an in-depth interview schedule.
  (c) Information from transcripts of discussions with long- and short-term groups of young people at school, youth club, unemployment scheme and on local estates, established over a period of one year as part of a larger project to identify young people's perceptions of life in the area and increase their say in issues and services affecting them.
2 A 1976 Home Office research study suggested that the increasing use of the caution by the police has in fact added to the total of young people appearing in annual criminal statistics (Ditchfield,

1976), while Taylor, Lacey and Bracken suggested its use in preference to a 'no further action' decision or 'on the spot warning' might
have a criminalizing effect on young people if they appeared in
court for some other reason, since 'cautions are used very much as
evidence of previous offences' (Taylor, Lacey and Bracken, 1979).
3 The teacher was paid out of the ILEA 'Disruptive Fund'; see Rock
and Taylor (1980).

References

APEX (1980) *Annual Report of the APEX Trust*, London, Apex.

Beresford, P. and Beresford, S. (1978) *A Say in the Future: planning
participation and meeting social need*, London, Battersea Community
Action.

Beresford, P. and Tuckwell, P. (1978) *Schools for All*, London, CMH/
MIND.

Ditchfield, J. A. (1976) *Police Cautioning in England and Wales*, London, HMSO.

Home Office (1968) *Children in Trouble*, London, HMSO.

National Youth Bureau (1980) *Intermediate Treatment Centres*, Information Paper.

Paley, J. and Thorpe, D. (1974) *Children: Handle with Care: a critical
analysis of the development of intermediate treatment*, Leicester,
National Youth Bureau.

Rock, D. and Taylor, N. (1980) Out of site, *Teaching London Kids*,
15, 19.

Smith, D. (1979) *Local Authority Expenditure and the Youth Service
1975–1980: a short review*, Leicester, National Youth Bureau.

Taylor, L., Lacey, R. and Bracken, D. (1979) *In Whose Best Interests?:
the unjust treatment of children in courts and institutions*, London,
The Cobden Trust/MIND.

Thorpe, D., Paley, J. and Green, C. (1979a) The making of a delinquent,
Community Care, No. 261 (26 April), 18–19.

Thorpe, D., Paley, J. and Green, C. (1979b) Ensuring the right result,
Community Care, No. 263 (10 May), 25–6.

3.6 Special provision in post-school education

JOHN PANCKHURST

The current inadequacy of provision for many young people leaving special education is acutely felt by themselves and their parents. Although a few local authorities have introduced imaginative innovations, the absence or unsuitability of much provision reflected in the studies described in this paper continues into the 1980s. What emerges from the surveys outlined by John Panckhurst is a feeling that the fight for access to post-school education on equal terms for handicapped young people is by no means won, even if some battles have given some students the advantage.

Post-school provision

The main concern of this review is the physically handicapped, although provision for that group cannot be seen in isolation from what is being done for other groups of young people with special needs. Developments in provision have often been unilateral as voluntary organizations, set up to further the needs of particular groups – for example, those with cerebral palsy, the visually impaired, the hearing impaired, those with spina bifida, the mentally handicapped . . . have argued the case for their young people and gone ahead and set up their own establishments. Such pioneering activities may be seen as a stage in a developmental sequence:

> In many cases the needs identified by voluntary bodies have in due course received public recognition, and responsibility for making provision for meeting them on a widespread basis has been assumed by local authorities. Thereafter they have often proceeded to identify new needs and to pioneer other services (Warnock Report, DES, 1978).

The point is illustrated by the Spastics Society which has recently translated two of its training establishments, at Lancaster in Lancashire

Source: Panckhurst, J. (1980) *Focus on Physical Handicap: provision for young people with special needs in further education*, Windsor, NFER–Nelson Publishing Company

and Tonbridge in Kent, to establishments of further education —
Beaumont College of Further Education and Dene College Continued
Education Centre — to cater for the education of less able, physically
handicapped 16- to 19-year-olds.

Further education for the physically handicapped may be seen to
date from the establishment of the Chailey Heritage and Craft School
for Boys in 1903 and the founding of Lord Mayor Treloar College,
with a vocational department, in 1908. Further initiatives were to wait
almost 20 years for Derwen 'Cripples' Training College, Oswestry, to
be founded in 1927.

Four other establishments, now funded to a large extent by the
Training Services Division of the Manpower Services Commission, have
made a distinctive contribution to the vocational training of disabled
adults and young people. These institutions are increasingly introducing
further education components for school leavers who may then
progress to more purely vocationally oriented courses: Queen
Elizabeth's Training College, Leatherhead, opened for male physically
handicapped school leavers and disabled men in 1934; St. Loyes
College, Exeter, in 1937; Finchale Training College, County Durham,
in 1943; and Portland Training College, Harlow Wood, in 1950. These
places, and others like them were established with a distinctly vocational
bent. Their aim was to give physically handicapped young people skills
which would allow them to lead purposeful and fulfilled lives with as
great a degree of economic independence as possible. The Spastics
Society, with its habit of initiative in developing provisions of various
kinds, has maintained an industrial training centre with specifically
vocational purposes while at the same time experimenting with new
approaches to further education, as distinct from vocational training,
in its two further education centres for spastic people.

The lead established by voluntary organizations — especially in
residential provision — was maintained through the 1960s. The founding of Hereward College of Further Education, the first residential
college for physically handicapped school leavers in the public sector,
in 1971, was a departure. The role of national residential colleges may
change to a regional one, if the Warnock recommendation 10:13[1] is
to be effected, but an innovative and experimental function on a
national basis seems likely to remain for the forseeable future. The
need for ordered involvement of the public sector in the further
education of handicapped school leavers was made explicit in the
report of a working party set up by the British Council for the
Rehabilitation of the Disabled in 1960. The report (Thomas, 1963)
recommended:

that local education authorities be urged to assess the extent to which facilities for further education are needed by handicapped young persons in their areas and to review their existing provisions in order to ensure that these needs are, wherever possible, met.

The Thomas Report noted that large numbers of handicapped children left school with an unsatisfactory standard of education and that there was therefore a *prime facie* case for continued education. This could be in special schools on a part-time basis but not to the exclusion of 'more adequate facilities for advanced and technical education' for which there was need. It would appear that the Thomas Working Party had 'special facilities' in mind, as a first step, rather than the opening up of ordinary colleges of further education to handicapped young people. One reason for this stance was the experience of the voluntary national residential colleges for the physically handicapped, which had found a need to experiment with the provision of courses of general education for groups of students as preparation for the vocational courses which were to be undertaken. Thus further education was perceived as a two-stage affair: general education first, followed by technical education and training.

Given that position, a further recommendation, which provided the rationale for the setting up of Hereward College of Further Education as a specialist national residential establishment for physically handicapped young people, was logical:

that local education authorities be urged to give consideration to the establishment, on a regional basis, of residential courses of general education as a preliminary to vocational training of the physically handicapped (Thomas, 1963).

The potential of the further education sector as a source of education and training for handicapped young people was voiced. For the physically handicapped, however, there was the dilemma of specialized residential provision versus provision in the main stream. Was it to be an either/or provision or were parallel and complementary facilities a possibility?

Integration at the post-school level

The question did not remain long unanswered. The right of disabled young people to further education was made quite clear in the Chronically Sick and Disabled Persons Act, 1970. This Act may come to be regarded as a watershed in the opening up of educational opportunity for the physically disabled. It made accessibility for disabled persons to, and within, new educational buildings, and the provision of parking facilities and sanitary conveniences, requirements 'in so far as it is in the circumstances both practicable and reasonable'. The Act was seen to contribute 'to a climate of opinion which increasingly accepts that handicapped people have a right to aids, that buildings should be accessible and other facilities should be available which will enable them to develop their talents to the full' (Coe, 1979). That, of course, does not rule out the place of the specialized residential college but it does open up the public sector and allow for diversity of provision and the possibility of genuine choice.

If there was any doubt about the direction which provision for the 16- to 19-year group should take, it was dispelled by the *Report of the Snowdon Working Party on Integration of the Disabled* (1976), which expressed unequivocal conviction of the rightness of integration: 'For us . . . integration is right not simply "where it can demonstrate a clear balance of advantage" but "unless there are plain indications to the contrary".' The Report recommended planned introduction of a system of integrated education for children and adults at all levels of education beginning as early as possible at the pre-school stage and extending upwards to post-school provision. To underline the point, it was stated that there should be no special sector for the handicapped in tertiary education but, rather, a clear set of policy goals with the object of 'improving the access of handicapped people to post-school education and ensuring that post-school educational institutions fulfil the needs of handicapped people'.

Clearly, much more was envisaged by Snowdon than mere physical access to institutions. There had to be positive discrimination in favour of handicapped people: 'equality of opportunity' meant significant concessions and provision according to need. Concentration of resources in a few centres of higher and further education (with its 'deceptive attraction for some') was gainsaid although the advantage of locating units for people with different kinds of handicap in particular colleges was noted. Nevertheless flexibility and maximum freedom of choice were espoused.

Viewpoints similar to those of the Snowdon Report were expressed in the research report, *The Disabled Student* (National Union of Students and Action Research for the Crippled Child, 1976), based on a survey of provision for physically disabled young people in 505 institutions in the tertiary sector: universities, polytechnics, colleges of education, colleges of further education and technical colleges, and other institutions. The research also sampled local education authorities on 'the range and quality of their specialist services to handicapped people' and special schools on the experiences of their 'academically and vocationally competent school-leavers in the tertiary sector'.

Bearing in mind that the NUS research had academically able students as its target group, recommendations were of an integrationist nature and explicitly opposed to segregation. The report noted that the tertiary sector had 'contrived largely to escape the attention of those who would make separate provision for the disabled and consequently no "special" segregated alternative framework has been devised'. This implied that the further and higher education sector was ripe for integration. The dozen or so national, specialized colleges — with the exception of Hereward College, all in the independent sector — were presumably not seen as constituting a 'framework' and, in any case, were not offering advanced courses.

Recommendations were designed to facilitate student choice of institution: all educational institutions should conform to the requirements of the Chronically Sick and Disabled Persons Act 1970 regarding access; furnishing, equipment and facilities must suit student needs, residential accommodation should not be segregated. The final recommendation encapsulated the philosophy of the report and the spirit of integration:

> The temptation to concentrate resources for handicapped students in a few isolated centres of higher and further education should be resisted. If the disabled person who wishes to study is to compete alongside his or her able-bodied counterpart then access must be widened to allow him or her the opportunity to study the widest possible range of courses in the full range of academic institutions (NUS and ARCC, 1976).

The extent of provision

To what extent was the post-school sector providing for the physically handicapped? The 1970s saw a number of surveys carried out which attempted to assess the scope and nature of provision. Concerted action had not yet been arrived at but the problem was being approached from several sources. Impetus for some of the work came from the appointment in 1974 of the Warnock Committee 'to review educational provision in England, Scotland and Wales for children and young people handicapped by disabilities of body or mind . . .' The resulting report (DES, 1978) brought together the main strands of thought and activity of the decade and made recommendations for co-ordinated development.

A 1973 study of handicapped school leavers

The first national study of handicapped school-leavers (Tuckey *et al.*, 1973) — from special schools only — was a follow-up of 788 young people who had left school 18 to 24 months earlier. Information was sought, by interview, on 'the range, availability and suitability of the facilities for the further education, training and employment' of these youngsters. [...]

Eighty-three per cent of the children in the sample were considered by their headteachers as suitable for further education and/or training. It should be noted that severely educationally sub-normal children were not included as they were then outside the education system. Thirty-seven per cent of the sample actually received further education (including higher education) and/or training: that is, approximately 654 young people were considered suitable of whom 292 received education or training and 362 did not. The figures were better for some categories of handicap than for others. The following show percentages considered suitable and (in brackets) percentages who got it: blind 93 (85) per cent, partially sighted 89 (85) per cent, deaf 95 (34) per cent, ESN 76 (19) per cent, physically handicapped 86 (56) per cent, epileptic 70 (30) per cent and maladjusted 86 (31) per cent. The visually impaired were better provided for than other groups of whom the physically handicapped were the next best provided for.

Taking the sample as a whole, one per cent went to higher education, 10 per cent to colleges of further education, nine per cent to special residential courses, 7 per cent to industrial rehabilitation units (employment rehabilitation centres), 5 per cent to training centres and a further 5 per cent to miscellaneous provisions. Fifty-one per cent, considered suitable, went nowhere.

This study showed that at the beginning of the 1970s post-school education and training were clearly inadequate. Tuckey *et al.* attributed a low further education take-up in part to inadequate co-ordination and co-operation among school, local authority and further education people. Efforts were soon made to assess the extent of provision within institutions of further and higher education.

Provision in universities and polytechnics

The National Innovations Centre: a 1972–3 survey

The National Innovations Centre conducted a survey of provision for disabled students in all universities and polytechnics in Great Britain in the academic year 1972–3 (National Innovations Centre, 1974).

Included in the disabled category were bedbound, wheelchair and ambulant physically handicapped, blind and partially sighted, hearing impaired, speech impaired, multiply handicapped and others. Questionnaires were sent to 150 institutions: 122 universities or university colleges, and 28 polytechnics. It was a particularly thorough survey, data being sought from six sets of respondents in each institution: admissions people, student health service, welfare/counselling service, appointments/careers advisory service, students union and disabled students. The aim of the study was to get a picture of the lives of disabled students in universities and polytechnics in the early 1970s, to identify short-comings and to suggest what was needed. As noted by the authors, the study gave a statistical base and a qualitative assessment previously lacking.

Fifty-three full returns were received from the institutions (38 universities and 15 polytechnics). There were 495 disabled students shown to be attending the 53 institutions; these were in the ratio of two per thousand in the universities and eight per thousand in the polytechnics (the ratio in the general population is nine per thousand). Returns were received from 242 disabled students. In the second stage of the research, interviews were conducted with 19 of the establishments and 62 disabled students.

This study conceptualized those issues which have since come to be regarded as the salient ones in assessing the adequacy of provision for the disabled in further and higher education: flexible and systematic admission policies and procedures, special facilities to aid study, access to the library, examination and assessment concessions, assured mobility (access, movement between buildings, parking), appropriate accommodation and paid professional help, good health and welfare provision (medical, academic, welfare services; prior information for intending students) and good employment/careers service.

Some particular points were stressed. The first was that institutions should have clear and well-known procedures for the admission of disabled students which ensure that the student makes his or her disabilities known and that the institution has a procedure for making it easier, not more difficult, for a disabled student to obtain a place: positive discrimination should be practised. Disabled candidates should always be seen by the institution's officers before being offered a place and those with motor disabilities or visual impairment should visit the site before accepting an offer.

The second was that every institution should appoint a recognized co-ordinator for disabled students, who should co-ordinate health, accommodation and tutorial services: 'The hard facts of providing suitable accommodation and proper health care, ensuring accessibility of the necessary buildings, and making available aids, mechanical and human, have to be dealt with by the institution' (National Innovations Centre, 1974). Universities and polytechnics should put their procedures for dealing with disabled students on a systematic basis from the admissions stage through to assistance with finding employment.

Thirdly, a strong point of principle was that provision for students with particular disabilities should not be located (as had been suggested) at one or two universities or polytechnics. Avoidance of isolation, and integration with ordinary students, were seen to be what disabled students needed and wanted. Fourthly, money should be available from central government to recompense institutions for disability-related expenditure and for grants for students, according to disability, for material and human aids. And finally, research was needed into many aspects of higher education for the disabled, with machinery to promote and co-ordinate it.

All of these activities, concludes the study, must be inspired by the aim of unleashing valuable human talent despite the physical constraints imposed by the disability.

University provision in the mid 1970s: a survey

A postal survey of provision for disabled students in 34 universities in the United Kingdom was carried out in the mid 1970s when Gunn (1976a, 1976b) circularized university physicians. Gunn's definition of disability, 'physical or sensory impairment or chronic sickness which could produce educational disadvantages', encompassed a range of disabilities similar to that of the National Innovations Centre study. The survey showed 258 disabled full-time students in 34 universities, a proportion (two in one thousand) similar to that of the National Innovations Centre study. The study sought to investigate six areas: admission policies, entry procedures, pre-entry information, facilities, examination procedures and careers advice. These were all canvassed in the 1974 National Innovations Centre study.

· Four universities only, including the Open University, had 'statements of positive intent' towards the *admission* of handicapped students. The University of Leeds' statement is sometimes taken as a model since it affirms that handicapped applicants (students and staff) will be treated fairly and not be 'unnecessarily prejudiced' on account of handicap. It makes explicit: a commitment to provide safe access and working conditions; an undertaking that no applicant will be turned down without an opportunity to discuss how he would overcome his difficulties; and an intention to establish a committee to review the needs of handicapped persons in the University. Gunn (1976) claims that declarations of intent are needed to encourage more applications and greater frankness by disabled applicants about their disabilities. The study showed half of the universities to have a firm policy in practice and half to have no policy at all.

Entry procedures were seen as inadequate, with communication gaps between student, admissions personnel and university medical staff. There were serious gaps in the information supplied to medical staff prior to the student's arrival. The design of pre-entry forms was considered to have priority.

Pre-entry information for students was seen as a problem because some universities gave no information for disabled applicants in their prospectuses. *Access to University and Polytechnic Buildings* (Central Council for the Disabled, 1977) was helping partly to overcome that problem, but a visit to the site was considered to be the best solution.

The universities surveyed were described as having 'a surprising number of special adaptations of the environment' for the physically disabled. The general picture was of hospitable environments. A wide array of special *facilities* and aids was available in half of the institutions. The other half had a positive attitude towards the provision of equipment. Perhaps the most important aid of all was largely lacking: the provision of care staff. This need will be discussed later, in the context of further education. Gunn argues strongly for the provision of nursing staff or of 'attendants' — who need not be qualified nurses — to make it possible for some students to attend university at all (see Panckhurst and McAllister, 1980 for a discussion on care provision at Hereward College of Further Education). He expresses reservations about segregated, purpose-built residential accommodation for the physically disabled on the grounds that integration into the university community is likely to be frustrated; better to provide adapted accommodation in a regular student environment.

The universities were shown to be extremely accommodating in assisting students to undertake *examinations*. All but two tailored the arrangements to the individual: secretarial assistance to type dictated answers (21), extra time (25) and secluded facilities (30) were among the things provided: and a range of mechanical and electronic aids was made available.

The provision of *careers advice* was less encouraging. Half of the universities accepted a responsibility to refer disabled students to their careers advisory services prior to graduation.

The over-all impression, from Gunn's survey, is of a benign university climate in general with some positive and active commitment to provide for the disabled, some acceptance of responsibility and some indifference. Without greater commitment the few disabled students in universities may be little more than novelty value, and can be coped with on an *ad hoc* basis, but if there is to be acceptance of more than two disabled students in a thousand (200 in a university of 10,000) provision must be more deliberately planned than it is now. It is perhaps relevant that the universities make good provision in areas which are traditionally their bread and butter (examinations, for example), in those which are seen to be related to learning (mechanical and audio-visual aids) and in physical modifications and adaptations (which are practical and visible). But in those areas which may be styled *guidance* (care staff, careers guidance, systematic admissions and entry arrangements . . .) there is much to be done. There would appear to be a good deal to be learned from the Open University on attitudes and understanding. And the National Bureau of Handicapped Students undoubtedly has an important educative function. How many disabled students are capable of full-time internal university study? If the Open University experience is an indication, many more than at present attend universities. Until the universities indicate that their doors are open for fair entry – perhaps on the Leeds 'Declaration of Intent' model – and until those provisions are made for disabled students after entry which the principle of equity (provision according to need) would indicate, it cannot be said that the university system is serving its community adequately.

Further education provision for handicapped school leavers

A 1975 survey

A questionnaire survey of further education, training, employment and leisure opportunities for handicapped school leavers was carried out, as a basis for a submission to the Warnock Committee, by the National Council for Special Education in 1975 (National Council for Special Education, 1975). Four sets of questionnaires were sent out. Colleges of further education and local education authorities were asked about further education provision; the Department of Employment, social services departments, voluntary organizations, the Institute of Careers Officers and sub-normality hospitals were asked about training; careers officers and the Central Youth Employment Executive were asked about employment; and 40 organizations were asked about leisure time needs.

In an 82 per cent response rate to the further education questionnaire it was established that ordinary colleges of further education offered special courses of various kinds: 15 had full-time courses of one-year plus (nine of these were work orientation or work preparation), nine had full-time courses of less than one year (six were work preparation), 46 had part-time courses (of which half were general education and a quarter on specific work skills) and 35 had part-time link courses with schools. In addition 77 colleges reported handicapped students in ordinary courses and 29 colleges had staff working with handicapped people on an out-reach basis in such places as adult training centres.

This survey recorded a good deal of activity in the further education sector but noted the importance of bridging courses into ordinary further and higher education, the need for more effective assessment procedures and records to improve choice of course, and the need for specialist facilities for the handicapped school-leaver in colleges of further education 'as a prelude to employment, self-development and self-fulfilment'.

The response to the questionnaire on training was only 19 per cent. Thirty-nine local authorities responded. Provision for handicapped school-leavers appeared desultory although awareness of the need for provision for ESN(S) young people and the physically handicapped was expressed. It was considered (by social services departments) that ESN(S) young people of between 16 and 21 years of age could be provided for by colleges of further education. Provision for physically handicapped 16- to 25-year olds was described as 'grossly inadequate and practically non-existent'.

> The severely physically handicapped young person has little choice – he must either stay at home – dependent upon an occasional visit by a social worker, or attend a day centre for all ages of disabled people and take part in diversionary activities for a few hours every week or attend an adult training centre for the mentally handicapped (National Council for Special Education, 1975).

There was a 46 per cent response rate to the employment questionnaire. Seventy careers officers responded. There was almost unanimous agreement on the difficulties of placing the handicapped in employment: what are the implications for further education? Inadequate preparation for work – in general attitudes as well as lack of vocational skills – was highlighted. An underlying theme was the need for properly planned 'transition from school to work' programmes. All handicapped young people, it was concluded, should have access to assessment, work preparation and vocational training courses. The question of who should provide them was posed but not answered: local authority? Department of Employment? Manpower Services Commission?

This was an important survey, in spite of the weaknesses of relatively open questionnaires and the frustrations of varying response rates, since it began the task of documenting local provision throughout England, Scotland and Wales, and the identification of needs. [. . .]

HMI survey of further and higher education: 1976–7

A comprehensive survey of further and higher education provision for handicapped young people in the maintained sector was conducted by Her Majesty's Inspectorate in 1976–7. The aim was to assess the extent and nature of provision. Local education authorities were also surveyed. The results of the survey, although not published (the DES has been strongly criticized for that: NATFHE, 1978a; Coe, 1979) were made available to the Warnock Committee, and may be taken to have influenced the findings and recommendations of that Committee.

Eighty-three per cent of institutions and 99 per cent of local authorities responded to questionnaires. A sample of establishments was visited by HMIs. The findings showed that one third of colleges and a minority of LEAs had a policy of provision for the handicapped; growth of provision had been sporadic rather than planned. One quarter of the institutions had a staff member responsible for the admission of handicapped students. The publicizing of available facilities and provision for the handicapped in further education was held to be inadequate, it was also thought that there was a need for LEAs to formulate policy and designate an officer to implement it.

After special school – what?

One study which went beyond the survey questionnaire was carried out by Brindley (1977), who interviewed 26 physically handicapped school leavers, and their parents and teachers, from three West Midlands special schools. Four students were very severely handicapped, 12 severely handicapped and 10 mildly handicapped. He was attempting to tap knowledge of, attitudes to, and aspirations about, further education; he also asked questions about personal care, occupations and social interaction. Sixty-five per cent of the group were considered by their teachers to be suitable for further education; of 90 leavers from the same three schools in the preceding four years 46 per cent had gone to further education. This suggests a gap between potential and take-up but not as serious as that revealed by Tuckey et al. (1973): in that study 27 per cent of the physically handicapped school-leavers went to higher education (one per cent), further education (13 per cent) and specialized national residential colleges (13 per cent); a further 29 per cent went to local facilities such as industrial rehabilitation units and training centres.

Sixty-two per cent of the students in the Brindley sample, and 74 per cent of their parents, had considered further education. When asked what sort of further education place they would like to attend on leaving school, if they were to take a course, 42 per cent of the sample opted for a special provision (half of that percentage in a residential college), 50 per cent for a full-time course at a local college of further education and eight per cent for a part-time course in a local college.

The study showed that pupils, parents and teachers all had expectations of local further education which could not be satisfied. In particular, provision for slow learning and socially immature pupils was seen to be lacking. Brindley noted that teachers were concerned that colleges of further education did not give high priority to non-vocational courses, that there was a shortage of specialized staff to deal with handicapped students and that curriculum development for handicapped students was lagging. Arrangements for personal care and for programmes designed to foster independence in personal care were areas of concern to parents and teachers alike.

Physical access problems, problems of mobility within colleges, inadequate transport arrangements and lack of personal care provision were cited as reasons why parents and teachers considered residential colleges over local colleges. Residential special education was sometimes specifically preferred because of the appropriateness of courses being offered and the opportunity for 'independence' afforded by leaving home.

Brindley reports that pupils, parents and teachers all saw further education as 'extra time': time to consolidate basic skills, to become personally more mature, and socially more adept, and to further undeveloped aptitudes. Further education may be seen for physically handicapped young adults as 'a bridge to society'.

National Association of Teachers in Further and Higher Education: a 1978 survey

NATFHE carried out a survey of provision for physically handicapped students in colleges of further education and polytechnics in 1978 (Bennett, 1978: NATFHE, 1978). The study, which was conducted through NATFHE branch secretaries, surveyed broad areas of provision, by questionnaire, in relatively open-ended fashion. The response rate was about one third, 182 institutions replying.

It was established that 98 institutions (54 per cent) had made some special *physical provision* for physically handicapped students: usually ramps, lifts, adapted toilets, hand-rails and reserved parking space. Twenty (11 per cent) assisted students on an individual basis to cope with existing facilities, and nine (five per cent) admitted physically handicapped students on the understanding that they could cope themselves with the college facilities. Sixteen colleges (nine per cent) did not admit physically handicapped students on the grounds that their courses were inappropriate (nautical and agricultural colleges; and some teacher training establishments). And 39 colleges (21 per cent) stated that they had no facilities for physically handicapped students and did not admit them.

A few colleges provided *aids* of various kinds, made special provision at examination times (typists, separate rooms, electric typewriters), had special workshops or (one college) residential provision, or made provision in specially built or adapted annexes.

'A small number' of colleges ran *special courses* for the physically handicapped but most adopted a policy of fitting such students into normal classes. Special courses were work-oriented or designed to help students to fit into the community whether employed or not.

Guidance for handicapped students was provided in various ways; sometimes teaching staff had guidance responsibilities, sometimes counsellors.

Transport arrangements varied: college minibuses, LEA or social services' transport and ambulances, voluntary organizations and individual volunteers. Some colleges made no special transport arrangements.

It was clear from the survey that the levels of provision varied widely among colleges which provided for the physically handicapped. 'A very small number adopted a highly positive approach, including physical adaptations and special courses, together with special promotional material aimed at the handicapped' (Bennett, 1978). Others referred to the facilities for handicapped students in ordinary college publications. Some institutions operated an 'academic criteria only' admissions policy, and met the special needs of handicapped students who were admitted. A few colleges had quotas on the number of students admitted.

This survey could not be taken as an accurate record of the national situation in England and Wales because of the relatively low return. However, it does illustrate the relatively immature state of provision for the physically handicapped in further education, and has added a little more to the quantification of provision.

The Open University

The Open University has a definite policy of provision for disabled students, the spirit of which is captured in the fifth point of its nine-point policy statement on disabled students: '5. Disabled students are equal members of the University for whom special provisions are made to enable participation (so far as is possible) on equal terms with all other students.' At present there are 1,200 students of the Open University in need of 'some sort of special service' (Tomlinson, 1979). This represents two per cent of the total enrolment of 60,000 (20 in 1,000) a figure dramatically in excess of the two in 1,000 cited in the National Innovations Centre study (1974) as attending ordinary universities.

There is a Disabled Students' Area of the University, with two full-time advisers, three administrators and eight secretaries, which supports disabled students directly, and co-ordinates the support given by the staff in the 13 OU regions. Adapted course materials are provided according to disability: for example, audio-tapes, tactile diagrams for visually-impaired students; transcripts of radio and TV programmes for the hearing-impaired. These are services in general, not tailor-made for the individual, who must also establish his or her own network of support. A study skills package, intended for use by visually-impaired, hearing-impaired and manually-impaired students is available. Personal support, in the form of a helper-care assistant or mobility helper, may be provided for physically handicapped students at the residential summer schools which are part of OU requirements. Special help is given to hearing-impaired students on certain specified weeks, and there are various direct advisory services to students, often in association with external agencies (Tomlinson, 1979).

As much support as possible is given to full-time and part-time regional staff, who are responsible for the guidance and teaching of students. In particular, staff are supplied with a compendium of information on the characteristics of students with special needs; and there is carried through a computerized information retrieval system monitoring of student progress, which enables quick identification of problems and the anticipation of incipient difficulties.

These support services are described as 'low-level', yet they are sufficient to support a large number of disabled students. But perhaps the most success-enhancing feature of the Open University is 'the open admission system with the built-in facility of guaranteed offer to disabled students'. That, in itself is a psychological boost to the morale of those who are more accustomed to barriers than to open doors. Tomlinson (1979) makes some general observations on the OU experience which are relevant to post-school provision as a whole. He emphasizes the importance of *people*: 'A tutor counsellor with only his native good sense and a little bit of information from us is more often than not able to cope with the specific problems thrown up by a disabled member of his group.' This is not to argue that training for work with the disabled is unnecessary but that such human qualities as acceptance and interest are fundamental. However, there must be 'at least one co-ordinator/administrator/counsellor appointed at a sufficiently high level to make his/her presence felt'. *Integration* is not an issue since it is already happening; 'the instrument of integration must be a common core of shared experience'. A clearly thought-out *admissions policy* is crucial. *Flexibility* in such things as examination procedures provides for individual differences without impairing the validity of a course.

Gunn (1976a) described the contribution of the Open University as producing 'the most remarkable inroads into the whole problem of further education for the disabled', with its 'positive and enthusiastic discrimination in favour of enrolment for the physically disabled'. Not the least of the contribution, he suggests, is the encouragement for each student to attend the residential element of the course being undertaken, and the glimpse of independence which that experience gives. He sees that sample of independence as perhaps starting a change in attitudes but not completing 'the metamorphosis from being homebound', that a three-year residential course could give. Residential attendance at a university he sees as having three elements for the disabled: intellectual training, independence and integration.

Note

1 'The national colleges which currently provide further education for young people with disabilities should in time all become part of their regional patterns of further education for students with special needs (paragraph 10.44).' Warnock Report, 1978. (Ed.)

References

Bennett, P. (1978) Patchy provision for handicapped students, *NATFHE Journal*, 4, 7.
Brindley, A. R. (1977) The physically handicapped school-leaver and further education. Unpublished MEd thesis, University of Birmingham.

Central Council for the Disabled (1977) *Access to University and Polytechnic Buildings*.

Coe, D. (1979) Planning further education courses for handicapped students at national, regional and local level, in K. Dixon and D. Hutchinson (Eds.), *Further Education for Handicapped Students*, Bolton, Bolton College of Education.

DES (1978) *Special Educational Needs. Report of the Committee of Enquiry into the education of handicapped children and young people* (*Warnock Report*), London, HMSO.

Gunn, A. D. G. (1976a) The Opportunities of the Physically Disabled Patient for a University Education, Reading, University Health Service (mimeographed).

Gunn, A. D. G. (1976b) Problems of disabled students, *British Medical Journal*, 2, 1948–9.

National Association of Teachers in Further and Higher Education (1978a) College Provision for Handicapped Students: Report of a Survey (1975–78), London, NATFHE (mimeographed).

National Association of Teachers in Further and Higher Education (1978b) NATFHE sceptical about DES commitment, *Education*, 22, 600.

National Council for Special Education (1975) Report of the Working Party on Handicapped School Leavers (mimeographed).

National Fund for Research into Crippling Diseases (1976) *Integrating the Disabled* (*Snowdon Report*), Horsham, NFRCD.

National Innovations Centre (1974) *Disabled Students in Higher Education*, National Innovations Centre. Out of print. Copies available in some libraries.

National Union of Students and Action Research for the Crippled Child (1976) *The Disabled Student*, London, NUS and ARCC.

National Union of Students and Action Research for the Crippled Child (1979) *Financial Assistance for Disabled Students*, London, NUS Publications.

Panckhurst, J. and McAllister, A. G. (1980) *An Approach to the Further Education of the Physically Handicapped*, Windsor, National Foundation for Educational Research.

Thomas, E. (1963) *The Handicapped School Leaver*, London, British Council for Rehabilitation of the Disabled.

Tomlinson, R. (1979) Student support services, in K. Dixon and D. Hutchinson (Eds.), *Further Education for Handicapped Students*, Bolton, Bolton College of Education.

Tuckey, L., Parfit, J. and Tuckey, R. (1973) *Handicapped School Leavers: their further education, training and employment*, Windsor, National Foundation for Educational Research.

PART 4

Parents, Children and Professionals

4.1 Parents and professionals

JOHN GLIEDMAN AND WILLIAM ROTH

In a world where professionals gain their livelihoods directly from their clients' purses they are usually compelled to act in their interests. Such in the case in the private practice of law and medicine. However, the relationship between the professionals of the welfare state and their clients is quite different; here the professionals' salary, status and advancement no longer depend only upon the satisfaction of the client. In this paper, Gliedman and Roth analyse the nature of educational and medical professions and the pressures on parents of handicapped children which create a relationship of unequal power in which the parents can neither control nor challenge the actions of the professional. They see the solution to this unsatisfactory position in changes in the power structure surrounding contact between parents and professionals so that the interests of the professionals are served if and only if they act according to their clients' interests.

If a single word could adequately sum up the status of the handicapped child in society − and no word really can − it would have to be *vulnerability*. Tensed between biology and society, every handicapped child is made vulnerable not only by the genuine limitations of his handicap but also by the destructive, demeaning, and entirely unnecessary stereotypes and role expectations that are the destiny of those who grow up handicapped.

Nowhere is this vulnerability greater than in the child's relationships with those who provide him with specialized medical, educational, and other services. In countless ways, large and small, many professionals define the child exclusively in terms of his handicap and teach him to identify his true self with the image contained in the handicapped role. Yet the child and his parents desperately need many kinds of help that only experts can provide.

Every disadvantaged group encounters a similar contradiction in the social services they receive: invaluable assistance conjoined with oppression. This contradiction is especially destructive for the handi-

Source: abridged and slightly adapted from *The Unexpected Minority: handicapped children in America* by John Gliedman and William Roth, copyright © 1980 by Carnegie Corporation of New York. Reprinted by permission of Harcourt Brace Jovanovich, Inc.

capped child because of the unique importance of services in his life. Even today, when many basic needs often go unmet because of lack of funds, professionals bear a day-to-day responsibility for the well-being of the child and his family that is without parallel for any other social group.[1]

The need for services — and their often oppressive character — dominates the concerns of many thoughtful parents and professionals. [. . .] Unfortunately, criticisms of services to handicapped children have underrated the ways that professionals confuse the relation between society and biology in their work. As a result, reformers have rarely perceived just how far their reforms must break with tradition if even the boldest moves — such as the legal and legislative gains in special education in the US during the 1970s — are not ultimately to prove hollow. Despite the advances of the past few decades, every handicap service still needs to recast its *conception* of the proper relationship between professionals and clients in terms that honour the dignity and humanity of the handicapped child and his family. Just as crucially, every nonmedical service, from education to social work, must systematically scrutinize its claim to possess expert scientific knowledge about handicap. All must purge themselves of a deviance analysis of disability and deal with the handicapped on their own terms.

A comprehensive overview of all services for the handicapped would be unmanageably long. We shall instead focus on what most discussions of services for handicapped children leave out — the many ways that traditional models of disability either promote pseudoexpertise or prevent the professional from establishing cooperative, nonoppressive relationships with the handicapped child and his parents. Again, for economy's sake, we will discuss the premier service areas of handicap: medicine and special education. It goes without saying that services we discuss briefly or not at all — such fields as social work, vocational rehabilitation, and research and development programs in technology for the disabled — are beset by similar problems.

While all these handicap services are deeply flawed because of their reliance upon traditional models of disability, it must never be forgotten that each of them still accomplishes far more good than harm. This point bears special emphasis in the case of medical services. Here a host of conceptually straightforward improvements — such as more funds for preventive medicine and programmes targeted at those children who are most likely to become handicapped — could accomplish prodigies in reducing the incidence and the severity of childhood disability.[2] It would be tedious to reiterate this point at every stage of our discussion. Yet as that analysis unfolds, it is essential that the reader keep in mind that our aim is not to be balanced or comprehensive; rather, it is to suggest a fresh way of thinking about service issues that can act as a supplement or a corrective to the traditional way that policy makers and civil rights advocates alike have approached the service needs of handicapped children and their parents.

The problem of client–professional relationships touches upon some of the most troubling issues of our age. In a society that routinely creates or expands its publicly funded social service organizations in response to perceived social needs, the question of the proper relationship between the client and the professional is increasingly synonymous with the question of the proper relationship between the citizen and the state. Our own position in these matters is conservative and is best stated beforehand. We are alarmed by the long-standing practice of service organizations viewing their clients through a medical or quasi-medical lens that transforms political or moral issues into apparently objective questions of 'social pathology' or 'preventive medicine'. This misuse of medical reasoning makes it especially easy for policy makers to think of handicap – or, indeed, any major social problem like crime or poverty – as a social disease.[3] On an individual level, the implications of the social pathology model make it equally natural for the professional to assume that because he is an expert in a technical speciality, he has the right (and, indeed, the obligation) to override or to undermine the client's judgements about himself or a parent's judgements about a child. In both realms moral choices that were traditionally assumed to be the exclusive prerogative of the individual have increasingly come to be seen by many professionals and laymen as falling within the boundaries of what Talcott Parsons has called the 'legitimate authority' of the professional and his service institutions.[4]

A similar transformation has affected the notion of expertise. To be acknowledged to be an expert, one must obtain formal credentials and formal licences. With few exceptions, neither laymen nor professionals respect the self-taught expert without proper credentials. The awe of credentials is widespread but also very recent in American culture, dating only from the rise of professional societies in the late nineteenth century.[5]

This enthusiasm needs two qualifications. To begin with, it is essential to distinguish between a professional's formal expertise and his ability or willingness to employ it on behalf of his client. Often, service institutions – such as the hospital or the school – severely constrain the professional's ability to use his or her expertise to full advantage. No other child demands more flexibility and ingenuity from the professional than does the handicapped child. Yet, as David Kirp and his colleagues note, 'organizations such as school systems devise routinized ways to handle recurring issues', even when there *is* no routine way to meet the child's special needs.[6] Like other institutions, the organizations that deliver services to handicapped children and their parents encourage their members to 'limit uncertainty, increase predictability, and centralize functions and controls'.[7] These pressures subtly tilt the professional's perceptions of the child's strengths, limitations, and needs in ways that ultimately serve the institution's self-interest.[8] The parent of a handicapped child labours under no such institutional constraints. Nor, despite the obvious complexity of all parental motives, is any other adult likely to have the child's best interests more constantly at heart.

Just as important, parents often know more about their children than the experts whom they consult. While many professionals acknowledge this fact, their training and ideology encourage them to ignore it in practice. All too often the only parents allowed relatively free give-and-take with professionals are parents who possess some independent professional standing as experts in a specialty that bears upon childhood — medicine, clinical psychology, social work, law, etc. A more striking abuse of our culture's concept of the expert cannot be imagined: to be taken seriously, the parents' claim to expertise about their own child must be backed by a socially recognized formal credential that 'proves' that they are experts about children in general.

Not that parents are, on the whole, any more rational about their children than the professional is. Quite the contrary; parents are at least as vulnerable to irrationality and to confusions of their self-interest with the child's interest as is the professional. Parents themselves may be influenced by the handicap role and the presumption that the handicapped are childlike. All of us are affected by the culture's presuppositions about disability, often in ways we do not even perceive. In focusing upon the professional's shortcomings, we do not wish to idealize or romanticize the parent's strengths. But we do wish to reassert certain traditional cultural priorities that are often forgotten by professionals: namely, that the parent's rights over the child take precedence over the professional's personal moral views. To put it bluntly, the professional exists to further the parent's vision of the handicapped child's future. Should the professional disagree, he has every right to try to *persuade* the parent to adopt a different view. He also has every right to give advice when the parent is confused and seeks guidance and emotional support. But except in the most extreme instances of parental incompetence and brutality, such as child abuse, the professional has no right to use his immense moral and practical power to intimidate or to manipulate the parent.

In every handicap speciality it is essential that parent and professional actively work together on the child's behalf. Co-operation may be essential for medical reasons: medication that is not given the child by the parent is medication that may as well not be prescribed. Collaboration is also necessary because neither the parent nor the professional possesses a monopoly on the truth, and each can serve as a check on the shortcomings and limitations of the other. But before a partnership can genuinely exist, there must be give-and-take, mutual respect, and something like moral and cultural equality. Both the parent and the professional must attempt to understand the other's point of view, special moral concerns, and culturally determined priorities for the child. Both must relate to each other as adults who possess complementary expertise and responsibility for the child. [We] shall [now] examine some of the most important obstacles to achieving this commonsensical – and very traditional – ideal of parent-professional co-operation.

The sick role and the parent

The occupational hazards in the relationships between experts and parents have been well summarized by the medical sociologist Eliot Freidson in his description of the average physician's conception of the patient: 'The customary professional characterization of the client [in medicine] . . . insists upon his ignorance and irrationality. Such characterization is the prime justification for the professional's inclination to make the client at best a passive participant in the work – to, in essence, remove from the client his everyday status as an adult citizen, to minimize his essential capacity to reason and his right to dignity. Expertise in general claims its privilege by claiming the client's incapacity.'[9]

This general tendency of experts inside and outside the field of handicap (a tendency shared by bureaucrats) is reinforced when the object of the professional's services is a child. Perhaps a child has cerebral palsy and needs physical therapy, or his hearing is impaired and he needs speech therapy, or he has a reading disability and needs special educational services – in each instance the average professional defines his relationship to the child in much the same way as would a physician treating a patient for an acute infection such as pneumonia. He views the child in accord with the dictates of the social pathology model. The child has a special problem. The problem falls under the umbrella of the professional's special expertise – his 'rational authority'.[10] The professional then seeks to approximate a service relationship in which the child obeys the strictures of the sick role.

At this point, however, the fact that the client is a child greatly complicates the picture. No matter how much the expert might wish to focus exclusively upon that part of the child that falls within the expertise — the child's muscular co-ordination, speech articulation, or chronic disease — he cannot avoid taking into account the child's parents. This need follows from the fact that as a rule children are not willing to follow the dictates of the sick role or, for that matter, any role formulated by an adult. The parents become the doctor's enforcers, seeing to it that the child obeys the doctor's orders. This doctor-parent collaboration is relatively inconsequential when it is short-term, but it becomes particularly crucial in the case of handicap because most interventions are long-term. [. . .]

The obligations of the sick role (as defined by Talcott Parsons, are):

1. The patient is exempted from normal role obligations.

2. He is not held responsible for his state.

3. The state of being sick is considered conditionally legitimate *if*—

4. The patient co-operates with the source of help and actively *works* to achieve his own recovery (i.e., follows the doctor's orders).

5. Implied but not stated explicitly by Parsons is the presumption that the sick role will be temporary.[11]

Unfortunately, most parents who take a handicapped child in for treatment are soon nudged into accepting most of these obligations for themselves. They get treated as if they were patients: proposition one gets reformulated, in effect, to read 'subordination of one's own idea of parental prerogatives and duties to the professional's conception of parental priorities and duties now that the child is under the professional's care.'

It is striking to observe how often the structure of the professional's relationship to the parent automatically transforms the parent, in the expert's eyes, into a kind of patient. A good example is provided by the role parents are usually forced to play when they are lucky enough to find a comprehensive diagnostic centre in a large hospital where a great variety of specialists can examine their handicapped child and where an overall plan of attack on the disability can be mapped out.[12] To begin with, during the several days in which the experts test the child, the parents are usually excluded. Finally, when the diagnosis and plan of attack are complete, the parents are summoned to a conference in which one professional — generally the social worker — 'interprets' the results of the diagnosis to the parents. But he also tells the parents that they will never be able to see the diagnosis. Only other professionals (with the parents' written permission) will be able to see it.

Speaking of this process, Beatrice Wright observes that it has three negative effects: '(1) The parent gets the feeling that much is being said and done behind his back. (2) Decisions and conclusions are made, albeit in the form of recommendations, without his active participation. This always carries the danger that the parent will be unable or unwilling to carry them out. (3) It places the parent in the position of a child who has to be told what to do without having a real say in the telling or doing.'[13]

Thus, from the very outset, the social worker's task in this encounter reduces to coping with the parent's negative reaction to being treated like a *patient* rather than like a *parent*. [. . .]

In recent years, sensitive professionals have expressed concern about the way services for handicapped children seem organized to exclude the parent from the decision-making process. This concern has been voiced in numerous calls for an increased awareness of the parent's rights as a parent and in a host of proposals for administrative reforms designed to include the parent in the decision-making process. However, even the most parent-centred administrative reform can be undermined by the many subtle pressures that often keep parents from speaking up and pressing their objections when asked to participate in a review process with professionals. Still more important are the obstacles raised by the professional's conceptions of his rights and prerogatives as a professional. These role expectations and norms of proper parental behaviour are often at serious variance with the parent's prerogatives concerning the child. As a consequence, many conflicts between parents and professionals hinge upon their basic disagreements about deeply felt personal values. These differences are highly unlikely to be resolved in favour of the parent in any simple review process in which the parent stands alone against an array of diploma-bearing experts.

The problem begins with the vast asymmetry in need between the parent and the professional — the fact that in most of these encounters the parent needs the professional far more than the professional needs any one parent. The parent's concerns are concentrated on one handicapped child; the professional has many children as clients and in almost no instance does his emotional commitment to a specific child come near the parent's. Handicap services are poorly organized, expensive, hard to find. For the parent, merely finding the threshold of the professional's offices requires inordinate time, money, and hard work. Professionals don't seek out parents; professionals are sought out, sought after, and treated with great care lest the parent find himself turned away from the threshold and forced to start the exhausting process anew. The very structure of the time pressures on the professional conspires to put the parent at a marked disadvantage. The half-hour spent discussing the child's problems with a physician is fraught with significance for a parent. It is anticipated. It is remembered. It is dwelt upon. The hopes and fears of the parent organize themselves around it. No matter how conscientious the professional, he must see the half-hour in a different, less intense light, if only to protect himself from the impossible strain of going through every minute of every day at the high emotional pitch the parent brings to his brief interview with the professional. These asymmetries are further magnified if what is at stake is not a consultation with one professional but a comprehensive review of the child's problems by a group of professionals. The structure of this event in the parent's eyes is even more likely to intimidate, to silence, and to push the parent toward compliance completely independent of the individual professional's intentions.

Yet these are not the only impersonal pressures that can subvert genuine dialogue. Perhaps the most common weakness of specialists is to overreach and mark out for themselves an area of expertise far exceeding their real special knowledge. Many a busy professional misperceives a conflict in personal values between himself and a parent as a challenge to his expertise and, therefore, to his professional identity. Does a mother expect the special education school to be accountable to her for the quality of the education it provides her child? The school's first impulse is to assert the primacy of its own bond with the child over the parent's by claiming that the question of the child's educational needs is far too complex to be dealt with seriously by a layman. Does the parent contemplate suing a vocational rehabilitation counsellor for malpractice (perhaps because the experts tried to persuade a newly blinded youth that the vocation appropriate for a blind man is to make brooms in a sheltered workshop)? The very idea of a malpractice suit brought by a client or on behalf of a client strikes the specialist as absurd.[14] As the professional sees it, the client's or parent's role is not to evaluate the quality of the service provided, it is to make the most of the opportunities provided by the service — to study hard or to encourage the child to study hard, to implement the advice of the rehabilitation counsellor, or to help the child pass through the rehabilitation process. In short, the professional rarely recognizes in his expectation that the parent ought to behave in a cooperative, patientlike way a personal value judgement rather than a necessity born of the professional's specialized knowledge. This error frequently leads the professional to equate a challenge to the sociological structure of the parent-professional relationship with a challenge to his claim to possess expert knowledge. The moment this confusion occurs, the professional may find himself employing a host of explicitly coercive strategies in what he believes to be a perfectly legitimate cause – defending his professional integrity against an 'irrational' parent.

A final twist is added to the professional's error – and the parent's predicament – by the ease with which models of psychological explanation lend themselves to viewing any perceived challenge to legitimate professional authority as a symptom of emotional 'maladjustment'.[15] In one stroke the professional erects a new tier of obstacles to learning from his firsthand experience with parents that he should not expect them to behave in a patientlike manner. As for the parent, the circle is closed and he finds himself in a double bind: either submit to professional dominance (and be operationally defined as a patient) or stand up for one's rights and risk being labelled emotionally maladjusted (and therefore patientlike).

Still other coercive pressures find their source in those great constants of American life which are often ignored in discussions of handicap – race and class. Even sensitive professionals who acknowledge the serious barriers to communication imposed by cultural differences sometimes seem to lose their heads when they talk about how they have overcome these barriers by spending enough time with the parents to work through initial misunderstandings and suspicions. For surely something more than time is necessary to bridge the gap between an upper-middle-class white professional and a family from the ghetto. Insight into the stereotypes, role expectations, and manners of the sub-culture to which the parents belong is also essential. Without this insight – and some way of learning from initial mistakes – even the best-intentioned and most time-consuming intervention can misfire. The professional may behave in ways that actually intimidate and threaten the parents even when he thinks he is being most open and flexible.[16]

The most subtle coercive forces often stem from what distinguishes the client–professional relationship at its best from a mere economic transaction in the marketplace – the feeling of a shared goal and a sense of community that can impart to the relationship an ethical and emotional quality and transform the bond into a kind of friendship.[17] Anyone who has ever experienced such a relationship with a professional will acknowledge that very often the preservation of the special bond becomes an end in itself. Even if one disagrees with the professional, one hesitates to go too far for fear of transforming the 'friendship' into a mere commercial transaction or an out-and-out political struggle. Precisely because the professional is sensitive and kind, he may encourage a process of self-censorship in the parent that conceals the professional's sociological mistakes and leads the parent to act against his own self-interest in the relationship.

Indeed, the tragedy of all the coercive pressures we have briefly surveyed is that the professional does not even notice them unless he takes great pains to probe beneath the surface of his relationships with parents. Between the intimidation he inadvertently practices on the parent, his tendency to equate differences in personal values with challenges to his expertise, his overuse of psychology to explain away parents' dissatisfaction with his prescriptions, and a host of other perceptual, cognitive, and structural factors, the professional is denied essential feedback, and a sociological misunderstanding of major proportions is perpetuated. The parent is the most immediate victim of this misunderstanding, but ultimately the child will suffer as well. [...]

Improving parent–professional co-operation: the political prerequisites

If one believes that parents require constant guidance and tutelage in order to act in the best interests of their children, the hazards of professional intervention we have explored will appear to be necessary evils. Our own position is quite different. We believe that the parent–professional relationship in handicap should be in accord with the traditions of civil society. Instead of professional dominance, there should be parental co-ordination, and not just by the affluent and well-educated parent who comes from the same cultural milieu as the professional. Parents should oversee and orchestrate the services that professionals provide their children. Parents of all races and social classes should be able to pick and choose among different experts, obtain outside opinions when dissatisfied with the services or advice provided by a professional, and constantly evaluate the professional's performance in terms of the overall needs of the growing child.

Every society seeks ways to distinguish between legitimate and illegitimate power. It does so by imbuing certain social roles – such as judge, policeman, and parent – with the moral right to exercise authority over other members of society in well-defined settings and circumstances. During the last century – and at an ever-increasing rate – the traditional moral justification for authority has been supplemented and frequently supplanted by a justification based upon expertise. Often, the expert's claim to authority is amoral. The engineer does not decide to build the bridge, he merely possesses certain specialized knowledge that makes it possible to build the bridge.

In the human services, however, the tendency toward specialization implicit in the concept of the technical expert has gone still further.

As even a cursory glance at such areas as child development will show, many professionals find it natural to believe that they are experts about the kinds of values that parents should possess and inculcate in their children. Much of the conflict and confusion that occurs between parents and professionals in handicap stems from the almost self-evident character of the professional's intuitive feeling that he is a moral expert as well as a technical expert.

Not the least of the benefits of urging the parent to assume an executive role *vis-a-vis* the professional is that this strategy takes the parent's traditional claim to moral authority and adds to it an appeal to the very different claim to legitimacy of managerial authority. Unlike the parent's moral claim, which often seems pallid and suspect when ranged against the professional's appeal to his expertise, the administrator's moral authority can hold its own. The administrator specializes, as it were, in being a generalist – in cultivating an ability to grasp the big picture that so often eludes the narrow specialist. By meeting the expert on the expert's own ground, the authority of the manager seems as natural, as self-evident, and as uncontaminated by arbitrary and subjective factors as the specialist's own claim to authority.

Unfortunately, what is culturally obvious often remains unexplored. Outside the field of handicap, the idea of parent-as-manager has obtained considerable currency in recent discussions of how to improve social services. Perhaps because the model seems so intuitively obvious, much less attention has been devoted to the need to empower parents in ways that permit them to exercise the discretionary and coordinating powers of the administrator in their encounters with professionals.

Insight into what the average parent needs in order to function as a manager is provided by mentioning some of the structural advantages that administrators possess when they consult experts. Our purpose in alluding to some of these advantages is not to tell the reader anything he does not already know but to suggest that what the reader knows about the realities of power and expertise in large organizations is of the highest importance in any discussion of how to enable more parents to function as executives in their relationships with professionals.

To begin with, when a professional advises an executive, the professional is dealing with an organization rather than with an isolated individual. As a consequence, even the outside consultant is likely to feel that his career is on the line every time he provides a service to the manager. The professor who consults for the government will be at his best because he wants to be asked to consult again, or perhaps because he also wants to be appointed to a prestigious government review panel. Since most individual parents are not rich, famous, or powerful, their satisfaction with the professional's services is much less crucial to the professional's career prospect. The different 'schedule of reinforcement' that the professional encounters in advising organizations is, of course, directly reflected in how seriously the professional treats the social side of his relationship with the administrator. It is only common sense to take pains in establishing a relationship that the administrator perceives to be satisfactory. Indeed, because the cards are so heavily stacked in favour of the administrator, the professional will often have to choose between speaking honestly and thereby harming his career prospects, or being 'realistic' and tilting his advice to make it more palatable to his employer's ears. Finally, professionals often share the culture's respect for the special kind of authority vested in the administrator. This respect is often a significant factor in conditioning the expert's behaviour toward an especially powerful administrator in government or private industry – i.e., the head of a large and powerful bureaucracy or a highly placed executive in a firm. As we have seen, professionals often lack an equivalent respect for the moral authority vested in the parent.

Here, then, is what it means to say that the parent should assume a managerial role. He must have power – the kind of power that comes with occupying a position of administrative authority in a large organization. Without it, even the best-intentioned attempts to reform the way professionals deliver their services risks frustration. Good intentions and a genuine desire to help are simply not enough if the deck remains stacked against the client. The parent, not the professional, should be the one to set the terms of the relationship.

For most people – all but the most wealthy, clever, and influential – this power must spring from the same source as that of the administrator – the group. Perhaps more than anything else, it is essential that parents of handicapped children organize themselves into self-help groups. These can provide the parent with access to alternate information about services in the community, consultations with outside professionals, and moral support. Just as important, membership in active local groups is likely to exert a subtle influence upon the weight professionals give to establishing a mutually satisfactory relationship with the parent. Viewed as isolated individuals, few parents are likely to seem important enough to the average professional to have much influence on his future career. As the member of a group of powerful local parents' organizations, the parent's ability to influence the professional's career prospects is greatly enhanced. [. . .]

A good grass-roots parents' group can accomplish many other things. It can provide the kind of continuity from year to year that fosters the emergence of a folk wisdom about how to meet specific crises in the family's life. It could be the place where parents swap ideas and experiences in the manner that parents have, from time immemorial, gotten together to share ideas about child rearing. By bringing together parents with similar experiences, it could go a long way toward reducing the sense of isolation and abandonment so often induced in parents by the strain of raising a child with a handicap. It could serve as a corrective to unrealistic hopes about medical miracles and educational breakthroughs. It could give parents the lowdown on the local social service agencies for handicapped children and provide the latest word on how to make the most of them. It could give parents a chance to meet successful disabled adults and to gain from them a more balanced understanding of the relative role of society and biology in their own child's handicap. In short, local self-help groups could be the place where parents with handicapped children came together to form a community of like-minded people – not a 'therapeutic community' managed for them by professionals, but a community that they themselves control.

Of course, parents' groups are not panaceas. They are just as vulnerable to the forces of decay, corruption, and ossification as other institutions.[18] What starts as a genuine 'participatory democracy' may turn into a private empire administered by a few politically astute parents for their own gain. And a sense of community can become a sense of oppression by a small-minded majority. Political inexperience is another problem. Parents of handicapped children are no more experienced in local political organizing than other parents. They are just as liable to make mistakes as any other group of politically inexperienced people. They may unnecessarily polarize issues between themselves and professionals in the community. And they may become easily discouraged when quick victories are not obtained, or when the group settles down to the often wearing day-to-day routine of practical politics. None of these hazards is unique to parents' groups, however. Indeed, they are common to all organized groups.

Discussions of parent–professional relationships hinge upon a fundamental question of values. Whose is to be considered as fully adult in the encounter: the parent and the professional or only the expert? All too often the social pathologist doesn't want to entrust parents with the power to make decisions on behalf of their handicapped children. He believes that he should routinely determine what is in the child's best interest. We hold to a different morality. We believe that professionals should treat parents as adults.

Notes

1 For overviews of funding needs, see Kakalik, J. S., Brewer, G. D., Dougharty, L. A., Fleischauer, P. D., Genensky, S. M. and Wallen, I. M., *Improving Services to Handicapped Children*, Santa Monica, Calif., Rand Corporation, and *The White House Conference on Handicapped Individuals*, vol. 1, *Awareness Papers* (1977) Washington, D.C., US Government Printing Office.

2 For a discussion of these issues that complements the psychologically and sociologically oriented analysis of medicine presented in this section, see Appendix 4, 'Medicine and Handicap: A Promise in Search of a National Commitment', by Katherine P. Messenger and John Gliedman, in Gliedman, J. and Roth, W. (1980) *The Unexpected Minority: handicapped children in America*, New York, Harcourt Brace Jovanovich.

3 This mind set is well illustrated by the tendency of the US federal bureaucracy to extend the traditional cultural definitions of groups of handicapped people to groups that have not traditionally been considered handicapped by the general culture. For example, the new HEW regulations for implementing Section 504 of the 1975 Vocational Rehabilitation Act define alcoholics, drug addicts, and juvenile delinquents as handicap groups. The framers of the regulations originally wanted to go further and also define homosexuals as a handicap group, but this decision was dropped in the final form of the regulations.

4 See Parsons, T. (1964) *Social Structure and Personality*, New York, Free Press, chapter 10, 'Definitions of Health and Illness in the Light of American Values and Social Structure', and chapter 12, 'Some Theoretical Considerations Bearing on the Field of Medical Sociology'.

5 For an overview, see Lasch, C. (1977) *Haven in a Heartless World: The Family Besieged*, New York, Basic Books.

6 Kirp, D., Buss, W. and Kuriloff, P., Legal Aspects of Special Education: Empirical Studies and Procedural Proposals, *California Law Review* 62, no. 40, 47.

7 Perrow, C. (1970) *Organizational Analysis: A Sociological View*, Belmont, Calif, Wadsworth Publishing Co.

8 For overviews, see Katz, E. and Danet, B. (Eds.) (1973) *Bureaucracy and the Public: A Reader in Official-Client Relations*, New York, Basic Books; besides many useful articles, the anthology contains an excellent general bibliography. Also see Crozier, M. (1964) *The Bureaucratic Phenomenon*, Chicago, University of Chicago Press, and March, J. G. (Ed.) (1964) *Handbook of Organizations*, Chicago, Rand McNally.

Some of the most interesting studies of professional behaviour have been carried out in medical sociology. See Freidson, E. (1971)

Profession of Medicine: A Study of the Sociology of Applied Knowledge, New York, Dodd, Mead, and (1976) *Doctoring Together: A Study of Professional Self-Control*, New York, Elsevier; and Millman, M. (1977) *The Unkindest Cut: Life in the Backrooms of Medicine*, New York, William Morrow. Millman's 'Suggestions for Reading' provide a brief overview of the burgeoning medical sociology literature.

Useful insight into the socialization influences to which professionals are subjected is provided by the concept of the 'deviant career'. See Becker, H. S. (1973) *Outsiders: Studies in the Sociology of Deviance*, New York, Free Press. For good discussions of the general structural and ideological pressures that often constrain or determine professional behaviour, see Hirschman, A. O. (1970) *Exit, Voice, and Loyalty*, Cambridge, Mass., Harvard University Press; Simon, H. A. (1957) *Administrative Behavior*, 2nd. ed., New York, Macmillan; and Simon, H. A. (1969) *The Sciences of the Artificial*, Cambridge, Mass., MIT Press. Also see Wolin, S. (1960) *Politics and Vision*, Boston, Little, Brown, chapter 10. 'The Age of Organization and the Sublimation of Politics'; and Rosenhan, D. L. (1973) On Being Sane in Insane Places, *Science*, 179, no. 4070, 250–8.

9   Freidson, *Profession of Medicine*, p. 353.

10   Parsons, *Social Structure and Personality*. The concept comes from Max Weber. See chapter 8, 'Bureaucracy', in Gerth, H. H. and Mills, C. W. (Eds.) (1958) *From Max Weber: Essays in Sociology*, New York, Oxford University Press.

11   See discussion of the handicapped role in chapter 2, of Gliedman and Roth, *op. cit.*

12   Gorham, K. A., Des Jardins, C., Page, R., Pattis, E. and Scheiber, B. (1975) 'Effects on Parents' in N. Hobbs (Ed.) *Issues in the Classification of Children*, vol. 2, San Francisco, Jossey-Bass, pp. 160–3.

13   Wright, B. A. (1960) *Physical Disability: A Psychological Approach*, New York, Harper & Row, p. 292.

14   See Scott, R. A. (1965) Comments about Interpersonal Processes of Rehabilitation, in M. B. Sussman (Ed.), *Sociology and Rehabilitation*, Washington, D.C., American Sociological Association, p. 135.

15   For the institutional extreme, see Rosenhan, 'On Being Sane in Insane Places'; for a somewhat overdrawn portrait of professional abuses outside the total institution, see Szasz, T. (1961) *The Myth of Mental Illness*, New York, Harper & Row. Perhaps the most sensitive and sophisticated discussion of the line between 'maladjustment' and legitimate difference is Oliver W. Sacks's (1974) extraordinary book about the victims of Parkinson's disease, *Awakenings*, Garden City, NY, Doubleday. Also see 'The Thera-

peutic Despair', in Farber, L. H. (1966) *The Ways of the Will*, rev. ed., New York, Basic Books.

16 See the many illuminating examples in Schorr, L. B., Lazarus, W., Weitz, J. H. and staff, (1976) *Doctors and Dollars Are Not Enough*, Washington, DC, Children's Defense Fund.

17 See Talcott Parsons's description of the 'affective component' in the traditional doctor–patient relationship in *Social Structure and Personality*. Also see the classic statements of a humanistic vision of the doctor–patient relationship cited in note 27 of chapter 11.

18 For more on the tendencies of all organizations to ossify, see especially Hirschman, *Exit, Voice and Loyalty*.

4.2 From normal baby to handicapped child: unravelling the idea of subnormality in families of mentally handicapped children

TIMOTHY A. BOOTH

Tim Booth argues that to understand the nature of mental handicap involves much more than a clinical diagnosis: subnormality is a social status acquired over a period of time during which parents and doctors negotiate a child's passage from normality to a deviant status. Drawing on a number of cases of families with severely subnormal children, he charts the parents' initial suspicions that something is wrong and the doctor's early caution and prevarication. In the interim the child is in a kind of limbo where neither his normality nor his deviance is assured. As the parents' certainty that their child is abnormal increases, the eventual passage to a new identity takes places, confirmed by the doctor's diagnosis, but elaborated by the parents.

[. . .]

In this paper I aim to illustrate and give body to [a] general discussion of the idea of subnormality in order to lay the foundations for a more detailed analysis of the social meaning of mental handicap. Specifically, by describing the sequence of events leading up to children being classified as severely subnormal I hope to indicate how the idea of subnormality is created and shaped by parents in the course of their everyday social experience. My intention is to show that the meaning of the term 'subnormal' is not exhausted by clinical definition but that, on the contrary, the label merely serves to identify a condition the reality of which is, for the families of retarded children, in large measure a social construction.

The material on which this paper is based has been drawn from the case-histories of 46 families each of which had at least one severely

Source: Booth, T.A. (1978) From normal baby to handicapped child: unravelling the idea of subnormality in families of mentally handicapped children, *Sociology*, the journal of the British Sociological Association, 12, 203–21

subnormal child. In half of these families the child was living at home; in the other half the child had been admitted to permanent residential care in a large subnormality hospital. [. . .] Over a period of five months, 132 interviews were completed with the parents and recorded on tape; each family was seen at least twice and most were visited on three or four occasions.

In this short account I have deliberately sought to condense the experiences of these families into a framework for analysis by omitting or overlooking the idiosyncracies in their case-histories and by drawing together and stressing the similarities. Of course, this approach does not do literal justice to the history of events or to the gradual unfolding of parental apprehension, anxiety, alarm and bewilderment captured in our records. It is not my aim, however, to try to narrate the personal drama acted out in the context of the mundane regularities of family life which typified the period leading up to the final diagnosis; nor to document precisely the different routes taken by families through the maze of health, welfare and educational services — involved at one stage or another in the screening and detection of developmental handicaps — before a conclusive assessment was made. Rather my purpose is to describe how what we call 'severe subnormality' emerges as a social status which can be defined in terms of how a mentally handicapped person is valued by others in the network of relationships which constitutes his social world.

Let me set the scene of this discussion by recounting the relevant fragments of two case-histories which reflect a pattern of events common to the experience of a large number of families who participated in the study.

CASE 1: When Bruce was 8 or 9 months old his mother Mrs. Gordon[1] noticed that he didn't seem to be sitting up very well. She took him to the family doctor who told her. 'He's a big baby and a bit lazy. He'll be all right.' Not until he was about 21 months old did Mrs. Gordon again voice the fear that something might be wrong with Bruce. Then she told her parents that she was worried because she didn't think he was 'keeping up to his stages properly'. They advised her to consult her doctor, but added that in their view there was nothing wrong with him. Mrs. Gordon took Bruce to her G.P. and told him of her concern. He said, 'You can't tell by looking at him' but 'if you're not sure and I'm not certain, I think we'll have him into hospital'. One week later Mrs. Gordon took Bruce to see a paediatrician. The child was admitted for 4 days of tests after which Mrs. Gordon was told that he was mentally handicapped.

CASE 2: Mrs. Mallin's suspicions were first raised when Martin was only a few weeks old, after she noticed that he wasn't following stimuli with his eyes. At this time, the district nurse was making the usual post-natal home visits and Mrs. Mallin took the opportunity to mention her fears about the baby's health — to which the nurse replied that she was worrying too much. However, the feeling that there was something wrong persisted. Mrs. Mallin remained convinced that the baby's reactions were altogether too slow. Eventually, she went to see the family doctor but again he merely assured her that there was nothing wrong and advised her not to worry. Still anxious, she took her worries to the doctor at the local Health Clinic. He discounted her fears as unfounded. When Martin was just short of a year old, they asked a specialist to examine him. After tests he confirmed that their suspicions were well-grounded and that Martin was in fact badly handicapped.

Each of these case-histories chronicles the crucial stages in a drama which prepares the ground for the creation of subnormality as a social state. In what follows, I want to discuss each stage in turn with the aid of short vignettes from the case-records. [. . .]

The arousal of suspicion: lay conceptions of irregularities in child development and behaviour

In most cases it is the parents who take the first initiative and instigate the process that eventually is to bring them into contact with the agencies that arbitrate on the question of what is to pass for normality. Only two children in the study were diagnosed at birth and both of them presented the more obvious physical stigmata of mongolism.[2] For the remainder, their transformation from normal baby into handicapped infant was more prolonged and devious.

The bulk of the clues which first prompted the parents' concern about their child referred to aspects of the child's physical condition or appearance — 'It was the smallness of his head that bothered me'; to the rate of physical or social development — 'He was a bit backward in coming forward'; or to the prominence of certain behavioural quirks and mannerisms — 'His reactions were so slow. He didn't ever seem to smile on cue.'

There was considerable agreement among the families on the nature of the clues which first occasioned their suspicion. Though there was often a wide variation in the age at which these clues were seen to become symptomatic of a more fundamental affliction. One family began to suspect there may be something wrong with their daughter when she showed no sign of attempting to sit up at six or seven months old while another did not refer their son to a doctor until he was 2½ years old and still incapable of sitting unaided and without support. In another case, the parents of an eighteen month old girl consulted their family doctor because she had not yet learnt to walk while another family delayed seeking advice until their son was three and still not walking. This points to a wide-ranging lay consensus on the milestones of growth tempered by a much greater measure of flexibility in timetables of normal development.

The interpretation of these clues as evidence for suspicion about the child's welfare was a crucial factor marking the first phase in the organization of parental doubt about the child. It was the meaning that the parents gave to these clues which determined the age at which the child entered the process from which he would emerge as 'severely subnormal'.

For those parents who immediately read the child's tardiness in keeping up to the timetable by which they charted normal progress as indicative of some underlying malaise, the age at which the child began the passage[3] into subnormality varied with the nature of the symptoms he displayed.

The Goochs say, 'It was when she wasn't sitting up that we began to get a bit worried.' They compared their daughter to a nephew who was three months younger. He was 'doing so much more and advancing so much more quickly' that they finally went to their doctor.

Mrs. Levy realized that there was something wrong with Guy when he reached the age of five or six months. As compared to his older brother when he was at the same stage, Guy didn't seem to 'respond' and he had kept his 'foetal face' much longer. Mrs Levy approached the clinic doctor for her opinion.

When Alan was nine months old, Mrs. Arnold noticed that he displayed no signs of attempts at speech. By the age of eighteen months she knew 'that there was nothing there' and she also noticed that his co-ordination of his hands and feet was bad. She sought her doctor's advice.

Mr. and Mrs. Gregory thought Kenneth was 'a very good baby' until they compared him with a relative's child when he was eight or nine months old. Whereas his cousin was 'climbing all over the place', Kenneth was 'doing nothing at all'. 'After that, everybody's baby seemed to be doing things and Kenneth not.' So the Gregorys took him along to the Welfare Clinic.

But many parents, by one device or another, managed to ignore or postpone judgement on the signs of irregular development which for these others had immediately been seen as cause for anxiety.

This was particularly the case among parents of children with manifest physical disabilities. Here, the known infirmity served for a time to avert suspicion about other aspects of the child's condition.

Michael was born with a cleft palate. He was very difficult to feed and very slow to put on weight and grow. When he was two years old he developed cataracts which left him with only partial sight. His parents say that they knew all along that he was backward for he was very slow to sit up, walk, and talk. He was still in nappies at the age of five. But they thought that all these difficulties were the result of his physical problems.

While David was still a baby, Mrs. Storthes noticed that he would periodically grimace or shudder. She took him to hospital where he was diagnosed as epileptic. He suffered frequent fits — as often as every twenty minutes — the worst coming when he was nearly two years old. But gradually, medication eased the severity of these fits until they gave no more trouble. Only then did Mrs. Storthes realize that there was more wrong than just fits.

For some of these parents the hardships and sorrows of learning how to cope with a physically handicapped baby undoubtedly closed their minds to the prospect that there might be something else wrong. For others, however, the physical handicap was the least threatening explanation for their child's behaviour. Although they were sensitive to the warnings and cues that pointed to a more fundamental malady they nevertheless struggled to reconcile their child's predicament with the most favourable long-term prognosis, even if this meant repressing the truth of their own feelings or colluding in an unspoken pact of mutual self-deception.

Nigel was born with a cleft palate which caused considerable difficulties with his breathing and feeding. Mr. and Mrs. Duncan saw the major problem as 'keeping him alive'. 'We deluded ourselves in thinking that once this had been corrected, Nigel would develop and grow better.' However, Mrs. Duncan admits that when she was eventually told by a paediatrician of the diagnosis of severe mental handicap, 'I wasn't a bit surprised I just knew. I knew already in my heart.'

Another group of parents, though heedful that their child was not as advanced as other children of the same age, succeeded for a time in interpreting the ambiguous cues they were given in an innocuous or benign way which did not seriously threaten to prejudice or impair his integrity. For some, this was made possible by the conviction that the causes of the trouble were organic in origin and that with proper treatment their child would soon catch up with others — 'I had thought her backwardness was due to some glandular trouble actually. I didn't think for a moment it was something that could never be put right.' Others were fully prepared to accept that their child was dull of understanding and slow to learn — 'We just thought he was ordinarily backward' — or, in less disparaging tones, that their child showed what amounted to an almost wilful reluctance to exert himself — 'He wasn't late enough on anything to really make us worry. We just put it down to being a lazy boy', or 'He was just a sleepyhead' — without seeing these qualities as signifying that anything more serious was amiss.

Some parents confessed that, looking back, they were either predisposed to ignore or quite blind to the evidence before their eyes — 'You don't realize they're not developing normally. He seemed normal. I don't know why because it's obvious now.'

In some cases this resulted from the deliberate decision to avoid falling into the role of worrisome parents. One mother, a former nurse, explained that 'having seen so many sick babies, the tendency is to think that all babies are like that. I was determined not to worry about my own child, not to be an anxious mother'. In order to uphold this attitude, these parents chose to suppress, overlook or play-down the signs of wayward behaviour which might have forced them to reconsider their responsibilities. In other cases, parents acknowledged that they simply failed to observe or discern those facets of their child's behaviour which, with hindsight, they could now appreciate had been unusual and irregular. For some of them, this was achieved by resorting to the common expedient of most parents: blocking their minds to the undesirable or unwanted traits that if admitted would tarnish their image of the child desired — 'I was looking for the things that were good about Leslie and I didn't see the others.' But more explained their omission in terms of their own ignorance or naivety, stemming in the main from the innocence as young mothers and their unfamiliarity with babies — 'I was slow to recognize her development wasn't quite normal. As a first child I'd nothing to compare her with.'

Mrs. Rodgers says that 'not knowing babies' at the time she 'didn't notice anything wrong' with Sidney although she 'knew he was slow'.

Mrs. Selby admits to being slow to recognize the signs of handicap in Christine but puts this down to being 'too young, too green . . . too young to make a fuss. If she'd been my second child, I would have known right away.'

In the light of their latter-day knowledge their past experiences assume a meaning that was not immediately evident to them at the time.[4] Certainly the more experienced mothers, who were swift in picking up the initial cues as warranting concern, confirmed that they had relied on their experience of rearing other children to guide them — 'I don't think I would have noticed if I hadn't have had the other children.' What the reality of the present testifies were the symptoms of handicap appeared to these new parents in their past context in a different less dogmatic guise:

'It didn't hit home that anything was wrong. Now you can look back and think, "Well, why didn't you question these things?" It just grew on us. As he got older we just accepted the problem. We were in such a problem that we couldn't see it.'

Finally, there was a group of parents who though wary of their child's progress nevertheless chose to procrastinate rather than follow up their suspicions. In spite of the fact that most of these parents were conscious of a strong sense of foreboding and feeling of uneasiness about what tomorrow might hold for their child — 'For a few months it had been dripping on my mind that something was wrong' — they nevertheless put their faith in an optimistic outcome to their worries; often backed by the reassurances and encouragement of relatives and friends. They hoped for improvement in the face of their fears; trusting that everything would sort itself out in time. As one family said who chose to defer searching out the truth which they feared they might not want to hear:

'We were both hoping that there was nothing really wrong with the child — always hoping for the improvements to happen next week. And of course the next week never came.'

However, for most parents the lee-way for these responses of pro-crastination, ignorance, circumvention or transference to the initial portents of handicap is limited. Sooner or later, as ad hoc explanations for the child's lack of progress are repeatedly discounted by the evidence of impaired development, and as the incongruity between the child's performance and parents' commonsense readings of the problem mounts, the last shadows of optimism fade into concern about the child's well-being and uncertainty about his future.

At this stage, an undefined question-mark hangs over the child. On the basis of the clues provided by commonsense timetables of child development, the parents have worked up a *generalized suspicion* about their child's well-being. Their interpretation of these clues at this point amounts to nothing more specific than the fear that there is 'something wrong'. This verdict, that all is not well with the child, provokes the decision to seek professional advice on the cause of the trouble and chronicles the beginning of the change in the status of the child.

The professional's response: prevarication

Only a few of the parents who took their suspicions for professional appraisal and consulted their family doctor or the local health clinic received an immediate diagnosis of retardation. For the remainder, the outcome amounted to the declaration of a moratorium on further change in the child's already fragile and vulnerable status.

> Mrs. Gooch's doctor told her that he didn't know if anything was wrong with her daughter because 'children varied so much'. 'He advised us to give it a month and see what progress she made.'

The doctor's responses were of two kinds: one dismissive, the other appreciative of the parents' anxieties.

In some cases, the parents' suspicions were dismissed with no more than a vague reassurance and the advice not to worry. These parents were offered no plausible alternative explanation that would nullify the fears which had brought them to seek the doctor's advice and help them to satisfactorily account for what they saw as oddities in their child's demeanour in a non-menacing way. The doctor restricted his role to the clinical task of finding out if there was any medical justification for what the parents held to be wrong or exceptional with the child and passed over the telling issue of why it was troubling them so much. Having certified that at this stage there was nothing about the child which called for any action on his part, the doctor terminated the case.

> Linda 'didn't speak on time' but when Mrs. Maxwell consulted her

family doctor she was told only that she expected too much and that nothing was wrong. When she didn't walk, Mrs. Maxwell again went to see her doctor to be told only, 'First you're worried about her not talking, now it's not walking.' She comments, 'He seemed a bit annoyed so I didn't go any more.'

When Geoff was two years old, Mrs. McCloud took him to the doctor on the grounds that he was too quiet for a child his age. The doctor told her that she worried too much and that she should feel lucky to have such a quiet baby. He advised her not to compare Geoff with other children.

The doctor's confident prognostications temporarily mollified the parents but left unanswered the questions that had been kindled in their minds by those features of the child's development which they had decided were out of the ordinary. They had referred to the doctor in the hope that his science would furnish them with a rational account of their child's apparent slowness which their commonsense reckoning had failed to provide. The attempt by the doctor to reassure the parents by fiat merely ensured that when the authority of his voice and his dogmatic tones began to fade with time, the sense of trepidation which had spurred them to call on his advice would occupy their thoughts again.

In other cases, the doctor was sympathetic and responsive to the feelings of agitation and alarm signalled by the parents' suspicions. But on examination he came to the conclusion that for the moment their concern was unfounded. What the parents had taken to be unusual enough to warrant the opinion of an expert, the professional disowned as belonging to the commonplace.

When Vicky was ten months old, Mrs. Castle noticed that she wasn't sitting up properly. She took her to the Health Clinic where she was told that Vicky was just 'a lazy baby'.

Mrs. Rymer realized that Stuart was 'slow' in maturing but when she mentioned this fact at the Health Clinic on one of her regular visits, they told her 'not to worry, he'll catch up'.

Mr. and Mrs. Harvey noticed that Eileen wasn't 'pulling herself up in her pram', 'beginning to be active' (or) 'grasping things'. Mrs. Harvey commented on some of these points to the doctor at the Health Clinic who concurred with her judgement – 'Yes, she is slow' – and advised that she consult her G.P. When they did raise these worries with their family doctor, he replied, 'Eileen's just a beautiful dumb blonde. She's not interested. She doesn't want to do these things yet.'

Here, the doctor ratifies the parents' lay judgement that their child is behindhand in his development but explains this fact in terms of the natural diversity of talents. The onus is put on the parents to adjust the phasing of the expectations they hold of the child. This signifies the first compromise in a whole series of concessions the parents will eventually have to make in the way they handle their child which plot his emerging status as a subnormal child. Without saying outright that something was wrong with the child the doctor managed to avoid the conclusion that all was well by placing him in an indeterminate position 'behind' others of his age.

But this outcome appealed to the parents' own reasoning and satisfied their immediate wish for a resolution to their troublesome doubts about their child. Unlike those parents whose worries, dismissed by their doctor, returned quickly when they found themselves unable to reconcile his assurances with their own observations, these parents were able to keep faith with this assessment by revising their estimates of their child's potential to fit the facts of his performance. Accordingly, it took longer for the discrepancies between opinion and fact to reach the limit beyond which it became more and more difficult to hold the view that the child was merely backward or slow, and to herald the revival of parental doubt.

The problem for the doctor at this stage is that so many of the symptoms described by the parents do not differentiate their child's development from the normal course of babyhood and infancy: 'Young handicapped children differ from normal children mainly in potential rather than in capacity.'[5] The insecurity which characterizes the parents' feelings about their child is mirrored in the uncertainty which the doctor faces in the clinical setting. He has to devise a strategy which allows him both to cope successfully with his own clinical uncertainty and to appease the parents who are nervously searching and pressing for a diagnosis. This means resisting all demands and pressures to commit himself one way or another to an authentic decision whilst relieving or neutralizing the suspicions which urge the parents to press for a definitive judgement. [. . .]

While in retrospect many parents were willing to believe that their family or clinic doctor 'didn't tell me sooner because they weren't sure themselves', others were sceptical about their openness and readiness to confide in them. As one father said, 'I often wonder why he didn't voice what he must have known earlier.' At this point the problem of clinical uncertainty begins to emerge and become confused with the way indeterminacy is invoked and used as a means of managing the parents.[6]

Several reasons were cited for this attitude of distrust. Some parents, like Mrs. Masterson, 'wondered if the G.P. put off telling us because we were doing so well with her'. In cases such as this, the implication is that the doctor knowingly withheld a diagnosis in order not to jeopardize the parents' sense of duty to the child and to permit the growing bonds of tenderness, constancy and love to foment and secure their relationship. Others believed that their doctor may have been 'trying to cushion us from the shock of diagnosis' during a particularly stressful or unsettled period of their lives when other strains and pressures were already falling on the family. For instance, one family who held this view had their eldest son in hospital with leukaemia at the same time as they first consulted their doctor about his younger brother.

Finally, there were parents who maintained simply that their doctor 'didn't want to talk about it' with them; that 'he didn't want to know'. A forceful illustration of this attitude is provided by the case of the Fletchers who only learnt of their daughter's mongolism from a locum G.P. when she was sixteen months old even though, as it turned out later, the diagnosis had been communicated to their regular family doctor immediately after Mrs. Fletcher was discharged from maternity hospital. Here the decision not to tell the parents, or to nurture their suspicions by suppressing information, seems to be informed by the idea that parents will be more ready to receive and grasp the diagnosis if they already are convinced themselves that something is wrong with their child. It is implied that until this dawning of awareness any effort to unmask the truth is likely to compound the shock for the parents and provoke resentment against the doctor and a rejection of the diagnosis.

But whether this prevarication was the result of clinical uncertainty or the attempt to programme the diagnosis, the effect was to consolidate the child's ambiguous and transitional status midway between health and sickness; normality and abnormality. He is left straddling two classifications of reality, one of which grants him a weak hold of his personal integrity while the other threatens life-long dependency. This stage then is characterized by a period of dormancy in the biography of the subnormal child during which events serve only to mark time.

The growth of conviction

Things do not remain static for long however and the passing of time puts strain on the transitional status negotiated for the child by doctors and parents, promising further movement and change in his public identity. Sooner or later it becomes evident to the parents that their child is falling further behind other children rather than holding his own. As one mother commented. 'Things began to get obvious then for other children were standing and Terry was still lying.'

Faced once again with having to find an explanation for their child's retarded development, the parents update their old suspicions. What had before registered as little more than an insinuation now turns into the conviction that the child's 'slowness' is evidence of some sort of deep-seated disorder.

> After being told that Sidney would 'catch up' given time, Mrs. Rodgers let things ride until she noticed that his younger brother was 'rapidly catching him up'. Then she 'went to the Clinic determined that something was wrong.'

Urged by a new spirit of determination and perseverance, the parents apply themselves to the task of working for a definite diagnosis.[7]

> Mrs. Castle rejected the opinion that Vicky was only a 'lazy baby'. She comments, 'I knew myself she wasn't a lazy baby' and adds, 'I started to fight from then onwards to see what was wrong with her.' She saw the family doctor and told him that she 'wanted to know what was really wrong with Vicky.'

> After having been told not to worry about Julie by the Health Clinic, Mrs. Conniston asked to see a specialist. He decided that she was physically handicapped and arranged for her to receive physiotherapy once a fortnight. But Mrs. Conniston wasn't satisfied and she asked for a second opinion. Her G.P. arranged an appointment at Great Ormond Street where they confirmed the diagnosis of physical handicap and offered physiotherapy every week. Mrs. Conniston was still unhappy however and when Julie was two and a half she asked that she be given an IQ test.

> When Christine was 3 years old she was put under the care of a psychiatrist. Mrs. Selby kept pressing him to commit himself and tell her what was the matter with her daughter but he warded off her

questions. She repeatedly requested him to arrange for Christine to be given an EEG but he declined to do so. Only when the Selbys moved house and Mrs. Selby asked her new doctor was Christine referred to hospital for an EEG.

These efforts mark the beginnings of the final negotiations between parents and doctor which are to precipitate the child into subnormality. On the basis of lay standards of normality, the parents have now passed beyond the threshold of tolerance within which they can indulge or excuse further transgressions or minor infringements of the normative criteria and moral rules distinguishing acceptable from deviant behaviour. This point seems to be reached when the child's behaviour, or the pitch and timing of his future development, becomes unpredictable for the parents in terms of their everyday knowledge of the wills and ways of children.[8] In approaching the doctor once again the parents are not, as on earlier occasions, asking for his professional opinion on whether or not there is something wrong with their child. This question has been concluded, outside the surgery or clinic, in the home; the parents are persuaded that their child is 'not right'. Their aim now is to make this judgement, and their child's fate, intelligible in terms of the language of medicine.

The vacuous label

'You know there is something wrong with your child and you're told there is nothing wrong with him at all and, "We don't know what you're worried about." Then nine months later your child is mentally handicapped. It's all wrong.'

Diagnosis completes the degradation of the child. A last consensus is reached on the reality of the child's condition which establishes his status as severely subnormal. He is finally and inevocably stripped of all claims to normality, past or prospective. As Garfinkel has put it, 'What he is now is what, after all, he was all along.'[9] Though the efforts made by the doctor to explain 'what sort of child he is' and the clarity and precision with which he communicated the diagnosis to the parents varied widely.

In a few cases, the parents were given a full clinical diagnosis of the origins and causes of their child's retardation; one mother acknowledged that her doctor 'spent a long time with me and really went into it'. More often, when evidence of aetiology was lacking, parents were offered a functional diagnosis — such as 'brain damage' — which provides a credible and publicly acceptable reason for the child's limitations without touching on their pathology. Finally, in a number of cases, parents were given what might be called a figurative diagnosis which described their child's condition in euphemistic terms using a vernacular rather than a specialist mode of expression: 'She said he was backward. They've never given it a name,' or 'They just said he was just backward. They never said he was mentally handicapped,' or 'They'd give you the impression that he was mental but they never spoke outright and said he was.'

In the light of this information given to them on diagnosis, the parents are at last enabled to make sense of their child's abstruse behaviour and irregular development which has puzzled them almost since his birth: 'Through this process the past was made to fit the present, so to speak'.[10]

Yet if the past becomes more accessible and easier to fathom after diagnosis, the future remains no less opaque and elusive. For the parents are in receipt of a label which testifies to the fact that their child will never be normal but which gives them no indication of how he will grow up; as one father said, 'It doesn't tell you what the child is going to be like.'

The problem now facing the parents is to translate the diagnosis of subnormality into terms that will vouchsafe its relevance in a social context. They were given little help by doctors, either family practitioners or hospital specialists, who were uniformly unwilling or unable to commit themselves to any sort of serious forecast of the likely effects of the child's handicap on his ability to look after himself in the future. Three types of prognosis were recollected by parents, all of which were typified by equivocation.

Some doctors were reported to have professed their ignorance and admitted to not knowing how the child's impairment might affect his competence: Mr. Hammond remembers the specialist saying, 'He'll never grow up properly. We'll just have to see how he grows up — I've no idea. Only time will tell.' Others were said to have given a counsel of despair, cautioning the parents against an optimistic evaluation of their child's prospects: 'We were told not to hold out any hope at all for her to do anything.' Or, finally, parents recalled their doctor giving them an ambivalent and inconclusive estimate of how their child might develop which left them with no firm idea of what they might realistically expect him to achieve: 'We were told that sometimes they develop better, sometimes they're not as good.'

At this point then the parents are in possession of a diagnosis which describes their child's handicap in a way that affords the insight into how he will fare in the routine world of daily life. It depicts the loss of bodily functions and mental capacity without relating the effect on social performance. The parents are not told how the child will suffer as a result of his handicap or what penalties and sacrifices it will impose on them.

Mrs. McCloud says, '. . . not taking much interest in children like that; not knowing about children of that sort; not knowing anybody like that, we just didn't know what it was all about. We just took his (the doctor's) word and said we'd wait and see how things progress.'

Mrs. Duncan says, 'You can't look into the future. You don't know what it's going to grow into so you can't picture it.'

Mrs. Gant comments, 'We never did have any real idea of just how much he would develop or how much he wouldn't develop.'

These quotations document the origins of subnormality as a social state. From this point onwards it is left up to the parents to build the social meaning of mental handicap by making the link between the diagnosis of subnormality and the social world of everyday life. A mother of two severely mentally handicapped sons evoked clearly the personal and domestic focus in which this task is painstakingly accomplished:

'They say to you your child will be handicapped. It doesn't dawn on you really. The most difficult thing for me was, when he told me, neither of them were walking or feeding themselves or toilet-trained and I couldn't see how they were going to turn out. When they were both about seven – or when Tommy was about seven and Jeff was about five – you could gradually see. By that time they'd learnt to walk; they'd changed from their baby ways and you could see that they'd sort of become little boys. It gave you somehow more idea of them. But they were a totally unknown quantity when they were so small and doing nothing and I thought, "Well, I don't even know what the handicap means".'

This link is forged in the course of the parents' efforts to reinstate the child into the family in a role which is compatible with the limitations imposed by his handicap and to establish predictable relationships with him based on their first-hand experience in practical affairs of his personal strength and weaknesses.[11]

Concluding remarks

In this paper, I have tried to step outside the clinical perspective on mental handicap which has informed most research, and dominated professional practice, in this field. Without doubt most of the advances in the care and treatment of mentally handicapped people have been achieved within this tradition. But the medicalization of our thinking about mental handicap has been so complete that it has blinkered our vision as to how other approaches might help to further our understanding.

I have attempted to show how becoming a mentally handicapped person is an intricate social process which turns on a series of critical decisions initiating gradual but perceptible changes in a child's social status and leading ultimately to the elaboration of a social role which cannot be defined in clinical terms. I have argued that in order to develop this approach it is necessary to break with the view that mentally handicapped people present a set of characteristics and potentialities which can be identified and assessed by the tools of diagnosis and medical evaluation and to examine instead the nature of the process by which qualities and capacities are ascribed to or withheld from them. In other words, to work from the premise that subnormality is not a quality within the person but a status allocated to them.

Using parents' own accounts of their experiences I have traced the evolution of the idea of subnormality up to the point of its emergence as a distinct social state. I have shown that subnormality is not a fact which comes into the world full-blown, but rather that it is framed and shaped by social activity. Children are not born ready classified as subnormal. They are assigned to the class of people called subnormal as a result of a series of decisions, spanning a period of time, involving parents, professionals and other people. By limiting attention to the period leading up to diagnosis, I have illustrated how the idea of subnormality is brought into being by the imputation of social meanings to physical states.

In the final section I indicated how, following on the diagnosis, it was left up to the parents to elaborate the idea of subnormality into an organized social role. For these parents, their child bears witness to the social reality of subnormality. From this point onwards, the child's actions and behaviour are assessed as those of someone who is subnormal and thereby work back on themselves to define in turn what subnormality is. In this sense my argument implies that the content of the social state we call subnormality cannot be defined in advance of an understanding of the social context from which it borrows its identity.

Notes

1 All names are, of course, pseudonyms. The same name is used to refer to the same family throughout.

2 It may be noted, nevertheless, that in the cases of three other mongol children in the survey a diagnosis was not made at the time of delivery but from four to sixteen months later. For a discussion of difficulties and delays in the diagnosis of mongolism see Kramm, E. R. (1963) *Families of Mongoloid Children* (HEW Children's Bureau Publication No. 401), Washington DC, US Government Printing Office.

3 For the sense in which this concept is used here see Glazer, B. and Strauss, A. (1971) *Status Passage*, London, Routledge and Kegan Paul. I have chosen to use the notion of status passage as a framework instead of the concept of the moral or deviant career because my intention is to focus solely on the sequence of changes, leading up to diagnosis, in the way mentally handicapped children are valued and judged by others, especially their parents. The concept of 'career' as it has been used in studies of 'adult socialization' and deviance refers also to the subjective changes in personal identity, in the person's image of his self, which accompany the changes in public status. This is an aspect that I shall not touch on here. See Becker, H. J. and Strauss, A. (1956) Careers, personality and adult socialization, *American Journal of Sociology*, 62, 253–63.

4 For a detailed discussion of the temporal foundations of experience, and of the ways in which the past may be re-interpreted in the light of present experiences, see Schutz, A. (1972) *The Phenomenology of the Social World*, London, Heinemann.

5 Davis, A. G. and Strong, P. M. (1976) Aren't Children Wonderful – A study of the allocation of identity in development assessment, in M. Stacey (Ed.), *The Sociology of the NHS*, Sociological Review Monograph 22, University of Keele.

6 See Davis, F. (1960) Uncertainty in medical prognosis: clinical and functional, *American Journal of Sociology*, 66, 41–47.

7 Burton, L. (1975) *The Family Life of Sick Children*, London, Routledge and Kegan Paul, also finds that in cases of cystic fibrosis 'diagnosis . . . required considerable parental effort to effect', p. 27.

8 Cumming, G. and Cumming, J. (1957) *Closed Ranks*, Cambridge, Mass., Harvard University Press, observe that the cut-off between the mentally ill and the mentally well in the eyes of the lay population seems to occur as soon as behaviour becomes non-normative and unpredictable.

9 Garfinkel, H. (1956) Conditions of successful degradation cere-
   monies, *American Journal of Sociology*, 61, 420–4.

10 David, F. (1963) *Passage Through Crisis*, Indiana, Bobbs Merrill,
    p. 115.

11 The analysis presented in this paper and concluded in this section
    contrasts sharply with the point of view put forward by Voysey,
    M. (1975) *A Constant Burden*, London, Routledge and Kegan Paul.
    She writes that 'what parents say about their child may reflect less
    their own constructions than the imputations of others, notably
    doctors, and especially once a formal diagnosis has been made'
    (p. 36). And, she adds, '. . . definitions of his condition in terms of
    the three dimensions of onset, diagnosis and prognosis may be
    initially and ultimately those of doctors. It is they who act to
    provide the basic rules in terms of which parents' evaluations of
    their child's behaviour must then make sense' (p. 39). I have sought
    to show that subnormality, as a social status, is not foisted on
    children by the arbitrary decision of professional diagnosticians.

4.3 Professionals and ESN(M) education

SALLY TOMLINSON

Multi-professional assessment has been much discussed lately, and it has become an orthodoxy that the surest determination of special needs is through close collaboration between professionals, each contributing their own distinctive skills. Sally Tomlinson documents how referral and multi-professional assessment of moderately educationally subnormal – ESN(M) – children actually worked in one LEA under the terms of the DES Circular 2/75. She reveals fundamental disagreements about the criteria for labelling a child as ESN(M), conflicts of professional and personal interest, and a considerable informal network of contacts designed to bypass and subvert the formal mechanisms. The people very often excluded from this network were the parents, who were informed of decisions rather than consulted about them and who felt frustrated by the army of professionals who were of little help to them. Tomlinson argues that the expansion of multi-professional assessment envisaged in the Warnock Report will increase professional powers still further and that it is now vital that they recognize the actual nature of their operations.

Professionals generally claim to know better than others the nature of certain matters and to know better than their clients what ails them or their affairs. They profess to serve the community – indeed the service ideal is usually taken to be a key professional characteristic. This is particularly true in special education, where an ever-expanding number of professional people work within an ideology of benevolent humanitarianism, which assumes that the discovery, assessment and treatment of more and more children who are handicapped or have 'special needs' is a hallmark of a civilized society.

But there is no reason to assume that professionals are more charitable or more altruistic than anyone else, as negotiations over professional fees and salaries, and anxieties over professional status demonstrate. Professionals, although often employed in areas of universal social concern, also have vested interests in defining the needs

Specially commissioned for this volume
©The Open University, 1981

of their clients and in expanding the number of clients they serve. The professionals who work in special education have very real interests in expanding their field — the more children who are potential candidates for special education, and the more kinds of provision, the more work for the professionals. Each profession involved in special education also has vested interests in consolidating its area of competence and in claiming that it does a vitally important job.

Within special education there is also an official ideology articulated clearly in the Warnock Report which claims that a process of 'smooth teamwork' operates between the many professions involved in referring, assessing and placing children in special schools or classes; any notion of conflict is conspicuously absent. Indeed, the development of extended 'multi-professional' assessment, advocated by both the Court and the Warnock Reports (DHSS, 1976; DES, 1978), assumes an unrealistic degree of communication, co-operation, and absence of professional conflicts and jealousies.

This paper looks at how professionals do actually work together in special education, at what sorts of power and expertise they wield and at the conflicts of interest and status that arise. The information presented is based on a study of forty children passing through the ascertainment process for special (ESN(M)) education, in Birmingham in 1976–7 (see Tomlinson, 1981). Some 120 professional people who had seen, tested or made decisions on the children were interviewed and asked not only about the children but about their dealings with and views about each other. The interviews were carried out with head teachers of referring and special schools, clinical medical officers, educational psychologists, and in some cases, psychiatrists, social workers, remedial teachers, assessment staff and education welfare officers. The parents of the children were also interviewed, partly to discover how the professionals treated them during the often lengthy process of assessment and partly to see how they viewed the professionals.

The city of Birmingham

In the mid 1970s the city of Birmingham was a rich city, and although by no means generous in its per capita expenditure, spent £86,129,590 on its education system in 1975/6. Roughly one million inhabitants, about 12 per cent of them New Commonwealth citizens, were living in what had become the industrial, financial, commercial and communications capital of the Midlands. The city had become, after the creation of the ILEA, the second largest education authority in the country, with 122,000 children in primary schools, 93,000 in secondary schools and 4,000 attending 42 special schools, 18 of them ESN(M) schools. The changeover from selection at 11+ to comprehensive schooling had provided a focus for party political debate from the 1960s and by 1972 the city council had introduced the consortium system, a grouping of secondary schools in eighteen geographical units. The affairs of each consortium were run by a committee of head teachers and principals, and local inspectors, with heads of special schools being invited to participate in their local consortium.

In the central education department seven sections formed the administration; one branch, the Special Services Section, was responsible for the management of special schools, the educational needs of 'handicapped and other disadvantaged children', the remedial teaching service and the schools psychological service. Provision for disruptive pupils had begun to be made in the city from 1972, two guidance centres and three suspension units being in operation by 1976.

The national issue of the over-referral of black children for ESN(M) education had not become a specific issue in Birmingham at any time. The West Indian community had focused their attention on London schools, where black children were likely to be four times more numerous in ESN(M) schools than their proportion in the total school population would warrant (ILEA, 1967). However with 18 per cent of schoolchildren in Birmingham being 'wholly non-European' by 1975, the education of minority group pupils was considered to be a growing problem in many respects, and in the inner-city ESN(M) schools West Indian pupils were over-represented.

The city had certain charismatic figures who had extended their influence over special education. One of the ESN(M) schools is still named after Dame Ellen Pinsent, an indefatigable worker for the subnormal, who started an after-care service for 'defective' school-leavers in 1901, and served on the Royal Commission for the Care and Control of the Feeble-Minded in 1904—8. Cyril Burt, a crucial figure in the development of mental testing for the educationally subnormal, carried out tests on Birmingham schoolchildren in the early 1920s. It was Burt who first suggested that an IQ score of between 50 and 85 points should be considered 'educationally subnormal' (Burt, 1935). The Wood Committee, which reported in 1929, and on which Burt and Ellen Pinsent both sat, put forward the figures of 50—70 as 'ESN' and this range of scores subsequently became associated with the category. Post-war, one of the head teachers of a city ESN(M) school worked with a senior lecturer at the university and together they produced a book which one reviewer claimed 'should be a standard text-book for all those working with ESN(M) children' (Tansley and Gulliford, 1960).

Tansley later wrote an influential book on remedial reading, became a city Inspector for Special Education and pioneered a scheme to discover children who were educationally 'at risk'. Gulliford became the country's first Professor of Special Education.

However, it is important to note that charismatic figures are often furthering charismatic professional interests. Burt's work on mental testing was very important in furthering the interests of the profession of educational psychologists who gradually came to take a major role in the assessment processes for ESN(M) education. Tansley was a representative first of the interests of special school head teachers, and then of the educational administration. Gulliford has furthered academic (psychological) interests in special education.

The official procedure

The official procedure by which children become classified as ESN(M) is very complex. The major professional people involved are educationalists, medical officers and educational psychologists. The notion of a 'team' decision dates back to the first selection procedures for schools for Special Instruction in the 1890s, when medical officers and educationalists vied with each other — at that time there was no advanced science of psychology. A rivalry of professional interests between medical officers and educational psychologists had, however, become noticeable by 1944, and in the Education Act of that year it was medical officers who were given the statutory powers to decide when children had a 'disability of body or mind' and needed special educational treatment. Medical officers were even empowered, providing they had done a short course on the administration of psychological tests, to test children and fill in the psychological section of the Handicapped Pupil (HP3) form. In 1976 the recommendations of the government Circular 2/75 (DES, 1975) on the discovery and assessment of children with special educational needs, were put into effect and the HP forms were discontinued. New Special Education (SE) forms were available for professional people to record their decisions and opinions about the children they had seen. SE1 was to be the 'report by a head teacher of a child who may require special education'; SE2 was a 'medical report on a child who may require special education'; SE3 was a 'report by a psychologist on a child who may require special education', and SE4 was to be a summary and action sheet on the needs of a child requiring special education — to be filled out by the local special education adviser or chief psychologist. SE5 was the 'certificate form' to be completed by a medical officer if the parents of a child objected to special education. This notion of compulsion, statutory since 1914, has always made the presentation of special education as solely 'for the good of the child' after equal consultation with parents, difficult to accept. Psychologists in Birmingham were quick to point out that these 'new' procedures still left statutory power over the educational destiny of children in the hands of the medical profession. The 'ideal' form of professional decision-making, as suggested by Circular 2/75 is illustrated in Figure 1.

However, local education authorities do have considerable autonomy in how to interpret central government recommendations. In Birmingham, the appointment in the mid 1970s of a new principal psychologist and a chief administrative officer who had formerly been an educational psychologist meant that the profession of psychology had particular influence on the way the procedures were implemented. Modified

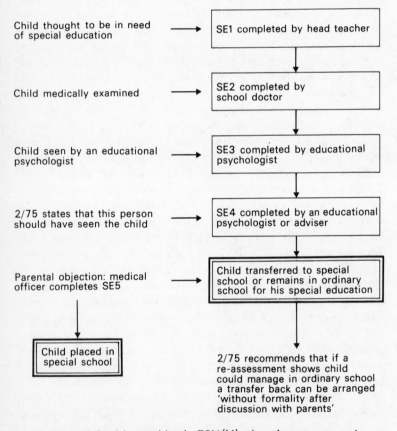

Figure 1 Decision-making in ESN (M) education as suggested by Circular 2/75

versions of the SE forms were to be used, and in the city's 'Notes for Professional Staff on the Educational and Health Services' the administrative procedures laid down were as follows: 'Referral may be made by schools, other agencies or parents, but the normal practice will be that children apparently in need of special education because of learning or behaviour difficulties will be referred to a psychologist in the first instance, whereas children with actual or suspected physical or sensory handicaps will first be referred to a medical officer.'

Although this suggested that officially the workload of assessment should be neatly shared into assumed psychological and medical areas of competence, educational psychologists were not particularly happy that the only statutory figures in the assessment processes were still medical officers. As one psychologist put it: 'At the smell of a medical decision, we will all be back working under the old medically dominated teams.'

The psychologists' professional anxieties may well have been justified. One head teacher interviewed during the study was annoyed that his educational psychologist refused to countenance the removal of a troublesome child from his school, and he had re-referred the child to the medical officer who was more sympathetic to his request.

The three departments in the city who are officially concerned with decision-making in special education are the Special Services Department, the Schools Psychological Service, and the School Health Service. The personnel who take responsibility for decisions are the Chief Administrative Officer (Special Services), the Principal Psychologist, and the Senior Specialist in Community Medicine (Child Health), formerly termed the Principal School Medical Officer. The reorganization of the health services in 1974 had not particularly pleased the doctors who examined children for special education. The Senior Specialist thought it had resulted in 'total muddle'. The city was divided into five Health Districts in 1974, which did not correspond to any educational divisions nor to the Special Services administrative divisions, nor even to the school clinic locations. By 1974 the central health area contained four school clinics, the southern area only one. The Warnock Committee spoke of co-operation being made 'more rather than less difficult' by Health Service reorganization, and this was certainly illustrated by one case in the study where a child was passed around between five doctors. A senior clinical medical officer explained the case thus: 'Dr. J. [the school MO] referred Mary to her own G.P., who referred her to Dr. O. [consultant paediatrician] who then passed her back to me. I told Dr. J. to refer the girl to Dr. B. [psychiatrist] but Dr. B. said she wasn't going back to that school any more; she felt she wasn't wanted or given a room to work in.' It was not surprising to find that this girl's parents were bewildered about, and antagonistic towards the whole assessment procedure. Yet the official policies of referral for special education have, particularly since the 1970s, stressed the necessity for parental involvement with professionals. Until 1974 the local authority sent a somewhat peremptory letter to parents telling them to bring their child for a medical examination. The letter was discontinued in 1974, and the procedures recommended via the SE forms are that 'parents should have been interviewed and the child's difficulties discussed with them well before this form is completed'. The Warnock Committee suggested that parents be allocated an SE form on which to record their views, but the official procedures to date do not require parents' views to be recorded. Nor is there any statutory requirement, as yet, to evaluate or follow up children in special classes or schools, with a view to transfer back to normal schooling.

Official practice in Birmingham was that, after assessment, 'Special Services place child in accordance with SE4 recommendations'. A clerk in the administration would be involved in contacting special schools and arranging a place, unless professional disagreement necessitated a case conference. Some professionals considered that this procedure was 'secretive' as the administration was not obliged to reveal the criteria which were used to place a child. One psychologist noted that 'we do all this professional work, we make careful decisions, then some 16 year old clerk decides what school to send a kid to'.

The Warnock Committee, reporting in 1978, suggested new procedures by which professionals could discover and assess children in need of special education. These are illustrated in Figure 2.

The implementation of some of the Warnock recommendations, outlined in the government White Paper of August 1980, will certainly extend professional involvement and cater for the interests of a variety of professional people. As Milo Minderbinder in *Catch 22* might have put it: 'everybody benefits', and Everrett Hughes (1971) made a similar point more academically: 'professionals do not merely serve, they define the very wants they serve.' Whether the clients of special education actually do benefit from increased professional involvement is problematic. For example, in the Birmingham study it took, on average, two years for a child to be seen by three professionals and placed in a special school; these professionals recorded their decisions on three forms. Suggested new procedures might necessitate six professionals seeing a child, and perhaps six forms being completed.

Official descriptions of policy and professional involvement may imply 'smooth teamwork', beneficial to the client, but reality is usually somewhat different. It is important to note that the clients of special

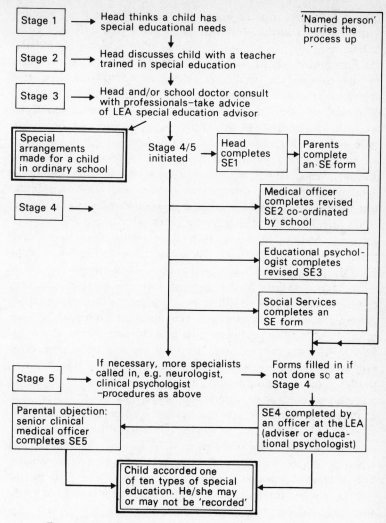

Figure 2 Decision-making in special education as suggested
by the Warnock Report

education, parents and children, are particularly powerless and vulnerable, and very dependent on professional judgements and opinions.

Professionals and the ascertainment process

How then do the professionals involved in the ascertainment of children for special education actually work together, and what are their opinions of each other? It was envisaged — and it turned out to be the case — that three aspects would provide possible areas for conflict. Firstly, it was thought likely that there would be a difference in the criteria used by the various professionals to recognize an ESN(M) child, given that official criteria are vague and confused. At the outset of the research ten possible 'accounts' of ESN(M) children were abstracted from the literature and from initial interviews. These were *functional accounts*, those stressing lack of attainment; *behavioural accounts*, particularly of disruptive or non-conformist behaviour; *statistical accounts*, describing children in terms of IQ; *psychological accounts*, stressing emotional problems or odd behaviour; *social accounts*, particularly stressing low socio-economic class, cultural or linguistic disadvantage, disorganized families and poor socialization techniques; *organic accounts*, including suggestions of innate incapacity; *school accounts*, maladaptation by or to school; *statutory* or legal accounts; *intuitive* accounts, that 'there is something wrong' and finally, *tautological accounts*. These last accounts tend to describe ESN(M) children as children in need of ESN(M) schooling.

Secondly, conflicts due to poor or difficult communication were envisaged, and thirdly, conflicts over professional encroachment on perceived areas of competence. The historical antipathy between medical and psychological personnel, each claiming a major role in the ESN(M) assessment processes, has been touched upon, and other professional antipathies emerged. The assumption that medical, psychological and educational personnel, each working with their own professional autonomy, theoretical models and belief systems can co-operate smoothly in the ascertainment process is problematic enough, but when other personnel — social workers, psychiatrists, education welfare officers, and so on — are also involved in seeing and reporting on specific children, the process becomes even more complex. The additional complexity is likely to be particularly felt by the parents, who are subject to more people visiting their homes and asking them to attend interviews in a variety of places.

Head teachers

Head teachers of ordinary schools are crucial elements in the ascertainment process for special education since it is their judgement that a child is potentially ESN(M) that sets it in train. Heads overwhelmingly use functional and behavioural criteria in accounting for ESN(M) children; they are not interested in causal explanation, they are interested in action. The heads used intuitive judgement and felt they could distinguish between a backward 'remedial' and a potentially ESN(M) child, although there was no consensus on whether backward children were also disruptive. There was some antipathy on the part of head teachers towards educational psychologists largely because of different accounts being offered and also because of poor communication. Psychologists seldom used behavioural accounts of ESN(M) children, whereas head teachers often do. It is very important to heads of normal schools to have children removed who are constantly disrupting their schools. Heads felt that while psychologists did possess special skills for assessing and testing children, and providing special learning programmes, they were 'too slow' or 'too busy' or such a scarce resource that one head remarked 'it's no bloody good referring children — it takes too long'. Some heads felt psychologists' skills amounted to a 'mystique of IQ and long words' which could baffle and frustrate the referring school.

Heads were less antipathetic towards the medical officers whose duty it was to examine children put forward for special education, partly because they had little contact with them and considered them less important than the psychologists in the decision-making process. They were often unaware that long delays for medical examination could hold up the assessment process and tended to blame the psychologists or the administration for delay. A few heads had realized that they could 'play off' psychological and medical personnel by re-referral, if they did not get satisfaction. Heads of ordinary schools did not have much contact with ESN(M) schools and they tended to have idealized views of the schools. One head said 'they have a better staffing ratio and specialized knowledge, the staff have all done a special one-year course' — of a school where only one member of staff had 'special' qualifications. They expressed the view that there ought to be more contact and information flow between normal and special schools but were reluctant to take a lead in this. Heads of normal schools tended to regard ESN(M) schools as places where children with learning and behaviour problems should go as speedily as possible. Heads thought that parents ought to be consulted over the referral process and by and large did discuss the referral with the parents. However, they did not fully understand how important the discussion was for parents as a way of getting information, and they were often more concerned to persuade parents not to object to special education. As one head put it 'no matter how we try to present it, it's still the barmy school we are sending their kids to'. Although the changeover to the new SE forms was being implemented in 1976, some heads had not heard about the new forms, although one was annoyed at a peremptory letter he had received from a psychologist which simply stated 'due to a change of procedure you now fill in an SE1'.

In common with all the professionals interviewed, the head teachers had an informal network of communication in addition to official forms. They relied on the telephone to 'get things done'. However the telephone had other uses — one head described how he became so enraged when the administration sent him the wrong forms, he tore them up in front of the telephone receiver! This head may have been expressing a feeling that as a method of communication no form was considered adequate. Heads complained of long delays after form-filling before they were contacted again and generally felt that once the referral had been made, events had gone beyond their control and they were relatively powerless to do anything but wait for other professional action.

It is interesting that while Circular 2/75 claimed that the assessment for special education had become more educational, the referring schools, whose business is education, do not feel they play a large part in supposedly educational decisions.

Educational psychologists

Psychologists are crucial figures in the process by which children move from normal to special (ESN(M)) education. It is psychologists, working within a 'scientific' model of mental testing, and possessing certain professional skills which schools do not possess, who may or may not legitimate the head teacher's judgement that a child is ESN(M). There is a strong potential for conflict between heads and psychologists. As one educational psychologist put it: 'There are some schools where if a kid is trouble, he's out so fast his feet don't touch the floor.' While heads traditionally have used behavioural accounts, psychologists tend to account for ESN(M) children in functional and statistical terms — an ESN(M) child has low attainment and a low IQ. They also use school accounts: an ESN(M) child may be one whom a school has 'rejected'. One psychologist said 'some secondary schools are notorious for their rejection, they want to run the school like the army and want to be rid of these kids'. Psychologists are able to act upon their beliefs that a school should cope with a child by not recommending ESN(M) schooling or by not visiting the school. One older psychologist who made a point of insisting that schools 'cope' generated a mixture of amusement and hostility in schools and was nicknamed Yogi Bear.

The personality and beliefs of individuals can affect the way they work and as a profession psychologists have considerable freedom to make decisions for which, given professional autonomy, they are not accountable to others. For example, although psychologists are 'supposed to' test children and give an IQ score, one psychologist remarked that he had 'given up testing West Indian children as the tests aren't valid'. This permitted professional idiosyncracy makes their decisions difficult to question and puts them in a powerful position in the assessment process. But their decisions may, on occasion, be over-ruled. One psychologist did test the child of the only middle-class family in the study. He gave an IQ of 67 and recommended ESN(M) schooling, but the parents arranged for the child to remain at normal school.

Younger psychologists tended to see themselves as part of a team. One said: 'The educational psychologist is really more a member of a team. An ESN head may want a psychological assessment of why a child has failed in ordinary school, so we may pull in other team members, for example, social workers, to help.' But older psychologists saw themselves more as individual professionals. By and large educational psychologists expressed satisfaction that by the 1970s they had achieved parity of esteem with the medical profession in the assessment process and regarded medical officers as fellow-professionals, but they were still wary of medical encroachment into what they now regarded as their province. 'The MOs are important in the initial screening of physical attributes, but they are annoyingly irrelevant if they duplicate information, particularly if they do IQ tests and don't pass the information on to us.' 'The doctors should not go around making educational decisions about children.' Psychologists' strongest criticisms were directed at the central administration. They felt that the assessment decisions were 'a mutual balance between medical and psychologist offices' and regarded what one psychologist described as a 'faceless administration' as a danger to their professional expertise.

Psychologists were the professionals most sensitive to the position of parents in the assessment process, although several saw parents as potential problems. One said that 'if parents don't agree, I've considered the certification procedure, although I don't see the point of sending a child to a school the parents don't approve of. My parents are usually frightened and anxious.'

Psychologists felt that communication between professionals would be improved with the new SE forms. They were unanimous in their condemnation of the HP (Handicapped Pupil) forms. As one said 'the HP was part of the structure — you read through the information and often it was out of date or totally inadequate — so you went about collecting your own information.' A major source of anxiety on the part of psychologists was that the summary form SE4 might be filled out by an administrator who had not actually seen the child to make a professional judgement.

Medical officers

Under the Mental Deficiency Act of 1913 and an Education Act in 1914 LEAs were required to ascertain and certify children who were considered to be defective, and to provide education for educable defective children. School medical officers, first appointed in 1907, were to play a primary role in the ascertainment and certification process. The medical profession was, after all, the most prestigious profession involved. After 1944 the requirement for a medical examination to determine whether a child was handicapped continued to be statutory and after the 1948 National Health Act the School Health Service remained under the aegis of the LEA – the Principal School Medical Officer being responsible to the Chief Education Officer. After the 1974 Health Service reorganization some confusion was created concerning the professional tasks and responsibilities of doctors who examined children put forward for special education. The Court Committee, reporting in 1976, had recommended the formation of District Handicap Teams to assess children in a hospital setting or a community-based medical centre. The Warnock Committee in 1978 said: 'We recognize that there would be considerable similarity between our assessment at stage 5 and assessment by a District Handicap Team' and recommended that multi-professional assessment should not be done in a hospital. In the Birmingham study one girl was being seen at a hospital by a district physician who had recommended her for ESN(M) education. Unaware of this, the professionals at the LEA child guidance clinic had tested the child and were trying to keep her out of ESN(M) schooling.

In the study, doctors tended to use rather deterministic social accounts of ESN(M) children, more so than any other professionals. In agreement with the Court Report, they did not consider that most ESN(M) children suffered from any medical pathology, but were likely to be of low socio-economic class – a 'rough child' as one MO put it. This accounting may be tautological, as the children referred as potentially ESN(M) are almost always of low socio-economic status and thus so, these are the only children the doctors will see.

Doctors' views of their own role in the assessment process were somewhat contradictory. They considered their role to be mainly 'physical', but at the same time thought it was their duty to involve themselves with the family and background of the child. As one doctor put it: 'We could be confined to just a medical role . . . but we extend beyond this, to look at the child in his whole environment.' Medical personnel were less willing to accept the intrusion of other professionals, particularly the psychologists, into what they considered to be traditionally their area of competence, and they were also less willing to see themselves as part of a team. Some doctors felt there had been an incursion into their role by psychologists. One older doctor, who in the 1950s had been one of only two MOs responsible for assessment, said: 'I felt the psychologists were taking over from us; they seldom followed up children as we did. I felt someone had to make the final decision and it was the doctor who was unbiased and could make a fair decision at a medical clinic.' Only one doctor, a young woman, thought the medical role should be subordinate to the psychologists: 'We should be on the periphery . . . . it amazes me to sit in case conferences and see people who are not concerned with education making educational decisions.'

In the study some conflict was noted between MOs and psychologists and between MOs and the central administration. In one case the school doctor and a psychiatrist thought a child should remain in his ordinary school, whereas the psychologist had recommended ESN(M) school. The head of the school was also pressing to have the child removed as he was disruptive, and eventually the doctors were over-ruled. In another case a doctor said: 'I didn't give a recommendation on principle, I was so cross at the change-over of procedures and no-one had told me what I was supposed to do.' On the other hand the doctors were also aware that the nature of the referral process made it possible for them to play a subversive role and collude with schools who might wish to circumvent a psychological decision about a child.

The doctors, in particular, felt that they were embroiled in administrative and communication problems, not made any easier by the 1974 reorganization. They felt they were not kept fully informed of decisions, that the central administration might manipulate their decisions, that forms did not arrive or were incomplete and that 'only the telephone keeps our heads above water'. They showed little enthusiasm for the SE forms. One doctor ascribed their own SE2 form as 'daft . . . it's more to do with teachers'. This comment may illustrate the doctors' anxieties that a medical role was being minimized. However, the doctors had developed strategies to overcome their problems. As one doctor put it: 'I ignore the headings, I write what I want', and another said: 'I write what I shouldn't. I write about behaviour and emotional problems on the forms.'

In the majority of cases, of course, there is co-operation between educational, medical and psychological personnel in the assessment processes, and praise for each other's professional skills. However, conflicts and antagonisms are present and demonstrate the idealistic

nature of the ideology of 'smooth teamwork'. The additional involvement of other professionals adds to the strains. As a psychiatrist put it:
'Between professional people working like this there are bound to be
resentments and jealousies.'

Special school heads

The heads of special schools, although not directly involved in the
assessment processes, do have powers to refuse a child entry, or hold
up entry to their schools. Thus they can shape the definition of an
ESN(M) child, in that such a child is literally one who has attended an
ESN(M) school. One of the tasks of special school heads is to collect all
the documents and forms on which other professionals have recorded
their decisions. But they are not too happy about the efficiency of the
administration. They noted that records often ended up incomplete
and did not think the new SE forms adequately recorded information
on children. One head of a special school remarked that the central
administration was 'more concerned with running an efficient
bureaucracy than with the needs of children.'

Parents and professionals

While professing a caring humanitarianism, professionals do have very
real power to affect the lives of whole families whose children are
referred for special education. Despite a rhetoric of parental involvement, to be found both in the Warnock Report and the 1980 White
Paper, there is as yet no formal machinery in the assessment process
for involving parents and no democratic structure which considers
parents as equal participants with a right to be involved in decisions
about their children. The working-class parents of educationally subnormal children in particular have always been regarded with some
apprehension by professionals. Since it was by no means certain that
parents would co-operate in the admission of their children to special
schools a certification procedure developed, was retained in the 1944
Act, and no change in 'enforceable procedures' is envisaged for the
future, certainly not for 'recorded' children. The rights of parents of
'non-recorded' children are also in doubt.[1]

Literature on the parents of handicapped children has tended to
stress their probable incompetence and need for professional help and
advice, and confidential files have always been the rule rather than the
exception. Social class is an important consideration in parental
involvement. Largely middle-class parental pressure groups working on
behalf of a variety of the more severe handicaps have developed, and
the journal *Parents' Voice* is influential. However the majority of

parents with children in special ESN(M) education have no voice. The connections between low socio-economic status, mild educational subnormality and badly behaved children, have probably contributed to inadequate parental involvement and consultation. Middle-class professionals do not generally consult as equals lower-class parents whom by and large they regard as incompetent.

The parents in the Birmingham study did not feel that they were sufficiently informed about professional decisions on their children, and did not feel the professionals discussed matters with them in a manner they could understand. They felt 'pushed around' by a complex system. One father, whose child had been seen by at least a dozen professionals, summed it all up: 'We were helped by one. The rest can go to hell.'

Even parents who had sought help were frustrated by what they saw as the indifference of professionals and their own lack of knowledge about the processes. Parents in the study regarded referring head teachers as the most important professional they had to deal with, and they depended on the referring school to let them know what was going on. However, they did feel that this was often a matter of 'being sent for and told' rather than being consulted. As one parent put it: 'The head sent for us but he didn't tell us what was wrong. Nobody tells us anything.' Although parents were uneasily aware of some legal compulsion concerning special education the position was rarely explained to them, and professionals were anxious to play this down and 'persuade' parents to accept special education. Parents did not really understand the educational psychologist's importance in the assessment process and only two out of forty parents knew about the significance of IQ testing procedures. They were clearer about medical involvement and anxious to have their children medically examined, but were confused when doctors introduced educational matters: 'The doctor knocked his knees and measured his head and said there was nothing wrong with him but his brain.' Parents were generally afraid to question the judgements of professionals even when they felt they were wrong, and professionals did not appear to do a very good job explaining their own role and discretionary powers. They did not appear to discuss the children in terms parents could understand or treat parents as equal and caring people in the process. Professionals, by and large, were more concerned to persuade parents to agree peaceably to their children entering special education and to play down the legal sanctions available if persuasion failed.

But this brings us back to the original point made in this paper. Professionals in general claim a right to practise the arts or sciences they 'profess' to know, and to give advice and help derived from their expertise. Professionals ask to be trusted by their clients. This, of course, poses problems in special education, where clients have little choice but to depend on professionals and have less power to question their judgements.

The increasing power of professionals

The new processes of referral and assessment for an expanded special education system will increase the number and type of professionals whose judgements are used to separate special children from ordinary children in schools. The adoption of the concept of 'special educational needs' as a rationale for this separation, and the abolition of statutory categories of handicap are likely to give more, not less, power to professional people. While the assessment processes beyond stage 3 will increase the numbers of psychological and medical personnel plus other professionals such as social workers, and speech therapists, it is educationalists, particularly heads and teachers in normal education, who will have increased powers to decide that larger numbers of children have special needs, and special educators who will have expanded professional interests in making provision for these children, in special units and classes as well as separate schools.

Teachers in special education were for many years regarded as the Cinderellas of the teaching profession, although the first special schools association was founded in 1903 and the NUT established a special section in 1922. Suggested new procedures and provision will enhance the status and powers of special educators in particular.

The expansion of the numbers of special children envisaged by the Warnock Report will be largely brought about by bringing children currently classed as remedial in ordinary schools, into a descriptive category with the current ESN(M) children – all to be known as children with learning difficulties. Children currently known as disruptive are also to be brought officially into special education. Thus, the profession of special educators, plus local authority advisers and educational psychologists who will take part in assessment up to stage 3, will be given a vastly increased clientele.

This clientele will largely be composed of the relatively powerless kind of people found in the Birmingham study – working-class and black parents who often lack understanding about what is happening to their children, can be mystified and persuaded by professional expertise and jargon, and have little legal redress in the face of professional judgements.

Given the proposed increase in their numbers and powers, it would seem desirable that all the professionals involved in special education should, despite their undoubted concern for individual children, recognize that much of what happens in special education is as much to do with their own particular vested interests as with the 'needs' of children.

This paper has attempted to show how professionals actually work together in referring and assessing children for one type of special education, and how the 'teamwork' of professionals is fraught with anxieties and problems. Professionals do have enormous powers over the lives of relatively powerless and vulnerable sections of the population. Professionals must be able to see their actions within a wider social and political context than that of simply helping individuals and catering for 'special needs'.

Note

1 Under the terms of the 1980 White Paper children already ascertained as requiring special education, and those proceeding beyond stage 3 of new assessment procedures will be deemed 'recorded'. Parents will have a right to appeal against recording to an LEA appeals committee established by the 1980 Education Act. The findings of the committee will not be binding on the LEA. For 'non-recorded' children (those who do not progress beyond stage 3 of assessment) arrangements governing the choice of schools and school attendance procedures established by the 1980 Act will apply.

References

Burt, C. (1935) *The Subnormal Mind*, London, Oxford University Press.

DES (1975) *The Discovery of Children Requiring Special Education and the Assessment of their Needs*, Circular 2/75, London, HMSO.

DES (1978) *Special Educational Needs. Report of the Committee of Enquiry into the Education of Handicapped Children and Young People* (Warnock Report), London, HMSO.

DES (1980) *Special Needs in Education* (White Paper), Cmnd. 7996, London, HMSO.

DHSS (1976) *Fit for the Future. Report of the Committee on Child Health Services* (Court Report), London, HMSO.

Hughes, E. C. (1965) Anomalies and Projections, *Daedalus*, 94, 1133–47.

Hughes, E. C. (1971) *The Sociological Eye*, Chicago, Aldine.

ILEA (1967) *The Education of Immigrant Pupils in Special Schools for ESN Children*, Report No. 657, London, ILEA.

Tansley, A. E. and Gulliford, R. (1960) *The Education of Slow Learning Children*, London, Routledge and Kegan Paul.

Tomlinson, S. (1981) *Educational Sub-Normality: A Study in Decision Making*, London, Routledge and Kegan Paul.

4.4 The provision of health services to handicapped children and their families

THE COURT REPORT

In 1973, the Committee of Enquiry into Child Health Services was set up by the Secretary of State for Health and Social Services under the chairmanship of Professor Donald Court. Although the official motivation for the committee was the need to solve some of the problems that came in the wake of the NHS reorganization in 1973, it was clear that child health services badly needed to improve. Britain had fallen behind many other Western countries in infant mortality and morbidity, there were wide variations in the health chances of children from different social classes, and services for handicapped children were fragmented, inefficient and ineffective.

The fate that befell the Court Report's recommendations was the combined opposition of professional medical organizations, insufficient public resources and government inaction. The Report has never been debated in the House of Commons and only three recommendations have been formally accepted. In the light of vague and general support for the Committee's 'philosophy' from successive governments, the health authorities have reacted slowly and partially; most recommendations await implementation.

In these extracts we have selected what the committee proposed as solutions to the problems of organizational divisions between preventive medicine and treatment, between hospital and community services and between different professions, and the need to protect the rights and responsibilities of parents.

A child and family-centred service

The special needs of children which arise from the fact that they are growing developing persons should be reflected in the facilities that are provided for them and, perhaps more important, in the training of those who care for them. *We want to see a service which is child-centred and we believe that this must be a service in which the profes-*

Source: DHSS/DES (1976) *Fit for the Future, Report of the Committee on Child Health (The Court Report)*, London, HMSO *sional staff are adequately trained and experienced in the special needs of children.*

This has implications first for the attitude of professionals. They should see their task not as usurping the responsibility of the family but as encouraging it, so that families are better able to exercise their responsibility for their children. They should see themselves as partners with parents: prepared and willing to give them explanation and advice about their children's health. And because parents have differing aspirations and backgrounds, they should help parents to make plans in ways which take account of family identity and individuality. Parents' understanding of children's development and illness varies widely and this is due in part to the poverty of professional communication. There can be no doubt that all too often parents feel they are passive bystanders rather than active partners in the care of their children. *The need is for a service that is geared to ensuring that parents are well informed and increasingly involved in their children's development and health, and which from the start will enable them to feel confident in their ability to care for their children.* [. . .]

An integrated service

It is a matter of providing a service which sees the child as his parents see him, as a whole person, whose life is a continuum rather than a series of segments. Parents should not have to draw distinctions between 'pre-school' and 'school'. *There should be one service which follows the child's development from the early pre-school years, through school and adolescence.* School may often present particular problems: if the child suffers ill-health a parent wants to be confident that his teachers will understand and be advised by doctors and nurses of the implications for his education and his care whilst in school. Parents should of course have ready access to the appropriate teacher, but they need doctors and nurses who can guide them with educational difficulties and unusual behaviour, and make sure that the child is not struggling with a developmental disorder or with physical illness, rather than with an educational difficulty. There is therefore a need for professional staff who not only have an understanding of educational medicine but can interpret the child's behaviour at school in the light of his behaviour out of it. A strong health service in school is an essential part of a good child health service. Similarly adolescence often produces renewed parental concern about personal behaviour. At a time when conventional adult attitudes and the authority of those who hold them may well be rejected, conventional health care may be rejected too. Yet professional help is often needed, and it has to be offered in ways which show understanding of the adolescent's particular problems of development and adjustment to the adult world.

The need for an integrated approach to health care is particularly great in the case of the handicapped child. Parents understandably want a single door leading to assessment, explanation and treatment. They need a coordinated service of care, therapy and education, with regular reviews of the child's progress leading to advice and support. They need an extension of services beyond the normal school leaving age until their child is effectively cared for by health services for adults, and by the Employment Medical Advisory Service. They also need ready access to the professional staff involved in treatment, especially to someone who has accepted personal responsibility for their child.

Equally parents should not have to attempt in making their first approach to the health services to draw a distinction between 'treatment' and 'prevention'. *The child health service should be able to provide families with a single identifiable source to which they can turn for skilled advice and where necessary treatment*, whenever they feel that they need to.

Some children will need specialized assessment and treatment. *So far as possible primary and specialist care should also be seen as a coordinated service.* Parents should not feel that there is a break in continuity of care when they are referred to the hospital-based services. Paediatric and specialist services are still for the most part hospital-based and concerned mainly with the treatment of acute illness. *In future we see these services having closer contacts with families, schools and communities in which children grow up.* They must continue to extend specialist interest to the problems of chronic illness, handicap, and problems of disturbed behaviour.

Equally if the specialist services are to play a full part in the child health services, *further efforts must be made to strengthen the practice of paediatrics within the hospital services.* Despite the fact that paediatrics, the recognition of the special needs of children, has largely developed in a hospital setting, there is still much that needs to be done to give practical effect to the principles on which it is based. Whenever admission to hospital is required it should be to a children's department which should be able to accommodate not only children with paediatric problems but those of the allied specialties too. Whatever hospital department a child attends the surroundings and facilities should be appropriate for children. There should be staff trained to meet both the personal as well as the technical needs of the child, and the need for play for younger, and teaching for older children, and for explanation and for comfort from a resident parent or visiting family, should be recognized. Above all these principles need to be applied to the care of the long-stay patient, and in particular to the handicapped.

We have argued that parents should feel that whether their child's problem is simple or complex, whether their need is for treatment or advice, guidance and support, and at whatever stage in his development it occurs, they are dealing with an integrated service. But the case for a more closely coordinated child health service can also be strongly supported on professional grounds as well. There is no place for hospital services which are separate from community services or community care which cannot move easily into a hospital setting. There is no place for developmental medicine which does not see the child also in educational terms. There is also no place for preventive or advisory services which are wholly divorced from treatment services. All trained doctors who are involved in the clinical care of children must be empowered to treat as well as to ascertain, diagnose or advise. Our argument rests on the nature of current health problems. Since so many of these have their origins in family or environmental circumstances, since so many have long term implications for a child's development, his ability to learn and benefit from education, we believe that their successful treatment and management cannot be carried out without understanding of the developmental aspects of child health and of the two major formative influences on a child's development, his family and his school. *An integrated service must include at every level both developmental and educational medicine as well as the treatment of acute illness.* [. . .]

[In Chapter 10 of the Report, the Committee turned its attention to the implications of the concept of an integrated service for health services in schools:]

Inter-professional collaboration

We stress the need for both doctors' and nurses' training to give greater understanding of the aims of education and the experience of teachers, and of the role of social workers, to pay more attention to inter-professional collaboration. These are required initially and again during post-graduate training. Joint in-service training of medical, nursing, teaching and social work staff should be arranged by AHAs, LEAs and LASSDs.[1]

The Committee was not empowered to consider the provision of social work services to schools. Nevertheless our recommendations concerning health services in schools presuppose a comparable development of social work services. We have been at pains throughout our report to emphasize the inter-relationship of health, educational and social factors in a child's development. The length of time that the majority of children spend at school makes it a unique setting in which preventive and remedial work may be carried out. Hence it is crucial that the balance between a child's health needs and his educational and social needs be understood, and effective cooperation between the three authorities and between their professional staff be established. Continuity of association as equals seems to us to be the surest method of obtaining this.

For the doctors and nurses in the child health services, this means that as far as possible they be appointed to provide services to specified communities of children defined with due regard to the schools and other institutions they may attend, and that they assume a more personal professional responsibility than has been customary for seeing that the necessary services reach 'their' children. This thinking informs both the proposal for the GPP[2] to have a special contract as school doctor to certain nominated schools in the vicinity of his practice and for the consultant community paediatrician[3] to be under contract to provide supporting services in educational medicine to schools within his district. *We recommend that such direct responsibility for a school or schools within a district be adopted as a matter of principle in the staffing and organization of educational health services.* Organizational obligations of this kind can only ensure that opportunities are created for inter-professional cooperation. We believe our proposals for the initial and in-service training of staff in general, and of health service staff specifically, will ensure that such opportunities are not ignored.

Conclusions [on health and education]

Our references to educational health services and the emphasis we have placed on the need for each school to have its own doctor and nurse might seem to imply that we visualize the continuation of a discrete school health service. This is not our intention, for it would be to depart from our central conviction that continuity of health care for school children no less than other children requires that their health services be based upon primary care by specially trained doctors centred in general practice, with close professional support from consultant paediatricians and allied specialists. This leads rationally to the primary medical component of educational health care being provided by GPPs.

We believe our recommendations would give the schools and the education authority a service that would incorporate the very best features of the school health service as it has developed since 1908[4] and allow necessary new developments in both primary and supporting care to take place as part of a new, integrated and much better trained child health service. Every school would have in first line support a school nurse and a school doctor both of whom would be appropriately trained, with time to maintain an interest in educational health care, the learning process and the aims of the education service, and both of whom would have the opportunity to assume a more personal professional responsibility than has been customary for seeing that the necessary services reach 'their' children. Every special school would have as their school doctor a consultant paediatrician experienced and skilled in the total health care of handicapped children; and that paediatrician would have the duty to provide consultant services in educational medicine throughout his district. Every LEA would continue to have the advice and expertise of the Area Specialist in Community Medicine (Child Health)[5] and the Area Nurse (Child Health)[6] who would be responsible for planning and ensuring the quality of the services.

The general change in climate of opinion regarding the role of parents in effective education needs to extend to the educational health service so that parents feel more able to understand and make use of the services and feel more supported and needed by them. We believe that our recommendations for the school entrance medical examination, regular health surveillance during school life and better training of and communication between doctors, teachers and parents should facilitate this change of climate. [. . .]

[Handicapped children and their parents perhaps require the benefits of an integrated service more than any other group. Chapter 14 considered their needs:]

Parents, professionals and handicapped children

Parents of handicapped children have much to gain, like their children, from the pattern of services we have proposed; but they also have their own special service needs, for they face problems in bringing up handicapped children which are additional to and to some extent different from the problems facing all parents. It is evident for instance, that families of handicapped children often get little relief from the economic and social difficulties that arise because they care for the handicapped child. These often mount as the child gets older and circumstances change. They are commonly worse off than families with children suffering from acute disease, though their burdens are usually more severe and last much longer. We foresee the advice, counselling, and practical help from NOs/CHV[7] and social workers, the improved domiciliary service, and the increased day and residential facilities which we have advised, as substantially meeting many of these problems.

However, parents of handicapped children have two other service needs of a different kind. First is the need to be treated as participants and not by-standers in the process of assessment and decision-making. When the child lives at home it is the parents who have to report on his function and behaviour, and monitor his progress. And because it is usually best for the child to continue to live in his own home, it is they who will be largely looking after the child from day to day. It is therefore as necessary for parents as for professionals to understand the child's level of abilities, his strengths and weaknesses, and the association between his handicap and behaviour problems that may exist or threaten. And to care for the child successfully at home they need support in their wish to keep him at home, for most of these parents are affectionate, and interested to make the most of their child's ability however limited this may be and despite the cost to themselves. Frequently they need to be reassured that just because he is handicapped, even severely so, this does not mean that he would be better off in hospital or cared for by professional people. And when residential care or schooling is thought to be necessary for either the child or, as more often, the parents or their family, they need time to consider the complex issues, to overcome their reluctance to part with the child, or to resolve to keep him at home against advice if they wish. To make a decision they need such information and advice as is available about the likely consequences for the child and for themselves and their family, of different courses of action: and they need to be allowed to change their minds without loss of face.

We are concerned that parents of handicapped children are not sufficiently involved or even consulted when decisions about treatment and management are made; they are simply told of them. Thus they frequently feel excluded from the treatment regime, caretakers of the child rather than partakers in his treatment. They are not given to understand how their day to day management of the child is an essential feature of therapy nor are they sufficiently often instructed in specific therapeutic procedures (e.g. physiotherapy, speech therapy, or behaviour therapy) to continue these at home. Consequently, they tend to see services as being offered too much as a substitute for, rather than a supplement to their own efforts. Successful care within the family would be much easier if the potential contribution of parents to assessment and therapy were more widely recognized and welcomed.

Arising from this partnership no less than because as front-line therapists they need access to health, educational and social service staff, *we think parents should have the right of direct access to the district handicap team*[8] *and others concerned in the treatment of their child.* It is usually thought that to open professional doors to parents might lead to problems of overlapping responsibilities and uncoordinated care. But the possibility of such administrative difficulties should not be an excuse for denying parents access to the help they feel they need. It should serve only to underline the importance of each professional, when approached, accepting a personal responsibility for coordinating any action he may advise or take with that programmed by the team. We are aware that some parents may 'shop' their handicapped child around, seeking for what professionals might regard as an unattainable cure but this is a manifestation of unmet need that should not be suppressed but recognized, and supported with the best advice and guidance.

We have referred to the sensitivity that needs to be shown in telling parents that their newborn child has a congenital defect. Similar understanding is required in discussing handicaps that may subsequently arise. At these times parents also need to feel that there is a network of people and services ready to help them. Such a network must include not only the statutory services but also self-help groups and voluntary bodies. These latter can be of particular importance in ameliorating any feeling of isolation and in providing continuing practical assistance when professional resources are limited. For parents to derive benefit from such groups, they must first be made aware of them. Hence professional health staff must see the dissemination of information as an important function of their job. Regrettably, in the evidence we received, lack of information was an often-mentioned criticism. The committee received one telling piece of evidence from the mother of a mentally handicapped child:

On reflection we feel that, medically, everything possible had been done for Rachel. Now we were left to cope with the problem alone, a problem which we and our families had never before experienced; for the first time in our lives we needed help, and none was offered. The doctors could only suggest we treat Rachel as a normal baby (!!) and the health visitor, though a good listener, could suggest nothing.

After the very, very unhappy months, literally torn between suicide or murder, as the only solutions to an otherwise insoluble problem, I happened to notice in the local paper a small advertisement for a Christmas charity dance — proceeds to the local playgroup for mentally handicapped children. I was staggered! Were there really enough of these children to support a playgroup? Why hadn't the health visitor known of such a group? This playgroup turned out to be my salvation . . . I met other young mothers of handicapped children, and through them I began to adjust to my problem and slowly to cope with it.

Notes

1 AHA: Area Health Authority; LEA: Local Education Authority; LASSD: Local Authority Social Services Department. (Ed.)
2 GPP: General Practitioner Paediatrician. The Report proposed this new position to be filled by GPs who have completed appropriate training in paediatrics. The GPP was intended to be the key part of the proposed comprehensive primary care. (Ed.)
3 This position was proposed as a new type of consultant paediatrician to be the specialist counterpart to the GPP. It was recommended that each health district should have at least one CCP. (Ed.)
4 1908 saw the implementation of the Education (Administrative Provisions) Act, 1907, which affirmed local authorities' existing duty to inspect children medically and empowered them to attend to the health of children in elementary schools. (Ed.)
5 Specialists in Community Medicine (Child Health) were created in 1974. Their responsibilities are to plan and organize child health services in the community and in hospitals, to advise LEAs on medical care, and plan and provide health services to LEAs. (Ed.)
6 The Area Nurse (Child Health): an administrative position responsible for the co-ordination of nursing services in schools. (Ed.)
7 NO: Nursing Officer; CHV: Child Health Visitor. (Ed.)
8 The Report recommended the establishment of multi-disciplinary teams in each health district to provide diagnostic, assessment and treatment facilities for handicapped children. (Ed.)

PART 5

Power and Policy in Special Education

5.1 Demystifying integration

TONY BOOTH

The outcome of debates about integration will influence not only the educational experiences of handicapped children, but also the lives and tasks of special educators, the nature of ordinary schools, the roles of professionals and the job of administration. There has been much talk of integration since the Warnock Report gave the idea qualified approval. Tony Booth examines official policy statements towards integration and recent trends in the placement of children with special needs, and he proposes some factors that may account for these trends.

Is integration occurring?

Introduction

I was prompted to examine the facts which form the basis of this article because many people were expressing views which were at variance with my own experience. I heard of fears that large numbers of handicapped children were being 'dumped' into ordinary classrooms without appropriate support; that there was a 'bandwagon' of integrationists who were pushing through plans for integrated education without careful preparation. My own experience of working as an educational psychologist for a local education authority and of watching special schools open and fill had indicated a trend in the reverse direction.

I noticed too that some people gained a different impression than I did from the reading of official pronouncements and reports. Thus plans for integration were said to be 'in line with Warnock'. Yet when I read the Warnock Report myself I was unable to derive any clear implication for a shift in educational policy to a position where fewer handicapped children would be educated in segregated forms of provision. I felt that both the official pronouncements and the trends in provision warranted further investigation.

However before we can make any assessment of whether integration is taking place we have to decide on the definition of integration we are using, the children to whom we are referring and the time period involved. I have defined integration in education as *a process of increas-*

Specially commissioned for this volume
©The Open University, 1981

*ing children's participation in the educational and social life of com-
prehensive primary and secondary schools.* Clearly this definition can
be applied to all children, not only those currently regarded as having
special needs. Most children could participate in education to a greater
extent and it would be interesting to know whether schools are now
more adept at responding to the needs and interests of children than
they were ten years ago. That would be one criterion on which to judge
whether the participation of children in education had increased though
it would be exceedingly difficult to gather evidence about it. I am
choosing to look at a rather simpler issue in this article. Is there a
tendency for children, conventionally regarded as handicapped and
often educated in special schools, to be educated in less segregated
forms of provision?

You can think of the continuum of provision for different groups of
handicapped children as represented in Table 1:

Table 1 Continuum of provision for handicapped pupils

Unsupported member of ordinary class in ordinary school
In ordinary class with support of teaching aide
In ordinary class + withdrawal to resource base
Ordinary class part-time special class part-time
Special class full-time
Day special school part-time
Day special school full-time
Residential special school
Hospital + hospital school

If integration were occurring we would expect to find a decreasing use
of forms of provision at the bottom of the list and an increasing use of
forms of provision nearer the top of the list. Of course such a change of
placement could not constitute integration by itself. It could only be a
first step in providing the opportunity for a handicapped child to
participate in ordinary school life through the development of an
appropriate curriculum and level of support.

The existence of an educational continuum does not imply a similar
'ideal' and point for each child. For each child there will be a point
along the continuum where a maximum level of participation can be
achieved, a 'least restrictive environment', as the Americans call it. For
some handicapped children the achievement of their least restrictive
environment might actually involve movement from the top of the
continuum to a point further down as their needs were identified and
met. However for any degree or category of handicap we can usually

find an example of education in the normal school in some part of the UK and this is strong evidence that many children could be educated in less segregated forms of provision. This must be an assumption behind any advocacy of the integration principle.

One indicator, then, of whether integration is occurring would be a decrease in the proportion of handicapped children attending special schools. I will consider the period 1950–77 for which the comparative statistics are readily available and which is sufficiently long for trends in provision to be apparent. It is a period which coincides, too, with a large overall growth in the numbers on school rolls. In looking at trends in the past people have neglected to relate changes in numbers of handicapped pupils to changes in the total school population. Is there, then, a decreasing proportion of handicapped pupils attending special schools?

The authorized version

Let us look at several publications in which our question appears to be answered. In the DES booklet (1974) entitled *Integrating Handicapped Children* we find the following statements:

> Opinion today is coming increasingly to favour the 'integration' into ordinary schools of more of the severely handicapped children who are usually placed in special schools.
> The extent to which this is already taking place is perhaps not commonly realized. (DES, 1974, p. 3)

The Warnock Report contains this clear statement:

> It has been long-standing government policy, confirmed in numerous official documents, that no child should be sent to a special school who can be satisfactorily educated in an ordinary one. There has in fact been a steady increase over time in the number of children ascertained as handicapped who have been placed in designated special classes and units in ordinary schools. It rose from 11,027 in 1973 to 21,245 in 1977, that is from 6.8% to 12.0% of all children ascertained as requiring separate special provision. The children placed in these classes and units have been mainly those with moderate rather than severe disabilities, but all categories of handicap are represented. They still form quite a small proportion of all handicapped children for whom special education is provided, but the trend is likely to continue. Although the existence of such classes and units does not necessarily entail integration in any

complete sense, nevertheless it is a proof that segregation is diminishing. (DES, 1978a, p. 99)

Chazan *et al.* (1980) in *Some of Our Children*, an investigation into early special needs and provision, tells us:

> However, in spite of the advantages of special schooling, there has been an increasing disinclination to remove children from the mainstream of education except where no viable alternative arrangements can be made. It is felt by many that the special school separates children from their fellows, so that they may lack the stimulation derived from mixing with the non-handicapped, and exacerbates the stigma often attached to handicapping conditions. Section 10 of the Education Act of 1976 firmly established the principle that handicapped children should be educated in ordinary schools unless it would be impracticable to arrange this. Although the full operation of this enactment has been left in abeyance, it has long been the policy of many local authorities to integrate as many handicapped children as possible in normal classes, and if this proves impossible, to place them in special units within, or attached to, ordinary schools. (Chazan *et al.*, 1980, p. 122)

And lastly the Government White Paper (DES, 1980) has this to say:

> There has been a marked shift in public attitudes towards separate provision for handicapped pupils. More and more people believe that, in order to give handicapped persons the same opportunities as other citizens, they should be involved in the ordinary processes of life and work to the maximum extent, and be integrated in their education with those who are not handicapped. An increasing number of LEAs and teachers are tackling in ordinary schools the additional needs of children, particularly those with physical and sensory handicaps, in every age group. . . . The Government intends that the process of planned and sensible integration of handicapped children into ordinary schools should continue. (DES, 1980, pp. 9 and 13)

I presume like me you take these extracts to state or imply an increasing reluctance to send children to special schools. However are they right? The answer is contained, surprisingly, in two of the sources I mentioned.

The reality

The last twenty-five years have seen a very considerable expansion of the provision made for handicapped children outside ordinary schools. The number of special schools (including hospital schools) in England and Wales increased from 601 in 1950 to 1,653 in 1977 and the number of handicapped children attending them full-time from 47,119 to 135,261. In Scotland the number of special schools increased from 84 in 1950 to 229 in 1976, the number of pupils attending them from about 10,000 to 12,322. (Warnock Report, DES, 1978a, p. 121)

Over the past two decades the number of handicapped children in special schools has more than trebled. (Chazan *et al.*, 1980, p. 122)

I find the juxtaposition of these two trends within the same publication and in the last case on the same page quite difficult to fathom. In Chazan's book we actually find them vying for control of the same sentence. in the opening paragraph of the introduction to his book we find this intriguing statement: 'Not only has the provision of special schools and units greatly expanded but it has been increasingly recognised that many children should and can be catered for in ordinary schools.'

But an inspection of the DES statistics for education does bear out the increasing use of special school placement for handicapped children. In Table 2 I have analysed the figures for placement in special school as a proportion of the total school population. The trend towards segregation is actually exaggerated by both Chazan and the Warnock Report since the school population increased by 50 per cent between 1950 and 1977.

Few people, of course, would suggest that the process of integration was occurring at the start of this period though government rhetoric in its favour was already in evidence. But clearly the proportion of children in special schools has increased throughout this time. There is an apparent easing off in the trend after 1972 but as the authorities have noted there has been a contemporaneous and rapid growth in designated special classes. There has also been a considerable increase in certain categories of special provision which are not included in the special education statistics. The growth of disruptive units described in an HMI survey (DES, 1978b) is the major example of such an increase.

In Table 3 I have analysed the trends in special school provision by official category of handicap. I have expressed the numbers in each

Table 2 Percentage of school population in special schools, 1950—77

Year	1950	1955	1960	1965	1970	1972	1975	1976	1977
Special school population (nearest thousand)	47,000	58,000	66,000	74,000	87,000	122,000	132,000	134,000	135,000
School population (nearest thousand)	6,315,000	7,199,000.	7,620,000	7,760,000	8,597,000	9,033,000	9,617,000	9,669,000	9,664,000
% of school population in special school	0.75	0.81	0.86	0.96	1.01	1.35[a]	1.37	1.38	1.39[b]

Source: DES, Statistics, 1976; 1977.

[a] The jump in the size of the special school population between 1970 and 1972 can be largely attributed to the incorporation of the severely mentally handicapped into education provision between those dates.

[b] The 1977 figures of approx. 1.4 per cent rises to 2 per cent if we include those children who have been ascertained as handicapped and attend special classes or are awaiting special placement.

Table 3 Pupils in category of major handicap expressed as prevalence per million, 1950—77

	1950	1955	1960	1965	1970	1975	1977	Comments
Blind	176	166	171	157	128	121	129	Decrease 50 – 70
Partially sighted	247	255	235	238	228	232	228	Slight decreasing trend
Deaf	515	543	454	401	391	395	375	Clear decreasing trend
Partially hearing	152	208	191	208	225	242	226	Overall increase No recent trend
Physically handicapped	1,013	877	926	965	1,207	1,271	1,354	Clear increase
Maladjusted	93	172	229	374	709	1,399	1,416	Clear increase
Educationally subnormal moderate severe	2,402	3,145	4,306	5,499	6,022	5,484 2,068	5,763 2,363	Clear increase
Delicate	1,704	1,704	1,394	1,091	750	491	456	Marked drop in numbers
Epileptic	117	110	98	105	118	229	217	Slight recent decrease
Speech defect	57	78	16	26	96	717	488	Recent decrease
Autistic	Figures not distinguished before 1974					56	58	No trend

Note: the figures for 1965 and 1970 include a single total for severely and moderately handicapped pupils.

category as a prevalence per million of the school population. The table indicates, quite clearly, that different groups of categorized children have been subject to different trends. Children with sensory handicaps, particularly the blind, the deaf and the partially sighted, appear to be less likely now to attend a special school than in the past. Certainly there has been a growth of units for children with sensory handicaps in ordinary schools and these sometimes take children who were previously sent away to residential special schools.

There is an equally clear trend for the physically handicapped, the educationally subnormal and the maladjusted. In each of these cases there has been an increase in segregated special schooling with the growth in numbers for the latter groups being quite spectacular.

The number of children categorized as delicate has dropped markedly. This is hardly surprising since the schools were established to provide an open-air cure for unhealthy children from inner-city areas. Children are generally healthier nowadays and we do not have quite the same approach to rigorous purging cures. Children identified as having a speech defect as their major category have experienced a promotion and subsequent demotion. Between 1970 and 1975 there was more than a seven-fold increase in children categorized in that way but after 1975 I suspect there has been a trend to reabsorb them into other categories, particularly the moderately subnormal.

Changes in prevalence

I have already suggested that the diminution of the group of children labelled 'delicate' is part of an explanation of the falling number of delicate pupils. There is one possible explanation for the trends in Tables 2 and 3 which would be compatible with a policy of increasing integration. For in my interpretation of the trends I have assumed that the proportion of handicapped children in the population has remained static. But if, for example, the proportion of the total school population with a physical handicap had actually doubled in the last ten years, as might be the case after an epidemic of polio, then an increase in placement in special schools might not indicate a policy of segregation. A greater proportion might be in special schools but an even higher proportion might be in ordinary schools. Equally a drop in the relative numbers of children with sensory handicaps in special schools might be related to a fall in total numbers of children with sight and hearing difficulties. Could all the trends I have depicted be explained by changes in prevalence?

There are other known variations in the prevalence rates for physically handicapped children which have affected the figures.

Children with spina bifida are a pertinent case. In the early sixties it became medical policy to enable babies born with spina bifida associated with hydrocephalus to survive through corrective surgery. By the mid-seventies, however, once the development of a generation of such children, encouraged to survive, had been watched with some disappointment by a large body of the medical profession, decisions were taken not to prolong the lives of many such infants. In 1967 Knox had estimated that for a town the size of Birmingham the numbers of children with spina bifida surviving into special education could vary per year from five with conservative surgical policies to forty if all children received operations. There is some indication that improved obstetric procedures and early paediatric interventions may be adding slightly to the chances of survival of some babies born with physical handicaps. There have also been suggestions that the same measures have contributed to a decrease in cerebral palsy as a result of birth complications.

The issue of prevention and the changes in incidence of physical handicap are discussed by Golding (this volume, Chapter 1.3) and by Potts (1982a) and Booth (1982). Estimates of changes in incident rates involve complex and difficult calculations particularly when the total numbers and amount of change is actually small. There is, however, little to suggest that the overall trends in provision for physical and sensory handicaps can be explained by changes in prevalence.

The estimation of changes in the numbers of candidates for the moderately subnormal and maladjusted categories is an even more hazardous procedure. There does seem to be a widespread belief that problems in school are increasing and both declining educational standards and rising disruption have been cited as contributors to teacher stress and one might suppose increased referral and placement of children in special schools.

Robert Thornbury, in *The Changing Urban School*, offers a sensational picture of schools on the brink of chaos:

Urban education in Britain in the 1960s and 1970s was devastated by a demographic landslide and ravaged by epidemic maladjustment. Some 21 per cent of boys and 16 per cent of girls in the inner city playground exhibited aggressive and abnormal behaviour. Juvenile crimes of violence multiplied seventeen times in the twenty-five years before 1977. Schoolchildren in London and other major cities were often a year behind the national average in reading attainment at eleven years. . . . Beyond doubt, in London, Glasgow and many urban authorities the schools system, especially in new comprehensives or multi-ethnic neighbourhoods, was on the edge of total collapse. (Thornbury, 1978, pp. 3–4)

But while it is true that terrible conditions do exist in some places, are children actually more villainous and difficult than they were previously? An apparently straightforward question like this is, in fact, extremely difficult to answer. In 1975 the National Association of Schoolmasters reported on an investigation into trends in violence in schools. In the foreword to the book, L. F. Lowenstein gave this summary of their findings:

> It was hoped, when commencing this study, to show the public, and teachers and parents especially, the trends that violence and obstructive behaviour have taken over a period of time. It was especially hoped that some answer could be provided to the question 'Are violence and disruption, as well as vandalism etc, on the increase or are they being contained or, even better, being successfully overcome.' I am sad to say that these questions have not been answered to my satisfaction and probably even less so to those of the critical and even sceptical teacher. (NAS, 1975, p. 5)

Nigel Wright (1977) reviewed this and other evidence on behaviour in schools. He could find no evidence of 'growing disorder' based on anything other than 'anecdotes and the personal impressions of influential people'. In fact he found continuous references to 'the growing disorder' in schools from 1870 onwards, though in earlier times it was the elite public schools which were the focus of public consternation. Wright argues that the misdemeanours of children have become more public rather than more prevalent as the growing numbers of comprehensive schools came under media scrutiny. But what of falling standards? Could they account for the growth of ESN(M) provision? If norms of competence dropped there would still be 50 per cent above and below the norm though a difficulty might arise if the distribution of competence changed; if there actually were a disproportionate increase in the numbers of very poor readers for example. But while there were five Black Papers published between 1969 and 1977 depicting and analysing the death of British educational excellence there is little firm evidence that educational standards had changed one way or another since 1960. Over a longer period there has been an indisputable improvement in standards of literacy. Before 1939 there were three million adult illiterates whereas in the sixties and seventies in a larger population there were only two million who could not read well enough for their everyday needs (Wright, 1977).

This brief examination of changes in prevalence of handicap is by no means exhaustive. It can be seen, though, that such changes cannot provide a clear explanation for the trends in provision which is consistent with a policy of integration. And whilst large changes in prevalence might have accounted for the figures there is no attempt within the official statements I have mentioned to use such a possibility to account for apparent contradictions.

The sources of official error

What then are the sources of the official error? It certainly seems that the authors of the Warnock Report and Chazan *et al.* have been misled by a superficial and temporarily isolated examination of the growth in numbers of special classes. For one might be led to a possible interpretation of this trend as indicating a transfer of handicapped children from special schools to special classes in ordinary schools and hence as evidence of integration. But, in fact, the growth in special school provision taken together with a growth in the number of special classes indicates a general movement of handicapped children towards increasingly segregated forms of educational provision. However, this suggestion, that the authors concerned have made a simple error of interpretation, does not explain why they allow contradictory views to rest easily within the same publication.

I suggest that one component of their mistake lies in the very existence of an official view. In 1954, at the very start of the rapid expansion of special school provision documented in Table 2, the Ministry of Education Circular 276 said 'no handicapped child should be sent to a special school who can be satisfactorily educated in an ordinary school', and subsequent reports have stated that the change in policy entailed by this injunction was actually occurring. It is not surprising that people believe what they read in official reports or that such views should form a background of 'knowledge' which other writers include uncritically in their own work.

The passing on of myths is a less mysterious process than their creation. After all we don't have time to question everything. But how does it come about that the writers at the Department of Education and Science with their ready access to statistics actually publicize false trends? Recently an HMI at the DES actually predicted that the trend towards segregated provision for handicapped children would continue until 1985. He was certainly aware of the figures. I cannot pretend to know how this particular myth was formulated. I do suspect that the principle of integration which has been officially espoused since 1954 is in direct contradiction to the wish by the government department to offer reassurances about the unhindered continuation of special schools. The simultaneous presence in the same person of conflicting wishes is almost certain to lead to contradictory utterances.

If we wish to be logical we cannot assert a proposition and its opposite. But in ordinary language we can appear to get away with it. For we can say integration is occurring and integration is not occurring without contradiction either if we use the word 'integration' to refer to different groups of children or we give it a different meaning in each half of the statement. At the beginning of the article I defined integration as a process of *increasing* the participation of handicapped children in normal schools. Clearly it is possible to increase the participation of some children whilst decreasing the participation of others. However 'integration' is often used, not to define a process, but to define a state. Thus handicapped children are said to be integrated if they are in a normal classroom irrespective of whether they were always there and irrespective of the level of support they receive. So it becomes possible to maintain that *integration* is occurring because some handicapped children actually are in normal classrooms and that *segregation* is occurring because there is a process in operation whereby more handicapped children are educated in special schools and classes. It should come as no surprise, to discover that people can use language to mislead, without actually committing an overt offence of insincerity.

In my more cynical moments I am led to doubt the sincerity of many, including those who write government reports, who argue for the integration principle. For, logically, the belief that handicapped children should be educated alongside others in principle entails a desire to see this occurring in practice. Conversely a desire not to see this occurring in practice, to any great extent, implies the absence of this principle. 'I don't want it to happen but I think it should' is a strange refrain for policy makers and academics. But if they are insincere why do they say it in the first place?

In my even more cynical moments and in my desire to make human sense of what goes on around me I see the espousal of the integration principle coupled with a suggestion that integration is actually occurring as a neat way of promoting the opposite process. For if integration is occurring we don't have to promote it. If we don't promote it the forces which have led to an increase in segregation can continue without hindrance.

Why has special school provision increased?

What then are the factors which have contributed to the overall growth of special school provision? One event with an unambiguous effect was the 1970 educability law. As responsibility for severely subnormal children was transferred to education there was a jump in special school attendance. However, most other potential factors are far less clear in their action, and I will review a number of candidates and come to some assessment of them before considering possible future trends.

The desirability of special schooling

The impression given by government statements since the fifties is that there is a general adherence to what the 1980 White Paper calls 'the integration principle'. There is said to be a widespread moral commitment for handicapped and non-handicapped children to be educated in the same schools. A clear distinction is drawn between this principle and the problems involved in putting integration into practice.

I have already cast doubt on whether an integration principle is at all generally held. For if there were such a widespread moral commitment it would have very definite implications at the level of action. We would expect to find that, since the fifties, local authorities had examined a range of alternative provision and then chosen the one that was both practicable and *least restrictive in its operation*. Where a successful practice has been in operation for a number of years, like the classes for the severely subnormal in schools in the London Borough of Bromley, we would expect to see an extensive policy shift in other areas. As new books and journal articles emerge which document the possibility and practicality of less restrictive forms of provision for the blind, the physically handicapped, the 'moderately subnormal', the 'maladjusted', we would anticipate teachers and policy makers trooping off to witness examples of good practice which they could adapt to their own local circumstances. We would find administrators eagerly reallocating money from special education budgets to support the education of handicapped children in normal schools. Handicapped children of nursery age would be discouraged from entering special schools and integrated within local nurseries, a sector in which, as a poll conducted for the Warnock Committee revealed, many teachers are only too happy to include such children in their classes.

We would expect to see some schools, with the aid of advisory services and special school staff, actively engaged in devising link curricula for children with sensory handicaps or slow learners, an exercise which with the appropriate use of remedial, special school and advisory staff might be done within existing staffing levels. We would hope to find professional groups attempting to solve their problems for the delivery of services to integrated provision. We should be witnessing careful costing of alternative schemes.

Above all, and at the very least, adherence to the integration principle would lead each local authority to devise a coherent long-term plan setting out stage by stage the redirection of special education services towards a policy of real practical and effective integration. All this I contend would illustrate the principle in operation.

In 1975 Jessie Parfitt surveyed the attitudes, intentions and practices concerning the integration of handicapped children in Greater London. Of the twenty outer London education authorities thirteen appeared:

> to be fully committed to a segregated system of special education and to be very well satisfied with and proud of their special schools. Most admit children from 3; some have reduced this age to 2. . . . Few of these 13 boroughs try to keep handicapped children in ordinary schools, and some only agree to do so for the mildly handicapped under parental pressure. In such cases they were unable to obtain financial resources to provide any welfare assistance. Some of the officers stated that they appear to have over-estimated the number of special school places needed. As a result it was apparent, and in some cases explicit, that the option for any one handicapped child being placed in an ordinary school was not really open as the special school vacancies had first to be filled. (Parfitt, 1975, p. 10)

Of the remaining authorities four were 'trying to see how they could be more flexible' and only three espoused a 'more positive and committed policy of gradually increasing integration'. Of the last group one, Bromley, has not expanded its initial promise of innovative integration. Jessie Parfit concluded her survey with this judgement:

> The DES has always maintained that special education should be a second choice . . . [but] except in rare cases, the chances at present are that ordinary schools will not provide satisfactory education and therefore the choice is not open. If the scales are not equally loaded — in other words, if adequate support, assistance and provision is not given to both alternatives — then the decision as to a child's real need cannot be unbiased. (Parfitt, 1975, p. 12)

The absence of efforts towards a policy of integration except on a very local and isolated scale suggests to me that the opposite principle is in operation. Special schools have expanded, in large part, because policy makers and their advisers have thought that separate schooling for handicapped children is a good thing.

The advocacy of a principle whilst acting on its opposite is indefensible. However, I am not suggesting there need be anything morally wrong in arguing for the advantages of special schools over other forms of provision. There are some quite compelling arguments for separate schools. One is that the real gains made in the education of some children, particularly the severely mentally handicapped, have emerged directly through the existence of schools established with the sole purpose of fostering the children's development. This argument is often used as part of a wider 'evolutionary' view that segregated forms of provision are a necessary stage in a process of identifying and meeting the needs of the handicapped. Increasing placement in special schools may follow an increased social and educational awareness that the needs of the handicapped should be recognized, and an increasing willingness to set aside additional provision to meet their needs. This idea may have particular force when one sees how remote the particular problems of the least competent class members may be from the minds of apparently excellent teachers. It is possible, then, to retain a concern and oversight for the needs of handicapped children in ordinary schools? Conversely can we afford to isolate our concern for vulnerable children away from the normal classrooms of normal schools?

A second view of the desirability of special schools concerns their atmosphere and rationale. Special schools, it is said, provide a haven for some children from the pervasive competitive ethos of ordinary schools. As a by-product they also give job opportunities to excellent teachers wishing to avoid working to the aims of mainstream education. Before we can assess the force of this argument we need to know whether it is possible for provision for handicapped children to be arranged so that they help to mitigate the prevailing competitive atmosphere within ordinary schools rather than suffer from it. And if special schools are to be used as alternative schools then these may be to the benefit of many children other than the handicapped. John Quicke (1980) has advocated their redeployment for this function.

We have to give special consideration to those children whose exclusion is most frequently desired from normal schools and who now are involved in a boom of provision, namely children involved in problems of discipline. This group highlight the diversity of issues surrounding integration and the possibility of holding very different views about different groups of children. But these children are not just segregated for their own educational benefit. They are separated in order to permit the classes they leave to run more smoothly. A wish for segregated provision for such children is frequently and openly expressed and I suspect that they are often not included when people talk of the integration principle. In looking at the arguments for the 'principle of segregation' we have to separate those views which are based on the needs of children from those which are rationalizations for the continuation of an expanding educational sector.

The efficacy of special schooling

I have pulled out the issue of efficacy from other reasons of practicality because it has the special status of a red herring. Some people would argue that children learn better in special schools and the expansion of such provision is a rational response to their educational needs. Peter Mittler, for example, appears to contrast the educational benefits of special schooling with an anticipated social gain from inclusion in an ordinary school: 'The question of whether mentally handicapped children should be taught in special or ordinary schools should be seen as one of reconciling the child's educational and learning needs with the need to maintain contact with ordinary children in the community' (Mittler, 1979). But there is no evidence to suggest that children reach higher levels of educational attainment in special schools as opposed to less restrictive arrangements with comparable levels of support. Despite the fact that much time, effort and money has been expended by researchers in attempting to prove the efficacy of a particular educational placement, a few moments' reflection might lead one to doubt the wisdom of their quest. Could the world really be constructed in such a way that groups of children learnt more because they were housed in a building called a special school? Helen Keller made rapid progress in her garden hut, but we wouldn't on that ground advocate garden huts as the universal special educational placement. The available evidence suggests that children can learn well in a variety of educational settings. Children who are perceived as different or undesirable are teased at times and sometimes discriminated against in the organization of school priorities and these problems may interfere with their educational progress. But these are not fixed qualities of schools: they are problems amenable to planned solutions. The efficacy issue reduces, then, to one of practicality. How can the provision for handicapped children be organized within ordinary schools to enable children to learn effectively?

The practicality of special schooling

The issue of practicality has two strands, only one of which is directly related to the needs of children. There may be many good reasons why the existence of special schools suits the needs of administrators and professional workers and I will look at the needs of the system and its managers in discussing the momentum of segregated provision, below.

When government reports refer to 'practicality' they imply, we must presume, that it is the effective delivery of services to children which is the prime consideration. They refer to cost, to the dispersal of professional support, to the joint development of resources for particular groups of children, to the establishment of special 'therapeutic' regimes.

I believe there are few reasons to suppose that integrated forms of provision are actually cheaper and there is every reason to suppose that the initial planning of such services is more complex. It is however difficult to argue for most groups of handicapped children that a less restrictive form of provision is not viable when we can point to an example of effective practice. As I have suggested, for any handicap irrespective of severity we can usually find an example of education within the normal school in some part of the UK. Such documentation is provided in Hegarty and Pocklington (1981) in some of the chapters in Booth and Statham (1981) in Jamieson, Parlett and Pocklington (1977) and in Cope and Anderson (1977). There is also a large body of literature on practice in other countries.

The momentum of the special education system

I have argued that one reason for the expansion of special schooling is that many people actually desired it in the past and still do today. However once a practice becomes systematized with forms and procedures and job specifications and recruitment drives and departments and departmental heads the practice may take on an organic growth of its own; it becomes an institution.

Segregated special education has its origins in the economic and educational climate of the nineteenth century and the desire for segregated schooling has rarely been so strongly expressed since. Mary Dendy, a woman of considerable educational influence and member of the Manchester School Board, spoke at the start of this century of a need for special schools where children could be incarcerated so as to 'stem the great tide of the feebleminded' (see Potts, 1982b). Despite this public rhetoric the actual numbers of children 'incarcerated' in special schools was relatively small then. The major growth of a special system from 1950 to 1980 coincided with the boom years and the upsurge of various professional groups whose work was specifically directed towards children with special needs. The growth in numbers of educational psychologists and speech therapists, for example, as well as the development of child guidance clinics, child development centres and child psychiatry departments all directed their efforts at resolving the problems for children whose disabilities and actions were a cause for concern. In collaboration with educational administrators it is not surprising that such groups viewed the prospect of segregated provision as a solution to the professional task. On the one hand it removed children from the sight and minds of the educators who could not cope with them and on the other it could be argued that segregated special education provided a total treatment environment.

This false identification of 'placement' with 'treatment' is crucial in understanding the way segregated provision has sometimes suited professional needs. Often the outcome of a protracted and highly populated case conference has been a recommendation for an education in a particular place. It became possible for hard-pressed school medical officers or psychiatrists or psychologists to believe they were fulfilling a professional aim in recommending children for special schools.

The very separation of special education from mainstream education produced a self-fulfilling process. For special education formed the sphere of activity of a number of people who interpreted their job aspirations and occupational satisfactions within its boundaries. Once people have become committed to the aims of an institution or organization then that organization will tend to expand as long as funds are available. Of course there is always the chance of a moral reappraisal forming the basis of new action, but unfortunately the competitive ethos and economic realities which launch people onto their chosen careers sometimes preclude the possibility of such a review.

The expansion of special school provision has had repercussions on the education system as a whole. Teachers in ordinary schools have been led to expect that some of their 'problems' can be resolved by removal of children from their classrooms. This then created a corresponding and increasing pressure from ordinary schools to gain the attention of the special school gatekeepers: the school medical officers and more recently the educational psychologists. Of course special schools could not expand if there were no children to fill them and at times recruitment has been actively sought from both sides. A special education administrator in one city interpreted his job as supplying head teachers with the forms on which to initiate special school referrals and explaining to them how this might best be achieved.

In actual fact, it has never been possible for schools to 'solve' more than a small proportion of their problems by arranging transfers to special schools. In such circumstances special schools may serve an important but misleading function. They may provide educators with *the illusion* that educational problems are being resolved in such a process, and they may permit the avoidance of a far more important and challenging issue: how can we meet the needs of all children in our schools?

Organizational and structural changes in mainstream schools

The growth of special school provision took place within a changing educational climate and certain of the developments within education may have made schools less able to cope with their problems and more eager to exclude children.

The growth of comprehensives. One might have supposed that the development of a comprehensive education system might have facilitated the integration of children with special needs. Circular 10/65 set out the guidelines for the establishment of comprehensive schools which would provide 'a school community in which pupils over the whole ability range and with differing interests and backgrounds can be encouraged to mix with each other, gaining stimulus from the contacts and learning tolerance and understanding in the process' (DES, 1965). However the government directive made no mention of handicapped children or special schools. This was a glaring omission in their underlying educational philosophy and there are reasons to suppose that the new comprehensives were not always havens of tolerance for deviant pupils.

The amalgamation of the segregated system of secondary modern and grammar schooling involved a large number of teachers in dealing with unfamiliar educational issues. Some attempted to avoid breaking step by incorporating their new comprehensives into a familiar image: a school of able pupils oriented towards and controlled by examinations which were to form the basis of their occupational selection. Some head teachers managed to pull it off. They had skill in controlling and guiding their pupil intake or good fortune in being based in an area imbued with middle-class aspirations. Nevertheless there were many career teachers who found their assumptions about their jobs challenged by the task of teaching children from the old secondary modern schools. This clash in expectations may have lead these teachers to define the futures of children they were ill-equipped to teach or control as outside their classrooms and schools. Certainly many of the new recruits to schools for the educationally subnormal and maladjusted were in this secondary age group.

Mixed-ability teaching. The growth in the use of mixed-ability teaching in the sixties and seventies is another development which has had ambiguous implications. In theory teachers of mixed-ability groups are expected to adapt the curriculum to the needs of each child. Where such child-centred education has been managed successfully schools have been able to include a wide range of handicapped children in ordinary schools. Some of the primary schools run on these lines attracted considerable interest from abroad as showpieces of integration (Levine, 1979). However mixed-ability teaching also brings its own constraints and the pressures of trying to cater to the interests of a diverse group of children may have lead some teachers to refer the most deviant for special education.

But it would be a mistake to presume that the breakdown of streaming and setting in schools is universal or even particularly wide-spread at the secondary level. Before 1920 streaming was rare but came into favour following the recommendations of the Hadow Report of 1931 and the Spens Report of 1938, both of which had been influenced by the educational theories of Cyril Burt. It was not until the sixties that the practice began to subside. The Plowden Report of 1967 advocated the abolition of streaming at primary level and this was facilitated by the introduction of comprehensive schools which removed the pressure of primary schools to selectively coach a few pupils towards success at the 11+ examinations (Wright, 1977).

Whilst national figures are unavailable, it is probable that streaming at the primary level has been largely abolished. In a study in the north-west of England only 13 per cent of primary schools still streamed (Bennett, 1976). However, the situation for comprehensive schools has been very different. In a survey of 1,051 schools conducted by the National Foundation for Educational Research, 50 per cent were unstreamed in the first year, 34 per cent in the second year and 25 per cent in the third year. But whilst these form groups were mixed ability in theory, the great majority of schools practised setting for some subjects from the first year (NFER, 1975).

The move towards comprehensive education is part of the process of integration. Where children remain in rigid bands or streams such integration may solely involve the sharing of a common location. But there is an opportunity within comprehensive schools, as in primary schools, to use mixed-ability grouping as a basis for including handicapped children within the normal classes for some of the time. This was clearly recognized in a DES discussion paper in 1978: 'The conditions for good mixed ability teaching if and when they exist are those which make allowances for individual differences and hence make it easier for handicapped children to fit into teaching groups in the secondary school' (DES, 1978c). What is needed to give this formula a basis in reality are the support teachers, resources and resource rooms that could make more schools truly comprehensive and this would require a redirection of special educational provision.

Assessing past and future trends

I have reviewed some of the factors which may have contributed to the increase of special school placement. The presence of a large number of people within local education authorities and of a smaller number of influential people outside them who have been committed to the growth and relative autonomy of a special education sector has certainly been an important driving force. Within this group are some who publicly advocate an integration principle which is plainly incompatible with their actions. They may or may not be aware of their reasons for doing this.

There are practical problems in integrating some handicapped children in some parts of the country. But often the practical difficulties have more to do with the reorganization of jobs and occupational aspirations, with the reallocation of money and resources, than with the needs of children. This inertia within the system is an important human issue and any change requires skill, sense and sensitivity. But it can only be tackled in an open and planned way if it is brought to the foreground of the integration debate. At the moment this matter often masquerades as practical difficulties in teaching handicapped *children* in ordinary schools. The provision for all sorts of mild and severe handicaps in ordinary schools testifies to the fact that many of the practical, *educational* problems voiced by policy makers can actually be overcome.

It is hard to estimate the contributory force of changes within the education system such as comprehensive schools and mixed-ability teaching. There is no evidence to suggest that the advent of comprehensives and changes of classroom organization have coincided with a drop in standards or a rise in disruptiveness of pupils. Such schools provide an opportunity for integration which was non-existent in the selective system. But they have grown at a time of rapidly expanding special provision and pertinently any specific reference to the handicapped was omitted from the blueprints for their establishment. Where secondary schools have taken on a wide group of handicapped pupils they have been incorporated successfully through judicious use of resource bases.

Conditions change and new economic and educational factors as well as government legislation may have a different effect on trends in the future. In fact there are several circumstances currently operating within education which may make an impact.

First, there is a real contraction in educational expenditure at present and there is unlikely to be any money available for new special schools or an expansion in professional services associated with special education. Any new separate provision is likely to develop in buildings already owned by local education authorities and hence to be on a relatively small scale. The growth of small disruptive units is, in part, a reflection of this situation. There may be a temptation on the part of some authorities to cut back on special educational expenditure even before the government promise of 'real' cuts in 1983–4 (DES, 1980). It is possible too that some may abuse the notion of integration to save money by not providing the appropriate level of support.

One effect of economic stringency is to make some people more cautious about change even where no additional money is involved. Many of the changes required to foster the process of integration are changes of attitude rather than finance but poverty is often pleaded by education authorities as a reason for not implementing integration. There is no doubt however that change does require personal energy and after current economies in schools where ancillary staff have been removed, allocation for books seriously curtailed, and now class sizes have begun to creep up many teachers are feeling hard pressed and aggrieved. Such circumstances are not the most advantageous for introducing broader professional roles. Even if in the long term a comprehensive approach to children with special needs would actually make teachers' jobs easier the short-term adjustments may be awkward. The NUT document on 'special education in ordinary schools' (NUT, 1977) certainly reflects the fears that economic shortages have fostered.

A second circumstance concerns the diminishing school-age population, a factor which until recently was able partially to mask the cuts in educational expenditure. In 1980 the bulge in the school population was in its final year of secondary schooling. Secondary schools now have an increasing amount of space available and are in the same position that has affected primary schools in the last few years. Special schools are also beginning to experience the effect of falling school rolls and some may close for this reason alone. The availability of space in schools provided a golden opportunity for educational innovation. In the past local education authorities have responded to the availability of space in primary schools by school closure. It is possible that the greater 'muscle' of secondary school heads may lead to the setting up of some special education departments within secondary schools as an alternative to school closure.

A third pressure affecting teachers is a current emphasis on 'accountability'. If teachers are to be held directly responsible for the progress of their pupils, then they may be increasingly willing to separate children they consider to have 'real' intractable problems from those amenable to 'ordinary' teaching.

The impact of legislation

I discussed earlier the considerable inconsistencies in official publications. Now if departmental policy is confused and confusing and the Department of Education and Science actually formulates legislation then we might expect that legislation relevant to the integration issue might also be ambiguous. It was widely believed and stated that section 10 of the 1976 Education Act, if enacted, would legally oblige local authorities to institute a process of integration. Section 10 was left to be enacted at a future date and in 1980 the Conservative government made it clear that they had no intention of doing this (DES, 1980). They referred to this intention in these words (p. 13):

> There are legitimate differences of view over where and how a child with special educational needs is best educated. . . . The right placement for a child with a serious disability can only be properly determined after careful assessment of his needs by competent professionals and in close consultation with his parents. For some children with special needs association, or full association, with other children is the wrong solution and to impose it would be unfair to the child, his parents, other children and the taxpayer. . . .
> Accordingly the Government does not propose to bring into force section 10 of the Education Act, 1976. (DES, 1980, p. 13)

And the day after the publication of the White Paper the *Daily Express* summarized the sentiments of many.

> *The Government firmly rejects the plan approved by the last Labour Government to put all handicapped pupils in the nation's 28,000 state schools.* (Bruce Kemble, *Daily Express*, 7 August, 1980)

But would the effect of implementing section 10 have been in the suggested direction? The 1944 Education Act had said that: 'The arrangements made by a local authority for the special educational treatment of pupils . . . shall so far as is practicable provide for the education of pupils in whose case the disability is serious *in special schools* appropriate to that category.'

Section 10 of the 1976 Act did substitute a clear change of emphasis. It directed that, unless such provision were 'impracticable or incompatible with the efficient instruction in the schools, or would involve unreasonable public expenditure . . . the arrangements made by a local education authority for the special educational treatment of pupils shall [be in] county or voluntary [i.e. ordinary] schools.'

But this change of emphasis was hardly new, as we have seen, and strange as it may seem, it was echoed almost word for word in the 1980 White Paper:

> *the proposed legislation will provide that a child with special educational needs shall be educated with children without such needs*, provided that the arrangements are capable of meeting his needs, are compatible with the efficient education of the children with whom he is educated, and with the efficient use of public resources, and take proper account of the wishes of his parents. (DES, 1980, p. 14, my emphasis)

The wording of these documents seems to provide further evidence of departmental games. Far from having different implications for integration the two documents appear virtually identical in this respect. The policy implications of either document turn on the precise numbers of children for whom education in ordinary schools is to be regarded as impracticable, incompatible with the efficient instruction of others or too expensive, though the 1980 White Paper does include an additional element of parental choice. How such terms are interpreted depends on the predilections, knowledge and beliefs of local authority policy makers. There appears to be nothing within either document which would intervene in the production of integration policy by personal, social and market forces. And at the time of writing this article these forces had continued to push and pull increasing numbers of children in the direction of special schools.

References

Bennett, S. N. (1976) *Teaching Styles and Pupil Progress*, London, Open Books.

Booth, A.J. (1982) *Eradicating Handicap*, Unit 14 of E241: Special Needs in Education, Milton Keynes, Open University Press.

Booth, A.J. and Statham, J. (Eds.) (1981) *The Nature of Special Education: people, places and change*, London, Croom Helm.

Chazan, M., Laing, A. F., Shackleton Bailey, M. and Jones, G. (1980) *Some of Our Children*, London, Open Books.

Cope, C. and Anderson, E. (1977) *Special Units in Ordinary Schools: an exploratory study of special provision for disabled children*, London, University of London Institute of Education.

Department of Education and Science (1965) *The Organisation of Secondary Education (Circular 10/65)*, London, HMSO.

Department of Education and Science (1967) *Children and Their Primary Schools: A report (Plowden Report)*, London, HMSO.

Department of Education and Science (1974) *Integrating Handicapped Children*, London, HMSO.

Department of Education and Science (1976) *Education Act, 1976*, London, HMSO.

Department of Education and Science (1978a) *Special Educational Needs, Report of the Committee of Enquiry into the Education of Handicapped Children and Young People* (Warnock Report), London, HMSO.

Department of Education and Science (1978b) *Behavioural Units: A survey of special units for pupils with behavioural problems*, London, HMSO.

Department of Education and Science (1978c) HMI Series: *Matters for Discussion. Mixed Ability Work in Comprehensive Schools*, London, HMSO.

Department of Education and Science (1980) *Special Needs in Education* (White Paper), London, HMSO.

Hegarty, S. and Pocklington, K. (1981) In preparation, Windsor, National Foundation for Educational Research.

Jamieson, M., Parlett M. and Pocklington, K. (1977) *Towards Integration: A Study of Blind and Partially Sighted Children in Ordinary Schools*, Windsor, National Foundation for Educational Research.

Levine, M. (1979) Some observations on the integration of handicapped children in British primary schools, in Meisels, S. J. (Ed.), *Special Education and Development*, Baltimore, University Park Press.

Ministry of Education (1931) *The Primary School: Report of the Consultative Committee* (Hadow Report), London, HMSO.

Ministry of Education (1938) *Secondary Education with Special Reference to Grammar and Technical High Schools: Report of the Consultative Committee (Spens Report)*, London, HMSO.

Ministry of Education (1944) *Education Act, 1944*, London, HMSO.

Ministry of Education (1954) *Provision of Special Schools, Circular 276*, London, HMSO.

Mittler, P. J. (1979) *People Not Patients*, London, Methuen.

National Association of Schoolmasters (1975) *Violent and Disruptive Behaviour in Schools*, London, National Association of Schoolmasters.

National Foundation for Educational Research (1975) *Mixed Ability Teaching Project*, unpublished survey results (see Wright, 1977).

National Union of Teachers (1977) *Special Education in Ordinary Schools*, London, National Union of Teachers.

Parfitt, J. (1975) *The Integration of Handicapped Children in Greater London*, London, Institute for Research into Mental and Multiple Handicap.

Potts, P. (1982a) *Biology and Handicap*, Unit 11 of E241: Special Needs in Education, Milton Keynes, Open University Press.

Potts, P. (1982b) *Origins*, Unit 8 of E241: Special Needs in Education, Milton Keynes, Open University Press.

Quicke, J. (1980) *The Cautious Expert: An empirically grounded critique of the practices of local authority educational psychologists*, PhD Thesis, University of Sheffield.

Thornbury, R. (1978) *The Changing Urban School*, London, Methuen.

Wright, N. (1977) *Progress in Education: A review of schooling in England and Wales*, London, Croom Helm.

5.2 Finance and policy-making in special education

J. R. LUKES

Special education's growth documented by Booth in the previous paper took place in a climate of considerable optimism about the power of education in general and at a time of ever-increasing public expenditure. Economic and political changes in the late 1970s have reversed the trends and in the early 1980s local education authorities find themselves being brought under ever-tighter financial control by central government.

In this paper, Lukes argues that the 1981 Special Education Bill will permit LEAs more scope for cutting spending on special education, as they will be forced to do as the cuts bite deeper. However the effects are likely to be unevenly divided, since the authorities that currently spend most on special provision – the ILEA and the Metropolitan Districts – are also likely to be hardest hit by the new methods of allocating central government funds to local authorities.

Special education is more complex and expensive than the rest of education. But the structure of power over decisions about its policy and finance is the same as that for the rest of education. So it is necessary to see how the whole system works, before considering what makes provision for special needs so complicated and costly – and what policy-makers may do about that in the 1980s.

The structure of power over policy

According to the main law still governing the system – the 1944 Education Act – almost all decisions on provision and policy are to be taken by the Local Education Authorities (LEAs). In practice these decisions are either taken or very largely shaped by central government in the form of the Department of Education and Science (DES). There is a gap between theory and practice and power has increasingly shifted to the centre.

The 1944 Act both designed the structure of provision, and allocated responsibility for it. Almost complete responsibility was given to the LEAs despite the fact, then as now, that over half of education's

Specially commissioned for this volume
© The Open University, 1981

funds come from central government, and that the Act gave it general oversight of the system. The only specific roles for the central department were to act as a court of appeal in disputes between LEAs, or between LEAs and parents, and to lay down minimum national standards on matters of physical provision such as school buildings, meals, transport and special education. The DES still does this with 'Regulations' which LEAs must obey.

LEAs were given, and still have, obligatory 'duties' and optional 'powers'. The duties refer mainly to primary, secondary and further education, the necessary, compulsory 'three stages of the system'.[1] They concern the provision of buildings and teachers, the provision and control of 'secular instruction' or the curriculum in its widest sense, the securing of attendance by five to sixteen year olds, and all sorts of extras such as duties over health and safety, free transport, boarding, clothing and meals for pupils in defined categories of need, student grants, and special education 'either in special schools or otherwise'.[2]

The optional 'powers' include the provision of nursery, higher and adult education, an educational psychology service, a youth employment or careers service, a youth service, work-experience schemes, community centres, sports and arts facilities, assistance to private schools and private pupils, extra school transport, meals, milk, boarding and clothing (all with charges), and discretionary grants to pupils, students, parents, teachers, voluntary bodies, community groups, and others, for many educational purposes.[3]

The corollary of these duties and powers, which have produced a system in large part LEA-financed, through the rates, has traditionally been the LEA right to decide how, and how generously, to exercise them.

Special education has been no different. The duty has been firm: to provide the education required by Regulations for the more serious categories of disability, in special schools if 'practicable . . . but where this is impracticable, or where the disability is not serious, the arrangements may provide for the giving of such education in any school'.[4] How to fulfil the duty, and what to see as practicable, has been up to the LEA.

An LEA is a local authority (a local government county or district council, consisting of elected councillors) which has been given statutory responsibility for education. In practice, the LEA is that council's education committee (a smaller number of the councillors) to which the council delegates its educational decision-making. Every education committee has an education department under a Chief Education Officer or Director of Education to administer its educational functions, i.e. to run the service and implement education committee policies.

The 104 LEAs fall into four groups: the 47 Non-Metropolitan ('shire') Counties, mainly rural and Conservative; the 36 Metropolitan Districts (for 6 conurbations: Birmingham, Leeds, Liverpool, Manchester, Newcastle, Sheffield), mainly urban and Labour; the 20 Outer London Boroughs; and the 12 Inner London Boroughs' shared Inner London Education Authority.

The relationship between the elected education committee and the appointed administration is complex. If it is asked which side within an LEA takes the decisions, the answer is that there tends again to be a gap between theory and practice. Formally the elected side, the education committee, takes the decisions at its periodic meetings. But considerable effective power rests with the administrators because unlike most councillors they have expertise, and continuity in office, are full-time, and above all can shape the committee's formal decisions by the reports, options, and recommendations they choose to present to it. After the meetings, it is they who implement the decisions so again they have relatively unfettered opportunity to secure their own objectives and to run the system as they want. There are obvious parallels with the relationship at national level between civil servants and ministers.

The Department of Education and Science

The DES's urge for power began in the 1960s for positive reasons, when the political climate was optimistic over education and economic growth, and intensified in the 1970s for negative reasons. By this time the climate had become distinctly pessimistic over both these things. Current government determination to cut public expenditure is the key to understanding DES policies and power in the early 1980s. Its role is to design and induce cuts in LEA provision and spending.[5]

Two examples must suffice. First, its new 'core curriculum' policy is related to its plans to restrict the number of teachers (and subjects) per school. It follows the Treasury's 1980 White Paper directive that 67,000 fewer teachers be employed by 1983–4, of the UK total of 527,000 in 1978–9: a 12.7 per cent cut within five years.[6] The DES has no rights over the curriculum. But in the 1980 Education Act it gave itself, via new Regulations, power to restrict every school's and college's teachers to a minimal core.[7]

Second, that White Paper said 750,000 school places must go by 1982–3, meaning school closures on the scale of say 1,000 secondary schools each with 750 places.[8] To this end the DES, in the same 1980

Act, restricted the 1944 Act's parents' rights of choice in their children's schooling, and community rights of objection to school closure.[9] The DES also commissioned a 1980 report urging LEAs to close schools in the interests of fewer, far larger schools, because they are cheaper. Falling pupil rolls are not the reason for these cuts, but only the rationale to gain public acquiescence.[10] The DES is deliberately careful to present educational not financial rationales, to avoid public resistance.[11]

But on one rare occasion the DES acknowledged that education, and its quality, was not its concern. It said it saw its policy role in terms of financial resources. To the criticism that 'this approach might over-emphasize economic aspects, with officials acting in too much secrecy', the DES agreed about the secrecy 'but argued that planning the allocation of resources was not an operation which lends itself to full and open consultation'.[12] Policy means cuts which mean secrecy about its intentions and plans.

Decision-making on education's income and expenditure

Funds for maintained ordinary and special schools come from LEAs. The source of LEAs' funds is the money central government gives local government (the Rate Support Grant or RSG) and the rates.

Officials from the Environment Department and local authorities agree on each year's 'total relevant expenditure' for all local services including education. This sum is the agreed necessary minimum expenditure to fulfil duties and main powers, so it is equivalent to the minimum income authorities need.

The Environment and Treasury ministers then decide what proportion of that total should be met by the RSG. A cut in RSG, for example, from 66.5 per cent in 1975–6 to 60 per cent in 1981–2, means more must come from rate income by raising the rates.

Second, the ministers decide on each year's 'cash limit': the allowance for extra spending due to inflation. The 1980–1 allowance was for 13 per cent yet the Treasury forecast for that year's inflation was 17.5 per cent. This annual underestimate of what local authorities will have to spend on the services agreed necessary, is an indirect way of making them provide less of those services. Each year's cash limit squeeze grows tighter; 1981–2's was 7 per cent, half the Treasury forecast.

Third, they now annually cut the total relevant expenditure itself. From 1974–5 to 1980–1, local government's share of public spending was cut by 14 per cent; central government's actually rose by 8 per cent.

A cut in RSG only forces an increase in rates if local authorities choose to give the provision officially agreed necessary. In fact, all three forms of cut in their annual income pose them with a dilemma. They can raise rates, to maintain services; or cut services, to avoid raising rates. Both courses are unpopular. Central government cuts in local funds reduce public spending but shift the political odium to local authorities.

The 1980 Local Government Act has changed the way the Rate Support Grant is calculated and allocated. The Environment Department now decides, within the total available, (a) what each local authority needs to spend and (b) what it can be deemed to raise from rates; the difference between the two is its RSG share. Both decisions — especially the former — are unavoidably arbitrary, subjective, political judgements, now made centrally and in secret.[13] Also, if an authority raises rates, to maintain services, its RSG share will be progressively cut and can even be removed: a severe new way of forcing cuts.

Before this Act, the RSG needs element combined an assessment of objective needs and past spending patterns, so that authorities spending more got more grant. One aim of the change is to penalize these 'higher spenders'. But whether they spent more because they were spendthrift, or because of greater needs, is arguable. The urban, Labour authorities were the biggest spenders. The new 'block grant', applying first to 1981—2, cuts those councils' RSG drastically more than the low-spending shire Counties. The London Boroughs and above all the ILEA suffer most.[14]

But all authorities' funds are cut in 1981—2. 'Total relevant expenditure', which used to rise annually, is cut by 3.1 per cent compared to 1980—1's planned spending, by 8.2 per cent compared with its actual spending — and by 16 per cent compared to its original planned spending.[15] Cuts on this extreme scale are likely to continue through the 1980s. The 1970s cuts in local services were because the total funds rose insufficiently. Real cutbacks in the total, since 1979—80, have created an unprecedented situation acutely relevant to education.

Cuts in local government funds mean cuts in education spending, since half of local recurrent spending is on education. The 1970s cuts in local government funds ended much of the LEAs' use of their optional powers. When the unprecedented 1979—80 decision was announced, LEAs unanimously said they could cut no more, without cutting the core — unless the law was changed, removing some of their duties.[16]

The 1980 Treasury White Paper cutting the basic core, teachers and schools, over the next five years needs to be seen in this light; likewise the 1980 Education Act which for the first time since 1944 removed duties, involving nursery education and school meals services and made them powers.[17] Simultaneously 1980–1's RSG was cut by over £220m on the assumption that LEAs would no longer provide those services. The RSG will continue to be specifically cut each year on the assumption that the LEAs obey central government over teacher cuts and school closures too. These assumptions compel obedience: LEAs have no alternative but to cut as ordered or to cut another part of the education service. Raising rates to replace central government funding will now be penalized. They thus face severer constraints and cuts pressures in the 1980s than ever before.

The legal removal of duties to permit spending cuts forced by RSG, may only have begun in education and other local services. Since 1980 the DES has been planning more, including school transport – and further education, for sixteen to eighteen year olds.[18] No duty is now sacrosanct.

The 1981 Special Education Bill

The 1981 Special Education Bill, produced in this financial context, does two main things. Firstly it repeals the LEAs' duty under section 33 of the 1944 Act to provide specified education, in any school practicable, for specified categories of serious disability. Who gets what is now wholly up to LEAs. They decide what counts as serious disability and thus who gets special education: children for whom 'statements' are made are defined as 'those with special educational needs which call for the LEA to determine the special educational provision that should be made for them'.[19] There will be no criteria for adequate provision for them because there will be no national standards or definitions. The new 'duty' for them and other children, 'securing that special educational provision is made for children who have special educational needs',[20] gives discretion to LEAs to provide as much or little as they want, because the definitions of special educational needs and special educational provision are up to them.[21]

Secondly, LEAs get far stronger directive powers over pupils, parents and schools. The 1944 Act's section 37 'school attendance orders' system, by which an LEA could compel truant pupils to attend school (and prosecute, fine and imprison non-complying parents), is extended to special education. LEAs can now compel any pupil to attend the school the LEA chooses for special education purposes, with these forceful powers.[22] The Bill gives the parents of children for whom statements are made, fewer rights over school placement than other parents under the 1980 Education Act appeals committees (because these decisions 'have substantial resource implications')[23] and fewer rights than under the 1944 Act.[24] The LEA decides whether to assess, whether to make a statement, what provision to make and can prevail.[25] Integration for these children is still up to the LEA, which can define 'efficient education' and 'efficient use of resources' as it wants.[26] A brand new duty is imposed on ordinary schools to accept whoever the LEA sends them. The explicit aim is to stop them objecting to handicapped pupils because they lack resources to meet their needs.[27]

Given the financial circumstances in which the Bill has been produced, and given the DES recourse to law already to release LEAs from duties for the explicit purpose of cuts, it is hard not to see the Bill's aims as firstly to enable LEAs to decide on whatever provision they think cheapest whether integrated or separate, and secondly to get their way over parents and schools who might object to either. If an LEA wants to send a child to a special school the statement system enables it to prevail over parents. If it wants to close special schools, it can prevail over their closure (which the Bill makes easier for LEAs than ordinary schools' closure),[28] over other schools' acceptance of the children, and by section 37 compulsion, over parents. Although the Bill requires special school closures to be referred to the DES, this is unlikely to offer any safeguards. The DES is likely to back the LEA, provided its aim is to cut expenditure.

This explains the Bill's origin in financial terms, as national and local policy-makers see it. The special education world sees the removal of categories in non-financial terms. One of its chief objections to them was that their specification of appropriate education for each single type of handicap overlooked the fact of multiple handicaps. But the solution was not to end all clear obligations on LEAs. It was on the contrary to oblige them to make provision for multiple handicaps in addition to existing obligations, as most Warnock evidence urged.[29] Now they are not bound to make provision for any group. The key to the Bill is this discretion for LEAs, freeing them from the section 33 duty in order to cut provision and spending, with added power to do so against any opposition. The Bill follows the Warnock Report in ending categories (though in nothing else) but the Bill's major new directive powers, and special school closure amendments, were not in the report.

DES policy on integration has vacillated ever since setting up the Warnock Committee in 1973, legislating for integration in the 1976 Act's section 10, ordering the planning for its implementation in 1977,[30] announcing its repeal in 1980's special education White Paper,[31] and confirming its repeal but in pro-integration terms in the

1981 Bill.[32] The explanation is the DES's shifting view about whether integration would be cheaper than separate special schooling or not.[33] The upshot in the Bill is that it leaves this to each LEA to decide, for each area and each child. The financial constraints described above ensure that every LEA is forced to seek the cheapest answer and that is all the DES wants.

Last, there is no reassurance for special or ordinary education in the fact that the 1980 Local Government Act block grant criteria for education 'needs' include unit costs for ordinary schools with an 'extra allowance' for special needs.[34] The criteria are merely assumptions about how each local authority's RSG share will be allocated between local services. It is still up to the authority's corporate management to give education more or less than nationally announced, just as it is up to the LEA not to spend the extra on special education. The financial squeeze on local authorities makes it unlikely education will get its announced share.

Every year since 1975–6 it has not; education has been cut by a greater annual proportion than the other local authority services and by more than the nationally announced guidelines for education cuts. For example, education's 1980–1 'programme' was £8539m, £400m (4.5 per cent) less than that for 1979–80.[35] With these acute pressures on LEAs' funds there is no guarantee that special education will not suffer, now that there is no longer a clear duty protecting it.

Special education spending and costs

To reach a clearer view of special education's future, it is useful to look at some relevant financial factors: its costs, LEA differences, and the relative cost of integrated or separate provision.

Although special school pupils are only 1.5 per cent of the total school population, they have 3.7 per cent of all teachers, 12.2 per cent of all educational support staff, 5.4 per cent of all schools, and 4.2 per cent of all education spending.[36] Special education costs more per pupil than ordinary education, as the unit costs comparison in Table 1 shows.[37]

Table 1 Costs per pupil of primary, secondary and special education (£)

	Primary	Secondary	Special excluding boarding	Special boarding
1978–79	337	505	1479	1763
1979–80	386	567	1648	2095
1980–81	436	629	1978	2370

Nine reasons for the higher costs of special education can be identified:

(1) Special education's pupil—teacher ratio, with roughly one teacher to every seven pupils, is more generous. DES Circular 4/73 withdrew special education's maximum class size Regulations in the hope of fewer teachers per pupil, but the ratios shown in Table 2 suggest LEAs have continued to give special pupils small classes. Between 1980 and 1981 the total number of teachers fell by 2.5 per cent; the number of special teachers by only 0.4 per cent.

Table 2 Pupil—teacher ratios (January 1981)

LEAs	Primary schools qualified teachers	Secondary schools qualified teachers	Special schools	
			Qualified teachers	Qualified teachers and other teaching staff
London (21 LEAs)	19.8	15.0	6.4	6.3
Metropolitan Districts (36 LEAs)	22.4	16.0	7.0	6.7
Counties (47 LEAs)	22.9	16.7	7.9	7.7
Total (104 LEAs)	22.4	16.3	7.4	7.2

(2) Special schools have not only more teachers but also more teaching aides and assistants, who form 3 per cent of their teaching staff and only 0.9 per cent of ordinary schools'. In 1980—1 their numbers in those schools fell by 7.6 per cent but in special schools rose by 0.5 per cent. Special education also has more administrative staff, as its administration is more complex. There are far more administrative options, over provision for the area and for each child, as well as more ancillary services to arrange, and co-operation with the health and social services to organize; 54.5 per cent of special education spending goes on staff.

(3) Special pupils need home-to-school transport more than others, and this takes 14 per cent of total special education spending. Ordinary schools' transport spending was cut to the legal minimum in 1980—1. Special's transport spending rose by 27.3 per cent over 1979—80.

(4) More is spent on boarding for special pupils, in two ways. Firstly, more receive it: 11.3 per cent of them are boarders, and secondly special boarding unit costs are almost double those of ordinary boarding.

(5) More is spent on special pupils' supplies. They have more equip-

ment, such as hearing aids and care materials, and some of it, such as sophisticated scientific equipment, is very costly.

(6) More is spent on discretionary grants to special pupils and parents because of their greater needs and expenses, for example over travel in connection with boarding.

(7) Twenty per cent of each year's special education spending goes on private schooling, which takes under 1 per cent of ordinary schools' annual spending. LEAs cannot control private special schools' fee rises, which were 19 per cent a year in 1979–80 and 1980–1.[38]

(8) The medical element in special education costs, shown chiefly by the high staff–pupil ratio, also makes it costlier. This is particularly true of hospital special schools and of education in homes and hospitals. The latter category has a pupil–teacher ratio of five to one.[39]

(9) A further reason for higher costs is the small number of special children in relation to the total pupil population. In urban areas where population is concentrated, special provision in any form, schools or units, is more viable. The problem of provision is most acute for towns and rural areas. But even in cities, the pupil numbers involved are small overall and smaller still for each category of disability.

There is a catch 22 for LEAs here. A special school big enough to be financially viable needs a big catchment area for pupils, which entails boarding, which is expensive. Boarding can only be avoided by a large number of small special schools, and that is the expensive situation which big schools with boarding were meant to avert.[40]

Differences between LEAs

How do LEAs resolve these difficulties of provision? Analysis of the 1980–1 statistics[41] reveals that LEAs fall into two camps. There are the providers of special education (the thirty-six Metropolitan Districts, and the ILEA) and there are the buyers of it (the forty-seven shire Counties and, unexpectedly, the twenty Outer London Boroughs). The contrast shows up in both the provision and the spending statistics given in Table 3. There is a consistent pattern of the ILEA and Metropolitan Districts dominating the league table of provision. Conversely the London Boroughs and Counties are the main buyers of special education. For both these groups of LEAs, spending on other LEAs' provision exceeds the income they receive from other LEAs for the use of their provision. In the Metropolitan Districts these figures balance and in the ILEA income exceeds expenditure.

This suggests that the Counties and Boroughs use the Districts' and ILEA's special school provision. That is borne out by comparing the numbers of pupils in other LEAs' schools with pupils from other LEAs

Table 3 Provision and expenditure on special education in LEAs in England and Wales

	ILEA	Metropolitan Districts	London Boroughs	Counties
Special pupils as a percentage of all pupils	2.8	1.7	1.5	1.3
Special schools as a percentage of all schools	10.7	6.7	6.0	4.6
Qualified teachers in special schools as a percentage of all qualified teachers	6.3	4.3	4.0	3.1
Special education spending as a percentage of total education spending	4.9	4.5	4.9	3.7
Proportion of special education net expenditure spent on private special school fees and on assistance to pupils in private special schools	9.0	9.0	26.9	20.9

Table 4 Special education net expenditure: what the spending goes on (percentages)

Provision	London Boroughs	Counties	Metropolitan Districts	ILEA	All 104 LEAs
Teachers and other staff	44.2	52.0	61.2	68.1	54.5
Transport	15.6	14.0	13.2	12.4	13.9
Premises	6.0	7.3	9.2	9.8	7.8
Supplies	1.6	2.2	2.6	5.0	2.4
Establishment expenses	0.4	0.6	0.6	0.7	0.6
	67.8	76.1	86.8	96.0	79.2
Private school fees	25.3	18.9	7.5	nil	15.5
Assistance to private pupils	1.6	2.0	1.5	9.0	2.3
Other agency services	0.6	1.8	3.6	0.01	2.0
Other assistance to pupils	1.2	0.3	0.9	0.8	0.6
Difference between spending on other LEAs' provision, and income	+3.5	+0.9	−0.3	−5.81	+0.4
	100.0	100.0	100.0	100.0	100.0

in their own schools. The Counties and Boroughs respectively have 2,436 and 4,767 more pupils in other LEAs' schools than the number they receive from other LEAs. The ILEA and Districts have 9,112 more pupils from other LEAs than the number they send out.

The contrast between the providers and buyers emerges clearly in their total special education spending profiles shown in Table 4.[42] These show that the ILEA and Districts spend 96 per cent and 86.8 per cent of their special education funds on actual provision, unlike the others.

Although the London Boroughs have relatively less special provision, they compensate for this by buying others'. It is the Counties which emerge as doing far less in every respect, buying as well as providing, in relative and in absolute terms. Their proportion of special pupils is the lowest; so is the proportion of their total spending which goes on special education. Why?

The striking feature of the analysis is the pattern in Table 3: the close correlation between the LEAs' different proportions of special pupils, ranging from 2.8 per cent in Inner London to 1.3 per cent in the Counties, and their provision, ranging from most provision in the ILEA, to least in the Counties. If there is a causal connection, not only a statistical correlation, is it that the urban areas' higher proportion of special pupils generates more provision? Or is it the reverse: that the greater financial feasibility of special provision in the urban areas generates the identification of more special pupils?

The former might be the case if there were links between urban areas, poverty, lower social class, and handicaps both physical and social. But there is rural poverty, and urban affluence, so urban poverty as a reason for more special pupils in urban areas seems unlikely.[43] Moreover this would not account for the fact that the wealthiest of the forty-seven Counties — the twelve south-east ones — are among those with the highest proportions of special pupils and of special provision.

Alternatively the latter might be the case; not for physical handicaps, but possibly for the social ones. If so, a further question arises. If financial feasibility of special provision is what generates special pupils, do the urban areas, which can more easily provide special education, have too much of it and too many special pupils — is the ILEA's 2.8 per cent too high? Or on the other hand do the rural areas, which cannot easily provide special education, have too little of it and too few special pupils — is their 1.3 per cent too low? The range among the 104 LEAs is actually much wider. The highest proportions of special pupils (and the most special provision) are in Manchester with 3.1 per cent and in six other cities with 2 to 3 per cent; the lowest proportions (and least provision) are in thirteen Counties with 0.5 to 0.9 per cent.

Paradoxically, both explanations might be true — for different handicaps. It may be that the Counties identify and deal with the obvious and more severe handicaps but not with the milder social ones, especially those of slow-learning pupils. To the extent that this is the case, there is a high proportion of County children whose special needs are not being met. This is important, because over 63 per cent of the total pupil population is in the forty-seven Counties.[44]

The costs of integration

Last, and more generally, would integration be cheaper? Might LEAs, in their search for spending cuts, do the right thing for the wrong reasons? There is argument but no adequate evidence. Some believe integration could be cheaper: putting special pupils and staff into ordinary schools would save on special school premises, and when retiring staff are not replaced, on staff.[45] To others it seems equally plainly more expensive: apart from initial new spending, on adaptations to 28,000 ordinary schools' buildings and retraining 471,000 serving teachers, 'the dispersal over many schools of the specialist teaching and supportive services at present concentrated in few schools will be considerably more expensive'.[46]

The argument for concentration of resources, which underlay the growth of special schools, is that it makes more sense to concentrate expensive, scarce and specialized provision on one site, for larger numbers, than to disperse it over many, for small numbers.[47] If the quality of provision is to be comparable to special schools', in terms of the number and specialized expertise of teachers, the amount and standard of materials and equipment, and the access to professionals from para-medical staff to special careers officers, then dispersing provision over ordinary schools must mean multiplying it: more staff and supplies of all kinds, albeit for few special pupils per school.[48] This is not an argument against integration. It is simply to say that if present standards are to be maintained for many groups of children with special needs then a structurally more expensive education system is entailed and should be faced. Conversely anything less than the multiplication and dispersal of provision would mean a fall in those standards.[49]

Two compromise ideas for integrating more cheaply are first 'the concentration of certain special classes or units in selected schools ... [given] the utility and desirability of a measure of concentration';[50] 0.28 per cent of all ordinary school pupils were in such units in 1980—1.

But units are not a universal solution; like special schools they tend only to be feasible in areas with sufficient numbers with common difficulties.[51]

The other idea is to make special schools (after closure) resource bases supplying materials to a group of ordinary schools, and to make their ex-staff peripatetic advisers to those schools – the aim being to avoid both the costly dispersal of provision and the dangers of integrating by special school closure and no new spending at all.[52] Resource base stocks would have to be small and circulating or the increased provision would cost as much as dispersal, and the same applies to special staff. But the occasional use of basic materials and the occasional advice of visitors would not compare with existing special education, nor would it mitigate those dangers for special and other pupils, or be an adequate substitute for more teachers and supplies in ordinary schools.

So it seems that integration can certainly be done cheaply, with financial gains but educational costs; or more expensively, with educational gains but financial costs. It can take numerous forms, each with its own cost ticket, but this basic clash between financial and educational considerations seems to remain. If for many reasons special education is expensive, whether in special or ordinary schools, it is tempting to say that we should accept this, like comparable European countries, and abandon the search for cuts in this field. Britain spends relatively less on special provision than for example the USA and Sweden where it is guaranteed to the age of twenty-one.[53]

Conclusion

Is it possible to forecast special education's financial future? The outlook for special education funds and the prospects for integration and special schools depend on the combined effects of two complex changes. First is the 1981 Bill, which releases LEAs from the duty under the 1944 Act to provide special education for specific children in special or ordinary schools, thus permitting the ending of such provision, and which gives them strong directive powers over pupils, parents and schools to secure either integration or special schooling, whichever they think compatible with 'the efficient use of resources'. LEA responses to the second change are equally hard to predict. It is the 1980 Local Government Act block grant's uneven allocation of the Rate Support Grant, cutting the urban authorities' grants to a far greater degree than the Counties'.

This new allocation of funds, within a sharply reduced total, transfers resources from the poorer areas to the richer. But the main problems, affecting all authorities, are caused by the cuts in the total. They have been devastating since 1979–80, after a decade of annual cuts of increasing severity. These cuts in LEA funds have forced a search for ways of cutting provision, first optional and then even obligatory provision, and this intensely straitened financial context is and seems likely to continue to be the main factor in LEA decision-making. Special education has been shielded from the cuts but is unlikely to be after 1981.

The Counties' funds are not exempt from the cuts; they only get more than the urban authorities within the lower total. So there is no reason to think their special education will expand, especially since they already spend less on it as a proportion of their total education spending than the urban areas, and provide less of it in every way. The relaxing of the duty on it could mean even less provision. Many Counties have hitherto seized every such opportunity to cut services and rates.

The urban authorities have hitherto sought to raise rates rather than cut services; and have spent more on special education in relation to their other education spending than the Counties. But offsetting these are the Act's new penalties against raising rates to make up for cuts in grant, and the far greater cuts in grant for these areas. So they will certainly use the directive powers and release from the duty to achieve whatever seems cheapest.

The DES assumes that to a large extent authorities will see integration as the cheapest option, and that special school closures will be the issue of the 1980s.[54] Since savings will only be significant if such integration is done with little or no new spending, the issue for the public may be to urge the spending. The 1981 Bill also assumes a greater use of private special schools on the part of both LEAs and parents.[55] The idea may be that LEAs may provide only for the most serious disabilities, by buying private places, after closing special schools for a wider range and larger number.

In making these decisions, LEAs may differ in their approach to different handicaps and special needs. They may see ESN and maladjusted children as the most feasible to integrate cheaply.[56] Putting them in ordinary schools without letting those schools employ more teachers for small extra classes is already proving unfortunate.[57] Yet this may increase because the pressure on LEAs is to cut not add to their teaching force. And 1980–1's 18 per cent cut in the number of remedial centre teachers reveals the low priority given to ordinary school pupils' special needs.[58] But LEAs seem keener to spend on 'behavioural' than on remedial or learning problems. Since 1974–6, ordinary school pupils regarded as 'behavioural problems' or trouble-makers have been ejected to separate behavioural units — an embryo new special education sector.[59]

All these possibilities and problems suggest the need for a national special education advisory council and for parallel local advisory committees, like those which already exist for local industry and teachers. Apart from supporting parents' rights, diminished by the 1981 Bill, they could protect the interests of those such as ESN and 'behavioural problem' children who lack pressure groups, and could try to ensure that integration is done decently with adequate spending.

Notes

1   1944 Education Act, sec. 7.

2   1944 Education Act, sec. 8(2) (c): the general special education duty.

3   Many powers, ambiguously, are duties to provide in response to demand or need.

4   1944 Education Act, sec. 33(2): the specific special education duty (with sec. 34).

5   House of Commons: *Tenth Report from the Expenditure Committee: Policy Making in the DES* 1976, HMSO or e.g. Hencke, D. (1978) *Colleges in Crisis*, Harmondsworth, Penguin; Lukes, J. R. (1975) Power and Policy at the DES, *Universities Quarterly*, 29, 132–65; cf. Pile, Sir W. (1979) *The DES*, London, Allen and Unwin.

6   *The Government's Expenditure Plans 1980–1 to 1983–4.* Cmnd. 7841, 1980, London, HMSO, pp. 90–9. The core curriculum policy is in *Framework for the Curriculum* (1980, DES). Its plans to restrict each school's teachers to the core, particularly by a 'secondary school staffing model', were accidentally discovered and revealed by the Chief Inspector of Audit (*The Times*, 19 December 1980).

7   1980 Education Act, sec. 27(1)(b).

8   See note 6, p. 94.

9   1980 Education Act, secs. 10–16, especially sec. 15.

10   Briault, E. and Smith, F. (1980) *Falling Rolls in Secondary Schools*, Windsor, NFER. Cf. Brooksbank, K. (Ed.) (1980) *Educational Administration*, London, Councils and Education Press, p. 40, gives the Chief Education Officers' collective view.

11   See the DES Secretary of State speech urging LEAs to do the same, in *Education* 14 July 1978.

12   OECD (1975) *Educational Development Strategy in England and Wales*, Paris, OECD, pp. 56–60: a critical international inquiry into the DES ending with a 'confrontation meeting' whose report is quoted. Compare, for example, the Warnock Report's statement that it was not possible to cost its recommendations (para. 19.4)

with Professor D. Kirp's comment, in *The Times Educational Supplement*, 19 September 1980, p. 4: 'These proposals cost money; the government knows just how much since a DES–DHSS task force prepared but did not publish cost estimates for each Warnock Report recommendation.'

13 McAllister, R. and Hunter, D. (1980) *Local Government: Death or Devolution?*, London, Outer Circle Policy Unit; Burgess, T. and Travers, T. (1980) *Ten Billion Pounds: Whitehall's Takeover of the Town Halls*, London, Grant McIntyre.

14 The Counties each lose grant equivalent to the sum of money that would be raised by a 1.1p in the £ rate increase. The Districts' loss is equivalent to about a 6.2p increase (some, more: up to 10.9p). The London Boroughs' loss is equivalent to about 10.4p, one up to 15.6p. Within this pattern, allocation is erratic; e.g. some Counties gain, up to the equivalent of 5.9p in the £. 'This year's settlement already shows that the new arrangement does not exclude the time-honoured custom by which Ministers do a good turn to ratepayers of their own political colour, at the expense of others' (*The Times*, 17 December 1980).

15 Association of Metropolitan Authorities: *Statement* (8 January 1981).

16 Announced in June 1979's Budget. The LEAs' response was at their July 1979 national CLEA meeting, and in the DES–LEA 'Expenditure Steering Group Education' *Report* to the Environment Department of July 1979. The dates in this section refer to each financial year 1 April–31 March. The sudden cuts for 1979–80 were announced in June after that financial year had already begun.

17 1980 Education Act, secs. 22–5.

18 Transport, in connection with the 1980 Education Act; F.E., in a private DES–LEA 'legal committee' set up in 1980. The 1980 Local Government (No. 1) Act removed many other local authority duties in order to permit cuts.

19 Special Education Bill, January 1981, secs. 4(1), 5(1), 6(1), 7(1).

20 Special Education Bill, sec. 2(1). Sec. 2 replaces the 1944 Education Act's sec. 8(2)(c) and sec. 33, and the 1976 Education Act's sec. 10, all three of which are repealed.

21 Special Education Bill, sec. 1 gives LEAs discretion over both definitions. *Special educational needs* are defined as learning difficulties worse than the majority in the LEA or disabilities preventing use of the LEA's normal facilities. *Special educational provision* is defined as anything extra to or different from the LEA's normal provision. The LEA decides what counts as normal for the majority and in its area.

22 Special Education Bill, 1981, sec. 16 and schedule 3.

23 *Special Needs in Education* Cmnd. 7996, 1980, London, HMSO,

para. 58, explaining why their appeals committee rights should be less.

24 Compare the Bill's sec. 7(1) with 1944's sec. 34(5), and the Bill's sec. 8 with 1980's sec. 7.

The 1980 Education Act's schedule 2 part 1 gives appeals committees an LEA majority (in membership), so appealing to them against LEA decisions is not a strong safeguard even for non-statement parents.

25 The Bill's secs. 4–9 together replace the 1944 Education Act's sec. 34 and sec. 38, both repealed.

26 Special Education Bill, secs. 2(2) and (3) say statement children should be integrated provided the LEA thinks it compatible with the phrases quoted.

For 'practicable' in the 1944 Act's sec. 33, as a way of letting LEAs decide between integration and special schooling, now read 'efficient'. Both are the legislative way of leaving this to the LEA. 'The wording of this clause is so loose that LEAs can easily avoid their obligation. . . .with the words "so far as is practicable" in the clause, anybody who wants to find a reason for not doing something can easily find it.' Sir F. Messer MP, in *Hansard*, 21 March 1944, vol. 398, no. 50, cols. 690–1.

27 Special Education Bill, sec. 14(6). Sec. 2(5) also gives schools a duty 'to use their best endeavours' to meet special needs, not actually to meet them.

White Paper paras 48, 47 and 45 revealed DES thinking. Placing a clear duty on LEAs might entail more RSG funds; placing it on the school might not: it must use 'the resources available to the school' and not demand more from the LEA. 'Where a school considers that it cannot meet the special needs of a pupil it will be required to inform the LEA' but 'it will be for the LEA to control, direct and adjust resources'.

Para. 47's duty on schools 'to meet special educational needs' became the Bill's duty to try to do so, lest even the former phrasing be construed as entailing more funds.

28 The 1980 Act's sec. 12 says LEAs must 'publish their proposals' for closure of county and voluntary schools and that 'any 10 or more local government electors' can object. The definitions used exclude special schools. The Bill's sec. 13 omits those two important points, openness and community protest. Although the Bill also requires referral of a special school closure to the DES, under present circumstances this is unlikely to prove a strong safeguard.

29 The Warnock Report, para. 8.29.

30 DES Secretary of State speech, 21 January 1977 (circulated to LEAs) ordering LEAs to make plans by September 1977.

31 White Paper, para. 36.

32 Special Education Bill, sec. 2(2), (3).

33 Its initial view that it would be cheaper was apparently changed
    when it received LEAs' plans after September 1977. Those plans,
    like 1976's sec. 10, assumed transferring sec. 33 obligatory provi-
    sion to ordinary schools. The high cost of doing so was partly what
    led the DES to decide to repeal the sec. 33 duty and 1976's sec.
    10: see White Paper, para. 36.

34 The special needs formula assumes 15 per cent of the pupil popula-
    tion to have special needs; 1.8 per cent in special schools, 13.2 per
    cent in ordinary. Each LEA's share of the grant allowed for the
    13.2 per cent depends on its share of the number of children
    nationally who (1) are non-white, (2) are in households overcrowded
    or lacking amenities, (3) are from one-parent families, (4) are from
    families with four or more children, (5) are from households of
    semi-skilled or farm workers, (6) get free school meals. Department
    of Environment Statement, 16 December 1980.

35 Cmnd. 7841 (Treasury White Paper), p. 90.

36 The percentages and calculations in this part are from the data in
    Chartered Institute of Public Finance and Accountancy, *Education
    Estimates Statistics 1980–81* (1980, London, CIPFA) and its
    volumes for earlier years. Unless otherwise stated, they refer to
    January 1981.

37 Unit costs are costs (spending) per pupil and are derived by divid-
    ing spending on a type of education by the number of pupils in it.

38 The amount LEAs spent on private school fees rose by 16 per cent
    and 17 per cent in those two years; by 19 per cent p.a. if LEAs'
    assistance to private special pupils is included.

39 Hospital special schools' spending is included in special education's.

40 There is no objective definition of the school size necessary for
    'financial viability'; it is a matter of LEA consensus or fashion at
    any one time. Over the past twenty years all LEAs have moved
    from boarding provision to a large number of small schools. (5.4
    per cent of schools for only 1.5 per cent of pupils shows that
    special schools are smaller than the norm).

41 The following calculations are from CIPFA figures for each LEA:
    CIPFA 1980, op. cit.

42 Boarding expenditure is excluded.

43 Poverty is seen as a factor in special needs (note 34 above) but not
    as peculiar to urban areas. The Counties have a higher proportion
    of the national total of low-income households than the Districts
    and London: Royal Commission on the Distribution of Income
    and Wealth (1980) *Final Report*, London, HMSO, part II.

    It is the concentration of population over a small area that
    makes special education provision relatively feasible. Norfolk, for
    example, has a larger pupil population than any of the twelve
    south-east Counties and a poorer one than many Districts, but a
    lower proportion of special pupils (0.9 per cent) and little special

provision. Its population is scattered over a wide area, which makes special education hard to provide.

44 5.5 million, out of 8.7 million (January 1981). On 'regional disparities' Sir George Godber once commented: 'The lower ascertainment rates in some areas were probably due largely to shortage of professional staff, insufficient special school accommodation or both.' In *The Health of the School Child 1964–5* (1967, DES), p. 65. The DES does not issue its own internal statistics on the numbers of children with different handicaps in each LEA.

45 E.g. Sir Edward Britton in *Education* 4 November 1977, quoting others.

46 Warnock Report, para. 7.56.

47 This argument is held by national and local administrators to apply generally to education; hence for example the DES efforts now to concentrate sixteen to eighteen provision in colleges and to end its costly dispersal over schools: Macfarlane Report (1981): *Education for 16–19 Year Olds*, London, HMSO, para. 112.

48 See for example Rowan, P. (1980) *What Sort of Life? UK Report for OECD Project 'The Handicapped Adolescent'*, Windsor, NFER; Cope, C. and Anderson, E. (1977) *Special Units in Ordinary Schools*, London, University of London Institute of Education; Warnock Report, para. 7.41.

49 Some pro-integrationists use this argument to urge the spending; some economizers use it to oppose integration: see for example the White Paper, para. 36; Warnock Report, paras. 7.55–6, 7.42.

50 Warnock Report, paras 7.37–8.

51 On problems for units mixing disabilities and ages: Warnock Report, para. 7.36.

52 Warnock Report, paras 13.21, 8.13; 8.6, 8.22; 19.3. Brooksbank (see note 10), p. 74, notes the failure of the same ideas for ordinary secondary schools' equipment and supplies (the aim being to avoid its costly dispersal).

53 Rowan (see note 48). France's special education, mainly residential, is relatively costlier: Halls, W. D. (1976) *Education Culture and Politics in Modern France*, Oxford, Pergamon, pp. 79–80, 168. W. Germany's is similarly expensive and wholly segregated, except in three 'high-spending' SPD (Labour) Länder now trying integration (personal communication from W. Tulasiewicz).

54 DES Minister's speech on the Bill, 14 January 1981 (Lady Young, in the House of Lords). The Bill's sec. 10 redefines special schools as DES-approved 'for the time being' only, and its schedule 2 applies this new definition to all existing special schools.

55 Special Education Bill, sec. 4, excludes children in private special schools from LEA special education duties and from the assessment and statement systems; 1944's sec. 34 had included them.

Sec. 12 extends DES approval of special schools to independent ones, in order to give LEAs an approved list for their use.

56   Integrating these could also cut LEA's special spending most sub-stantially because they constitute 75.4 per cent of all special school pupils: see the White Paper, para. 20. ESNs are 64.3 per cent of the total, maladjusted 12.1 per cent, physically handicapped 9 per cent, and the other categories of handicap only 1 to 3 per cent each.

57   Compare Taylor, G. and Ayres, N. (1970) *Born and Bred Unequal*, London, Longman, p. 107.

58   CIPFA, 1979, 1980 (see note 36).

59   HMIs: *Behavioural Units* (1978, DES). Most of these 239 units were set up by LEAs in 1974—6.

5.3 Handicap in Northern Ireland: a special case?

FIONA STEPHEN

Debates about education in the United Kingdom are often debates about England and Wales. Northern Ireland in particular receives very little attention: similarity is tacitly assumed. Yet, as Fiona Stephen demonstrates, the combined effects of social, economic, political and religious forces have produced in special education a dramatically different scenario. Not only is provision quite distinct, and in many ways several years behind developments in the rest of the UK, but the incidence of certain handicaps is also substantially greater. This analysis provides a paradigm case of the social and political determinants of special education systems.

Introduction

Continuing political unrest has highlighted the obvious fact that Northern Ireland, whilst linked in a constitutional, legal and economic sense to the rest of the United Kingdom, has a definite history, social structure and cultural tradition of its own. Nevertheless, most studies of education in the UK ignore Northern Ireland and its special position.

There has been some discussion of the effect of the troubles on the behaviour, attitudes and levels of stress and anxiety of Northern Ireland's children. A recent collection of papers: *Children under Stress* (Harbison and Harbison, 1980) concentrates almost exclusively on the characteristics of children, particularly truants and offenders, but has little to say about educational provision for troubled children. There is an almost total absence of studies on children with physical, mental and sensory handicaps in Northern Ireland, and a lack of investigations into special educational provision for these groups. It is on these groups that I shall concentrate my attention in this article. I shall attempt to document the important ways in which special education in Northern Ireland differs from that in the rest of the UK. I shall examine the incidence of handicaps, levels and forms of provision and the legal, constitutional and critical framework within which special education operates.

Specially commissioned for this volume
©The Open University, 1981

Incidence of handicaps in Northern Ireland

Northern Ireland has a higher rate of congenital handicap (and infant mortality) than the rest of the UK and most other economically developed countries. In 1978, governmental concern at the gravity of the problem prompted Lord Melchett, the then Minister of State for Health and Social Services, to appoint an advisory committee to examine the problems, with a view to reducing the number of perinatal deaths and handicapped births (DHSS, Northern Ireland, 1980). Their report, *You and Your Baby*, documented the seriousness of the situation and the radical steps that the Committee suggested would improve the position.

Comparative figures for Northern Ireland and the rest of the UK are difficult to obtain owing to differences in the modes of reporting and the availability of statistics. Comprehensive figures on congenital handicap in Northern Ireland are not available and mental subnormality and some other handicapping conditions such as muscular dystrophy are not identifiable until later in childhood. Further, no statistics have been kept on babies that have suffered cerebral palsy at birth. However there is no doubt that overall rates of congenital malformations are considerably higher in Northern Ireland. The *You and Your Baby* Report stated an incidence rate of all fatal and potentially handicapping conditions of 42.0 per 1,000 total births. This compares with a rate for all notified congenital malformations in England and Wales in 1979 of 21.0 per 1,000 total live births (OPCS, 1980). Thus the overall rate of congenital handicap in Northern Ireland is double the rate in England and Wales. Since perinatal and infant mortality in Northern Ireland is higher as well, one would not expect the prevalence rates in early and later childhood to differ by so much. In 1978, for example, the rate of deaths of children under one year per 1,000 live births was 13.2 in England and Wales and 16.0 in Northern Ireland.

Incidence rates of specific handicapping conditions are more difficult to compare. It is known, however, that the incidence of spina bifida and related central nervous system malformations in Northern Ireland is one of the highest in the world (see Golding, Chapter 1.3). A table in the *You and Your Baby* Report (Appendix 9) gives an incidence rate of all CNS malformations of 8.4 per 1,000 total births. This compares with rates in England and Wales in 1978 and 1979 of 2.9 and 2.5 (OPCS, 1980).

Chromosomal abnormalities show a correspondingly high rate in Northern Ireland. The incidence of Down's Syndrome at 1.7 per 1,000 total births is higher than that in England and Wales, currently standing at approximately 1.1 per 1,000 total births. Also showing a dramatically higher incidence rate are cardiac malformations, put at 6.5 per 1,000 total births in the *You and Your Baby* Report. This compares with a rate of 1.2 in England and Wales for the wider category of cardio-vascular malformations (OPCS, 1980). Showing closely comparable or slightly lower incidence rates are ear, eye and skeletal deformities.

What reasons can account for the high incidence of the congenital handicaps in the province? There are a number of possible contributing factors, many of which are in need of much fuller research. First of all, the scattered population in isolated rural areas is inadequately served by good antenatal and perinatal care. The system at present relies on mothers coming to regular antenatal clinics early on in pregnancy. It is not clear that this is occurring in many outlying areas where many of the women are isolated on small farms. This problem is compounded by the shortage of health visitors. Between 1975 and 1977, there was an increase in the numbers of health visitors from 380 to 391 in Northern Ireland. (CSO, 1979) The absolute figure however still remains low. Furthermore, there is inadequate genetic counselling and screening. The *You and Your Baby* Report suggested that one of the most important ways by which the incidence of handicap could be substantially reduced was by effective genetic counselling and antenatal diagnosis. The Report argued that 40 per cent of disorders due to a single gene defect could be prevented in this way; that approximately one-third of disorders due to gene defects (cystic fibrosis of the pancreas, phenylketonuria, or Duchenne muscular dystrophy) could be prevented; that about a 30 per cent prevention rate was possible in the case of Down's Syndrome and congenital heart disease; finally it was argued that the incidence of spina bifida and related central nervous system abnormalities could be reduced by 10 per cent per annum (i.e. twenty-five cases a year in Northern Ireland). In the case of anencephaly, the Report claimed proper screening would permit the detection of nearly 90 per cent of all cases, and almost 80 per cent of cases of open spina bifida.

Second, more women give birth in Northern Ireland beyond the ages of thirty and thirty-five. This is partly the result of religious opposition to contraception. Table 1 compares live birth rates in five age groups in the four countries of the UK.

It is known that several congenital malformations show a higher incidence in older women (see Golding, Chapter 1.3), but it is difficult to estimate precisely how far the different patterns of fertility

Table 1 Live birth rates per 1,000 women in five age groups in 1977

Country	20–4	25–9	30–4	35–9	40–4
England	105	119	59	18	4
Wales	109	115	54	18	3
Scotland	109	120	58	18	4
N. Ireland	132	174	103	48	14

Source: CSO, 1979, p. 41.

contribute to the higher incidence rates. Probably contributing to these rates are the strong anti-abortion and anti-contraception attitudes of some sections of the religious community in Northern Ireland.

Dominating all these factors is the widespread and chronic social deprivation in the province. Northern Ireland has by far the greatest socio-economic problems in the United Kingdom, and the known association of many congenital malformations and prevalence rates of handicap with social conditions makes poverty a major contender as an explanation for higher incidence rates. The priority recommendations from the *You and Your Baby* Report recognized this association in calling for a policy of positive discrimination in favour of socially deprived areas in the provision of health and personal social services.

The Report linked two specific socio-economic variables to the incidence of handicap in Northern Ireland: poor housing and inadequate diet. About the first it was said:

Using a definition of housing stress based on households living in substandard of dwellings, overcrowding and economic disadvantage, the highest incidence of such stress in Northern Ireland is in the Belfast area and the Western part of the Province. . . . These same areas have the highest rates of infant mortality and handicap (p.10).

Secondly, inadequate diet and nutrition was seen as an important factor in the incidence of certain handicaps: 'There is evidence that on average in Northern Ireland an individual eats less non-root vegetables and less fruit than in other parts of the United Kingdom' (p. 10).

As they went on to suggest, the danger of vitamin deficiency had been shown to be a potentially crucial variable in the high incidence of spina bifida and anencephaly. They surmised that: 'If this is confirmed by subsequent studies it could clearly make a significant impact on the incidence of spina bifida and anencephaly' (p. 10).

Provision for special education in Northern Ireland

Special education in Northern Ireland is governed by similar laws and superficially appears comparable to provision in England and Wales. However it differs in certain crucial respects. First of all in most statutory categories, there is much less provision. Table 2 shows the number of children ascertained (or 'determined' as they are called in Northern Ireland) in statutory categories and educated in special schools in Northern Ireland compared to England and Wales.

Table 2 Provision of statutory categories of special needs, 1978, in England and Wales and Northern Ireland: number of children in special schools per 10,000 school population

Category	Northern Ireland	England and Wales
Delicate	3.8	4.9
Physically handicapped	8.1	13.7
Educationally Subnormal (ESN(M))	45.3	61.6
Maladjusted	1.9	14.8
Blind	0.7	1.3
Partially sighted	2.5	2.3
Deaf	1.3	3.9
Partially hearing	1.9	2.2
Speech defects	1.0	4.2

Sources: DES, 1980; Department of Education (Northern Ireland), 1980.

It is apparent that in all categories with the exception of the partially sighted, provision is substantially less in Northern Ireland. This is clearest for the 'maladjusted', indicating a clear difference in the criteria for allocation to this category. This explanation cannot be so readily invoked to explain, in particular, the lower level of provision for the physically handicapped children, which given higher prevalence rates, one would expect to be higher than in England and Wales. Provision in ordinary schools compensates the lack of special school provision for the hearing impaired. The number of children who are deaf or partially hearing in some form of special provision is 9.2 per 10,000 school population in Northern Ireland and 8.7 in England and Wales. But for other categories, special provision in ordinary schools does not compensate. In particular the small numbers of children determined as maladjusted are not explained by high numbers of maladjusted children in units and classes. In January 1980 there were only forty-two children determined as maladjusted in ordinary classes of ordinary schools, and none in special units in ordinary schools (figures provided by the Northern Ireland Department of Education, Statistics Branch).

The second respect in which special education is significantly different in Northern Ireland concerns the position of severely mentally handicapped children. In England and Wales the special educational needs of all children are the responsibility of the Department of Education and Science. The Education (Handicapped Children) Act of 1970 gave local education authorities the responsibility for educating all children irrespective of the severity of their handicap, and parallel legislation applies to Scotland. No such legislative change took place in Northern Ireland. Although there has been intense debate since, severely mentally handicapped children continue to be classed as being in need of special care and as unable to benefit from education. These children attend 'special care schools'. The administration of these falls under the Department of Health and Social Services, not the Department of Education. The majority of other handicapped children attend special schools.

Special schools

Prior to the 1948 Health Service (Northern Ireland) Act, mentally handicapped children and adults (as well as many of the physically handicapped) had no defined service. The majority were cared for in the home. Some were accommodated in psychiatric hospitals, others in the work houses. In an age when the general attitude towards the handicapped (particularly the mentally handicapped) ranged from support for euthanasia to pity, it is not surprising to discover that in Northern Ireland (and Europe as a whole) government policy hardly existed. However, with the post-war growth of the welfare state and the development of a more scientific, and humane, approach to educational psychology and the learning process, certain changes began to take place.

We can compare the improvement by looking at the following figures. In 1939 only seventy four children with physical and sensory handicaps received institutional treatment in the Belfast area. Of this number, seventy were classified as deaf and dumb and the remaining four as cripples. In 1936 Haypark School for backward children had opened. the only one of its type. As one writer rather naively put it:

> It seems now rather difficult to understand why there had been so little done for such children by the Authorities . . . . These children were simply disregarded. . . . It had become customary to regard the problem as one for the medical profession rather than the teacher. (McNeilly, 1973, p. 44)

After the war there was a gradual increase in provision. In 1952 the first provision was made for educating (at pre-school level) the physically handicapped, established by a voluntary body, the Northern Ireland Council for Orthopaedic Development (NICOD). In 1956 the Belfast Education and Library Board established the Fleming Fulton School which took over responsibility for the nursery established by NICOD five years earlier. This early example illustrates a trend, which has been general in the United Kingdom, of voluntary bodies first establishing provision, which were then taken over, or subsidized by governmental bodies. The same occurred with Mitchell House, Belfast. This was established by NICOD in 1956 and in its first phase was a voluntary school dependent on charity and grant-aid. Only in 1973 did it become a full state school. By 1971–2 nine special schools had been established in Belfast. Half of these catered for ESN children. In total 95 teachers were engaged to teach 1,126 pupils. (McNeilly, 1973) In the following eight years one special school was opened. The main expansion occurred within the existing schools. Present government expenditure cutbacks have inevitably slowed this process down. In Northern Ireland as a whole there now exist twenty-four special schools. However, these show a marked unevenness in regional distribution. Figure 1 shows that of the twenty-four existing schools seventeen are situated in, or within, a ten-mile radius of Belfast. This means that approximately 50 per cent of the population that live outside this area are catered for by only seven special schools. It is not surprising to discover therefore, that eight of the seventeen Belfast area schools offer boarding facilities.

Special care schools

After the Education (Handicapped Children) Act 1970 took effect in England and Wales, the Department of Health and Social Services gave long careful consideration to its implications and to whether a similar transfer of responsibility to the Department of Education (Northern Ireland) should be made. A Consultative Document on Services for the Mentally Handicapped was produced in April 1976 and the resulting policy document *Services for the Mentally Handicapped in Northern Ireland: Policy and Objectives* was published in July 1978 (DHSS, Northern Ireland, 1978a). The general tenet of the documents was that the Northern Ireland health and personal social service administration was in an advantageous position, unlike that in England, in having a unified responsibility for all aspects of care (medical, social, educational and training) thus ensuring a continuity of care, which was the prime concern. The Area Health and Social Services Boards argued that 'since mentally handicapped people by definition require care throughout

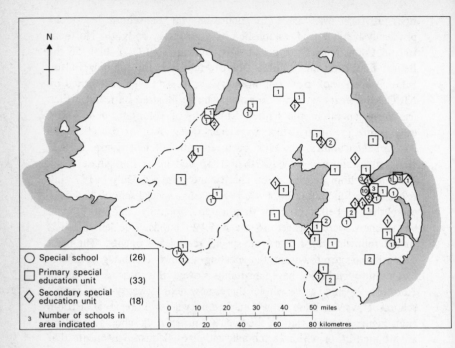

Figure 1 Distribution of special schools and special education units
(primary and secondary) in Northern Ireland, 1978
(Data from statistics of the Department of Education,
Northern Ireland)

their lives, while schooling covers only a few years and then only for
the period of actual attendance, there is less disruption in the
continuity of care if these schools remain as social services facilities'
(p. 14).

One factor that played a decisive role in maintaining the old system
was the fact that 50 per cent of the 2,000 special care school places
were filled by adults (aged sixteen–fifty years old). To change over
was not feasible without a massive increase in day-centre places. As the
two documents revealed, special care is in a dire state, with a serious
shortage of residential and day-care provision. The move towards
'normalization', with more adults in the community in adult training
centres, has and would have entailed great expenditure on building
programmes.

Northern Ireland's DHSS's limited budget has meant that the major
priority is to create more adult places and get the adults out of the

schools into centres providing suitable occupation and work training. (To meet this, the DHSS have put their own proposal to double nursery and day-care provision for the under-fives to one side.) It seems ironical that bearing in mind the official emphasis on the continuity of care, special care is unable to make provision for those already under the Boards' responsibility, not to mention all the handicapped children in other categories currently provided for by the education authorities, who will require provision on leaving school.

The continued classification of children as 'educable' or 'special care' creates problems and anomalies. It can become a critical issue for parents for practical as well as emotive reasons. Many mentally handicapped children are physically handicapped as well. When a child with multiple handicap is ascertained as 'borderline special care', placement in a special school for the physically handicapped rather than in a special care school can be advantageous.

Special care schools are staffed by qualified teachers who since 1978 are inspected by the Northern Ireland Education Inspectorate. This was a direct response to the teachers in the special care schools, and the parents of school-age mentally handicapped children ('the minority body', which the 1978 policy document described as having persuasively argued for the transfer of the schools to the Department of Education). The special care teacher/pupil ratio is 1:10 overall, but may vary within a school. Child-care attendants have also been introduced since 1978, to leave the teachers free to teach. All this is similar to a special school for the physically handicapped. The difference is in the provision of therapeutic paramedical staff. In the schools for the physically handicapped the Area Health and Social Services Boards provide full-time physiotherapists and occupational therapists, who are attached to a particular school. In special care schools, which are themselves the Health Boards' responsibility, physiotherapists and occupational therapists are employed on a peripatetic basis. When a child with a multiple handicap requires daily treatment, the special school can offer it, whereas the special care school cannot. Thus the placement of children determined as borderline can increase or decrease their potential physical achievement.

Provision in ordinary schools

In January 1980, 2,023 children determined as handicapped were being educated in Northern Ireland's ordinary schools, representing 0.54 per cent of the school population of 370,000. Table 3 shows their distribution.

Many of the special units providing for handicapped children are of

Table 3 Handicapped children in ordinary schools in Northern Ireland
(January 1980)

		In special units	In ordinary classes
Primary schools	Partially hearing	143	89
	Other handicaps	322	660
Secondary schools	Partially hearing	104	53
	Other handicaps	236	416
	Total	805	1,218

Source: Northern Ireland Department of Education, Statistics Branch.

recent origin, but of a total of forty-seven, thirty-three have only been established since the mid-1970s.

Thirty-two of the units are for the partially hearing. The other twelve are mainly for the ESN, with a few catering for the physically handicapped and those with speech defects. In some cases they are fully integrated with the rest of the school (as at Ballygolan Primary School with its partially hearing units). In many however, the units are effectively self-contained in separate buildings and attached to a particular school in little more than name.

These units may be seen as an effort to distribute special educational help more widely throughout the province. Prior to the establishment of these units hardly any special education provision existed outside Belfast. In Derry (the second city) the units constitute two-thirds of the special provision.

Preschool provision

Provision for handicapped children at this level cannot be separated from a discussion of the more general problems of preschool education in Northern Ireland. Nursery school and playgroup places are few and far between. Many nursery and playgroup facilities are run by voluntary bodies such as the NSPCC and the Save The Children Fund. In 1974, in Northern Ireland, full and part-time nursery education was available for only one child in every seventy-five, compared with one in thirteen in England and Wales.

Furthermore provision is particularly lacking in the most socially deprived areas. The Belfast Education and Library Board in their *Report on Nursery Education* (1978) said that 'The level of provision is alarmingly low in the Lower Falls, Upper Falls, Andersonstown, Ballymurphy, Whiterock, and Lenadoon areas.'

In the areas of greatest economic hardship, particularly the urban working-class Catholic districts where the potential need for nursery facilities is greatest, such provision is lacking. Part of the explanation for this has been the attitude of the local Roman Catholic church which is reluctant to provide or encourage nursery education in any form as it is deemed to undermine the role of the family and to bring into question the woman's proper role in the home, as wife and mother. In rural areas and indeed in many Protestant working-class districts the situation is similar. Here again, a strong pro-familial ideology prevails.

In October 1978 a government White Paper *Policy and Objectives: Day Care and Education for the Under-fives* (DHSS Northern Ireland, 1978b) proposed a doubling of nursery and playgroup places by 1983. However, government departmental cuts in allocations to Area Boards have resulted in a trimming down to the most 'essential' services by statutory provision. In this situation, preschool provision has been and is seen as an extra which may be cut without too much controversy.

In this general lack of provision, special preschool facilities are scarce. Fleming Fulton and Mitchell House remain the only special nurseries catering for the severely physically handicapped in Belfast. The Jordanstown school is the only school in Northern Ireland which provides nursery facilities for the profoundly deaf. The net effect of both the paucity and unequal distribution of special nursery facilities is twofold. First, although such a problem is not quantified, there clearly exists a general imbalance between demand and provision. The specialized preschool facilities simply do not correspond to needs in and out of Belfast. Second, the concentration in Belfast of the special nursery facilities which do exist, such as the three mentioned above, means that parents outside Belfast are faced with the choice (where places are available) of having no nursery provision readily available, or sending their children into board on a five-day basis. In short, the present situation is unsatisfactory at all levels and in all situations.

The context of special provision

The question of special provision for the handicapped cannot be abstracted from the constitutional, socio-economic and religious-cultural framework. Without some understanding of these issues, the reason why special provision has evolved in the way in which it has done would remain obscure. Three generalizations can be made. First the unique constitutional situation of Northern Ireland within the UK has created the institutional autonomy within which traditionalism could persist. Second, the religious cultures of the province only reinforce many of the basic problems, and third, socio-economic deprivation not only helps to explain the high incidence of handicap in the province and the difficulty of its eradication, but also affects the priority given to services for the handicapped.

The constitutional framework

> The general posture of successive British governments may be summarised in a single phrase, let sleeping dogs lie. Having extricated herself from the Irish imbroglio, Britain by and large left political leaders in Northern Ireland to deal with the difficulties that remained after British rule. (Lawrence, 1975)

The six counties of Northern Ireland, having resisted incorporation into what the Protestant majority feared would be a Catholic-dominated nation, remained part of the United Kingdom, but not in a full and integrated sense. The resulting constitutional arrangement, which at the time was regarded by many as a temporary compromise, in fact lasted until Stormont was prorogued by the Heath government in 1972. Since then, Northern Ireland has been ruled wholly from London, and British civil servants have been 'drafted in' to the Northern Ireland administration. Under the Stormont system, the province, whilst governed by the British parliament from Westminster, had its own local parliament. Unlike other regions of the UK therefore, it possessed a large, although by no means total, degree of autonomy. The attitude in London was to leave Northern Ireland to itself, as long as it remained stable and conformed in the broadest sense to UK standards. W. D. Flackes has commented:

> Some British Ministers regarded the old Stormont system as nearer to dominion status than to simple devolution. Thus, while the 1920 Act declared that the power of Westminster in Northern Ireland was not diminished in any way by local self-government, the reality was somewhat different. Westminster Ministers considered their responsibilities in Northern Ireland to be *limited* [my emphasis] to issues such as foreign trade, defence, major taxation, customs and excise and the High Court. (Flackes, 1980, p. 185)

Parliamentary rules, at least until the troubles, did not therefore permit discussion on the province. Legislation for the UK did not automatically apply to Northern Ireland. This had to be discussed at Stormont where it could be amended. By no means all UK legislation was applied in the province. The result has been to create notable legal differences. For instance, the 1967 Act on homosexuality was not applied in Northern

Ireland. Divorce law has remained very restrictive. Abortion has never been made legal. How has this constitutional and administrative situation affected the problem of special education in and for Northern Ireland?

In general the effect of devolved government in Northern Ireland (and this has persisted even since the introduction of direct rule in 1972) has been to create definite anomalies between practice in the province and the rest of the United Kingdom. Where it was believed that administrators and the populace as a whole would resist innovations and changes, these were not introduced, or were only introduced in a modified form, usually at a later date. It has inevitably led to the situation that special problems could persist for a longer time, without being either recognized or tackled.

I have already noted how the 1970 UK legislation was not enacted for Northern Ireland. It is also worth noting that the subsequent UK enquiry into special educational needs did not apply to Northern Ireland either. The Warnock Report (DES, 1978) provided further indication of the problems arising from Northern Ireland's peculiar situation within the UK. Its terms of reference specifically excluded studying Northern Ireland either as a special case, or as part of UK provisions as a whole. The function of the Committee was to:

review educational provision in England, Scotland and Wales for children and young people handicapped by disabilities of body or mind, taking account of the medical aspects of their needs together with arrangements to prepare them for entry into employment; to consider the most effective use of resources for these purposes; and to make recommendations.

Northern Ireland was thus ignored in this most important of reports. The Committee's composition reflected the same bias, for although there were five members from Scotland and Wales, there were none from Northern Ireland. Whilst three assessors from the Scottish Education Department and one from the Welsh Education Office were attached to the Committee, there was no equivalent appointee from Northern Ireland. Of the fifteen co-opted members two were from Scotland, one from Wales but none were from Northern Ireland. The Committee went on 'many visits, individually or in groups, to a wide range of institutions in England, Scotland and Wales', but none, apparently, were made to the province. Even though other fact-finding tours were made to the United States, Canada, Denmark, Sweden, Holland and West Germany, none were made to Northern Ireland.

Of course, it is possible to suggest that this exclusion of Northern Ireland was because of the political disturbances at the time. However, it seems much more likely that another and more profound influence was at work — the persistence of the view, which was almost unstated, that Northern Ireland should be left alone to sort out its own problems.

The religious and cultural context

I have already mentioned the role of the churches in the higher incidence rates of congenital handicaps, by their opposition to abortion and contraception. However, they also have played a role in the way in which special provision has developed in Northern Ireland.

There is high involvement of the churches (particularly the Catholic church) at all levels of the general education system. Religious control of appointments and the curriculum is strong. All state schools have 50 per cent of the seats on management committees reserved for the clergy or their appointees. In Catholic schools, the proportion of reserved management seats is 66 per cent. Perhaps a less obtrusive although possibly a more effective form of clerical control is the actual appointment of clerics to top teaching posts. A 1977 survey showed that a high proportion of principals in Protestant schools are involved in 'church duties', such as organists, lay preachers, Sunday School teachers and elders. In Catholic schools, nuns and clerics predominate in posts of responsibility as well as principalships.

One might expect that this pervasive religious influence would be at least as strong in special schools. Given the Christian ethic of compassion and charity, it might be supposed that their influence would be stronger. However, this is not the case. It is a curious fact that special schools for the physically and mentally handicapped, deaf and blind, represent (apart from the technical schools) the only non-sectarian schools in Northern Ireland. This low profile cannot be ignored, for it illustrates a particular attitude of the churches in Northern Ireland to the handicapped. The lack of interest in the religious education of the handicapped seems to suggest that these children are not regarded by the churches as full and adequate members of society who have a potential for development. In a more general sense (although quite unconsciously and for the best of motives) the churches reinforce the attitude that the best approach to the problems of the handicapped is charity and care.

The effects of this attitude are manifold. The churches do not really act as a pressure for increased provision by the state. In general they assume and spread the view that the handicapped are a cross to bear. Given their strong pro-familial ideology, it is almost certain that they believe that the real place for the handicapped is in the family. Again, this demobilizes pressure for increased and more adequate provision of nurseries, schools and pre-industrial training facilities. By encouraging passive acceptance of the situation and thus lowering aspirations in the communities, they tend to undermine the efforts of parents and children who want to achieve and who are seeking change. In short the strong religious influence in Northern Ireland has acted as a force for conservatism where the handicapped are concerned.

The social and economic context

One of the few beneficial effects of the 'troubles' has been to focus attention on, and direct research towards the social and economic structures of Northern Ireland. The province is the poorest region of the UK and suffers from chronic regional underdevelopment. The problem of deprivation in Northern Ireland is clearly not a simple by-product of post-war economic decline. Living standards in general have always been lower in Northern Ireland compared to the rest of the United Kingdom. In the inter-war years, in social security and housing the levels of public expenditure were lower than in the rest of the United Kingdom. The unemployment insurance scheme was far narrower in application than in Great Britain. It excluded a larger proportion of workers and the contribution conditions were more severe. As a result a far larger proportion of people were forced to seek help from the Poor Law. Expenditure under the Poor Law, however, was considerably lower than in other parts of the United Kingdom. In housing, local authorities only provided 15 per cent of all new housing built between the wars, compared with 25 per cent in England and Wales. This has contributed to the deep structural crisis in Northern Ireland housing which has persisted to the present day. The Northern Ireland Housing Executive conducted a Housing Condition Survey in 1974 and found that 19.5 per cent of houses were unfit for habitation. Unemployment rates in the province are among the highest in the UK. In January 1980, when the unemployment rate in the south-east of England was 3.9 per cent and in the north 9.0 per cent, it was 11.5 per cent in Northern Ireland. However, these figures conceal great variations. Certain Catholic areas of West Belfast and west in the River Bann experience Third World levels of unemployment (see, for example, Boal, Doherty and Pringle, 1974).

Improvements have obviously occurred in the post-war period. Yet Northern Ireland still remains the key problem area in the United Kingdom. This was the conclusion reached by Townsend (1979). He compared household incomes in the regions of the UK as percentages of the supplementary benefit scales. Table 4 shows the results for Northern Ireland, the North West, the East Midlands and Greater London. Northern Ireland emerged as having the highest level of poverty of all regions in the UK.

Table 4 Percentages of population in different regions according to net disposable income

| | Household income as % of supplementary benefit rates | | | |
	under 140	140–99	over 200	no. of people in sample
N. Ireland	44.3	29.3	26.4	239
North West	33.9	31.6	34.6	612
Anglia and East Midlands	24.9	33.6	41.5	497
Greater London	23.1	28.3	48.7	697

This conclusion was recently endorsed in a short but systematic study by Eileen Evason (1980):

> The position of Northern Ireland as one of the smallest (population one-and-a-half million) and poorest regions in the United Kingdom is by now well known. The striking volume of income deprivation noted in survey after survey is a product of high unemployment, low wages, higher prices and slightly larger households. No other region in the United Kingdom is trying to cope with the combined effects of such a range of problems (p. 9).

Evason's pessimistic conclusions were supported by recent research into low pay in Northern Ireland by Black, Ditch, Morrissey and Steele (1980). Their research showed that low pay among men in Northern Ireland stood at twice the United Kingdom average; that expenditure on various durable household goods was significantly lower in Northern Ireland; that about one-third of all households found themselves living below needs level and that all measures adopted by the state to alleviate low pay in the province had had very little effect. As the recession bites deeper in Northern Ireland, the percentage in the poverty trap is bound to increase.

In this situation, less pressure arises to provide facilities for the severely handicapped. This has been particularly evident in the provision of pre-industrial training and work experience. In the whole of Belfast there is only one work centre for physically handicapped people, which provides 'sheltered employment' for some thirty-five disabled young people. It is not equipped to provide them with skills that would permit them to go into open employment. There is no place in Northern Ireland that provides training for moderately or severely disabled people.

Conclusion

Northern Ireland must be treated as a distinct problem area; the failure to develop fully adequate services is due to profound and persistent structures. In Northern Ireland we not only confront a crisis created by current public expenditure cuts, but also deeper and longer-term problems — the result of historical neglect, structural deprivation unequalled anywhere else in the UK and resistance to change by conservative interest groups.

However, the situation is not entirely static. The political unrest of the past decade has inevitably led to an intense questioning of the old *status quo*. Pressure for change is growing, and the demand for equality with the rest of the UK is bound to increase the longer direct rule continues. In the final analysis the shape of special education in Northern Ireland will be formed by broader political forces, and will be determined by the outcome of the present conflict and its final resolution.

References

Black, B., Ditch, J., Morrissey, M. and Steele, R. (1980) *Low Pay in Northern Ireland*, London, Low Pay Unit.

Boal, F. W., Doherty, P. and Pringle, D. G. (1974) *Social Problems in the Belfast Urban Area: an Exploratory Analysis*, London, Queen Mary College, University of London.

Central Statistical Office (1979) *Regional Statistics, No. 14*, London, HMSO.

DES (1980) *Statistics of Education, Volume 1*, London, HMSO.

Department of Education, Northern Ireland (1980) *Northern Ireland Education Statistics: Schools, Pupils, Teachers, Scholarships and Awards*, Belfast, HMSO.

DHSS, Northern Ireland (1978a) *Services for the Mentally Handicapped in Northern Ireland: Policy and Objectives*, Belfast, HMSO.

DHSS, Northern Ireland (1978b) *Policy and Objectives: Day Care and Education for the Under-fives*, Belfast, HMSO.

DHSS, Northern Ireland (1980) *You and Your Baby. Report of the Advisory Committee on Infant Mortality and Handicap in Northern Ireland*, Belfast, HMSO.

Evason, E. (1980) *Ends that Won't Meet: a Study of Poverty in Belfast* (Poverty Research Series 8), London, Child Poverty Action Group.

Flackes, W. D. (1980) *Northern Ireland: a Political Directory, 1968–1979*, New York, Gill and MacMillan.

Harbison, J. and Harbison, J. (1980) *Society Under Stress: Children and Young People in Northern Ireland*, London, Open Books.

Lawrence, R. J. (1975) Northern Ireland, in Thornhill, N. (Ed.) *The Modernization of British Government*, London, Pitman.

McNeilly, N. (1973) *Exactly Fifty Years: The Belfast Education Authority and its Work, 1923–1973*, Belfast, Blackstaff.

Office of Population Censuses and Surveys (1980) *OPCS Monitor: Congenital Malformations* (Reference MB3 80/4), London, HMSO.

Townsend, P. (1979) *Poverty in the United Kingdom: a Survey of Household Resources and Standards of Living*, Harmondsworth, Penguin.

5.4 Education can compensate

A. H. HALSEY

In the 1960s and early 1970s in Western Europe and the USA there were many attempts to use education as a weapon to combat social and economic inequality. Most of the effort of compensatory education was aimed at preventing later school failure by providing concentrated doses of structured preschool experience for disadvantaged children. But the initial results were disappointing: gains were made, but they tended to disappear after a few years of primary schooling. In this paper, A. H. Halsey describes the recent and much more optimistic results of the long-term effects of compensatory preschool education, in particular its effect in reducing the likelihood of a child's referral for special education.

Educational budgets are now under siege all over the western world. Ministries of Education have been dominated by optimism for a century. They pursued policies of expansion in the belief that national wealth, and the reduction of social inequality, would inevitably follow.

The official ideology of liberal progress was never undisputed, but it was dominant. The consensual political middle trudged on in Britain, through the 1870, 1902 and 1944 Education Acts, slowly developing a state system of common schooling from infancy to adolescence, topped by selective and voluntary education beyond school.

Optimism reached its apogee in the easy affluence of the 1950s and early 1960s, with education steadily increasing its share of both the gross domestic product and the public purse, until at the end of the sixties it was halted. Schools and colleges now stand in the shadows, convicted of high promises and low performance.

Professor Jensen convinced many Americans that the intelligence of black children could not be boosted by pre-school programmes. In Britain this abrupt reversal of fortune was rationalized mainly by the Black Paper pessimism of the right, compounded by economic depression and now by a monetarist government bent on cutting public

Source: Halsey, A.H. (1980) Education can compensate, *New Society*, 24 January 1980. Copyright © New Society, London. Reprinted by permission.

expenditure. Nursery education — formerly and ironically a darling of Margaret Thatcher when Secretary of State — is now a prime target.

But the defences of the educational expansionists were also undermined from the left. Christopher Jenck's *Inequality* (published in 1972) was a powerful American blow against what he took to be the misguided faith of the schoolmaster turned President in Lyndon Johnson's Washington:

'As long as egalitarians assume that public policy cannot contribute to economic equality directly but must proceed by ingenious manipulations of marginal institutions like the schools, progress will remain glacial. If we want to move beyond this tradition, we will have to establish political control over the economic institutions that shape our society. That is what other countries usually call socialism. Anything less will end in the same disappointment as the reforms of the 1960s.'

The most publicized 'ingenious manipulations of marginal institutions' in America in the 1960s was Headstart — a programme of pre-schooling. Disappointment with 'Headstart's early results were the starting point of Jensen's researches. All the more interesting, then, to have a study published a decade later by the American Department of Health, Education and Welfare, in which the question is elaborately asked whether there have in fact been *Lasting Effects After Pre-School* from the euphoric educational reforms of the 'war on poverty'.

In Britain, pre-schooling developed sceptically and tentatively (in the wake of Headstart) within the action research programmes of Education Priority Areas. It was greeted with hostility from both left and right. 'A research smokescreen', declared John Barron Mays, Professor of Sociology at Liverpool. 'Nursery education has been tried in America and doesn't work', was the crude opinion of a high-ranking Tory minister. Moreover, and unhappily, one of the most influential and deservedly respected sociologists of education, Professor Basil Bernstein, could also be involved in opposition to the Headstart idea. He entitled an influential article 'Education cannot compensate for society' (Bernstein, 1970); warned against treating children as 'deficit systems'; against distracting attention from the reform of schools on to the shortcomings of parents and families; and against the sanctifying of concepts like 'cultural deprivation' as labels which would add further to the burdens of the children made to wear them.

Bernstein's were humane cautions linked to sophisticated argument. But they were easily and fatally assimilated to the holy proletarianism of a then-fashionable left, with its ideologically *a priori* rejection of the possibility that anything could be wrong with a working class child.

Those who were more concerned with practical reform than with ideological purity preferred to notice that 'deficit' could be socially created. They inferred that it could therefore be socially remedied. But, as has so often happened with Bernstein's research, the message was vulgarized by others. In the popular and political mind what stuck was his:

We should stop thinking in terms of 'compensatory education' and not the rest of the sentence, which read:

but consider, instead, most seriously and systematically the conditions and contexts of the educational environment.

The Education Priority Area projects in London, Liverpool, Birmingham and the West Riding were well described by the neglected half of Bernstein's sentence. They also, however, contained crucial elements of 'compensatory' (even though the participants preferred to call it 'complementary') education. More precisely, the EPA researchers had been impressed by the principle of positive discrimination, put forward in the Plowden report of 1967.

They tried, with resources that have to be described as miniscule by comparison with the American programme, to apply positive discrimination to the educational environment of slum children. The EPA projects — which were directed from Oxford — began when and because Anthony Crosland was Secretary of State at the Department of Education and Science, and Michael Young was chairman of the Social Science Research Council. They ended and reported when Mrs Thatcher was established at the DES and Sir Keith Joseph at the DHSS. Most precisely they recommended positive discrimination in pre-schooling.

The experience of three years in four districts had led to the conclusion 'that pre-schooling is *par excellence* a point of entry into the development of the community school as we conceive of it. It is the point at which properly understood, the networks of family and formal education can most easily be linked.' And three years of action research supported the contention 'that pre-schooling is the most effective educational instrument for applying the principle of positive discrimination and this conviction rests partly on the theory that primary and secondary educational attainment has its social foundations in the child's experience in the pre-school years, and partly on the evidence that positive discrimination at the pre-school level can have a multiplier effect on the overwhelmingly important educative influence of the family and the peer group to which the child belongs.'

We can now go some way further towards testing the validity of an adherence to optimism, retained in the teeth of opposition both then and since. The new American study has been produced by a consortium of twelve research groups, carrying out studies of the *long-run* effects of the early education programmes of the 1960s (Lazar and Darlington, 1978). The group was led by Irving Lazar and Richard Darlington. Having pooled the data from their originally independent experiments, they collected common follow-up data in 1976–7. In this way they have assembled records of the experience and performance of 3,000 children, mostly black and all poor, who were involved in early education programmes in the 1960s, either as 'experimental' or 'control' subjects, and who by 1976–7 were between 9 and 19 years old.

This is valuable and rare evidence. It would take another 15 years and millions of dollars to re-create it. Of course, it has its imperfections, quite apart from the dangers of any transatlantic passage. The original Headstart experiments were not designed to collect common information. They varied in size, starting point and content; they were, to varying degrees, experimental; and there has been a lot of attrition. Moreover, those in the Lazar–Darlington study are not just any old Headstart projects, but ones which are usable because they were properly designed and recorded. They include, for instance, the famous projects by Susan Gray in Tennessee, and by Deutsch in New York. Nevertheless, remarkable trouble has been taken in producing the final sample, and measuring its relation to the original population. Exceptionally rigorous rules have governed the testing for the long-term effects. It is, in short, an evaluation done with meticulous care.

The upshot is that the Lazar–Darlington consortium has established the existence of lasting effects from pre-schooling (i.e. nursery schooling) in four main ways.

First, they show that the beneficiaries are less likely to be assigned later to special or remedial classes. This effect of pre-schooling was shown to be there for children of the same initial IQ, sex, ethnicity, and family background. It persisted even when the comparison was controlled for IQ scores at age six.

Second, there has been the same lasting effect with respect to dropout from school, and what the Americans call 'retention in grade' – i.e. being held back to repeat a year's work because of poor performance. According to the evidence of the eight projects which had collected the relevant data, early educational experience protects against these failures. The protection holds for all poor children regardless of sex, ethnic backgrounds, early IQ and family circumstances.

Third, achievement in mathematics at age ten (fourth grade) is significantly improved by pre-schooling. The evidence also suggests a trend to better scores on reading tests at the same age.

Fourth, children from poor families who went to pre-school

programmes scored higher than the 'control' children on the Stanford Binet IQ test for up to three years afterwards. In some projects, this superiority was maintained, but not among those who were aged 13 or over.

Finally, it has emerged that pre-school children retain more 'achievement orientation', and their mothers tend to develop higher vocational aspirations for them than they have for themselves – a discrepancy not found among 'control' children.

The first and second effects are shown in Table 1. Those who had the 'treatment' – i.e. went to one of these well-planned programmes, are compared with a control group of socially and racially matched children who did not. Table 1 tells us that, ordinarily, 44 per cent of children from disadvantaged homes have had to be given special remedial education, or are made to repeat a year, or have dropped out from school: but among those given pre-school education of a certain kind the proportion is reduced to 25 per cent. Altogether, if you send children to a good nursery school, they are twice as likely afterwards to stay above the minimum level of school success as a similar group of children denied the opportunity.

It is true, as I have noted, that these impressive findings come from high-quality pre-school arrangements, and not from a random sample of Headstart programmes. It is true, too, that to use avoidance of remedial classes and 'grade failure' as measures of effectiveness is to focus on the minimal aspirations of a school's work. On the other hand, these are appropriate measures from two points of view. They point to characteristic failures of the children for whom the pre-school programmes were designed – typically, the black child from a poor family. And they are measures of actual educational experience, rather than abstractions like measured intelligence, which may or may not issue in practical performance.

Educational policy makers on either side of the Atlantic may be justifiably disappointed that research has still failed to discern any particular feature of pre-schooling which accounted for success: for example, age of entry, parental involvement, type of teacher or type of teaching. The programmes varied in all these respects. What they had in common was enthusiastic and careful organisation. These qualities also made them usable for comparative and retrospective research.

But what Headstart and the EPA experience do show is that a pre-school programme, properly devised, can be a most economical investment for a government wishing to save money on schools. And for a government determined to relieve the handicaps of those who come from poor families, a pre-school programme discriminating in their favour seems to be one of the crucial weapons in the armoury. In that way, education *can* compensate for society.

Table 1 How many under-achieving students did better after Headstart?

Headstart project	Failure rate of project children	Failure rate of control children	Reduction in failure by attending project	Total
good experimental design				
	%	%	%	No.
Gordon	39.1	61.5	36.0	82
Gray	55.6	73.7	24.6	55
Palmer	24.1	44.7	46.1	221
Weikart	17.2	38.5	55.3	123
median	31.6	53.1	41.1	481
quasi-experimental design				
Beller	48.6	53.1	8.5	69
Levenstein	22.1	43.5	49.2	127
Miller	20.6	11.1	–	125
Zigler	26.6	32.3	17.6	144
overall median	25.4	44.1	36.4	920

NB: 'Failure' is defined as being placed in special education classes, and/or retained in grade, and/or dropped out of school. 'Reduction' is % control minus % project, divided by % control. Children's data were collected in different grades. The design of the Miller project permits no 'reduction' conclusion. The numbers in the total are of project children plus control children.

References

Bernstein, B. (1970) Education cannot compensate for society, *New Society*, 26 February.

Jencks, C. *et al.* (1972) *Inequality: Reassessment of the Effect of Family and Schooling in America*, London, Allen Lane.

Lazar, I. and Darlington, R. (1978) *Lasting Effects after Preschool*, A report of the Consortium for Longitudinal Studies.

5.5 The end of a quiet revolution: the United States Education for All Handicapped Children Act, 1975

ALAN ABESON AND JEFFREY ZETTEL

No legislation in special education has been more thoroughly debated than the United States' Public Law 94–142, although in Great Britain there remains little awareness of its nature or effects. In this paper, written before the law was implemented, Abeson and Zettel, members of staff of the US Council for Exceptional Children, analysed the policy failures and litigation that preceded PL 94–142, described the principal provisions in the new legislation and looked forward to a better future for America's estimated eight million handicapped children.

On the opening day of school in September 1978, a quiet revolution will end. The end will not come silently, easily , nor dispassionately. The officers and soldiers who led and fought the revolution will not fade away for they recognize that the passing of this revolution may merely be signalling the beginning of the next. Accompanying this end, however, will be celebration — celebration for children who are handicapped and who, since the beginning of public education in the United States, have been the victims of discrimination that often prevented them from receiving an education. On that day in 1978, it will be a violation of federal law for any public education agency to deny to a handicapped child in need of a special education an appropriate programme. As stated by the National Advisory Committee on the Education of the Handicapped (1976), 'In law and as national policy, education is today recognized as the handicapped person's right' (p. 143).

The beginning of the end of the final phase of the revolution to achieve public policy affirming the right to an education for every child with a handicap was on November 29, 1975, when President Gerald

Source: The end of a quiet revolution: the United States Education for All Handicapped Children Act, 1975, by Abeson, A. and Zettel, J., *Exceptional Children*, 44 (1977), 115–28. Copyright 1977 by the Council for Exceptional Children. Reprinted with permission.

Ford signed into law Public Law (P. L.) 94–142, the Education for All Handicapped Children Act of 1975, which becomes fully effective in September 1978. This law, which concluded the policy revolution begun in 1970, was built heavily on the policy victories that were won since that time in the Nation's courts and state legislatures. Additionally, the Act is based upon principles of sound educational practice that, although applicable to all children including the handicapped, were often pioneered and articulated by special educators.

Since the enactment of P. L. 94–142, it has been a central theme of discussion for virtually every element of the education community in the United States. The discussions have centred around strengths and perceived weaknesses of the Act and the implications for professionals and for parents. [. . .] The settings of these discussions have extended from the Congress, the United States Office of Education, state legislatures, and state departments of education to local school boards and local education agencies.

Too frequently, however, the topic not discussed is implementation. It is implementation that begins for some children in October 1977 but that must be extended to all school age youngsters in September 1978. Too frequently as well, discussions of P. L. 94–142 have been based on misinformation or misinterpretation. Too often during these debates, the history is forgotten, administration reigns supreme, and the danger of this law becoming a comprehensive set of empty promises looms large. [. . .]

In large measure, the burden for overseeing the effective implementation of this Act rests at least in part with special educators, many of whom are the veterans of the battles just concluded. Teachers, administrators, psychologists, therapists, and parents, for example, are all members of the implementation community. So too are all other members of the education community who may not be aware nor think of themselves as having responsibilities for children who have handicaps. [. . .]

A recent history of the inadequacy of educating children who have handicaps

With minor exceptions, mankind's attitudes towards its handicapped population can be characterized by overwhelming prejudice. [The handicapped are systematically isolated from] the mainstream of society. From ancient to modern times, the physically, mentally or emotionally disabled have been alternatively viewed by the majority as dangers to be destroyed, as nuisances to be driven out, or as burdens to be confined. [. . .] Treatment resulting from a tradition of isolation has been invariably unequal and has operated to prejudice the interests of the handicapped as a minority group. (*Lori Case* v. *State of California*, 1973, p. 2a)

The manifestations of these attitudes occurred in schools in a variety of ways including the exclusion of children who have handicaps, incorrect or inappropriate classification, labelling or placement, and the provision of inappropriate education programmes, as well as arbitrary and capricious educational decision making. While this listing is not exhaustive, it is illustrative of the major practices in use prior to the initiation of the quiet revolution. To a large degree, the Congress designed P. L. 94—142 to respond at least in part to these illegal and inappropriate practices.

Exclusion, postponement, and the right to an education

The Congress of the United States in the statement of findings and purposes that are a part of P. L. 94—142 (1975), indicated that 'one million of the handicapped children in the United States are excluded entirely from the public school system and will not go through the educational process, with their peers' (Sec. 3, b, 4). Related is an analysis of 1970 census data done by the Children's Defense Fund (1974) who concluded that 'out of school children share a common characteristic of differentness by virtue of race, income, physical, mental or emotional "handicap" and age' (p. 4). [. . .]

Beginning in 1970 and continuing today, the legality of denying a public education to a child with a handicap by exclusion, postponement, or by any other means has been successfully challenged in both state and federal judicial systems. The rationale for such litigation has been primarily derived from the equal protection clause of the Fourteenth Amendment of the United States Constitution, which guarantees equal protection of the law to all the people. In other words, where a state has undertaken to provide a benefit to the people, such as public education, these benefits must be provided to all of the people unless the state can demonstrate a compelling reason for doing otherwise. The language most often used to express this concept in education was the 1954 *Brown* v. *Board of Education* Supreme Court decision that proclaimed:

In these days it is doubtful that any child may reasonably be expected to succeed in life if he is denied the opportunity for an education. Such an opportunity, where the state has undertaken to provide it, is a right which must be made available to all on equal terms. (74S. Ct. 686, 98L. Ed. 873)

Two of the most heralded and precedent setting right to education lawsuits occurred in the early 1970s in Pennsylvania and the District of Columbia. It was in fact these cases that initiated the quiet revolution. In January 1971, the Pennsylvania Association for Retarded Children (PARC) brought a class action suit[1] against the Commonwealth of Pennsylvania in Federal District Court for the alleged failure of the state to provide all of its school age children who were retarded with access to a free public education. The court decreed the state could not apply any policy that would postpone, terminate, or deny children who were mentally retarded access to a publicly supported education. Further, it stated that all retarded children in the State of Pennsylvania between the ages of 6 and 21 were to be provided with a publicly supported education by September 1972 (*Pennsylvania Association for Retarded Children* v. *Commonwealth of Pennsylvania*, Consent Agreement, 1972).

Following the *PARC* decision, a second, similar federal decree was achieved in 1972. In *Mills* v. *Board of Education of the District of Columbia* (1972), the parents and guardians of seven District of Columbia children brought a class action suit on behalf of all out of school handicapped children. The outcome of the *Mills* decision was a court order providing that all school age children, regardless of the severity of their handicap, were entitled to an appropriate free public education.

In both the *PARC* and *Mills* cases, allegations were made regarding the manner in which identification, evaluation and placement activities, and decisions were rendered regarding the education of children who have handicaps. Consequently, both the *PARC* consent agreement and the *Mills* decree required specific due process procedures to be established. Also litigated in these cases was the issue of where children with handicaps should be placed in relation to nonhandicapped children for receipt of their education. Both of these policy areas will be examined later in this article.

Following the precedents established by these two cases, the right to education principle became further solidified through the passage of a number of state statutes and regulations, thus adding to the impetus and policy breadth of the revolution. By 1972 it was reported that nearly 70% of the states had adopted mandatory legislation requiring the education of all children who have handicaps as defined in each state's policies (Abeson, 1972). By 1975 all but two state legislatures had adopted some form of mandatory law calling for the education of at least the majority of its handicapped children (US Congress, Senate, 1975). Today all but one state has enacted such legislation. Further, the Education Amendments of 1974; P. L. 93—380, required that, in order for states to participate in the financial assistance available under the Act, they were to establish a goal of providing full educational opportunities to all children with handicaps.

Incorrect or inappropriate classification or labelling

A major component of the quiet revolution, the labelling and classification dilemma also became the subject of litigation. It must be recognized, however, that Dunn in 1968 published an historic article that described the issue and brought it to the attention of the field. For purposes of litigation, however, substantial evidence was gathered which supported the claim that schools too often assigned labels, subjected children to individual psychological assessments, and altered their educational status without the appropriate supporting data and often without parental knowledge.

The classification of children with handicaps by categorical labels was shown to produce major problems (Abeson, Bolick, and Hass, 1975). Among the adverse effects of inappropriate labelling are first, labelled children are often victimized by stigma associated with the label. This may be manifested by isolation from usual school opportunities and taunting and rejection by both children and school personnel. In the latter instance, it may be overt or unconscious. Secondly, assigning labels to children often suggests to those working with them that the children's behaviour should conform to stereotyped behavioural expectations associated with the labels. This often contributes to a self fulfilling prophecy in that a child, once labelled, is expected to conform with the stereotyped behaviour associated with the label and ultimately does so. When a child is labelled and placement is made on the basis of that label, there is often no opportunity to escape from either the label or the placement. Thirdly, children who are labelled and placed in educational programmes on the basis of that label may often not need special education programmes. This is obviously true for children who are incorrectly labelled, but it also applies to children with certain handicaps, often of a physical nature. The fact that a child is physically handicapped does not mean that a special education is required.

Other researchers questioned the alleged preponderance of minority group children found in special education classes. Studies conducted by the California State Department of Education, for example, discovered that while Spanish surnamed children comprised only 13% of their total school population, they accounted for more than 26% of the students in their classes for the educable mentally retarded (Weintraub, 1972). Mercer (1970), examining the process of special educational placement in Riverside, California, found three times more Mexican Americans and two and a half times more Black Americans in those programmes than would be expected from their percentage in the general population. [See Mercer, this volume, Chapter 1.2]

In January 1970, *Diana* v. *State Board of Education* was filed in the District Court of Northern California. The suit, brought on behalf of nine Mexican American students aged 8 through 13, alleged that the students had been improperly placed in classes for the mentally retarded on the basis of inaccurate tests. Coming from homes where Spanish was the predominant or only spoken language, the plaintiffs argued they had been placed in classes for the educable mentally retarded on the results of an IQ score obtained from either a Stanford-Binet or Wechsler intelligence test. When the nine were retested in Spanish, however, seven scored higher than the IQ cutoff for placement in classes for the educable mentally retarded.

On the basis of this data, the plaintiffs argued that the tests relied primarily on a verbal aptitude in English and ignored their learning abilities in Spanish and that the tests were standardized on White, native born Americans and related in subject matter solely to the dominant White, middle class culture (Ross, DeYoung, & Cohen, 1971).

A similar landmark decision regarding the testing and classification of students was filed in late 1971 on behalf of six Black, elementary students attending the San Francisco Unified School District. The plaintiffs in *Larry P.* v. *Riles* (1972) alleged they had been inappropriately classified as educable mentally retarded on the basis of a testing procedure that failed to recognize their unfamiliarity with the White middle class culture and that ignored learning experiences they might have had in their homes.

In resolving these suits, various agreements were established requiring the use of the following types of practices: children were to be tested in their primary language and interpreters were to be used when a bilingual examiner was not available; Mexican American, Black American, and Chinese American children already in classes for the mentally retarded were to be retested and evaluated; the state was to undertake immediate efforts to develop and standardize an appropriate IQ test.

As with right to education, these cases and the growing literature led to the concept of nondiscriminatory evaluation. This concept was also added to state law in many states particularly in the form of requiring school districts to consider multiple data and sources for consideration by teams of professionals prior to making classification and placement decisions. In addition, mandates appeared requiring that parents of children suspected of being handicapped be provided with notice and the opportunity to approve or reject evaluation of their child. These principles were also articulated in P. L. 93–380. Specifically required of the states was that they were to adopt procedures to ensure that testing materials and procedures used for classification and placement of handicapped children were to be selected and administered so as not to be racially or culturally discriminatory.

Provision of inappropriate education programmes

While the quiet revolution at times seemed to be focusing on major rights issues, attention was also focused upon more than simple access to the public schools. The evidence that emerged in the process of documenting the effects of classification and their resulting placements seemed to suggest that many assignments were made as a function of administrative convenience rather than an awareness of the individual needs of children. Consequently, the goal of access was modified and expanded to include the concept of access to appropriate programmes.

This concern was reflected in the judicial orders that emerged from both the right to education and classification litigation. Similarly, the emerging statutes qualifying the nature of the education to be provided to children with handicaps were abundant with the words 'suitable' and 'appropriate' and the phrases 'specialized instruction', 'appropriate to the child's capacity', and 'designed to develop the maximum potential of every handicapped person'.

These qualifiers were further translated principally in state statute and regulation into requirements for the development of some type of individually designed and delivered programme. A notable example comes from Illinois, which adopted a regulation (State of Illinois, 1974) requiring that educational plans be developed that include specific objectives to be attained by each child.

Such directives were clearly related to the use of multiple professionals in the evaluation process. Without such a procedure and goal, much of the valuable individual information acquired about each child was lost and never considered in relation to the unique needs of individual children. Further, it became apparent as the revolution progressed that the spectre of accountability was also going to be applied to the education of handicapped children.

A major aspect of the suitability or appropriateness of a handicapped child's programme, which was further addressed in the litigation, was where children with handicaps should be placed for educational purposes in relation to their nonhandicapped contemporaries. The conceptual basis for considering this issue came largely from Reynolds (1962) who portrayed the existence of a continuum of placements for children with handicaps ranging from the least restrictive (i.e., being placed in a regular classroom setting with considerable opportunity to interact with nonhandicapped children) to the most restrictive setting (i.e., a special school or a nonpublic school placement, such as a private institution, that would provide little if any contact with nonhandicapped individuals). It is well recognized, however, that the implementation of this continuum was never intended nor should be interpreted to mean that all handicapped children should be placed in regular classrooms. What is intended is that individual children, possessing individual needs, will be placed on the basis of these needs in the least restrictive setting.

As of 1974 only six states were required by law and eleven by regulation[2] to adhere to the principle of least restrictive placement (Bolick, 1974). However, by October 1975, the National Education Association reported that twenty-two or half of their state affiliates reported having statutory or regulatory language requiring that children with handicaps were to be placed in regular classes at least some of the time.

Perhaps one of the clearest and most comprehensive statutory definitions of least restrictive environment as it applies to children with handicaps can be found in the following 1972 Tennessee state statute, which was essentially echoed in P. L. 94–142:

> To the maximum extent practicable, handicapped children shall be educated along with children who do not have handicaps and shall attend regular classes . . . . Special classes, separate schooling or other removal of handicapped children from the regular educational environment, shall occur only when, and to the extent that the nature or severity of the handicap is such that education in regular classes, even with the use of supplementary aids and services, cannot be accomplished satisfactorily (Tennessee Code Annotated, Sec. 23, Chap. 839, 1972).

Inappropriate educational decision making

As has been briefly mentioned, the quiet revolution also was concerned with the manner in which education decisions were being made about children with handicaps in the public schools. The litigation revealed students were frequently misplaced and misclassified not only as a result of inappropriate evaluation instruments and procedures, but also because of inappropriate decisions. Traditionally, school administrators were able to decide whether a child with behavioural problems, a child restricted to a wheelchair, or a child who was especially difficult to teach could come to school and, if so, where that child was to be placed. Often these decisions were made unilaterally, without data, without legal basis, and without parental involvement or notice.

When these practices were brought to the attention of the court in Pennsylvania, the court ruled first, prior to consideration of the right to education question, that such practices must cease. To remedy the situation, the court first established the right of all children who are mentally retarded to the protection of procedural due process (in accordance with the 5th and 14th Amendments). This was contained in the 1972 *PARC* consent agreement which decreed that no child who is mentally retarded or thought to be mentally retarded can be assigned initially or reassigned to either a regular or special educational status or excluded from a public education without a prior recorded hearing before a special hearing officer.

Second, the court approved as part of the agreement a 23 step process to meet the due process mandate. Some of the requirements included: providing written notice to parents or guardians of the proposed action; provision in that notice of the specific reasons for the proposed action and the legal authority upon which such actions can occur; provision of information about the parents' or guardians' right to contest the proposed action at a full hearing before the state secretary of education or his designate; provision of information about the purpose and procedures of the hearing, including parents' or guardians' right to counsel, cross examination, presentation of independent evidence, and a written transcript of the hearing; indication that the burden of proof regarding the placement recommendation lies with the school district; right to obtain an independent evaluation of the child, at public expense if necessary (Weintraub and Abeson, 1974). [. . .]

The Education for All Handicapped Children Act of 1975, P. L. 94–142

By April 1975, [. . .] the quiet revolution to win for every handicapped child an appropriate education had reached something of a crescendo. Over half of the states by that time had either been through or were in the process of going through litigation. Increasingly, parents of handicapped children and professionals were forming statewise coalitions to file and maintain lawsuits, to advance state and local policy, and to implement newly won policy directives.

Despite this momentum, however, these congressional committees learned that over 1.75 million children with handicaps in the United States were being excluded entirely from receiving a public education solely on the basis of their handicap; that over half of the estimated 8 million handicapped children in this country were not receiving the appropriate educational services they needed and/or were entitled to, and that many other children with handicaps were still being placed in inappropriate educational settings because their handicaps were undetected or because of a violation of their individual rights.

It became clear that, although federal and state judicial and legislative actions had brought about progress since 1970 there remained a need for greater effort. The Congress decided this effort should take the form of legislation that would later be referred to as the 'Bill of Rights for Handicapped Children'. Approved by an 83 to 10 vote of the Senate on June 18, 1975, and a subsequent 375 to 44 affirmation of the House of Representatives on July 29, President Gerald Ford signed this historic bill on November 29, 1975. P. L. 94–142, the Education for All Handicapped Children Act, had become law. [. . .]

Right to education

The intent of the Congress to ensure that this Act will provide for the education of all children with handicaps is reflected in its statement of purpose:

> It is the purpose of this Act to assure that all handicapped children have available to them, within the time periods specified, a free appropriate public education which emphasizes special education and related services designed to meet their unique needs (Public Law 94–142, 1975, Sec. 3, c).

The time periods specified are that beginning in September 1978 all handicapped children aged 3 to 18 shall receive a free appropriate public education. The law further orders that by September 1, 1980, such an education shall be available to all handicapped children aged 3 to 21 (except in instances where the education of the 3 to 5 and 18 to 21 age ranges would be inconsistent with state law or practice or any court decree).

Inclusion of this right in P. L. 94–142 makes abundantly clear that it is as the National Advisory Committee[3] stated, national policy. After the dates specified occur, there simply will not be any grounds for depriving a handicapped child who, because of that handicap, possesses unique learning needs requiring special education. No longer will it be permissible for school persons to exclude or postpone the education of such handicapped children on the grounds that they cannot learn, their handicap is too severe, programmes do not exist, or for any other reason.

This civil rights principle can also be clearly expressed in educational terms. First, it means that no child is ineducable or stated in another way, all children can learn. Closely related to this statement is that education cannot be defined traditionally but rather must be considered as a continuous process by which individuals learn to cope and function within their environment. [. . .] Translated to curriculum planning, it means that to provide mobility training for blind children, adaptive physical education for physically handicapped children, or instruction in bodily functioning for some mentally retarded children is no different than teaching driver education, physical education, or health and hygiene to nonhandicapped children.

The right to education also means that children with handicaps are eligible for participation in all programmes and activities provided or sponsored by the schools as all other children are eligible. The presence of a handicap no longer can mean automatic ineligibility for music, athletics, cheerleading, or other extracurricular activities. By the same standard, children with handicaps may no longer be considered for non-inclusion in all course offerings, most notably vocational education. Similarly, if the presence of a handicap and related special learning needs leads to the provision of special education, it does not render the child ineligible for other special services.

Included within the mandate of the right to education for all children with handicaps are those children who possess learning needs that require programme delivery in public or private day or residential settings that operate on a tuition basis. In the past, some or all of these costs were, because of various state statutory approaches, partially or totally a family responsibility. [. . .]

[Under P. L. 94–142] placement in tuition based programmes at public cost does not occur as a function of parental option. It is only when it has been determined either through public school recommendation or as the result of due process that a tuition based setting is required to provide a child with an appropriate education. [. . .]

Right to nondiscriminatory evaluation

[. . .] The policy directives contained in P. L. 94–142 are straightforward and clear in their intent to remedy these negative practices that have had impact not only upon minority group children but also upon some handicapped children.

Essentially, the Act requires that the testing and evaluation materials and procedures that are used for the purposes of evaluation of children with handicaps, will be selected and administered so as not to be culturally discriminatory. Further, the law specifies that such materials and procedures are to be provided in the child's native language or mode of communication. Finally, no single procedure or test can be the sole criterion for determining the appropriate educational programme for a child. This last requirement clearly builds upon the maxim that standardized procedures including tests are not in themselves evil but, rather, become so if inappropriately used.

[. . .]

Inclusion in P. L. 94–142 of the 'mode of communication' requirement is an important addition to the nondiscriminatory policy requirements. While the culturally and linguistically discriminating attributes have been recognized, no attention has been directed to the problems of children with handicaps who [were at a disadvantage in tests designed for the able bodied children]. Because a youngster can not stack or rearrange the blocks does not mean the child does not know what is required nor how to do it. Consequently, evaluators under P. L. 94–142 must consider the child's mode of communication.

Right to an appropriate education

To deal with the past problems of inappropriate educational services being provided to children who have handicaps, the Congress included as a major component of P. L. 94–142 a requirement that each child be provided with a written individualized education programme known as the IEP. The IEP required for each handicapped child is the central building block to understanding and effectively complying with the Act. In order to understand the IEP, it is important that the following progression, as described by Weintraub (1977), be understood.

Handicapped children are defined by the Act as children who are 'mentally retarded, hard of hearing, deaf, orthopedically impaired, other health impaired, speech impaired, visually handicapped, seriously emotionally disturbed or children with specific learning disabilities who by reason thereof require special education and related services' [Sec. 4 (1)(1)]. This definition establishes a two-pronged criterion for determining child eligibility under the Act. The first criterion is whether the child has one or more of the disabilities listed in the definition. The second is whether the child requires special education and related services. Not all children who have a disability require special education, many can and should attend school without any programme modification.

Special education is defined in P. L. 94–142 as '. . . specially designed instruction, at no cost to parents or guardians, to meet the unique needs of a handicapped child, including classroom instruction, instruction in physical education, home instruction and instruction in hospitals and institutions' [Sec. 4 (16)].

The key phrases in the above definition of special education that impinge upon the IEP are 'specially designed instruction . . . to meet the unique needs of a handicapped child.' Again, by definition, then, special education is special and only involves that instruction which is specially designed and directed to meet the unique needs of a handicapped child. Thus, for many children special education will not be the totality of their education. Furthermore, this definition clearly implies that special proceeds from the basic goals and expected outcomes of general education. Thus, for example, intervention with a child does not occur because he is mentally retarded but because he has a unique educational need that requires specially designed instruction.

Equally important to understand is the concept of related services which are defined in the Act as: 'transportation, and such developmental, corrective, and other supportive services as may be required to assist a handicapped child to benefit from special education, and includes the early identification and assessment of handicapping conditions in children' [Sec. 4(1)(17)].

The key phrase here is 'as required to assist the handicapped child to benefit from special education'. This leads to a clear progression: a child is handicapped because he or she requires special education and related services; special education is the specially designed instruction to meet the child's unique needs; and related services are those additional services necessary in order for the child to benefit from special educational instruction.

The term 'individualized education programme' itself conveys important concepts that need to be specified. First, 'individualized' means that the IEP must be addressed to the educational needs of a single child rather than a class or group of children. Second, 'education' means that the IEP is limited to those elements of the child's education that are more specifically special education and related services as defined by the Act. Third, 'programme' means that the IEP is a statement of what will actually be provided to the child, as distinct from a plan which provides guidelines from which a programme must subsequently be developed (p. 27).

Finally, a specific definition describing the components of an IEP is included within the Act:

A written statement for each handicapped child developed in any meeting by a representative of the local educational agency or an intermediate educational unit who shall be qualified to provide or supervise the provision of, specially designed instruction to meet the unique needs of handicapped children, the teacher, the parents or guardians of such child, and, whenever appropriate, such child, which statement shall include (A) a statement of the present levels of educational performance of such child, (B) a statement of annual goals, including short-term instructional objectives, (C) a statement of the specific educational services to be provided to such child, and the extent to which such child will be able to participate in regular educational programmes, (D) the projected date for initiation and anticipated duration of such services, and appropriate objective criteria and evaluation procedures and schedules for determining, on at least an annual basis, whether instructional objectives are being achieved (Public Law 94–142, 1975, Sec. 4, a, 19).

The IEP requirement of P. L. 94–142 has received much attention in terms of its potential for achieving the goal of the Act – appropriately educating every handicapped child. Inclusion of the teacher, for example, in the development of the IEP is designed to ensure that realistic teacher concerns and needs will be considered as part of the IEP development process. It is appropriate that teachers have a major voice in programme planning since they have major responsibility for programme provision. Similarly, parent participation is designed to ensure that the extensive amounts of information parents possess about their children and their judgements as to the education programme needed will be considered. Establishment of jointly determined expectations for individual children that are known to all involved and interested in the form of goals and objectives is highly regarded because with such specificity comes a clear basis for assessing a child's progress so that inappropriate programmes do not continue and necessary programme changes will occur.

[. . .]

No discussion of appropriate education for children who have handicaps is complete without consideration of the least restrictive placement principle. As noted, the statutory definition of the IEP itself requires consideration of 'the extent to which such child will be able to participate in regular educational programmes'. In addition, each state must establish procedures to ensure that, to the maximum extent appropriate, handicapped children, including children in public and private institutions or other care facilities, are educated with children who are not handicapped and that special classes, separate schooling, or the removal of handicapped children from the regular education environment occurs only when the nature or severity of the handicap is such that education in regular classes with the use of supplementary aids and services cannot be achieved satisfactorily (Public Law 94–142, 1975, Sec. 612, 5, B).

Implementation of this portion of the appropriate requirement has been interpreted by some to mean that all handicapped children, regardless of the severity of their handicap, are to be placed in regular classroom programmes. To others, these mandates mean that all handicapped children are to be placed in self contained special education classes. Neither of these is correct. What must exist is school system capacity to provide programmes that are appropriate for individual children in the least restrictive alternative setting. Conceptualizing the requirement in this manner indicates that, although placement decisions must be indicated in the child's IEP, it must follow determination of the child's learning needs and programmes. Available placement options no longer can dictate placement decisions for individual children.

Right to due process of law

During the revolution, the manner in which identification, evaluation, and placement decisions were made about children with handicaps were reviewed virtually throughout the country. To solve these problems, the courts ordered adherence to procedural due process. It was this solution that was also selected by the Congress as part of P. L. 94–142. Like most of the elements of this law, due process has received wide attention and discussion. It is included in the Act to ensure that all of the rights created by the Act are in fact made available to children who have handicaps, their families, and the public schools. One way of expressing this intent is to suggest that the presence of due process is designed to allow for equal consideration of the interests of a handicapped child – the child, the family, the schools.

The specific elements of due process the Congress included in the law are as follows:

(1) Written notification before evaluation. In addition, the right to an interpreter/translator if the family's native language is not English (unless it is clearly not feasible to do so).

(2) Written notification when initiating or refusing to initiate a change in educational placement.

(3) Opportunity to present complaints regarding the identification, evaluation, placement, or the provision of a free appropriate education.

(4) Opportunity to obtain an independent educational evaluation of the child.

(5) Access to all relevant records.

(6) Opportunity for an impartial due process hearing including the right to:

    (a)   Receive timely and specific notice of the hearing.

    (b)   Be accompanied and advised by counsel and by individuals with special knowledge or training with respect to the problems of children with handicaps.

    (c)   Confront, cross examine, and compel the attendance of witnesses.

    (d)   Present evidence: (1) Written or electronic verbatim record of the hearing. (2) Written findings of fact and decisions.

(7) The right to appeal the findings and decisions of the hearing.

The procedural safeguards section of the Act includes two provisions that are of special importance. First is the requirement that, for children whose parents or guardian 'are unknown, unavailable or the child is a ward of the state' and who are being considered for service under this Act, procedures must be established to assign an individual 'who shall not be an employee of the State educational agency, local educational agency, or intermediate educational unit involved in the education or care of the child to act as a surrogate for the parents or guardian' (Public Law 94–142, 1975, Sec. 615, 6, 1, B). Without this requirement children without parents or guardians would essentially be deprived of access to their rights of due process.

Until P. L. 94–142 was enacted, the circumstances under which due process could be invoked was limited to identification, evaluation, and placement. Under this Act, however, the Congress has extended the due process opportunity by providing 'an opportunity to present complaints with respect to any matter relating to the identification, evaluation, or educational placement of the child, or the provision of a free appropriate public education to such a child' (Sec. 615, b, 1, E). [. . .]

The future

Beginning in 1970 and continuing until the opening of school in September 1978, the quiet revolution effectively established in policy the educational rights of all handicapped children. With the conclusion of this revolution or at least one aspect of it, the efforts of all educators and particularly those in special education who have long worked to establish these rights must shift to achieve implementation of these rights. P. L. 94—142 is the national policy — it is specific as to what is to occur and it appropriates some funds to assist state, intermediate, and local education agencies in carrying out their state mandated responsibilities of providing for the education of all the children residing within each state. Clearly that mandate now applies equally to children who have handicaps.

[. . .]

Of crucial importance in undertaking the implementation task is for all elements of the education community to correctly understand the Act and the reasons for its creation. Misinterpretation and misinformation is a critical danger. Citizen voters, legislators, school board members, administrators, teachers, support personnel, and parents of children with handicaps must be aware of what the law does say, not what someone thinks it says. What will happen inside the schoolhouse door will largely depend upon members of this population who have had little or no exposure or knowledge about children with handicaps.

[. . .]

When all is said and done and historians examine the quiet revolution, they may well determine that, while P. L. 94—142 is the premier educational policy attainment for the handicapped, the most notable overall policy for this group is Section 504 of the Vocational Rehabilitation Act of 1973 (Public Law 93—112). This small section of law prescribes that:

> no otherwise qualified handicapped individual in the United States . . . which solely by reason of handicap be excluded in the participation in, be denied the benefit of, or be subjected to discrimination under any programme or activity receiving Federal financial assistance.

While this law requires that virtually the total society must provide handicapped persons with equal rights, it is of special importance in the implementation of P. L. 94—142. The regulations that accompany Section 504 contain a portion devoted totally to preschool, elementary, secondary, and postsecondary education. These regulations, which to a large degree conform to many of the P. L. 94—142 requirements, will enhance the implementation process because virtually every education agency received federal financial assistance. To be in violation of P. L. 94—142, in most situations, also will mean a violation of Section

504, which in its finality can mean the withholding of all federal funds. This is particularly true in relation to the basic educational rights of children who have handicaps. Section 504 in concert with P. L. 94–142 will be the substance of implementation. How well that effort occurs will determine if there will be need for another revolution, and if so, the magnitude of its volume.

Notes

1 An action brought by one or more plaintiffs on behalf of a class of citizens. This is a common method for challenging the constitutionality of an action. [Ed.]
2 A law refers to a general statement of rights and provision, whereas a regulation, having the force of law, defines the interpretation of these laws more specifically. (Ed.)
3 A non-governmental body without legal power which reports and makes recommendations to the President or Congress. (Ed.)

References

Abeson, A. (1972) Movement and momentum: Government and the education of handicapped children, *Exceptional Children*, 39, 63–6.

Abeson, A., Bolick, N., and Hass, J. (1975) *A primer on due process: Education decisions for handicapped children*. Reston VA, Council For Exceptional Children.

Bolick, N. (Ed.) (1974) *Digest of state and federal laws: Education of handicapped children* (3rd ed.). Reston VA, Council For Exceptional Children.

Brown v. *Board of Education* (1954) 347 U.S. 483, 74 St.Ct. 686, 98L. Ed. 873.

Children's Defense Fund (1974) *Children out of school in America*. Cambridge, MA, Author.

Diana v. *State Board of Education*. Civil Action No. C-70 37 R.F.P. (N.D. Cal., Jan. 7, 1970 and June 18, 1973).

Dunn, L. M. (1968) Special education for the mildly retarded – Is much of it justifiable?, *Exceptional Children*, 35, 5–22.

Larry P. v. *Riles*, Civil Action No 6-71-2270 343F. Supp. 1036 (N.D. Cal., 1972).

Lori Case v. *State of California*, Civil No. 13127, Court of Appeals, Fourth Dist. Calif., filed December 14, 1973.

Mercer, J. (1970) The ecology of mental retardation, in *The proceedings of the first annual spring conference on the institute for the study of mental retardation*, Ann Arbor, Michigan.

Mills v. *Board of Education of the District of Columbia*, 348F. Supp. 866 (D.D.C., 1972).

National Advisory Committee on the Education of the Handicapped (1976) *The unfinished revolution: Education of the handicapped*. Washington DC, GPO.

National Education Association (1975) Schools must face serious problems posed by integrating handicapped, NEA president says. (NEA Press Release). Washington DC, Author.

Pennsylvania Association for Retarded Children v. Commonwealth of Pennsylvania, F. Supp. 279 (E.D. Pa. 1972, Order, Injunction and Consent Agreement).

Public Law 93–112, *Vocational Rehabilitation Act of 1973*, Section 504, July 26, 1973.

Public Law 93–380, *Education Amendments of 1974*, August 21, 1974.

Public Law 93–142, *Education for All Handicapped Children Act*, November 29, 1975.

Reynolds, M. C. (1962) A framework for considering some issues in special education, *Exceptional Children*, 28, 367–70.

Ross, S. L., Jr., DeYoung, H. G. and Cohen, J. S. (1971) Confrontation: Special education placement and the law, *Exceptional Children*, 38, 5–12.

State of Illinois. *Rules and regulations to govern the administration and operation of special education*, Article X, 1974.

Tennessee Code Annotated, Sec. 1, 8A, 23, Chap. 839, 1972.

US Congress, Senate, *Education for All Handicapped Children Act*, S.6., 94th Congress, 1st Session, June 2, 1975, Report No. 94–168.

Weintraub, F. (1972) Recent influences of the law regarding the identification and educational placement of children. *Focus on Exceptional Children*, 4, 1–10.

Weintraub, F. (1977) Understanding the individualized education programme (IEP), *Amicus*, 23–7.

Weintraub, F. and Abeson, A. (1974) New educational policies for the handicapped: The quiet revolution, *Phi Delta Kappan*, 55, 528.

5.6 Street-level bureaucrats and institutional innovation: implementing special education reform

RICHARD WEATHERLEY AND MICHAEL LIPSKY

One of the state laws on which P. L. 94–142 was modelled was the Massachusetts Chapter 766.[1] Many provisions, such as the requirements for multi-disciplinary assessment, individualized treatment plans and education in ordinary classrooms, were paralleled by provisions in the federal law. In this paper, Richard Weatherley and Michael Lipsky examine the implementation of Chapter 766 in three school districts, each of which developed its own distinctive strategy for coping with the immense burdens created by the new law. They show how the realities at the 'street level' constrained and distorted the reforms hoped for by the state legislators.

This paper focuses on the introduction of innovation into continuing practice. Chapter 766 required adjustments in the behaviour of public employees and in the working conditions established for them in their agencies. While we focus in this paper on the implementation of a statute affecting educational personnel, our case study includes governmental efforts to change the work requirements not only of teachers but also of police officers, welfare workers, legal-assistance lawyers, lower-court judges, and health workers.

These 'street-level bureaucrats', as we have called them, interact directly with citizens in the course of their jobs and have substantial discretion in the execution of their work.[2] For such public workers, personal and organizational resources are chronically and severely limited in relation to the tasks that they are asked to perform. The demand for their services will always be as great as their ability to supply these services. To accomplish their required tasks, street-level bureaucrats must find ways to accommodate the demands placed upon

Source: Weatherley, R. and Lipsky, M. (1977) Street-level bureaucrats and institutional innovation: implementing special education reform, *Harvard Educational Review*, 47, 171–97

them and confront the reality of resource limitations. They typically do this by routinizing procedures, modifying goals, rationing services, asserting priorities, and limiting or controlling clientele. In other words, they develop practices that permit them in some way to process the work they are required to do. [. . .]

In a significant sense, then, street-level bureaucrats *are the policy-makers* in their respective work arenas. From this perspective it follows that the study of implementation of policy formulated at the federal or state level requires a twin focus. One must trace the fate of the policy in traditional fashion, from its authoritative articulation through various administrative modifications, to discover the ways this policy affects the context of street-level decision making. At the same time, one must study street-level bureaucrats within their specific work context to discover how their decision making about clients is modified, if at all, by the newly articulated policy. [. . .]

Local-level responses

The major threat to the Massachusetts Comprehensive Special Education Law, and what makes it truly innovative, is the requirement that children with special needs receive individualized assessment and treatment. This thrust is reflected in a number of provisions: the required assessment of children by interdisciplinary teams with parental involvement; the requirement that a specific educational plan be tailored to the needs of each child; the replacement of generic descriptive labels by behaviourally specific inventories; and the accommodation, insofar as possible, of children with special needs in regular educational settings rather than in segregated classrooms. At the same time, certain provisions of the law are directed toward achieving uniform and nondiscriminatory treatment and comprehensive coverage of all children with special needs. As we will discuss later, these two aims of individualization and comprehensiveness are not entirely compatible in practice.

The requirements of the law created severe problems for local school districts. Extending school responsibility to persons aged three to twenty-one and requiring identification, assessment, and service provision to be accomplished in the first year posed challenges well beyond the capacity of any school system at the time. Special-education administrators began the 1974—5 school year without specific guidelines for constituting assessment teams, evaluating children, or writing educational plans. The regulations stipulated what needed to be done but provided no blueprint for administering the process. Both the division and organized parent groups had taken an adversarial stance toward local schools, and, as a result, administrators feared numerous court suits and appeals, which they believed they would lose. Parents, for the first time, were to be involved in educational planning for their own children, thereby challenging the autonomy of educators. Schools were to provide social, psychological, and medical services that many educators believed to be well beyond the legitimate purview of educational institutions. There was considerable doubt that full state reimbursement would in fact be available to pay for such services, and the likely competition for resources within school systems threatened to exacerbate underlying tensions between regular and special education. Furthermore, each step in implementing the law called for numerous forms to be completed, creating an enormous paperwork burden.

Under Chapter 766, what had formerly been a simple procedure informally worked out by the teacher, the specialist, and perhaps the parents, now became a major team undertaking with elaborate requirements governing each step. The process officially begins with a referral for assessment which may be initiated by a parent, teacher or other school official, court, or social agency. Before that, however, 'all efforts shall be made to meet such children's needs within the context of the services which are part of the regular education programme.'[3] The referral must document these efforts. Within five days of the referral, a written notice is to be sent to the parents informing them of the types of assessments to be conducted, when the evaluation will begin, and their right to participate in all meetings at which the educational plan is developed. Parents have the right to meet with the evaluation-team chairperson to receive an explanation of the reason and the procedure for the evaluation. The parent must give written consent for the evaluation and its individual components before the assessments may be initiated.

In the case of a full core evaluation, required when it is expected that a child will be placed outside of the regular class for more than 25 percent of the time, at least five assessments must be completed. An administrative representative of the school department must assess the child's educational status. A recent or current teacher must measure 'the child's specific behavioural abilities along a developmental continuum, . . . school readiness, functioning or achievement, . . . behavioural adjustment, attentional capacity, motor coordination, activity level and patterns, communication skills, memory and social relations with groups, peers and adults.' A physician must conduct a comprehensive health examination. A psychologist must provide an assessment, 'including an individually appropriate psychological examination, . . . a developmental and social history, observation of the child in familiar surroundings (such as a classroom), sensory, motor, language, perceptual, attentional, cognitive, affective, attitudinal, self-image, interpersonal, behavioural, interest and vocational factors.' A nurse, social worker, guidance counsellor, or adjustment counsellor must make a home visit and evaluate 'pertinent family history and home situation factors'. Additional assessments by psychiatric, neurological, learning-disability, speech, hearing, vision, motor, or any other specialists will be carried out if needed.[4]

For each assessment, a detailed, written report of the findings must be forwarded to the chairperson of the evaluation team and frequently to the evaluating specialist's supervisor. After the individual assessments are completed, team members may, if they choose, come together in a pre-core meeting to discuss their findings. Finally, there is another team meeting, with parents in attendance, in which the educational plan is developed. The educational plan must include a specific statement of what the child can and cannot do, his or her learning style, educational goals, and plans for meeting them during the following three, six, and nine months. This entire process, starting from the day the notification letter is mailed to the parents and ending with the completion of the educational plan, is to take no more than thirty days.

These requirements presented school personnel with an enormous increase in their workload in several ways. There were suddenly many more children to be evaluated. Many more individuals had to take part in each evaluation. Educational plans had to be written in much greater detail, completed faster, and circulated to a wider audience. Because team members had different schedules and other responsibilities, getting everyone together for a meeting became a difficult task. An evaluation of a child that might previously have taken two or three people a few hours to complete now took as many as ten to twenty hours for the chairperson and two to six hours for each of the other team members.

From the standpoint of implementation, the chief difficulty presented by Chapter 766 revolved around the tension between the requirements for an individualized approach to educating children and the strong pressures for mass processing created by requirements for comprehensiveness. This tension between individualization and mass processing is not unique; it is characteristic of many street-level bureaucracies which attempt to reconcile individualized service with high demand relative to resources. Since street-level bureaucracies, particularly schools, may not officially restrict intake, other means must be found to accommodate the workload. Workload pressures in the past were at least partially responsible for many of the abuses that Chapter 766 was intended to correct: special-needs children were subjected to arbitrary assessment, being labelled and dumped into segregated special classes, exclusion, denial of appropriate services, and unnecessary institutionalization. The workload pressures did not disappear with passage of the law. If anything, they increased under the substantial burden of added demands.

School personnel put forth extraordinary efforts to comply with the new demands. However, under the current system of public education there was simply no way that everything required could be done with the available resources. In the following sections we examine the objectives of the law against the reality of its implementation. The behaviour described below indicates the limits of school organization. It does not so much reflect negatively on school personnel as it demonstrates how new demands are accommodated into the work structure of people who consistently must find ways to conserve resources and assert priorities to meet, in some way, the demands of their jobs.

Mainstreaming

Martin J. Kaufman and associates summarize the case for mainstreaming as based on the belief that it will remove stigmas; enhance the social status of special-needs children; facilitate modelling of appropriate behaviour by handicapped youngsters; provide a more stimulating and competitive environment; offer a more flexible, cost-effective service in the child's own neighbourhood; and be more acceptable to the public, particularly to minority groups.[5]

Chapter 766 requires that, to the maximum extent feasible, children with special needs be placed in regular-education programmes, even if for just a small fraction of the school day. If possible, special classes are to be located within regular school facilities.[6] This provision, designed to end the practice of segregating handicapped children, originally

Table 1 Special-needs children by programme prototype

	October 1974	October 1975
Per cent of special-needs children in regular class with support (i.e., no time out)	35.9	19.8
Per cent of special-needs children in regular class with up to 25 per cent time out	43.9	56.2
Per cent of special-needs children in regular class less than 75 per cent of the time	20.2	24.0

Source: Data supplied to the author by an official of the Massachusetts State Department of Education.

evoked fears that special classes would be closed and large numbers of difficult-to-manage children would be returned to regular classrooms.

The spectre of hordes of handicapped children being loosed upon regular class teachers never materialized. To begin with, there were probably not that many children in full-time, self-contained, separate programmes. Furthermore, the regulations contained a 'grandfather clause' whereby all children in special programmes as of September, 1974, were presumed to be correctly placed unless evidence was presented to the contrary. Data obtained from an official of the state department of education indicate that children were actually shifted from less to more restrictive programmes during the first year of implementation. In part, this shift probably reflects increased use of resource rooms. Ironically, by providing separate rooms staffed by specialists to provide special-education services, school systems *decreased* the proportion of fully integrated children by sending them out of the regular classrooms for special help. Table 1 shows the percentage of special-needs children in various programmes as of October 1964, as implementation was getting under way, and as of October, 1975, after implementation.

With regard to mainstreaming, the law's major impact follows from its procedural barriers proscribing the inappropriate assignment of children to self-contained classes. While several instances of active recruitment of children by special-class teachers were noted during the study, such instances were rare. This was true not only because of a lack of space in existing special classes, but also because of a genuine commitment to mainstreaming on the part of special-education administrators and most special-class teachers. Chapter 766 provided special educators the necessary leverage with principals and other administrators to expand and revamp services. There was, however, evidence that a subtle kind of dumping was taking place: there appeared to be a wholesale shifting of responsibility for troublesome children from the regular-class teacher to a special or resource-room teacher.

We observed many close working relationships between regular-class teachers and specialists. Specialists would sometimes consult teachers on how to handle particular classroom problems and how best to work with individual children. Some efforts were made to coordinate learning in the regular class with the specialist's intervention programme. However, the maintenance of such relationships requires time, which was in short supply. Far more frequently, the teacher had little contact with specialists, had no knowledge of the content of the educational plan, and demonstrated an attitude that the child's learning or behaviour problem was the responsibility of someone else, namely, the specialist.

Even when specialists sought to work closely with teachers, the pressures of increased caseloads and the vastly increased time spent in the assessment process prevented them from doing so. Thus the law, while limiting the segregation of handicapped children, resulted in a further compartmentalization of students needing special services and increased the danger that they might be stigmatized on the basis of their need for help from specialists outside the regular classroom.

More efficient identification and processing

According to estimates from the state department of education, only 50 to 60 per cent of children with special needs had been identified and provided services by Massachusetts schools prior to the passage of Chapter 766.[7] The present regulations require local education authorities to undertake a range of activities to identify children in need of special services, although there was no shortage of referrals from teachers and parents. The school systems studied varied in the way they translated this requirement into action.[8] System B derived more than half of its referrals from pre- and in-school screening, while screening accounted for but a small fraction of the other two systems' referrals. Furthermore, in all three systems, the kinds of disorders identified through screening were directly related to the speciality of the person doing the screening. For example, System B, which relied much more heavily on speech specialists to conduct screening than the other two systems, referred more than twice as many children for evaluations because of speech problems. In many instances, those doing the screening were actually referring children to themselves. That is, the speech specialist conducting screening would more than likely participate in the core evaluation and eventually treat the child. This overlap of functions suggests that the local systems need to guard not only against failing to identify children in need of special services, but also against unnecessarily recruiting children not in need of special services.

One measure of the relative efficiency of the assessment process is the time required to complete an assessment. The regulations require that the evaluation take place within thirty working days after the parents are informed, or in no more than thirty-five days after the child is referred. Despite substantial differences among the three systems with regard to procedures and staffing, there was surprising uniformity in the time taken to complete assessments. The mean number of months taken to complete the assessments was 6.9 in System A, 7.8 in System B, and 7.9 in System C — all considerably longer than the time permitted under the law and longer than the three months permitted until the plan must be signed by the parent. In systems B and C, where data were available, only 11.9 per cent and 21.2 per cent of referrals, respectively, were completed within three months. This is an index of the overwhelming scope of the task confronting the schools.

Equity, uniformity and comprehensive coverage

Chapter 766 seeks to end arbitrary and discriminatory practices through an individualized approach to the classification and assignment of children with special needs. This is to be accomplished in a way that assures a measure of equity — equal treatment for children with the same needs — as well as responsiveness to parents and teachers. Fiscal constraints and the governance procedures of local school systems impose the additional requirements of accountability, efficiency, and fiscal integrity. These aims constitute conflicting bureaucratic require-ments.[9] In the absence of specific guidance from the state depart-ment, the three school systems we analysed pursued different strategies, each of which maximized one or more of these requirements at some sacrifice of the others. The differing approaches to the core-evaluation process taken by the three systems warrant brief description.

System A, with the smallest enrolment, designated a psychologist, a social worker, and a learning-disabilities specialist already on the staff as the primary core evaluation team. Several additional part-time specialists were hired to supplement this team, and existing school-based specialists and teachers were brought in when appropriate. This system has a strong tradition of principal[10] and school autonomy and professionalism. Thus, while the primary team did conduct most of the evaluations in the central district offices, many evaluations were done in the schools, sometimes without the participation of any of the primary-team members. This two-tiered arrangement produced wide disparities among schools in the identification and assessment of children. The team and administrators adopted a largely reactive stance toward evaluation and, for the most part, simply processed referrals coming to them. Personnel at all levels rationalized this reactive posture with the belief that most children with special needs were already being served and that the services provided by the system were superior to those found in most other systems.

System B hired an outside business consultant to design a procedure for central oversight of the work flow. New forms and other required documents were developed for personnel involved at each step of the referral and evaluation process. Central files made it possible to determine which forms were outstanding for any particular child, and follow-up procedures were instituted to assure completion of the process. On the whole, the record-keeping system was excellent. Assessments and educational plans were forwarded to administrative supervisors to ensure central quality control. An aggressive case-finding effort was enhanced by the thorough orientation of teachers and principals. School psychologists were designated as chairpersons of the core evaluation teams, and to accommodate this added responsibility the number of psychologists was doubled. The procedures adopted by System B tended to be dominated by a concern for completing forms properly and speedily. As a result, assessment meetings were conducted hastily and with a minimum of genuine deliberation.

In System C, the largest of the three but with the smallest per-pupil expenditure, most evaluations were attended by the special-education administrator or one of the programme directors. Their presence assured a high degree of quality control. These administrators viewed their participation as a means of training school-based staff through their example and interactions in the meetings. The evaluations were regarded as belonging to the schools, and the chairpersons of the core-evaluation teams had a much more varied array of backgrounds than chairpersons in the other system. Whereas in systems A and B the outcome of an evaluation was usually predetermined, System C held relatively few of the 'pre-core' meetings in which team members would meet, usually without the parents, to discuss the assessments and educational plan. As a result, the core meetings in System C tended to be characterized by a great deal of give-and-take, a high level of parent involvement, and genuine group problem solving. The deliberations were longer, with more people involved, and this system conducted a much higher percentage of full-core rather than pre-core evaluations.

One indication of the differences in style among the three systems is shown in a comparison of numbers of persons involved and time spent in the core-evaluation meetings. Of meetings observed, the mean duration was forty-two minutes in System A, fifty in System B, and seventy-four in System C. The mean number of participants was 6 in System A, 5.7 in B, and 9.5 in C. While the three systems developed idiosyncratic procedures for identifying and processing special-needs children, all confronted the same serious problem: no explicitly mandated system of priority in referral, assessment, or provision of services accompanied the requirement for uniform treatment of children with special needs. It seemed as if all children were to be processed at once without official regard to the seriousness of the individual situation; a child with multiple physical and emotional problems was to be processed no sooner than a child with a slight hearing impediment.

In practice all three school systems made unofficial distinctions between routine and complex cases. Routine cases were viewed by school personnel as those in which the completion of the educational-plan form was necessary in order to provide the services of a specialist. In these cases, an implicit decision would be made prior to referral that a service was needed. The evaluation was then viewed as a bureaucratic hurdle to be gotten over as quickly as possible, in some cases even without the supposedly mandatory participation of parents. Many of these meetings took on a contrived, routine character. The more complex cases were those in which the assessment of the child was in fact problematic — there was some disagreement among school personnel regarding the assessment or educational plan, considerable expense to the school system might be involved, or the parents were viewed as potential 'troublemakers'. Troublesome parents were those thought likely to disrupt the process by complaining, questioning, or rejecting recommendations of professionals; or those whose higher socioeconomic status suggested to school personnel that a threat might be forthcoming. The percentage of complex cases varied considerably among the three school systems. In System C the majority of cases fell into this category, while in systems A and B complex cases constituted perhaps no more than 15 to 25 per cent of the referrals.

In addition to making distinctions among kinds of referrals, the three systems employed a variety of unofficial rationing techniques to hold down the number of referrals. First, teachers sometimes failed to refer children despite evidence of problems that should have indicated the need for evaluation. Classroom teachers were deterred by the necessity of completing the forms and justifying their assessment of the problem to the principal and specialists. For some teachers, acknowledgement of a problem they could not handle themselves represented failure. They could look forward to the end of the school year when they would pass the children on to the next teacher in line; consequently, many tended to refer only those who were most trouble-some. Second, a principal would occasionally dissuade parents from requesting a core evaluation with assurances that the child was doing fine or that services were already being provided. Third, referrals from teachers were submitted through the principal and/or specialist, and in a number of instances the principal or specialist would simply fail to follow through. Finally, administrators sometimes gave instructions to cut back on referrals. In one of the systems, principals having the largest number of referrals were told by the central administration to curtail evaluations because of the costs of services being recommended.

In general, these rationing practices resulted from unsanctioned, informal categorization of potential referrals. Such categorization reflected the personal priorities of the individuals making the referral decisions. In weighing the relative costs and benefits of referring a child for core evaluation, individuals implicitly appeared to act on several criteria. Concern for the well-being of their children was without question the foremost consideration for the great majority of school personnel. Without such concern, implementation of Chapter 766 would have broken down completely, for in all three school systems administrators and specialists kept the process going by working extraordinarily long hours under constant stress with little hope of catching up, at least during the first year or two.

The institutional rewards system provided another criterion. Some principals believed that they themselves would be at least informally evaluated on the number and handling of referrals. In System B and System C principals were encouraged to refer; in System A they were not.

The degree to which children were creating problems for teachers or other personnel because of their disruptive behaviour also affected decisions. Teachers interviewed generally stated that they referred the 'loudest' children first. This general criterion was supported by an examination of the dates of referral for learning and behaviour problems: in systems B and C, where sufficient data were available, behaviour referrals occurred with greatest frequency in the first three months of the school year.

The speed of processing tended to be affected by the position of the person making the referral. In general, parent and principal referrals, while accounting for a relatively small percentage of total referrals, were processed more rapidly than those from teachers.

Finally, the availability of services within the system influenced decisions. In one system, school-based specialists decided informally whether or not a child should be referred on the basis of the presumed solution rather than the presented problem. If they foresaw a need to buy the services of additional specialists, a quick evaluation would be held.

Both systems and individual schools varied in their rate of referral and processing. By the end of June, 1975, System A had completed evaluations on approximately 3.8 per cent of its students; System B, on 5.5 per cent; and System C, on 2.8 per cent.[11] Some individual schools in these systems did not refer and evaluate any children, while others processed many. Of the schools in systems B and C which had evaluated at least five children, some completed nearly half of the evaluations within the required three-month period, while others completed none. There were also variations in the reasons for referral. Speech problems were the primary referral reason for about 20 per cent of children evaluated in System B, only 5 per cent in System A, and fewer than 2 per cent in System C. While learning referrals were relatively constant across the three systems, ranging from 58.1 to 65.9 per cent of referrals, behaviour referrals constituted 22.2 per cent in System A, 13.6 per cent in System B, and 29.2 per cent in System C.

Thus, a law and its administrative regulations, intended to produce uniform application of procedures, instead yielded wide variations in application. The chances of a child's being referred, evaluated, and provided with special-education services were associated with presumably extraneous factors: the school system and school attended, the child's disruptiveness in class, his or her age and sex,[12] the aggressiveness and socioeconomic status of the parents, the current availability and cost of services needed, and the presence of particular categories of specialists in the school system.

Parent involvement and interdisciplinary team assessment

Chapter 766 seeks to regulate arbitrary and inappropriate classification and assignment of children by placing restrictions on the use of standardized tests and by requiring joint assessment and planning by an interdisciplinary team that includes parents. The net effect of these required procedures in the three systems has been greater involvement of parents, more careful assessment of children, and some genuine team decision making. But, at the same time, both teachers and parents have played a secondary role to specialists in the evaluation process.

The impact of parent participation was as much a function of the team's anticipating pressures from parents as it was a response to their actual involvement. In numerous instances parents made substantial contributions to the assessment or planning processes; however, school personnel frequently took actions aimed at placating or avoiding conflict with parents. For example, one of the authors observed administrators in a lengthy meeting developing a defensive strategy for handling an angry mother whose child's referral papers had been lost by school personnel. Their primary concern was not why the referral did not get processed but rather how to absolve themselves of responsibility.

The parent was usually in the position of joining an ongoing group; generally, the core-evaluation team had met as a group during other assessments, and its members worked together on a continuing basis. The parent, in addition, might confront a sometimes unsubtle implication that the child and parent were somehow at fault for creating a problem. This was particularly true when the problem involved disruptive behaviour or a learning difficulty of which the nature was not readily apparent. Perhaps defensive about their lack of time, training, and skills to work with special-needs children, some teachers we observed assigned blame to parents and children, and they were frequently joined in this by other personnel. In fact, the deliberations in assessment meetings often revealed an underlying preoccupation with the assignment of blame. Here, for example, the teacher asked to describe a child's strengths and weaknesses responds with negatives:

> Academically, he is below grade; he has a short attention span and a severe learning disability, poor handwriting, poor work habits; his desk is disheveled, and he never puts anything away. His oral is better than his written work. He never gives others a chance. He is uncooperative, ignores school rules – due in part to his frustration with learning. He can't stay in his seat. He won't accept pressure. He is interested in smoking, drugs, and alcohol and has a security problem. He has difficulty with all the specialists. He fights . . . .

There were additional factors which put parents at a disadvantage. Often there were status differences between a poor or working-class parent and the middle-class professionals who might dress differently and speak a different language. The use of technical jargon lent an aura of science to the proceedings while making much of the discussion unintelligible to parents and, frequently, to teachers as well. One psychologist explained test results to a working-class parent in this way: 'He is poor in visual-motor tasks. He has come up [improved] on sequencing-object assembly-completions which may reflect maturation in addition to training – that is, his visual-motor improvement. . . .' In another meeting, a tutor began, reading from a report: 'Reading, 2.1 level; comprehensive language skills, good; daily performance, erratic. He is the type of child with learning problems – he has difficulty processing short sounds, auditory sequencing, and so forth. The visual is slightly better than the auditory channel.' In another meeting, a teacher and psychologist, trying to convince a reluctant parent that her child should be held back for a year, produced a computer printout showing the child's performance on test scores in comparison to other children the same age. The parent immediately capitulated.

The regulations governing the core-evaluation meeting call for assessments to deal equally with the child's capacities and strengths as well as with deficiencies. However, an assessment was principally the result of someone's concern about deficiencies. Furthermore, the assessment provided official certification that the child had 'special needs' that required services over and above those provided for most other children. Most of the core evaluation was devoted to verifying the child's negative functioning through the recitation of test scores, anecdotal information, and observations. The presentation of negative data appeared to serve two functions. First, teachers frequently presented negative data about a child in an apparently defensive strategy aimed at absolving themselves of responsibility for the child's problem. Second, the negative assessment of a child might prepare the way to obtain parents' compliance with whatever plan school officials wished to impose.

Increased services

While much of the controversy and effort in the first year's operation of Chapter 766 revolved around the assessment process, the ultimate goal of the law is the provision of services. School systems are required to provide whatever services are recommended by the core-evaluation team for an individual child, without being constrained by cost considerations. If appropriate services are unavailable, the school system must develop them or send a child at local expense outside the system where such services may be obtained. Because of its remarkable comprehensiveness we might have expected this provision to break down in practice through informal imposition of cost or referral restrictions. Nonetheless, we may still legitimately inquire into the extent to which the spirit of the provision was honoured.

The requirements immediately expanded the range of options for special education and did lead to some expansion and redesign of special-education services. In some respects, however, the implementation of Chapter 766 actually resulted in a reduction of services, at least during the first year. One problem was the wholesale withdrawal of services to schoolchildren by the departments of welfare, public health, and mental health, the Massachusetts Rehabilitation Commission, and other state agencies. Special-education administrators bitterly complained of instances in which services previously offered to children at little or no cost were now being withdrawn or offered on a fee basis.

Even more demoralizing for school personnel was the reduction of in-school specialist services which resulted from the assignment of these specialists to complete core evaluation. In general, the specialists who were involved in assessment and educational-plan meetings were the same persons who would be called upon to provide the recommended services. These specialists, along with other team members, faced two problems: the sheer volume of new assessments; and the vastly increased time required to test or otherwise evaluate a child, write up the assessment report, attend the team meetings, and write the educational plan. Specialists were caught in a particularly difficult bind. Their contribution was essential to the assessment process. At the same time, a conscientious discharge of these responsibilities meant less time available to work with children and more time spent completing forms. One specialist said, 'It just kills me to walk by those kids with them saying, "Aren't you coming to see us today?" '

The most frequent response to this overwhelming workload burden was to work harder and longer hours completing paperwork at home. The considerable personal strain on those engaged in implementation at the local level was apparent. While additional staff members were hired in all three systems, this increase in numbers was rarely sufficient to meet the increased demand. That the law was carried out as well as it was is due to the dedication of those at the local level whose extra efforts constituted a sizeable hidden subsidy to the school system.

However, the magnitude of the workload often forced specialists to shortchange the assessment process. When assessments could not be bypassed, they were routinized. Meetings became cursory. Parent signatures were obtained on black forms to cut down the time required to get the signed educational plans returned. Educational plans, instead of providing individually tailored programmes, were most often little more than road maps routing children to one or more specialists during the school day.

Earlier we discussed the rationing of attention to assessments in response to the overwhelming demand. For the same reason, special educators rationed the services they provided to children. One form of such rationing was that services that in previous years had been offered on an individual, one-to-one basis were now delivered to groups. This practice was rationalized on the grounds that group treatment is more beneficial, which of course it may be. However, it is hardly accidental that this theoretical breakthrough was coincident with the additional burdens placed on special-education personnel by Chapter 766. Also, the number of hours a specialist would see a child per week was reduced. There was increased reliance on student trainees to fill service gaps. And, finally, initiation of services might simply be postponed until later in the school year.

Team members often failed to respond to very obvious service needs voiced by parents, particularly those involving counselling for emotional problems. For example, upon hearing the results of the testing of her child, a mother looked up and said: 'You know I have another boy, William. He probably has that same problem, but they didn't give him those tests. I thought he was lazy and thoughtless, but he was afraid to go into third grade. He wanted to go back to second.' The teacher responded, 'There is nothing wrong with going back to second.' This was the end of that discussion.

The relationship between classroom teachers and specialists is also a source of tension. The specialist can provide some relief for the teacher in handling a classroom problem; however, there are costs to the teacher in seeking such help. Classroom teachers resent the added paperwork burden involved in initiating referrals and the amount of time it takes to get specialists' services through the core-evaluation process. They too may be intimidated by the specialists' technical jargon. Like parents, they may be unfamiliar with the assessment process and outnumbered in evaluation meetings.

There are several additional factors inherent in the respective situations of specialists and teachers which contribute to this tension. Classroom teachers and specialists have differing perspectives. Teachers often regard special-needs children as contributing to their difficulties at work, whereas specialists regard these children as clients they were specifically trained to assist. Teachers have only one school year during which to accomplish their objectives for individual children or the class as a whole, but specialists can take a longer view. They may work with children over a period of years spanning the children's entire school careers. Thus a problem of some urgency to the teacher may be seen by the specialist as one that may be put off until some time in the future.

Status differences add to the tension. Specialists typically have qualifications as classroom teachers but also have additional education and certification and, in some cases, higher pay. Furthermore, specialists and teachers are responsible to different lines of authority. The classroom teacher is responsible to the principal, while the specialist reports to a programme director or division head who is generally located both physically and administratively close to the top of the system's hierarchy.

An additional source of tension is the discrepancy between teachers' expectations and results. Teachers look to the assessment process to provide some relief from disruptive children, but this expectation frequently remains unsatisfied. Teachers reported that 58 per cent of the children they referred for evaluation exhibited behaviour problems. However, only 21 per cent of these children were reported by the teachers to be getting any help either outside the school system or from the specialist within the system whose job it was to deal with behaviour problems. Responsibility for children is also a source of conflict between classroom teachers and specialists. Teachers are subject to conflicting pressures. On the one hand, they may wish to relinquish responsibility for an individual child whom they view as disruptive. On the other hand, they may view themselves as having primary responsibility for the child and may resent intrusion from outsiders. One teacher put it this way:

> The first- and second-grade teachers here had a list of five or six kids who ought to be retained. However, the psychologist recommended promotion on the basis of IQ tests. Teachers are losing their identity. We used to have teacher aides here who were paid $100 a week and that worked fine. Now they hire tutors at $6.75 an hour.

Elimination of labelling

The Chapter 766 requirement to discontinue the use of descriptive labels conflicts with the limited capacity of street-level bureaucracies to classify and differentially treat clients. Labels function as client-management aids and also help define worker-client relationships. Many classroom teachers and specialists were educated in an era when diagnosis ended with the assignment of a label, which in turn provided the sole basis for placement and treatment. Such terminology is not easily unlearned. Under the new regulations, there was some reduction in the use of labels and a very definite shift to individual behavioural descriptions. However, the use of labels persisted, as is indicated by the following statements made at assessment meetings:

> The Bender showed her to have an equivalent score of a five-year-old. However, I don't think she is a trainable.

> John was getting an awful lot of special help. He used to be, with an IQ under 50, according to state law, in a trainable class, but he has been in an educable class and has been progressing beyond what one would expect based on test scores alone.

Chapter 766's aim to eliminate labels was also foiled by federal requirements demanding continued use of the traditional designations. Thus, the State Division of Special Education compelled local school systems to report, as they had in the past, the numbers of and expenditures for children specifically classified as mentally retarded, physically handicapped, partially seeing, speech-hearing handicapped, emotionally disturbed, and learning disabled.

Even as old labels persisted, new ones were invented. When a psychologist and counsellor were contrasting programmes for 'LD [learning disabled] kids' and 'our kids', the observer asked who 'our kids' were. The psychologist replied, 'Oh, they used to be called retarded.' In another instance one teacher said that she ran a programme for 'substantially independent' girls. When asked what that meant, she replied, 'Well, we used to call it the EMH [educable mentally handicapped] class.'

Conclusion

[. . .]

That the systems we studied processed hundreds of children while maintaining the levels of services they did provide is a tribute to the dedication of school personnel and to the coercive, if diffuse, effects of the law. However, in certain respects the new law, by dictating so much, actually dictated very little. Like police officers who are required to enforce so many regulations that they are effectively free to enforce the law selectively, or public-welfare workers who cannot master encyclopedic and constantly changing eligibility requirements and so operate with a much smaller set of regulations, special-education personnel had to contrive their own adjustments to the multiple demands they encountered.

While not, for the most part, motivated by a desire to compromise compliance, school personnel had to formulate policies that would balance the new demands against available resources. To this end, school systems, schools, and individuals devised the following variety of coping patterns.

They rationed the number of assessments performed. They neglected to conduct assessments; placed limits on the numbers that were held; and biased the scheduling of assessments in favour of children who were behaviour problems, who were not likely to cost the systems money, or who met the needs of school personnel seeking to practice their individual specialities.

They rationed services by reducing the hours of assignment to specialists, by favouring group over individual treatment, and by using specialists-in-training rather than experienced personnel as instructors. They short-circuited bureaucratic requirements for completing forms and for following the procedures mandated and designed to protect the interests of parents. They minimized the potentially time-consuming problem of getting parents to go along with plans by securing prior agreements on recommendations and by fostering deference to professional authority.

In short, they sought to secure their work environment. As

individuals, teachers referred (dumped) students who posed the greatest threat to classroom control or recruited those with whom they were trained to work. Collectively, they sought contractual agreements that the new law would not increase their overall responsibilities.

These responses are not unique to special-education personnel but are typical of the coping behaviours of street-level bureaucrats. Chapter 766 placed additional burdens of judgement on roles already highly discretionary. [. . .]

The case of special education in Massachusetts provides a sober lesson in how difficult it is to integrate special services for a stigmatized population, particularly when that population is attended by professional specialists, funded through separate channels, championed by people fearful that they will lose hard-won access to decision making, and perceived to cause work-related problems for those responsible for managing the integration. In such a situation the role of law in legitimizing new conceptions of the public order and in mobilizing resources should not be overlooked.

Notes

1 Chapter 766 of the Acts of 1972, The Commonwealth of Massachusetts.
2 This formulation is elaborated in Lipsky, M. (1976) Toward a Theory of Street-Level Bureaucracy, in Hawley, W.D., and Lipsky, M. (Eds.), *Theoretical Perspectives on Urban Politics*, Englewood Cliffs, N.J., Prentice-Hall, pp. 186–212.
3 Commonwealth of Massachusetts, Department of Education, 'Regulations for the Implementation of Chapter 766 of the Acts of 1972: The Comprehensive Education Law', 28 May 1974 (henceforth referred to as 'Regulations'), para. 314.0, p. 17.
4 The procedures for a full evaluation are set forth in the 'Regulations', para. 320.0, pp. 21–2. An intermediate core evaluation may be given, with the parent's approval, in those cases in which it is expected that the child will *not* be placed outside a regular class more than 25 per cent of the time. It differs from the full core evaluation only in that fewer assessments are required ('Regulations', para. 331.0, p. 34).
5 Kaufman, M. J., Gottlieb, J., Agard, J. A. and Kukic, M. B. (1975) Mainstreaming: Towards an Explication of the Construct, *Focus on Exceptional Children*, 7, 1–12.
6 'Regulations', para. 502.10 (a), p. 58.
7 Thornton, M., Regulations on Special Education to Hike Taxes, *Boston Globe*, 22 February 1974. These estimates, it should be noted, were derived by applying the widely accepted national incidence figures of about 12 per cent to the state's school population.

8 Seven elementary schools, three in each of two school systems and one in the third, were selected for study. These are referred to as Systems A, B and C. (Ed.)

9 See Wilson, J. Q. (1967) The Bureaucracy Problem, *Public Interest*, 6, 3–9.

10 Headteacher. (Ed.)

11 Statewide, systems completed evaluations in a range from 2 per cent to 20 per cent.

12 The mean age of children evaluated varied from 12.6 years in System A to 7.5 in System B and 10.3 in System C. In all three school systems, males evaluated outnumbered females by between two and three to one.

PART 6

Research, Theory and Practice

6.1 The role of psychological research in special education

CHRIS SINHA

Received wisdom has it that the way to make use of research in the practice of special education is to develop the means to apply it: to translate academic knowledge into practical knowledge so that the teacher can boldly rise to the challenge of new insights discovered by the researcher. This naive and somewhat imperious view is challenged in this paper. Chris Sinha argues firstly that psychological theories themselves in part reflect the same assumptions as those that underpin current social and educational practices. Secondly, he shows that the differing contexts of pure and applied research mean that whilst the former thrives on change and development, the latter survives by conservatism. More important, research and practice promote quite different views of what counts as valid and useful knowledge. Mutual comprehension and collaboration will thus depend upon the negotiation of a meeting point for these ways of working and thinking.

Psychology, the child and special education

There is an exceptionally close relationship between psychology and special education, in which the influence of psychological thinking upon educational practices is more marked than in any other sphere except pre-school education. Of course, the educational system as a whole is profoundly 'psychologized'; its theory and practice is sustained and rationalized by appeal to psychological concepts and evidence. Selection criteria, learning and teaching methods, curriculum development, remedial techniques, classroom organization and layout, 'educational' toys and materials and training courses for teachers; all these diverse facets of the educational enterprise are imbued by the products of psychology. Yet, the impact that psychology has had is unevenly spread throughout the educational system. As a general rule, the younger and less able the group of children being catered for, the greater the extent to which educational theory and practice is psychologized. It is no exaggeration to say that our contemporary received notions of infancy and early childhood are primarily *psycho-*

Specially commissioned for this volume
©The Open University, 1981

logical, and both teachers and parents look to psychology as the prime source of information and guidance regarding early child development.

Throughout history, every culture has entertained educational, social and moral concepts of childhood (Ariès, 1973). Twentieth-century Western culture is unique in that it accords a *scientific* status to psychology's pronouncements, and constructs the image of the child after a fashion that 'science' dictates. It is also unique in the value it places upon *educational* intervention in the pre-school years.

This has not always been the case. Until the latter half of the nineteenth century, the classic treatises on education concerned themselves principally with the education and training of boys and young men, only secondarily with that of girls, and relegated infancy and early childhood to the realm of nature, myth and magic. Usually, this relegation was accompanied and justified by reference to the seemingly pre-ordained sexual division of labour. Rousseau, at the beginning of Book 1 of *Emile, or on Education* (1762), while acknowledging the importance of 'the earliest education', maintained that it 'undoubtedly is woman's work. If the author of nature had meant to assign it to men, he would have given them milk to feed the child.' Early childhood, then, was a matter of nurturance and care, within which Nature would take her course until such proper time that education would interpose itself between the child and society.

Insofar as there was considered to be a role for intervention in what we would now call the pre-school years, this was held to be the proper domain of the medical sciences, rather than of the educational and moral ones. The advent of psychology, with its claims to be 'the proper science of mankind', effected a profound transformation of this view of childhood. Psychology, while drawing its earliest concepts from philosophy, natural and bio-medical sciences, laid claim to and occupied a new and unique space in the intellectual constellation, seeking to render a scientific account of the mental and behavioural facts of human life. From its inception, it sought to wrest the territory of human childhood from the grip of folklore, superstition and cultural tradition on the one hand, and the pronouncements of somatic medicine, on the other.

One of the first fruits of the encounter between the emerging discipline of psychology, and the equally new cultural domain of 'early childhood', was the concept of 'scientific pedagogy', a practice of teaching and learning informed by psychological theories and findings. And, as is illustrated by Lane's superb study *The Wild Boy of Aveyron* (1977), the fundamental concepts of 'scientific pedagogy' were themselves developed in the context of practices of diagnosis, classification and remediation of childhood psychopathologies. Psychology and special education, then, can be seen to have emerged together; not only did psychological theories underpin special educational practices, but the 'subjects' of special education provided the subject matter for the emerging specialization of developmental and child psychology.

Since these early days, of course, both psychology and special education have undergone profound changes − not always, it might be said, for the better. The closeness of their relationship, however, has not diminished; the changing fortunes of psychological theories − behaviourism, psychoanalysis, psychometric testing, cognitive developmental theory − have been mirrored in the selection and classroom procedures advocated at different times in the field of special education. By now, the relationship is institutionalized in myriad organizational, administrative and ideological forms; the conceptual tools at the teacher's disposal, and the vocabulary in which curricular objectives are set − discrimination, cognitive development, reinforcement, motor skills − are those of psychology. Not unnaturally, a major feature of this institutionalized relationship has been the growth of a massive research industry in the field of the psychology of special education and childhood disability. The rise of the research industry, in the years following the post-war boom, has in turn posed the problems of *dissemination* and *implementation* of research findings in the classroom context.

Research and practice in the psychology of special education

In this paper, I wish to explore some of the problems inherent in prevailing models of the relations between research and practice in special education. I shall argue that these problems stem from three principal sources: first, an inadequate conceptual framework for understanding the relation between 'pure' and 'applied' research; second, an institutional inertia and inappropriately rigid division of labour; and third, an unsatisfactory and inadequate theorization by psychology of what are its own appropriate aims and methods in the sphere of special education. In reality, these three foci of the 'research/practice problem' are not independent, but mutually reinforcing and deeply intertwined. Any attempt to resolve or transcend the contradictions and inadequacies of current theory and practice will require attention and energy to be paid to all of them.

To begin with, however, let us examine some of the assumptions currently held about the relationship between 'pure' and 'applied' research. A commonsense view sees the former as working out fundamental problems and formulating general principles, and the latter as applying these solutions and principles to particular practical problems. In this view, a one-way transmission belt is assumed from research to practice; a well-formulated and consistent body of theory and evidence is taken for granted, and the main problem is seen to be that of isolating the specific parameters, or dimensions, of the real world problems, and of setting specifiable and realistic goals. This can be labelled the *operational* view of the relation between research and practice, in that it conceives the main problem to be that of operationally implementing a theory in a practical problem area.

In the real world, things are more complicated than this. In the first place, scientific disciplines are historically developed as systematizations and legitimizations of *practices*, either pre-dating the science or newly emerging in response to some historical situation. This is true of all sciences, but very clearly and markedly so in the case of the social or human sciences. The object of study of 'scientific psychology' – the abstract and universal psychological individual – was not just hanging in the air waiting to be 'discovered' by science prior to the birth of the discipline of psychology. Rather, psychological theorization can be seen as a systematic *response* to, and *intervention* in, an emergent way of seeing and acting in relation to certain groups of people and social 'problems' designated as being in need of certain types of intervention.

Put very simply, the relationship of psychology to special education has been *interventionist*, and not merely *theoretical*, from the very beginning; and the type of theory adopted or advocated by psychologists has been as much a product of their particular view of intervention as it has been the result of 'pure' experimental work. We can see quite clearly in the case of a concept like intelligence how socially determined values underlying current practices become translated into a theoretical construct, which in turn lends scientific legitimacy to the self-same practices. What I am arguing is that this state of affairs, far from being an aberration, is in fact the norm in the relationship between a theoretical discourse and a social practice.

Many psychologists fiercely reject the suggestion that the scientific enterprise has more to do with the theoretical systematization and legitimation of socially embedded practices than it does with the unveiling of timeless truths; they detect underlying charges of ideological bias, and, worse, the hint that truth is 'only relative', which, they believe, undermines the whole basis of objective inquiry. My point, however, is not to discredit psychology – it has often enough shown itself perfectly capable of doing that unaided. Nor do I wish to suggest that rigour and objectivity are not desirable and attainable. Rather, I want to point out that an understanding of psychology's role in special education (and in society generally) demands that we pay attention to the *context* of the pursuit of science, and the *negotiation* in practice of its goals and methods in particular areas of both pure and applied research in relation to that context.

I shall return below to the notions of context and negotiation; for now, let us focus again upon the problem of 'pure' and 'applied' research. Although, as I have argued, the history of a particular discipline demonstrates the fundamental and unbreakable link between the theories advanced and the practices advocated, the very success of a 'unifying' project, the attempt to systematize and synthesize many different domains of practice under a single theoretical rubric, is contradictory and in a sense self-defeating. For no sooner has a particular discipline, such as psychology, established its reputable place in the pantheon of knowledge, than the fragmentary and disparate nature of the collection of practices which it subsumes tends to reassert itself. This is, of course, inevitable: reality *is* complex, and the types of problems faced by researchers in human memory, mental retardation, ergonomics and inter-group behaviour require very different concepts and methods.

Consequently, however, a complex division of labour becomes established, in which both a horizontal (social vs. experimental cognitive vs. developmental vs. ethological) dimension of sub-discipline, and a vertical (pure, experimental vs. applied, practical) dimension can be distinguished. Although each of the compartments of this honey-comb selectively borrow and exchange concepts and methods from each other, they also do so from other disciplines (sociology, anthropology, neurology, physiology, psychiatry, linguistics, computer science, etc.), with which they share certain common concerns. What has emerged, in the case of psychology, is a set of theories, concepts and methods, applicable to different domains and problems, which bear more of a 'family resemblance' to each other than a relationship of logical coherence or necessity. This situation is not only inevitable, but desirable, for no single theory can comprehend the whole range of psychological phenomena, although there has been no shortage of takers for that prize.

Often, however, this diversity of concepts and methods poses a serious problem for the 'applied' researcher, who, as in the case of special education, tends to be concerned with a *range* of psychological problems and issues, rather than a strictly limited research question. The pressures of practical necessity, and the need for comprehensibility and communicability to practitioners in the field, often mean that the *version* of a theory (or theories) actually applied to real problems differs in certain ways from that developed in a 'pure' research context.

What is more, the pure and applied disciplines may then develop in different ways, in different research and institutional contexts, so that by the time a particular application of a theory has become widely established, that theory has long since become discredited or superseded in the pure research field. Something like this can be said to have occurred in the case of behaviour modification in special education. Few active researchers in developmental psychology would nowadays consider behaviourism to be an adequate theory. Yet, because it has been developed as a useful tool in special education, and incorporated in many programmes devised by applied psychologists, this theoretical inadequacy has not substantially affected its institutionally legitimized role in applied clinical and educational psychology.

It is often the case, then, that pure and applied research diverge greatly in their aims and methods, and that new developments in pure research may take many years to filter through to the practitioner. In fact, whereas pure research often appears to be characterized by the more or less rapid exchange of one hypothesis for another, and the continual competition between one general type of theory and others, applied research often appears very much more consensual, conflict-free and enduring. Having developed a technique which 'works', at some level, which conforms to the norms of legitimate practice, and which confers or maintains the professional status of the specialist in the sub-discipline, the applied researcher will be reluctant to abandon it on purely theoretical grounds, particularly if no obvious candidate for its replacement offers itself.

There are evident dangers in this situation. Applied research in a particular area, such as special education, may become an isolated sub-culture, in which exotic and expensive techniques, based upon outdated theories, compete for scarce resources, while genuine innovation is stifled under the weight of a conservative consensus. The same problem of the institutionalization of the division of labour presents itself at the point at which the applied research actually becomes translated into practice — by teachers, educational and clinical psychologists, speech therapists and so on. Each of these groups of people will have been trained in particular ways, reflecting the current or past institutional consensus within their own discipline. Each group will tend to assimilate new research findings to the models to which they have become accustomed by virtue of their training and experience. Often, too, different groups of practitioners will have different professional status. Both these factors contribute to friction and misunderstanding between practitioners and researchers, and between different groups of

practitioners. Further, the working conditions and day-to-day professional aims of the practitioner differ from the priorities and time-
scale of the researcher, and this too will promote conflict. Teachers,
for example, are often heard to voice the opinion that research findings
are irrelevant to classroom practice, or that suggested techniques are
impracticable. Researchers, on the other hand, are prone to the belief
that their own professional norms are the only legitimate ones, that
deviations from their recommended modes of intervention are
necessarily harmful rather than constructive, and that the evaluative
evidence offered by practitioners has only 'anecdotal', as opposed to
scientific, status.

The Bristol Teacher Research Group

It was with the aim of short-circuiting these institutional barriers that
Dr Norman Freeman and I initiated in October 1976 a Teacher
Research Group on the topic of 'Language and Representation in
Mentally Handicapped Children', at the University of Bristol School of
Education. Both of us had been working, separately, on aspects of
children's linguistic and cognitive development. Neither of us had any
significant experience of working with mentally handicapped children,
but we were both convinced that the work that we were doing had,
potentially, some interesting implications for special education,
although at the time we would have been hard put to have justified this
conviction. We were fortunate in that the School of Education had for
some years been encouraging and funding the formation of teacher
research and development groups, largely as a result of the initiative of
the late John Taylor. Accordingly, a leaflet outlining the aims, as we
saw them, of our proposed group was circulated to local special schools.

We were astonished by the response: some twenty-odd teachers and
speech therapists turned up on the first evening. Obviously, what we
were offering tapped a felt need by teachers which was not catered for
elsewhere. With some trepidation, we attempted to find out what kind
of activities the teachers had in mind when they answered our circular
and confessed our deep ignorance of special education. We also tried to
explain how we thought developmental psychological research might
bear upon their professional concerns. Not surprisingly, we found that
their image of relevance was rather different from ours. We saw the
problem as being one of *applying* psychology; they saw it as being one
of *using* psychology to deal with real children and their problems. We
tried to explain that we dealt in generalities and abstract processes, and
they countered by asserting the uniqueness of the children. Yet the
descriptions they gave of the children which they talked about were

psychological ones, not just in that many of the teachers were familiar and fluent with psychological jargon, but also because, as we gradually recognized, the terms of reference of special education *are* basically psychological, in a non-academic sense.

It soon became clear, though, that the teachers did not see it in this way. Psychology, as they saw it, meant academic psychology, and their own knowledge and expertise did not count as academic and scientific knowledge. For our part, we felt that our academic psychology was not particularly well suited to analysing the difficulties of individual children, and we were impressed by the ability of the teachers to deploy their understanding over such a wide range of different problems. I shall return in the next section to the problem of dealing with individuals; for now, I want to emphasize that it was not, in fact, simply the case that our knowledge was theoretical and theirs practical, for we possessed *practical* experience in a range of skills and knowledge (working with children in test situations; designing and analysing experiments) which the teachers did not share; and they were familiar with the concepts and theories of special education of which we were relatively ignorant.

In fact, a major feature of the split between the researcher and the teacher seemed to be the different notions of *evidence* in research and practice, and of the status of different types of evidence. Research evidence is public and subject to the scrutiny of other researchers through academic journals and such like channels; it is evaluated according to norms of truth and consistency, and it is seen as having a significance independent of the particular circumstances and occasions of its production (thus, for example, experiments should be *replicable*). The particular subjects who provide the data are only of importance as *representatives* of a population (leaving out of account, for the moment, clinical case studies; and even here, the individual case is often seen as representative of a syndrome). Research evidence is accorded a high status — it is *science*, and research workers are (high status) *scientists*.

The evidence used by the practitioner, on the other hand, is *private* and rarely rendered in an explicit way. It is evaluated according to criteria of *usefulness* and *relevance*, and its significance is largely in terms of the particular individual or group from which it has been gathered. And these individuals and groups are the focus of an intervention, so that, far from statistically ironing out the idiosyncracies and peculiarities of the subject group, it is in the interests of the practitioner to emphasize them. Finally, practitioners are often seen, and see themselves, as being of relatively low status in relation to researchers; and their kind of evidence tends to be dismissed as merely 'anecdotal'.

In our teacher research group, we found ourselves having to *negotiate* both a set of common rules for evaluating evidence, and a set of aims which would be relevant to the contexts of both research and practice. We decided, in fact, to carry out a series of experiments, and to try together to evaluate their significance in the classroom context. This is not the appropriate place to give a full account of these experiments (see Freeman and Sinha, 1977), but it is important to point out that they were all carried out by the teachers, sometimes with our assistance, using the children they taught as subjects. Our Monday evening sessions became clearing houses, at which everyone would report their own results, and the pattern of experimental data was constructed and analysed on the spot; vigorous discussion about how to interpret the findings followed, and often continued over coffee or beer.

Gradually, we learned, as psychologists, how to use our 'academic' knowledge to analyse constructively the way in which the individual children performed in the experiments, and to suggest teaching and remediation techniques. The teachers learned to render their own observations explicitly, and to relate them to various theoretical propositions that we were exploring. We all learned a great deal — some of which I shall summarize in the final section — about the nature of learning processes in mentally handicapped (and normal) children, and how we might best capitalize upon the strengths of individuals in order to help them overcome their weakness in other areas.

But we also learned something about the co-operative enterprise of putting research into practice. We came to question the framework of 'applied research' as traditionally conceived, and to understand the need for a much greater involvement of practitioners in the definition of the goals and procedures of psychology in the special education context. We became more critical of received wisdom, less ready to accept assertions just because they were couched in technical jargon, or just because they were consecrated as habit and wisdom. At the same time, we became more open and receptive to ideas and experiences which we might have dismissed as uninteresting or unimportant before, and we learned to check 'instinctive' responses of dismissal: not to think or say 'that's just theory', or 'that's just anecdote'. And, most importantly, we discovered that we had problems in common, and tried to understand from where they stemmed; and in some cases the support of the group helped us to gain the confidence and awareness to challenge 'the system' and start to change it.

These were rather intangible benefits of working in a democratic and collective way, in an environment which was both supportive and critical, to try to apply psychological research to special education problems. Nonetheless, they were real benefits, and point the direction to an alternative practice of applied research, which consists as much in negotiating aims and raising consciousness as in implementing and evaluating controlled studies. Furthermore, the teacher research group which I have described did not take place under ideal conditions: we (the researchers) were not experienced workers in this field, we were not working in it full-time, and we received only minimal (though very essential) funding. Yet the benefits of working in this fashion were apparent to all of us, and I believe that it is within such contexts that research can most readily be put to use in practice. I am not offering a model, for every research problem and every practical setting demands its own specific approaches and procedures. As one of the teachers remarked at a meeting: we started out looking for recipes; we ended up realizing that what we needed were *strategies*. The strategy which underlay the Bristol teacher research group differed from the usual model of applied research, in that it did not take for granted a strict division of labour, to be rigidly applied in all circumstances, but based itself upon the mutual negotiation of areas of expertise with respect to particular problems. Collaborative work, for us, meant extending one's knowledge through being educated by others, and re-negotiating our roles, so that the teacher became a researcher, the researcher a resource, and all of us educators.

Theoretical and practical reasoning

In the previous section, I stressed that there is a considerable divergence between the way in which researchers and practitioners habitually view evidence. The problem seems to be that each group evaluates the evidence offered by the other in its own terms, which may be inappropriate: research is seen by practitioners as 'irrelevant' and 'too theoretical', while the observations of practitioners are seen as 'unsystematic' and 'unscientific' by researchers.

From the point of view of an effective interventionist psychology, neither of these two ways of seeing is wrong in itself; the goal must be to attempt to combine them, or at least to make them mutually intelligible. Applied psychological research needs to incorporate the insights and experience of practitioners, while conserving the rigour and objectivity of the experimental method. It may be, however, that our notions of 'insight' and of 'objectivity' will require some examination if this goal is to be achieved, in order that both of them can be made *explicit* components of a useful methodological approach.

The notion of 'insight' has itself been the focus of psychological investigation in the past. It usually refers to a kind of sudden or immediate understanding of a problem, an unreflective understanding produced not by a chain of logical reasoning, but by a simultaneous seeing of all the elements of a problem, together with its solution. We all know of occasions when the behaviour of somebody (even ourselves) can be described as 'insightful', but we usually find it difficult to express the process by which the insight came about. Insight is a highly valued quality in professionals working with young children, but again difficult to quantify or articulate. Yet we recognize it when we see it; and, further, experienced workers employ the same kinds of insight when trying to help a child through a task, yet find it extremely difficult to teach to those with less experience.

I would suggest that there is, in fact, nothing particularly mysterious about what we refer to as *insight*: the difficulty lies in communicating about it. Insight, in fact, can be viewed as a particular way of applying *knowledge*, but a form of knowledge that is generally not recognized as objective or scientific. The sort of knowledge which comes into play when insightful interventions are made is *context-specific*, or *embedded* knowledge, as Margaret Donaldson (1978) calls it, and it is extremely difficult to communicate. It can be contrasted with the context-free, disembedded knowledge which in our culture is highly valued as the norm of intellectual discourse.

It often appears to be the case that 'embedded' or 'context-bound' knowledge is mysterious in its processes of application; but the sense of mystery is essentially a result of our familiarity with the idea that 'disembedded' knowledge is the most valid and powerful way of representing information. This idea, however, is itself a cultural product; in other cultures, 'embedded' thinking is the norm, and 'disembedded' thinking presents great difficulties for individuals. On the other hand, the power and flexibility of embedded thinking when used habitually by other cultures can seem astonishing — quite as mysterious as the processes underlying 'insight'. Here is what Thomas Gladwin (1964) says about the cognitive processes of the Trukese, an island people of the South Pacific:

Voyages spanning over one hundred miles of open ocean are still regularly made in sailing canoes, and longer ones were made in the past. The destination is often a tiny dot of land less than a mile across, and visible from any distance only because of the height of those coconut trees which may grow in its sandy soil . . . . the crew usually rely on one of their number who has been trained in a variety of traditional techniques by an older master navigator . . . . these techniques do not include even a compass . . . to say nothing of chronometer, sextant or star tables.

Essentially the navigator relies on dead reckoning . . . having memorised for this purpose the knowledge gleaned from generations of observation of the directions in which stars rise and fall through the seasons . . . . through the night a succession of such stars will rise or fall . . . . between stars, or when the stars are not visible due to daylight or storm, the course is held constant by noting the direction of the wind and the waves. A good navigator can tell by observing wave patterns when the wind is shifting its direction or speed, and by how much. In a dark and starless night the navigator can even tell these things from the sound of the waves as they lap upon the side of the canoe's hull, and the feel of the boat as it travels through the water.

Gladwin says this about the types of thinking embodied in the norms of Western and Trukese cultures:

In our culture we value (and measure crudely with intelligence tests) . . . abstract thinking in which bodies of knowledge are integrated and related to each other through unifying symbolic constructs . . . developing an overall principle or plan from which individual steps towards a solution can be derived deductively. In contrast, the Trukese' work towards a solution involves improvising each step, but always with the final goal in mind. The Trukese start with a simplified *gestalt*, whether or not they can describe it in words, and fill in the details as they go along. We prefer to look a situation over and design a somewhat special gestalt which will at the outset embrace all the essential details. (Gladwin, 1964; 1973)

Starting with the initial and end points in mind, and filling in the details of the route to be travelled as you go along, is not only something which we all habitually do in a literal sense − though not with the same facility and efficiency as the Trukese navigator; it can also stand as an apt metaphor for the sort of activity skilled practitioners engage in when doing remedial educational work with young children, which we often refer to as 'insightful'. There is, however, a difference: the end point here is often only vaguely defined as 'development', 'progress', 'better understanding' and so forth.

This mode of reasoning, however − which modern cognitive psychology often refers to as 'procedural', as opposed to 'propositional' reasoning (Johnson-Laird, 1980) — does not at all fit the classical description of the scientific method; although it may be said that the actual practice, as opposed to the theory, of doing research, *is* often quite like this, too. Every psychology student, however, is taught that the goal of science is to abstract, classify, generalize and quantify; and to derive, by a succession of steps which *logically* flow from each other, universally applicable or at least statistically generalizable laws. It would seem, at least at first sight, that the concerns of psychological research, and those of the practitioner — for whom every journey possesses its own unique goals and contours — are almost completely divergent. Yet this cannot in fact be so, for a fairly simple reason: the scientific method (leaving aside for a moment the problematical question of what that really is), when appropriately applied, is able to generate *new evidence* and to *change the theory* in a way in which the practical reasoning of everyday contexts cannot do. As Weisstein (1971) succinctly puts it: 'The problem with insight, sensitivity and intuition is that they can confirm for all time the biases that one started out with. People used to be absolutely convinced of their ability to tell which of their number were engaging in witchcraft. All it required was some sensitivity to the workings of the devil.'

Practice *does* change, and part of what motivates the change is new findings and theories emerging in basic research. What needs to change is the *relationship* between research and practice, in such a way that the rigour and objectivity of research methods can be incorporated into practice without doing violence to the nature and complexity of the practical task itself. If such a change is to come about, psychology must see its role as being one of articulating and making explicit the goals and processes of interventionist practices; in enabling communication to occur about what these goals and processes may be; and thereby enabling practitioners to relate what they do to a shared set of concepts and theories and agreed ways of organizing and analysing their perceptions so that these can attain the status of evidence, and no longer be dismissed as anecdote. In the next, and final section, I shall try to suggest what sort of psychological concepts are currently good candidates for this role, drawing upon recent research in developmental psychology.

Process models in psychological research

Perhaps the most important lesson to have emerged from recent research in developmental psychology is that the *context* in which a task is presented to a child, and the way that context is established through *communication*, are at least as decisively important in determining how the child will go about it, as is the logical structure of the problem incorporated in the task. Many of these recent findings are summarized in Donaldson (1978), Sinha and Walkerdine (1978; 1979) and chapters in Wells (1981), and I can only give the briefest of outlines of their most important features; in particular, I would refer the interested reader to Margaret Donaldson's *Children's Minds,* both for further information and for her excellent discussion of these issues.

What immediately concerns me, however, is the way in which some of these recent findings challenge ideas which have come to dominate both developmental psychology and psycho-educational theory in the last twenty years or so. These ideas stem above all, directly and indirectly, from the work of the great psychologist and epistemologist Jean Piaget. I want to stress, at the outset, that it is not my intention to discredit, far less dismiss, Piaget's massive contribution to our understanding of developmental processes. His work is, and will remain for the foreseeable future, the basic reference point for all developmental psychologists; and I would strongly advise anyone who wishes to read the recent critiques of Piagetian theory also to read Piaget himself (e.g. Piaget, 1953; Piaget and Inhelder, 1969).

In particular, it is important to point out that in the field of special education, Piagetian developmental theory is only now partly displacing the previously unchallenged hegemony of behaviourism. In my opinion, this is an unqualified step forward, and nothing that I say should be taken to endorse the view that 'the behaviourists were right all along', which I have at times heard expressed in response to recent developmentalist criticisms of Piaget. Behaviourism, whatever the merits and demerits of behaviour modification as a specific technique, is *not* a developmental theory, and, as I shall argue, it is a developmental theory that is required.

Having said that, what is at issue is the relationship between what is traditionally called 'cognitive development', and the social context and social relations which confer what we may as well call 'meaning' upon what is learned, and how it is learned. For Piaget, the child exists as a solitary individual, a biological/cognitive organism interacting with a physical environment. From these interactions stem new and more complex ways of organizing actions, and these action—co-ordinations, when internalized, form *cognitive structures*, existing in dynamic equilibrium with the products of their application to the environment. The sort of concepts in which Piaget was interested, and the development of which he devoted his life to investigating, were those like space, time, motion, causality, class-inclusion and conservation, which are widely applicable across very many circumstances and situations. They are structures of great power and generality.

There is much that is truly revealing about this sort of analysis; in particular, the idea of intelligence as a *structuring activity*, common to all individuals, as opposed to a static quantity or attribute possessed, once and for all, in varying amounts by different individuals. But there is also much that it neglects. In Piaget's work, we find little reference to the equally complex structures governing the infant's and the child's social interactions with mothers and other caretakers; nor to the role which these structures play in the strategies that children employ to find out about the nature of the world around them (Bruner, 1975; Trevarthen and Hubley, 1978).

Nor, at least in his later work, do we find much reference in Piaget to the acquisition and development of language. Yet, it is increasingly becoming clear that the role of social interaction, communication and language is crucial in the cognitive development of the child. What is more, the way that children *use* language and communication, to understand the world, is very largely governed by their extraordinary sensitivity to *context*. Children interpret the problems that adults pose for them according to their evaluation of the intentions of the experimenter, their familiarity with the structure and materials of the task, and the linguistic encoding of the task-demands given by the experimenter. Linguistic and cognitive development are largely processes of *social interaction and negotiation* (Wells, 1981).

If this is the case, the sort of psychological theory that we need for practical intervention is one which gives due weight to the subtlety and complexity of these contextually governed, negotiative processes. Children's thinking, it seems, is *embedded* in context, in the sense used by Donaldson, and in the sense that I have used the term to characterize the rather woolly notion of 'insight'. It seems, then, that the new findings in developmental psychological research point in precisely the same direction as the requirements for an interventionist psychology in special education practice: the need for *process models*.

We do not yet really possess such models, but there are clues to their possible form. Half a century ago, the Soviet developmental psychologist Vygotsky made the suggestion that 'every function in the child's development appears twice: first, on the social level, and later, on the individual level; first *between* people, and then *inside* the child' (Vygotsky, 1978). In this way, Vygotsky maintained that 'learning awakens a variety of internal developmental processes that are able to operate only when the child is interacting with people in his environment and in cooperation with his peers. Once these processes are internalised, they become part of the child's independent developmental achievement.' The difference between what the child can do, today, with help, and will be able to do tomorrow independently, Vygotsky called the *zone of proximal development*, the zone within which remedial intervention should take place. He used this concept in his own pioneering work in special education. We now possess a wealth of data on normal children's development upon which we can build and extend Vygotsky's ideas, yet we know rather little about, for example, mentally handicapped children's specific similarities and differences. Are they more or less context-bound in their development? How relatively sensitive are they, in attentional terms, say, to the negotiative cues offered by adults?

I would suggest that these are the crucial issues for both research and practice in the future, in special education, and indeed in every area of education where attention needs to be paid to specific and individual learning strategies. In the past, psychologists' excessive preoccupation with *standardizing* — tests, responses and teaching methods — has led them to neglect processes. Now is the appropriate time to redress the balance; and in so doing, to construct a psychological approach which is adequate to bridge the gap between research and practice.

Note

Thanks are due to many people with whom I have discussed the ideas in this paper. Rather than single out names, I would like to record my especial gratitude to all the participants in the Bristol Teacher Research Group, and my hope that I have accurately reported at least some of the experience of the group. It's their paper too. The paper was written with the support of a grant from the Social Science Research Council.

References

Ariès, P. (1973) *Centuries of Childhood*, Harmondsworth, Penguin.
Bruner, J. S. (1975) From communication to language — a psychological perspective, *Cognition*, 3, 255–87.
Donaldson, M. (1978) *Children's Minds*, London, Fontana/Collins.
Freeman, N. H. and Sinha, C. G. (1977) Language and representation in mentally handicapped children, Teacher Research Group Report, University of Bristol School of Education.
Gladwin, T. (1964) Culture and logical process, in W. Goodenough (Ed.), *Explorations in Cultural Anthropology*, New York, McGraw-Hill, reprinted in N. Keddie (Ed.) (1973), *Tinker, Tailor . . . the myth of cultural deprivation*, Harmondsworth, Penguin.
Johnson-Laird, P. N. (1980) Mental models in cognitive science, *Cognitive Science*, 4, 71–115.
Lane, H. (1977) *The Wild Boy of Aveyron*, London, Allen and Unwin.

Piaget, J. (1953) *The Origin of Intelligence in the Child*, London, Routledge and Kegan Paul.

Piaget, J. and Inhelder, B. (1969) *The Psychology of the Child*, London, Routledge and Kegan Paul.

Rousseau, J.-J. (1762, 1969 edn) *Emile, ou De L'Education*, London, Dent.

Sinha, C. G. and Walkerdine, V. (1978) Children, logic and learning, *New Society*, 12 January, reprinted in M. Hoyles (Ed.) (1979), *Changing Childhood*, London, Writers and Readers Publishing Co-operative.

Trevarthen, C. and Hubley, P. (1978) Secondary intersubjectivity: confidence, confiding and acts of meaning in the first year of life, in A. Lock (Ed.), *Action, Gesture and Symbol: the emergence of language*, London, Academic Press.

Vygotsky, L. S. (1978); M. Cole, V. John-Steiner, S. Scribner and E. Souberman (Eds.), *Mind in Society; the development of higher psychological processes*, Cambridge, Mass., Harvard University Press.

Walkerdine, V. and Sinha, C. G. (1978) The internal triangle: language, reasoning and the social context, in I. Markova (Ed.), *The Social Context of Language*, London, Wiley.

Weisstein, N. (1971) Psychology constructs the female, or the fantasy life of the male psychologist, in *Liberation Now: writings from the women's liberation movement*, New York, Dell.

Wells, G. (Ed.) (1981) *Learning through Interaction: the study of language development*, Cambridge, Cambridge University Press.

6.2 Theory and research in classrooms: lessons from deaf education

DAVID WOOD

David Wood explores in detail the negotiations between teacher and researcher that can lead to valuable outcomes for both. Using two extended examples of investigations into teaching strategies with hearing-impaired children, he illuminates the contributions both parties make at various stages of the research process. By treating the teacher as an equal partner, the researcher gains insights that might otherwise be denied to him, and the teacher can put the researcher's knowledge and expertise to useful purposes. Thus, by negotiating the aims and methods of the work from the outset, its relevance is greatly enhanced.

Introduction

Psychology was, until fairly recently, a merely academic study, with very little application to practical affairs. This is all changed now. We have, for instance, industrial psychology, clinical psychology, educational psychology, all of the greatest practical importance. We may hope and expect that the influence of psychology upon our institutions will rapidly increase in the near future. In education, at any rate, its effect has already been great and beneficial. (Bertrand Russell, 1926)

Heartened though many psychologists may be by Russell's strong faith in their discipline, few would be bold enough to claim that its influence on our institutions has been as rapid or as positive as Russell envisaged in his essays *On Education*. Throughout the field of educational psychology and many other branches of the subject there are currently many debates both about the past value and the future course of the discipline. What should the psychologist interested in education be studying — what is his subject matter — and how should that study proceed? Such questions are the focus of much contemporary debate and the starting point for the issues considered in this paper.

Over the past twenty years or so, the major basis of psychological

Specially commissioned for this volume
© The Open University, 1981

activity has been the analysis of human performance in laboratory situations. A great deal of work on the development of learning and reasoning in young children (much of it inspired by the work of Jean Piaget) has attempted to enrich our understanding of the young child and his educational needs by investigating his abilities to solve, or not to solve, a variety of problems. Such problems have usually been set by an unfamiliar adult to an individual, isolated child, encountered in specially contrived situations. The performances of children in such situations and the changes that occur in their ability to solve problems at different ages have formed the primary data base or subject matter from which theories have fashioned their hypotheses about the nature of mental activity in the young learner. Over the past few years, however, it has become increasingly clear that attempting to generalize findings about children from such situations to the classroom is difficult and hazardous. One contemporary view, derived both from laboratory study and more naturalistic observations of children at home and in school, holds that the apparent competence of a child — for example, his ability to solve a particular type of problem — is influenced not only by the logical nature of that problem but also by a range of social factors such as who sets his task, how they try to help him handle it and where he is when that task is introduced to him. His ability to reason rationally, solve problems or even talk freely to an adult varies as a function of the social situation (e.g. Donaldson, 1978; Labov, 1970; Tizard *et al.,* in press; Wood *et al.*, 1981).

Appreciating the extent and potential significance of the gulf between behaviour in the laboratory and classroom, many researchers in education have started to move away from the laboratory as the principal and sole context for gathering insights into the nature of the learning process to work in classrooms. But it has generally been the case that the description and evaluation of what has been observed there has remained the sole responsibility of the researcher-theorist. One practical result of this has been the proliferation of a large number of 'coding systems' for categorizing and analysing classroom activities.

The many different descriptions of teaching and learning in the school that have arisen out of this new line of research illustrate the wide range of interests, assumptions and theories embedded in the sub-culture of research workers. It is now generally recognized in science that a description made of any phenomenon does not reflect an 'absolute reality'; it also embodies a contribution from the mind of the person who makes the description, revealing their interests, goals, assumptions and even, perhaps, their moral judgements about the nature of that reality. If the assumptions and objectives of an observer and those he observes coincide, then this state of affairs is not, perhaps, a vital problem. However, given that the training, objectives and experiences of teachers on the one hand and researchers on the other are often so very different, one suspects that such coincidence in class-room research is rare. This helps explain, perhaps, why teachers often find the analyses and recommendations of research workers irrelevant, overly abstract and of little practical value.

In some situations, of course, the differing perspectives of teacher and researcher may of necessity be different in kind. For example, if a researcher is attempting to study the relationship between general levels of pupil performance and differences across different school environ-ments (e.g. Rutter *et al.*, 1979), he may well work with a model of the hypothetical, 'average' pupil who exists in no classroom and is recognized by no teacher. However, if the researcher is attempting to say something specific about the nature of teaching and learning in a particular classroom, is explicitly or tacitly evaluating an individual teacher's methods, or where he is attempting to discover the specific problems faced by children trying to learn in school, then the relation-ships between the perspectives adopted by both teacher and researcher must be investigated and articulated.

So, the argument proceeds, if a researcher is interested in the description and evaluation of particular styles of teaching behaviour and their impact on the learning experiences of children, then he must work co-operatively with the teacher to negotiate a shared language for analysing what goes on in the classroom. In so doing, I shall argue, teacher and researcher together will also lay the foundations for the development of a much richer and useful account of the educational process.

The focus of this paper, then, is a consideration of the nature of effective working relationships between teachers and psychologists in developing ways of describing and evaluating teaching–learning activities. Although the aim is a general one, the actual case studies discussed concern specific problems in the education of deaf children. Before embarking on this main theme, a few words need to be said about the nature of those problems.

All the children involved in the studies I shall describe are severely or profoundly deaf and were either born deaf or became so before they developed language. On entering school they possessed, at best, a few words and were unlikely to be putting even two words together in a single utterance. On leaving school, judging by past evidence (e.g. Con-rad, 1979) they will not be able to make themselves understood through speech nor will they understand much of what is said to them.

The majority of them will probably achieve a reading age of around eight or nine years.

The enormity of the problems facing the severely deaf child as he tries to acquire language are, as one might expect, a major concern of his teachers, and the co-operative research I shall describe is addressed to the question of how the teacher might best help the child to learn and to develop his powers of language.

One final caveat needs inserting before we consider this work. Although all the research discussed stemmed from a desire to work in close harmony with teachers, it was far from clear at the start how such a working relationship might be established. Looking back after five years of research, it is now clear to us ('us' being a team of eight researchers) that our initial approaches to the task fell short of what we now see as the best way to proceed. However, these digressions are themselves informative and will be used to illustrate the problems facing both the teacher and the research worker committed to working together.

Working in the nursery

In the first year of our research, we spent most of our time simply sitting in classrooms, observing children with their teachers, talking to teachers about their objectives, ideas and methods and generally familiarizing ourselves with what life in classrooms with hearing-impaired children is like. We had already developed a number of guiding ideas about the possible impact of pre-lingual deafness on the child's abilities and, particularly, on his relationships with others, but we did not try to move directly to test these. Rather, we worked much more informally and tried to develop a general picture of the child's experiences in schools.

Most of our time in this initial period was spent in nursery classes. There were two main reasons for this. First, we simply wanted to start from the beginning and see how the child was assimilated into school life, to discover what kinds of tasks and experiences he encountered and what sorts of developments took place in his language and his inter-personal relationships. A second reason for focusing on the early years was that we were also involved at that time in studies of pre-school hearing children in nursery schools and playgroups (Wood *et al.*, 1980) and this provided an ideal opportunity to compare the experiences of deaf and hearing children in a general way.

Eventually, we undertook systematic observational studies of a number of children in different classrooms, observing them over periods of half to one hour, day by day until we had built up an extensive picture of each child's day at school. The observations proved invaluable. They not only provided a data base for comparing the experiences of deaf and hearing children in great detail but they also sharpened *our* intuitions and perceptions of young children. Such observational techniques are currently being used by the Pre-School Playgroups Association (Sylva *et al.*, 1980) to help train adults in the task of caring for under-fives. Detailed observation is itself a powerful training instrument and it helped us to identify some of the problems and abilities of deaf children. We also undertook a quasi-experimental study of the techniques used to teach young deaf children and this, eventually, led us into our first really close co-operative work with teachers.

Before coming to work in classrooms, we had undertaken a number of laboratory studies of mothers teaching three- to five-year-old hearing children. All these experiments involved the same task; we had designed a construction toy — a set of twenty-one blocks that fitted together according to a recurrent rule to make a pyramid (Wood, Bruner and Ross, 1976; Wood and Middleton, 1975; Wood, Wood and Middleton, 1978; Wood, 1980). This task is a useful one for studying teaching and learning with young children. It is quite difficult, and children below the age of four or five years of age are generally incapable of putting it together alone. But children enjoy the task and will work at it for long periods of time. It appeals to a wide age range — three year olds enjoy it, particularly when parents help them to make it, and eight year olds will work for half an hour or more with it alone and are generally capable of working out how to do it without help. It can also be taught to children in a variety of ways. It engenders quite a number of teaching strategies from both mothers and teachers and these vary widely in their relative degrees of success. Some mothers are able to teach in such a way that their child is able to do it alone after instruction while others teach in such a way that children are largely incapable of doing it alone after being taught. We had also developed a system for analysing the interactions between adult and (hearing) children which enables us to predict how well a child will do with the task after a particular episode of teaching. Mothers who teach the task well manage to key most of their instructions to their child's momentary successes and failures. When their child makes a mistake, they immediately step in to offer more help; if he succeeds, their next offer of help leaves him more scope for initiative. Some mothers, however, teach too much — they continually offer a lot of help when the child should be allowed to try and take over responsibility for himself. Others teach too little — failing to offer help when the child encounters a problem.

Although this rule of teaching sounds obvious and easy it is in fact very difficult to follow. Indeed, we have tried to teach children ourselves according to this rule and, though generally successful, we have found it virtually impossible to teach 'perfectly' all the time. It is simply too difficult in the midst of teaching to think quickly enough, observe the child carefully enough and act fast enough to provide optimum instructions on every occasion.

How would teachers of the deaf teach their pre-schoolers how to do this task? Would they teach in a similar way to mothers with hearing children or have they developed special techniques? Would the young deaf child learn as quickly or in the same way as the hearing child or would he too exhibit special 'deaf' learning methods?

These were the questions that led us to the study. We made video recordings of teachers instructing their children how to do the task and subsequently analysed these according to our original system of analysis. It failed to predict how well children were being taught.

Our initial expectation, based on observation and the existing literature, was that deafness would engender different patterns of teacher–child relationships from those operating with hearing children. It would have been easy at this point, then, to write the study up and reach such a conclusion on the basis of our evidence. What works well in teaching the hearing child does not work in teaching the deaf child, so it seemed reasonable to conclude that different teaching-learning principles governed effective instruction of young deaf children. Fortunately, however, we had said at the start of our work that we would discuss any findings and our evaluations of them with the teachers who had participated in the study. We already knew that some of the teachers who had co-operated with us would not like the conclusion we were then likely to reach. They firmly believe the deaf children are basically normal and that they develop in similar ways to hearing children, if at a slower rate. Any suggestions that they and their children behaved 'abnormally' would not fit in with their own philosophy.

One of the teachers, who was later to become an integral member of the research team, was extremely critical of our analysis. She argued that it simply did not fit the reality of the situation. With a keen analytical mind she was able to translate this general intuitive feeling that we had got things wrong into explicit statements about where our coding system had failed.

Our coding of teacher–child interactions analysed each instruction or suggestion from the adult in terms of the degree of 'control' or 'help' it offers the child. For example, if the teacher simply says, 'Do you want to make something with the blocks?' she is attempting to induct the child into relevant activity but not specifying what material he should use nor what he should do with it — a 'general verbal prompt'. However if she says, 'Get the big ones together' she *is* specifying the criterion that a child should use to guide his selection of material — a 'specific verbal instruction'. She might actually pick up or point to material thus effectively solving the problem of selecting which blocks to use for the child, and so on. By looking at each successive move from the teacher and seeing how far any increase or decrease in control was contingent on the child's momentary success and failure, we were able to calculate how well she followed the teaching rule stated above.

However, the teacher concerned, Margaret Tate, argued that our descriptions of 'general verbal' prompts and 'specific verbal instructions' was invalid. She argued that our classification of such supposedly verbal instructions was wrong because we had ignored the subtle non-verbal cues she gave to children as she talked. For example, when saying to a child, 'Now you make one with the big blocks', she would follow her statement with a deliberate movement of her head and eyes towards the blocks in question.

It took almost a year for these criticisms to really take hold of our thinking to the extent that we could translate them into action. Eventually, we hit on the brilliant idea of looking at all the tapes with the sound track off! These children are deaf, we sagely observed, perhaps we could get better insights into how they responded to the teacher by crudely approximating their experiences of the situation. Immediately we did this we became aware of a whole new dimension of non-verbal activity that our attention to speech had masked from us. We were soon able to see how the majority of the general and specific verbal instructions were accompanied by readily interpretable non-verbal routines. One example will illustrate the point.

A child was attempting to put two blocks together to make the first stage of a level of the pyramid. He knew that the pieces had to be the same size, but did not yet know all the constraints that determined which two blocks of the same size should be fitted together. In fact, he had selected two pieces that had pegs on them (construction works by fitting pegs into holes), when, in fact, he needed one with a peg and another with a hole. Mrs Tate said to him, 'No, you need one with a hole', but as she did this she also picked up two blocks of the same size with pegs and tapped the two pegs together. The child looked at her, both smiled and shook their heads.

This strategy, making deliberate and informative mistakes, provided a precise non-verbal meaning for what she was saying. There were, in fact, a variety of non-verbal moves that served this function. When we had classified all the tapes using a modified, non-verbal coding system, we were able to recalculate our scores of teaching 'contingency' – how often teachers followed the rule outlined earlier. This time we *did* discover correlations between teaching styles and children's learning (Wood, 1980). This, in turn, implies that the basic strategy for teaching the deaf child how to do something is fundamentally similar to that with hearing children. The result completely overturned our first conclusions. Thus, Margaret Tate had not only played a vital role in *evaluating* our research findings, she also helped to lead us on to new insights, and eventually to new hypotheses about some of the relationships between language, non-verbal behaviour and teaching.

But the evaluative process was not entirely one way. In looking at the tapes of the experiment, and at our observations of the same teachers and children in more natural classroom situations, we noted a number of general features, of which the teachers were not conscious. For example, Mrs Tate had used a good deal of non-verbal deliberate mistakes in teaching the blocks task. She also did this a good deal in her everyday teaching. In fact, we were able to isolate a number of quite specific strategies that she used in her interactions with children that led them to use language at (for them) new and more advanced levels. Mrs Tate was, of course, aware that she often made such deliberate mistakes in interacting with her children, and knew that these ploys were useful in getting communication off the ground. However, she had not realized how systematic the relationships were between her non-verbal activities and the children's language development. She found the analysis of her non-verbal behaviour illuminating and important. Although they were already a *natural* part of her teaching style she was now made consciously aware of them and their specific effects on her children's responses to her.

This 'illumination' and consciousness-raising has, in turn, led on to a number of important consequences. Mrs Tate often lectures and demonstrates to trainee teachers about how to work with pre-school hearing-impaired children. After we discussed her non-verbal support for her language with her, she concluded that in future she would modify her training to draw attention not simply to what she said to children, but also to get trainees to attend to what she *did* as she spoke. She has also produced her own video tapes for teacher training, and here too she now lays particular stress on the importance of establishing shared meanings and joint activities with children at a non-verbal level, as well as keying in her speech to these activities.

This experience underlines a number of general features of a productive, co-operative relationship between teacher and researcher. The teacher in these studies was not simply a subject of the experiment. Nor was she expected to be a passive consumer of received wisdom. Indeed, as we have seen, our initial wisdom proved to be far from wise and was poorly received. By recruiting the teacher as an *evaluator* of research findings, we came to a different set of conclusions, and to new hypotheses about the nature of the phenomena we were interested in. She had changed our perception of what we were seeing, and raised *our* awareness of features of the teaching process about which we were originally ignorant. She also helped, then, in the generation of new hypotheses and lines of research. But she had not yet reached the stage where she dictated the actual *questions* worthy of attention.

Later, however, Mrs Tate went further and deeper into the research process. She came to us one day, and said how important she felt *singing* was for deaf children. We had never considered the possibility. But her suggestion that she should look systematically at singing lessons was an interesting one. She felt that the children's voice quality in singing was better than in speech, and that they enjoyed singing in a way that they did not enjoy conversation – particularly the younger, less able, children. She also pointed out that singing was a good way of getting the child to play with his voice – to hear whatever he could of his own sounds, clearly a vital experience when sound is so poor and often unrewarding and uninformative. She wanted to undertake systematic observations of singing lessons to see if they did, indeed, help children in the way she thought.

But another thought struck us. In our experimental study and our observations we had been struck by the tremendous problems that the children faced in conversation. To take part in discourse it is necessary to know *when* to talk and *what* to talk about. It is a complex, interactive process, and one that cannot take off until the child has mastered basic 'turn taking' skills (Bruner, 1976). He must know when his turn comes, when another's turn is in progress, what their turn means, and so on. Most of the pre-school deaf children we had observed lacked this basic knowledge of conversation and, hence, met immense problems when they were expected to speak. Their problem was not only one of sound reception and production, but also involved the discovery of the inter-personal structure of language use which develops in hearing children *before* they start to talk (Bruner, 1975). It occurred to us that another important aspect of singing is that it involves sound production in *parallel*, with no turn-taking requirements. In prospect, then, singing offers a situation for enjoyable use of the voice and production of words and activities with the turn-taking rules waived. Conceivably, then, it is an easier and potentially more enjoyable language-using situation than conversation.

Mrs Tate has now spent nearly two years recording singing lessons, development of the voice, and comparing these to developments in the child's conversational abilities. We have not yet managed, together, to test all her hypotheses about singing, but it is interesting how, now, Mrs Tate herself has discovered the importance of the turn-taking aspects of singing, whilst we, in turn, have been convinced that her ideas about voice quality, sound production and singing have real weight.

Here, then, the teacher has moved on from consumer and evaluator of research to become the *hypothesis generator*. Her knowledge of children is much wider, far more personal and much more 'developmental' than ours. She has seen the same children over long periods of time in a way that we have not been able to do because we simply do not have the responsibility for caring for children over such long periods. She brought a new perspective and, indeed, a different sort of knowledge about children to our discussions. From this, hypotheses have arisen that had not occurred to us. Of course, it is quite possible that other researchers, with a background, say, in music rather than language development as we had, would have come to a similar hypothesis. But the breadth and depth of the teachers' experiences makes them a rich potential source of new ideas and insights – if they are listened to and taken seriously by those trained as professionals in research.

Conversations with the primary school deaf child

Our second experience of working alongside teachers also began in our first year – indeed, in our first weeks of research. Since we knew at the outset of our work that we would need the co-operation of both heads and teachers if our work was to take place, we agreed to address a meeting of the newly formed British Association of Teachers of the Deaf. At that meeting we talked about the ideas that we hoped to investigate in schools, the background to our thinking and we made some preliminary suggestions as to the sorts of activities we might want to focus on (Howarth and Wood, 1977).

At that meeting there was a young teacher of the deaf, who had taken a first degree in psychology and later gone on into teaching. She had recently undertaken a course inspired by the work of Joan Tough (e.g. Tough, 1977) and was actively thinking about her own styles of conversation and teaching with her primary school children. In our address we had talked about the nature and value of conversation in language development. We asked those at the meeting, 'What are the effects of a child's deafness upon the *adult* who tries to interact with and teach him?' We knew from the work going on into language development in hearing children that adults, interacting with and talking to children, spontaneously adjust the structure and content of their language to fit the child's level of linguistic and intellectual ability (e.g. Snow and Ferguson, 1977). It seems that most of us know tacitly how to modify our speed of speaking, the complexity of our grammar and the topics about which we talk to successfully integrate our activities into the young child's ongoing activity. We seem to know what sorts of things to talk about and how to talk about them in a way that the young child will comprehend. We are also skilful in using the child's non-verbal behaviour and his general demeanour to help achieve an understanding of his far-from-perfect speech.

But these natural abilities, we suggested, rest on the integrity of the child's intellectual level of development and his speech. For example, although an eighteen-month-old hearing child may only be speaking one or two word utterances, we can usually understand what he is saying by exploiting the context of his utterances. Children of this age are almost invariably talking about that which fills their senses − not the past, the future, the imaginary, or the hypothetical. The young child is simply not capable of these demanding intellectual activities. Thus, he can be understood because what he is talking about is in context. This is not the case with the deaf child, however. He may be speaking two words at six, seven or even eight years of age when he *can* remember, plan, reason and imagine. So his words are a poor guide to his meanings and the immediate context often does not help to achieve understanding − for he is not talking about it.

How are our abilities as natural teachers and language models influenced, then, by this rendering of language and thought by severe pre-lingual deafness? Do our natural capacities as teachers go out of the window, and, if so, what takes their place?

The primary school teacher, Jean Lees, had been thinking along somewhat similar lines herself, and she came up to us after the conference to suggest some joint research. On the course designed by Joan Tough she had been led to taperecord her conversations with her children. A brief extract of one such recording is presented below.

Sally	Mummy write a letter lots.
Teacher	Mummy wrote a long letter. Where did she put the letter?
Sally	Er.

Teacher	She posted it? Where's the letter?
Sally	There book.
Teacher	There in the book. In the green one or the blue one?
Sally	Blue.
Teacher	In the blue book. So this morning when you were asleep Mummy wrote a long letter.
Sally	Me sleep . . .
Teacher	When you were asleep?
Sally	(no response)
Teacher	What time did you wake up?
Sally	Seven o'clock
Teacher	Seven o'clock. What about Mummy?
Sally	Mummy six o'clock.
Teacher	Mummy gets up very early at six o'clock.
Sally	Mummy me me mummy shaking.
Teacher	And she shakes you.

The recordings surprised and disappointed her. She felt that she was asking too many questions and leaving children too little time to answer before coming in with another, usually more specific question and generally failing to solicit as many spontaneous ideas from her children as she wished. This pattern was not what she had expected — it did not square either with her philosophy or her self-image. She suggested to us that she should try to change her style of talking to her children to see if it was in fact possible to generate more spontaneous and interesting conversation from them.

We helped her to design such a study, so that she could properly monitor the effects of her changes in style. She adopted a number of different styles with the same children, maintaining each of them over a period of some weeks, and systematically taking taperecordings at specific times.

Eventually we developed a number of coding systems to help her to describe her various approaches. One style, for example, was very high in questions and what we called 'repair'. She might ask a child, 'What did you do at the weekend?' (short pause). 'Did you go out with Mummy?' (Child — 'out, Mummy'). 'Oh, you went out with Mummy — you went out with Mummy' (Child — 'yes'). You say, 'I went out with Mummy'.

This style of talking to children, we were to find, is not uncommon in classrooms for the deaf. It is also an abnormal style as we know from comparisons with conversations involving hearing children. From subsequently detailed analyses we have concluded that the style of teacher talk effectively robs the child of any initiative, and any real interest in the interaction. For example, the initial, open question: 'What did you do . . . ?' was immediately simplified by the teacher to a closed, yes–no question, 'Did you go out with Mummy?' After an answer, the teacher first checked the meaning – which she had more or less dictated in the first place, and then 'repaired' the child's grammar by trying to solicit a better formed sentence.

Mrs Lees was able to change this style dramatically by asking fewer questions and demanding less repair and, above all, by increasing the frequency of what we called her 'personal contributions'. She started to tell the children something about herself. When she did this, children were given a chance to ask *her* questions, to elaborate the topic of conversation spontaneously and generally to be more active and talkative.

This brief account illustrates how a teacher can both change her teaching styles *and* help to evaluate the effects of different styles on children's patterns of language use. Jean felt that she had improved her own practice, and improved her children's chances for development. The study also advanced *our* general knowledge about the deaf child's abilities. For example, we now know that he often appears linguistically impoverished not only because of his impairment as such, but because of the effects that it exerts over the natural abilities of his teacher. Change the style of the teacher, reduce the incidence of highly controlled and abnormal moves from her, and the child immediately becomes more active and forthcoming. We have yet to show that in doing this the teacher can engender long-term improvements in the child's language and his social development, but it seems like a strong bet and our current research is putting it to the test.

Jean Lees showed, then, that she at least could modify her style and improve the fit both between her philosophy and practice and her objectives and the methods she uses to achieve them. The research worker here acts basically as a consultant and confidant. He maintains a dialogue with the teacher helping her to explicate her own goals, methods and effectiveness. His training and background also helps in the development of coding systems and statistical analyses to check the effects of any changes the teacher might want to initiate. And, given that he has the time and resources to work in other classrooms, he can help by collecting information about other children with similar problems so that any changes in the teacher's children's language can be compared with suitable 'controls'.

But one case study, however carefully done, is clearly not generalizable. If Mrs Lees was to prove her point, it was necessary to show that similar effects could be engendered in other classrooms with teachers less committed to a particular outcome. Fortunately, we were also undertaking studies along these lines, and were able to recruit another group of teachers (Wood *et al.*, 1981). We taught them how to modify their teaching styles in various ways. We found that they also met with the same pattern of change in their children's enthusiasm and loquacity to that found by Mrs Lees.

This second, brief account, illustrates other roles that can and, indeed, arguably *must* be played by teachers in educational research. Here we saw a teacher not only generating hypotheses but going on to test them systematically by controlled classroom intervention studies, in which normal practices were changed and their effects noted. Other teachers also helped to determine how far the effects of changes in style found by Jean Lees occurred with other children. They were relatively impartial about the various strategies suggested (though some found one or two of them distasteful and 'unnatural'), and by participating in the research they helped us to determine how far findings from one study could properly be *generalized* to other classrooms. Thus, they not only act as controls for possible contaminating factors, they also carried the research on one stage further to test the general applicability and relevance of our findings.

Before leaving this second study, we should perhaps mention that the research process did not end here. In our various contacts with teachers we found individuals who *violated* some of the predictions from Jean Lees's study. In general, the predictions held up, but there were some interesting exceptions. These led us back in the research cycle to try and formulate hypotheses about the nature of their departures from the general pattern. This will enable us to refine our knowledge of the factors that make it worthwhile for the deaf child to talk and those that stimulate him to learn. We do not yet know whether the exceptions we have noted will prove important and informative. But one thing is sure, without the further, active, involvement of teachers, we shall never find out.

Stages in co-operative research

The case studies just discussed are just two examples of several joint research projects being pursued with teachers. They were selected because they illustrate how teachers can be involved in each of several distinct stages of research, as it moves from observation, intuition and hypothesis creation through to evaluation and dissemination. The stages suggested are as follows:

Observation and hypothesis formulation

We have argued that teachers have access to quite different types of knowledge about children to that possessed by researchers. The institutional constraints that place them, and not the professional researcher, in protracted periods of care and responsibility for children, breed a quite different relationship between them and the child. The researcher, given his job and his lack of direct responsibility for children, occupies quite a different relationship with them, and this, in turn, is likely to foster quite different perspectives and hypotheses. By putting the two forms of knowledge together — the teacher perspective and the researcher perspective — the synthesis can both accelerate the formulation of new ideas, and extend the basis upon which new intuitions and the precursors of explicit hypotheses are based.

Hypothesis testing

Having formulated a hypothesis, the next step is to subject it to a realistic and valid test. In education this ideally means working in classrooms and other naturalistic contexts. Here the researcher meets with other constraints imposed by his limited professional role. He cannot work in an extended way in schools. He probably lacks the professional qualifications and skills, and his own job imposes other demands on him that limit his time in schools. The teacher has first-hand knowledge of his or her children; is already entrusted with their care and well-being and potentially has the time and opportunity to test out hypotheses in the natural context. Thus the more realistic any experimental test of an educational hypothesis is to become, the more the researcher *needs* the teacher as a colleague.

Evaluation of evidence

The transition from evidence derived from a hypothesis-driven piece of research to a confident general statement about the validity or value of the hypothesis, its relevance and workability in the classrooms, involves a number of other stages, the first of which is an initial judgement about the significance and potential of the outcome of the research. We listed one example where active co-operation with a teacher during this phase of the research not only led to a complete re-interpretation of the data but also generated new hypotheses and fresh insights into the phenomena in question. Whereas the researcher is better armed with statistical techniques and methods for evaluating the internal coherence and reliability of his measures, the teacher may well be in a better position to offer evaluations about the *validity* of any conclusion drawn from those measures.

Productivity or generalizability of findings

The first stages of research, just outlined, rest fundamentally on the quality of the *relationship* between researcher and practitioner. It must be frank, egalitarian and trusting. But these qualities, we know from other research sources, may well be themselves the primary ingredients in any success and not the hypothetical processes and practices deemed to be important. The researcher, unlike the teacher, has the freedom to work in many educational contexts, and is able to establish working relationships with other teachers who may, or may not, share the same commitments to the hypothesis held by the teacher-researcher. It is important that they should be enjoined to participate in a further evaluation of findings, to see how any methods or practices really do have the effects that are claimed. Here too, the active involvement of another cohort of teachers is a fundamental requisite for the success of the research.

These four stages of research are, of course, highly idealized and somewhat artificial. However, they do help to illustrate the potential role for the teacher in formulating and developing the theory of education. At no phase in this idealized cycle of research is the teacher unable to participate. Indeed, at certain phases he or she is indispensible. The process just outlined is *not* the researchers' sole possession. To be sure, they have the time, the experience and the knowledge to collect samples, develop measures, do the statistics and argue the case. But these ingredients are of little value without some sense of what is worth looking at, what is likely to be significant, what can be generalized and built upon. And for these activities, we have argued, the teacher is a valuable and often a *necessary* partner.

In conclusion, then, whilst effective research in education may demand some degree of specialization and division of labour, without an active, co-operative relationship between practitioners and researchers it is difficult to see how *all* the stages of research can be fulfilled. Furthermore, any one stage will be fulfilled more effectively with collaboration. Until the various professionals involved in education work together in this way, it seems inevitable that we shall continue to spawn unworkable, unrealistic or invalid theories and that the teachers' intuitions about what works and what does not will go unheard and untested. Co-operative research is difficult and fraught with many methodological pitfalls. But it is our best way forward.

References

Bruner, J. S. (1975) The ontogenesis of speech acts, *Journal of Child Language*, 2, 1–19.

Bruner, J. S. (1976) From communication to language – a psychological perspective, *Cognition*, 3, 255–87.

Conrad, R. (1979) *The Deaf Schoolchild*, London, Harper and Row.

Donaldson, M. (1978) *Children's Minds*, London, Fontana/Collins.

Howarth, C. I. and Wood, D. J. (1977) Research into the intellectual development of deaf children, *Teacher of the Deaf*, 1, 5–12.

Labov, W. (1970) The logic of non-standard English, reprinted 1972 in Giglioli, P. P. (Ed.) *Language and Social Context*, Harmondsworth, Penguin.

Russell, B. (1926) *On Education*, republished 1976, London, Unwin Paperbacks.

Rutter, M., Maughan, B., Mortimore, P. and Ouston, J. (1979) *Fifteen Thousand Hours*, London, Open Books.

Snow, C. E. and Ferguson, C. A. (Eds.) (1977) *Talking to Children: language input and acquisition*, Cambridge, Cambridge University Press.

Sylva, K. D., Roy, C. and Painter, M. (1980) *Childwatching at Playgroup and Nursery School*, London, Grant McIntyre.

Tizard, B., Hughes, M., Carmichael, H. and Pinkerton, G. (in press) Children's Questions and Adults' Answers, *Journal of Child Psychology and Psychiatry*.

Tough, J. (1977) *The Development of Meaning*, London, Allen and Unwin.

Wood, D. J. (1980) Teaching the young child: some relationships between social interaction, language and thought, in Olson, D. (Ed.), *The Social Foundations of Language and Thought*, New York/London, W. W. Norton.

Wood, D. J., Bruner, J. S. and Ross, G. (1976) The role of tutoring in problem-solving, *Journal of Child Psychology and Psychiatry*, 17, 89–100.

Wood, D. J., McMahon, L. and Cranstoun, Y. (1980) *Working with Under-Fives*, London, Grant McIntyre.

Wood, D. J. and Middleton, D. J. (1975) A study of assisted problem solving, *British Journal of Educational Psychology*, 66, 181–91.

Wood, D. J., Wood, H. A., Griffiths, A. J., Howarth, S. P. and Howarth, C. I. (1981) The structure of conversations with 6–10 year old deaf children, submitted for publication.

Wood, D. J., Wood, H. A. and Middleton, D. J. (1978) An experimental evaluation of four face-to-face teaching strategies, *International Journal of Behavioural Development*, 1, 131–47.

6.3 Principles of curriculum and methods development in special education

D. J. POWER

One of the most fundamental aspects of recent thinking about child development has been a growing awareness of the social nature of language and reasoning. In parallel, we have come to see that many early school tasks prove difficult not because the logical structure of the task is complex, but because the social setting breaks the rules of language use that children have gradually acquired through interaction with other people.

Power argues here that it is particularly important that these insights are applied to the teaching of handicapped children; he focuses on the hearing-impaired and mentally handicapped.

Introduction

It is clear that in very general terms any opportunity for learning is followed by one of two outcomes as far as the recall of the material is concerned: either over time the material is gradually forgotten or it is not. While this may seem a trivial distinction, it becomes important if it can be demonstrated that the differences in recall are preceded by systematic differences in the circumstances under which the learning took place. I believe such differences in the learning circumstances[1] preceding different recall outcomes do exist and that examination of these differences throws light on the conditions necessary for designing better curricula, teaching methods and settings for handicapped children.

In his *Reflections on Language* Chomsky (1976) points out that the learning of language is significantly different in nature from the learning of many other aspects of human knowledge.

He has likened the learning of language to the learning of 'common sense' (and I would add social behaviour and 'daily living skills') and compared it with what he sees to be a very different matter, the learning and understanding of such 'subject matter' school subjects as physics and chemistry. As he points out:

Specially commissioned for this volume

There are striking differences between these systems. Knowledge of physics[2] is conscious knowledge. The physicist can expound and articulate it and convey it to others. In contrast, the other two systems (i.e. common sense and grammar) are quite unconscious for the most part and beyond the bounds of introspective report. Furthermore, knowledge of physics is qualitatively distinct from the other two cognitive structures in the manner of its acquisition and development. Grammar and common sense are acquired by virtually everyone, effortlessly, under minimal[3] conditions of interaction, exposure, and care. There need be no explicit teaching or training, and when the latter does take place, it has only marginal effects on the final state achieved. To a very good first approximation, individuals are indistinguishable (apart from gross deficits and abnormalities) in their ability to acquire grammar and common sense. Individuals of a given community each acquire a cognitive structure that is rich and comprehensive and essentially the same as the systems acquired by others. Knowledge of physics, on the other hand, is acquired selectively and often painfully, through generations of labour and careful experiment, with the intervention of individual genius and generally through careful instruction. (Chomsky, 1976, p. 144)

This provides a valuable insight into the reasons why traditional approaches to teaching communication and other living skills to handicapped pupils have not been as successful as we would wish. Because of the customary pedagogical practice and theoretical orientation that most of us bring with us from our training and experience, we, as teachers, have tended to treat communication and social skills as being 'subjects' just like any other subject in the school curriculum, and hence ones which can be taught in the same way as other school subjects. It is now becoming clearer that this is not the case. As Chomsky states, language is qualitatively different, both in its final knowledge state and its method of acquisition, from other school subjects such as chemistry, physics and so forth. Hence, I wish to argue that we need to revise our view of what it means to know and use language and social skills and the methods whereby that knowledge is acquired.

It therefore becomes necessary to discover a pedagogy for fostering the acquisition of competence in 'functional' subjects such as language and social and daily living skills because it is crucial for the development of handicapped pupils that they not forget what they are taught in these fields, as they more often than not have done when taught via

traditional approaches. These approaches are typified in the communication area by what Van Uden (1977) has called 'constructivist'
approaches: sentences are built up from 'paradigm lists' of words as
parts of speech according to certain formulae (Noun + Verb + Noun =
Sentence, etc.) via conscious repetition and drill in situations quite
removed from real life use. A recent example is the language skills
curriculum of the Board of Public Education of Pittsburgh (1978)
which sets out that as far as *grammar* is concerned the student will be
able to, among other skills:

> recognize major parts of speech and how they function in sentences
> [and]
> write grammatically correct sentences and transformations.

> Intensive instruction in the grammar of the English language is
> necessary for severely hearing impaired students with language
> retardation. The acquisition of the grammar or syntax of a language
> occurs as a result of repeated exposure to oral language from the
> earliest years. The severely hearing impaired student, lacking such
> exposure, must develop syntactic expression through highly struc-
> tured instruction. This instruction must include auditory and visual
> channels of communication, using traditional methods of teaching
> grammar as well as refinements brought about through recent
> linguistic studies. (Board of Public Education, Pittsburgh, pp. v.
> and 1)

This is followed by a detailed sequential curriculum examining the
parts of speech and their function in sentences, and so forth. The
emphasis is on written language, but there is a clear expectation that
this kind of procedure will benefit the pupil's oral language as well.

Ecological validity and the special curriculum

I suggest that we need an alternative curriculum based on the principles
of appropriateness to the learner's age and developmental level, to the
social settings in which they live and to their view of and needs within
that setting. In current parlance, I am calling for a curriculum that is
'ecologically valid', that is, relevant and true to the children's lives
within their own social milieux.

These principles are probably valid for all curriculum areas, including
'content subjects' like science, mathematics and social studies, but in
special education settings they are crucial for the 'functional subjects'
whose retention and proper use is central to the personal and social
development of the individual. Paramount among these are language

(both verbal and non-verbal), social skills of inter-personal conduct and manners, and 'daily living skills'.

What is appropriate to the learner's age is not immediately apparent when chronological age may be radically out of step with developmental level. This was exemplified by the considerable deterioration of the language and behaviour of a twenty-year-old severely intellectually handicapped young man in a residential setting who was finally transferred to an adult ward because he was of that age. In fact he looked and acted like an eight year old, liked being with a children's group, and was making greater progress there than he did in what might *a priori* have seemed a more enhancing setting. In some cases, movement towards age appropriate settings may be a very long-term goal underlying the educational programme.

Similarly, the situation also needs careful analysis. For many severely handicapped individuals, special settings may bring about idiosyncratic and deviant ways of behaving which are nevertheless facilitative and useful adjustments to life experiences and demands. The controversy over the extent to which deaf children should be exposed to or even inducted into 'deaf culture' provides an example of this: for those who support a purely oral approach such induction would be retrograde and stifling; but in the recent literature, it is being increasingly argued that membership of the deaf culture is enhancing for both the personal/social and intellectual development of many deaf individuals, even though culturally distinct ('deviant') from the point of view of the majority hearing culture (Freeman, Boese and Carbin, in press; Furth, 1973). Similarly Strom (1980) has argued that although the American 'Special Olympics' for intellectually handicapped individuals in some ways perpetuate their differentness, they can also be a source of pride and enhanced self-worth for those taking part in them, with a consequent eventual improvement in their ability to cope with life's demands. I would presume that supporters of Jean Vanier's 'quasi-segregated' *L'Arche* settings for the intellectually handicapped would make a similar kind of argument about their approach, where the mutual support and respect obtained in their 'deviant' settings are nevertheless facilitative for their intellectually handicapped members.[4]

The curriculum also needs to be commensurate with the learner's own view of what knowledge is of most worth in his situation, and not one arbitrarily imposed upon him by the organizers of his learning. Thus, although teachers must have a view of what is desirable for a pupil to learn, they must also be alert and sensitive to feedback from pupil behaviour which indicates whether he is responsive to teaching or not, for if he is not, then he is not likely to internalize his learning, and the loss of correct recall that I spoke of above will be the outcome.

Scheffler (1968) has urged that there are pressures on teachers to concentrate on the external performance of behaviours and thus to bypass developing the intelligent understanding and application of these activities:

> A crude demand for effectiveness easily translates itself into a disastrous emphasis on externals simply because they are easier to get hold of than the central phenomena of insight and the growth of understanding. In an important essay of 1904, John Dewey distinguished between the inner and outer attention of children, the inner attention involving the 'first-hand and personal play of mental powers' and the external 'manifested in certain conventional postures and physical attitudes rather than in the movement of thought'. Children, he noted, 'acquire great dexterity in exhibiting in conventional and expected ways the *form* of attention to school work'. The 'supreme mark and criterion of a teacher', according to Dewey, is the ability to by-pass externals and to 'keep track of [the child's] mental play, to recognize the signs of its presence or absence, to know how it is initiated and maintained, how to test it by results attained, and to test *apparent* results by it'. The teacher 'plunged prematurely into the pressing and practical problem of keeping order in the school room' Dewey warned, is almost of necessity 'to make supreme the matter of external attention'. Without the reflective and free opportunity to develop his theoretical conceptions and his psychological insight, he is likely to 'acquire his technique in relation to the outward rather than the inner mode of attention'. Effective classroom performance surely needs to be judged in relation to the subtle engagement of this inner mode, difficult as it may be to do so. (Scheffler, 1968, p. 137)

Although this was said of normal children, it is no less true of handicapped children, except that the 'engagement of the inner mode' with many is all the more difficult. I suggest however that customary curricula for functional subjects have actively discouraged this engagement by failing to reflect the nature of the knowledge they communicate and the settings in which it is to be applied. I shall now examine the application of these principles to the content, structure and methods of special curricula.

Content

It is important that the content accords with 'real world use', probably the least well understood, and hence least attended to, aspect of ecological validity for curriculum development. Sociologists have pointed out that much of our awareness of our actual language use and social behaviour in real settings is 'pre-reflective'. We believe we know what we do when, for example, we greet others or take leave of them, but we have not in fact objectively observed ourselves or others in actual greeting and leave-taking. Hence we tend to continue to teach handicapped children what we consider to be the norm in these areas, but it may not accord with what actually occurs in real-life settings. This may account in part for the often-noted 'stiltedness' or 'oddness' of deaf and mentally handicapped adolescents to whom we may have taught only stereotypic, formal and even archaic modes of greeting and leave-taking which are rarely used outside classrooms.

Beveridge and Brinker (1980) reported, for example, that in initiating contact with others, mentally handicapped children very frequently gave unsolicited information. As they note, 'giving unsolicited information to people who are already in possession of it does not represent the use of language in accordance with the normal rules of adult conversation'. Similarly, I have seen hearing-impaired children taught to say, 'Good morning, Miss Smith. How are you today?' or some such formula in the belief that this is how people greet one another, when in fact observation indicates that this formula is rarely used, and when it is, may be met with suspicion as an attempt at levity or sarcasm. (This also happens with second-language learners, as instanced by the report in the Brisbane *Courier Mail* (19 July, 1979) of an Australian Vietnamese migrant: 'Being polite has brought unexpected problems . . . . We say to someone "Hello, sir", and he thinks we are being funny. But it says in the English book to say, "Hello, sir". Mr Nguyen said: "We need advice on what to do and what not to do".')

Problems in this area are compounded by the fact that such formulae are often taught out of the context of their authentic use, so that pupils may have a particular greeting rote-learned, but use it in settings or ways outside the classroom or clinic that are seen as odd, or in fact never use it outside the classroom unless specially prompted because generalizability of such formulae to other social settings is invariably very low.

In the first case one gets such odd happenings as those reported by Rees (1978) where a mentally retarded girl who had received 'psycholinguistic' training was handed a cup, and responded: 'It's a cup, it's pink, it's plastic, you drink out of it', or the teenage blind girl, who when introduced to a new teacher greeted her: 'How are you, Miss

Ferguson, how are you, are you fine, oh dear God, I hope you're fine': good examples of what Van Uden (1977) has called 'baked sentences' — syntactic forms set hard in the child's knowledge, but without any context of authentic use. Rees (1978) presents a particularly good review of this whole area of the 'pragmatics' of language use and its implications for teaching language to handicapped individuals.

Generalizability of language and social training may also be low because of non-use of skills in real-life settings: the 'transfer distance' is just too great for pupils to be able to make the jump from classroom or clinic to real life (Hart and Rogers-Warren, 1978).

Although these examples have been taken from the language area, parallel ones can be drawn from social and daily living skills and a great deal of research needs to be done to establish exactly what is 'authentic use' in such contexts of activities that Jakobovits and Gordon (1978) have termed the 'daily round' of commonly occurring transactions among individuals and small groups. The establishment of a taxonomy of such transactions must be seen as one of the highest priorities for special education curriculum research.

Two other problems in the social skills learning area also need considerable attention from special educators. First of all, there is the frequent and redundant (and hence boring and off-putting) painstaking teaching in school of skills already naturally and easily learned from parents and siblings at home. The need for very close liaison between school and home in this area cannot be overemphasized. Secondly, it must be asked whether schools are desirable environments for teaching social and life skills anyway. Much of the content of 'Daily Living Skills' curricula for severely mentally and physically handicapped children is to do with domestic tasks and skills which would be much better learned away from school (like cooking and laundering) and/or which (like fixing fuses and mending taps) are ones which are not needed at that stage of life (indeed may never be!), and which probably have to be relearned later when needed in adulthood. More spectacular examples of ecological *invalidity* would be hard to find (unless it be the incongruous movement of the school beginner from the enormously rich oral and (read-to) print literature of his pre-school years to trivial inanities of the 'Run, Spot, run' variety). It could be argued that schools are forced to teach many social and daily living skills largely because the pupils are there and that we would be better devoting our energies to the development of adequate adult programmes where such learning will be more effective because it is now relevant.

Structure

As far as the structure of curriculum content and sequence is concerned, account must be taken of the normal process of development. For example, in the language area, a considerable amount is now known about the form and sequence of acquisition of complex syntactic structures.

The case of negation is particularly instructive in that it can be readily shown that children go through various non-verbal ways of negating the world (turning away, pushing away, etc.) often accompanied by vocalizations, before coming to syntactic oral expression of negation, within which again a number of stages may be found: typically, the child moves from just putting a negative element before a sentence 'nucleus' ('No me home now' for 'I'm not going home now'), to putting that element within the sentence ('Me no home now'), until with the emergence of the auxiliary verb system, he can achieve something close to the final adult form. Thus it seems clear that pupils move through stages of development of syntax, propelled by a process that may be broadly characterized as one of adults 'seizing' the child's actions or utterances to give 'reflective feedback' (Van Uden, 1977; Brown, 1977); for example, Child: 'Allgone milk'; Mother: 'Yes, love, your milk's all gone. I'll get you some more', where the mother takes the child's immature utterance, accepts its meaning and message, but reflects it back to the child, pointing out, as it were, how the same meaning could be coded in a more mature way. Thus children need actively to construct these syntactic representations of their thought from exposure to a very large amount of (primarily maternal) language in meaningful settings. Those programmes which advocate direct teaching of correct forms without taking into account the child's current developmental status may be in danger of teaching splinter skills (the 'baked sentences' I noted above) which the child cannot use in real life because he cannot relate them to his previous understanding and representation of these particular concepts. Thus such approaches as 'Distar' (Engleman and Obsborn, 1976) are in danger of not providing an adequate link to the child's understanding and real-life needs, particularly when applied to mentally handicapped children whose pattern and rate of development is quite different from those for whom the materials were originally intended. Approaches to language teaching via programmed instruction (Wolff, 1973) have the same problem, unless perhaps the programme is used solely for follow up practice drill.

An example from a non-language area is task analysis of such skills as self-feeding with a spoon for moderately or severely intellectually handicapped children. Adherence to the structure of development in this sphere would mean not the analysis of the task as done by a skilled adult and the application of a set of sub-skills so derived to sequencing part-tasks to build the whole for the handicapped individual, but rather analysis of the developmental sequence of self-feeding in normal infants and the sequencing of activities for handicapped pupils to follow that normal sequence of development.

Method

In the cases of both materials and techniques, the development of curricula needs to be informed by adherence to the principles of developmental appropriateness as far as both the 'social age' and the level of cognitive development of the learner is concerned.

For materials this means provision, for example, of age and interest appropriate readers for teenagers and adults with reading problems, who now need not be embarrassed about their reading materials because of the recent proliferation of readers suitable to their needs and interests. Much more still needs to be done in this way as far as oral language teaching materials are concerned although I feel that our own recent efforts in this regard, based upon the principles evolved by Jakobovits and Gordon (1974) and the *Challenges* TEFL materials (Abbs and Sexton, 1978) are a move in this direction (Power and Hollingshead, 1977, 1978, 1979, 1980). These materials attempt to sequence materials for language learning so that they are socially interesting and cognitively challenging to handicapped language learners of various ages.

Another aspect of ecological validity has been pointed out by the University of Lancaster group (who produced the *Challenges* materials mentioned above): each medium used for teaching must be faithful to its own style. For example, audiotape should not attempt to do exercises better done in writing, written materials should reflect real-world newspaper and magazine styles, and so forth. Thus the *Challenges* audiotapes are simulated radio broadcasts; their films use amateur actors improvising dialogue from real-life problems, their printed materials simulate real newspaper and magazine style. The implications of this for special education teaching seem to me again to be virtually unexplored, and much more work needs to be done on the impact of various media upon the learning of handicapped pupils.

As far as techniques are concerned, I have argued above that that kind of learning which is not followed by forgetting needs a pedagogy different from what we traditionally use for school content subjects, and I believe that Jakobovits and Gordon's (1974) notion of learning in 'authentic transactional environments' provides a key to such a pedagogy. Jakobovits and Gordon's (1974) discussion is couched in terms of language, but I believe it to be generalizable to social and daily living skills. In fact Jakobovits and Gordon (1978) have themselves discussed the notion of analysis of the 'daily round' of ordinary activities which could provide a context for social and daily living skills curricula — just as their notions about teaching in authentic transactional environments would provide a pedagogy for teaching in this area.

Essentially, what Jakobovits and Gordon are advocating is that classroom experiences[5] should be organized in such a way that pupils and their mentors[6] interact in meaningful and necessary exchanges in growing approximations to a target language (or social skill). Such meaningful input will, over a period, provide the child with linguistic and social behaviour data that will enable him to construct for himself more nearly correct representations of the target skills we wish him to acquire:

> The authentic . . . teacher performs in the classroom the authentic use of the target code, thereby providing the relevant learning opportunity for practising the target skills. 'What is your sister's name?' is an improvement over 'What is your name?' (i.e., I already know your name, and you know that I know it, so to ask you is to lack real involvement and authenticity). 'With whom did you play ball during recess this morning?' is preferable to 'Who did Jane throw the ball to?' 'What did you and Johnny talk about on your way to school today?' is more authentically relevant than 'What did Mr Jones eat for breakfast?' (i.e. when Jane and Mr Jones are the characters depicted in the course book). The authentic . . . teacher avoids emphasis on the cognitive aspects of study in favour of its experiential aspects. Thus, he minimizes linguistic explanations . . . and linguistic practice exercises and assignments. Instead, he finds ways of increasing the student's performative practice of authentic language use. He does this in a number of ways. By talking to each student in a personally relevant way . . . By splitting the class into dyads or triads so that each student has the opportunity to perform. By enlisting the help of student aides, parents and para-professionals. By making use of the mass media and audio-visual aids as stimulants for subsequent authentic interactions (discussions, projects, games) . . . .
>
> *We cannot over-emphasize the fact that the teacher's attitude towards this technique of teaching . . . must be different from the usual one in one particular essential feature. She must not attempt*

*to teach . . . directly. This means that she may not be seen to display
an interest in the 'correct' use of [a certain skill] . . . as would be
the case were she to correct the pupil's [performance] in the usual
manner. Instead, the claim she must continue to maintain is that she
is interested in transactional performance, not in 'correct' communication, pronunciation, or syntax [or social behaviour].* (Jakobovits
and Gordon, 1974, pp. 51–2; 260–1, author's emphasis)

Jakobovits and Gordon go on to point out that it is obviously not
possible entirely to replicate outside settings in the classroom and still
be authentic. However, as they also say, it is not necessary to duplicate
exactly outside conditions, because the enactment of himself by the
student in real settings is the necessary condition for authentic transactions to take place.

This kind of transaction authenticity allied with the detailed
examination of development to determine curriculum content and
structure, with the faithfulness to the medium of the thematic
Challenges materials and with the 'gamesing' and simulation approach
of Power and Hollingshead (see also Quigley and Power, 1979) should
provide a firm foundation for a step forward in curriculum development for special education. It is now incumbent upon us to do the
research and development work to turn this promise into reality.

The central importance of our doing so is underlined again by a
statement of John Dewey (1916) about the centrality of communication to human development:

Society not only continues to exist . . . *by* communication, but it
may fairly be said to exist . . . *in* communication. There is more than
a verbal tie between the words common, community, and communication. Men live in a community by virtue of the things they have in
common; and communication is the way in which they come to
possess things in common. (Dewey, 1916, 1966 edition, p. 4)

If we are to fulfil our aims of providing a place in a community for
our handicapped pupils, then it is necessary indeed that we provide
them with good linguistic and behavioural communication, and I
believe we now have the theoretical tools considerably to improve our
pedagogic performance in this regard.

Notes

1 'Learning circumstances' must include teacher, setting and curriculum as well as pupil variables. In this paper I concentrate mainly on
those to do with curriculum and setting.

2 Ron Boxall of the Queensland Education Department has pointed out to me that this is only strictly true of the formal technical description of physics. The learning of 'the physics of the real world' (e.g., that released objects fall, that some objects are moveable or malleable, and others not) falls into Chomsky's other category of language and common sense. In this passage, therefore, Chomsky is really talking about the learning of *language*, not 'grammar', if 'grammar' is taken to be the formal description of our knowledge of language.

3 One would now, of course, argue that the conditions of 'interaction, exposure and care' under which language and common sense are learned are far from 'minimal'. Research of the last decade indicates quite clearly that a lot of very intense, albeit unconscious, effort is put into learning language, both by children and by their mentors (mainly their mothers) (Snow and Ferguson, 1977; Schiefelbusch, 1978).

4 A Canadian, Jean Vanier, has established a series of group homes in several countries, usually in villages or small towns, where severely intellectually, physically and/or socially 'deviant' people may live with sympathetic others for mutual support and development.

5 And, I would add, many out-of-class experiences; classrooms are often not the best places to learn the kinds cf language use and social and living skills we are talking about. They are frequently better learned in the real world environment outside the classroom.

6 Who need not always be professional 'teachers'; most more mature individuals than the learners have much to offer in this kind of pedagogy. Parents, grandparents, older pupils, peers (Beveridge and Tatham, 1976; Strom, 1980), and other recruits can well be used for their general and expert knowledge to widen the range of interactive experiences of handicapped pupils — thus avoiding the growth of a restrictive 'intimate dialect' and 'deviant' behaviours in the special education classroom.

References

Abbs, B. and Sexton, M. (1978) *Challenges: Student's Book,* London, Longman.

Beveridge, M. and Brinker, J. (1980) An ecological developmental approach to communication in retarded children, in F. M. Jones (Ed.), *Language Disability in Children*, Manchester, Manchester University Press.

Beveridge, M. and Tatham, A. (1976) Communication in retarded adolescents: Utilization of known language skills, *American Journal of Mental Deficiency*, 81, 96–9.

Board of Public Education, Pittsburgh, Pennsylvania (1978) *Language Skills Development for the Hearing Impaired Student*, Belmont, Calif., Fearon-Pittman Curriculum Development Library (SE7*–005).

Brown, R. (1973) *A First Language: the early stages*, Cambridge, Mass., Harvard University Press.

Brown, R. (1977) Introduction, in C. E. Snow and C. A. Ferguson (Eds.), *Talking to Children: Language Input and Acquisition*, Cambridge, Cambridge University Press.

Cazden, C. B. (1972) *Child Language and Education*, New York, Holt, Rinehart and Winston.

Chomsky, N. (1976) *Reflections on Language*, London, Temple Smith.

Dewey, J. (1916, reprinted 1966) *Democracy and Education*, New York, Free Press.

Engelman, S. and Osborn, J. (1976) *Distar Instructional System: Distar language 1*, Chicago, Science Research Associates.

Freeman, R., Boese, R., and Carbin, C. (in press) *Is your Child Deaf?*, Baltimore, University Park Press.

Furth, H. G. (1973) *Deafness and Learning: A Psychosocial Approach*, Belmont, Calif., Wadsworth.

Hart, B. and Rogers-Warren, A. (1978) A milieu approach to teaching language, in R. L. Schiefelbusch (Ed.), *Language Intervention Strategies*, Baltimore, University Park Press.

Jakobovits, L. A. and Gordon, B. (1974) *The Context of Foreign Language Teaching*, Rowley, Mass., Newbury House.

Jakobovits, L. A. and Gordon, B. (1978) *Society's Witnesses: experiencing formative issues in social psychology*, Manoa, University of Hawaii, Department of Psychology.

Power, D. J. and Hollingshead, A. (1977) *Systematic Language Instruction Package, SLIP 1: Passive*, Burwood, Burwood State College, Institute of Special Education.

Power, D. J. and Hollingshead, A. (1978) *Systematic Language Instruction Package, 2: Verb phrase negation*, Burwood, Burwood State College, Institute of Special Education.

Power, D. J. and Hollingshead, A. (1979) Methods for language development in deaf students, 3: Conjunction, *Research Report No. 1*, Centre for Human Development Studies, Mt Gravatt College of Advanced Education.

Power, D. J. and Hollingshead, A. (1980) Methods of language development in deaf students, 4: Determiners, *Research Report No. 2*, Centre for Human Development Studies, Mt Gravatt College of Advanced Education.

Quigley, S. P. and Power, D. J. (Eds.) (1979) *TSA Syntax Program* (9 vols), Beaverton, Ore., Dormac.

Rees, N. S. (1978) Pragmatics of language, in R. L. Schiefelbusch (Ed.), *Bases of Language Intervention*, Baltimore, University Park Press.

Scheffler, I. (1968) University scholarship and education of teachers, *Teachers College Record*, 70, 1–12.

Schiefelbusch, R. L. (Ed.) (1978) *Bases of Language Intervention*, Baltimore, University Park Press.

Snow, C. E. and Ferguson, C. A. (Eds.) (1977) *Talking to Children: language input and acquisition*, Cambridge, Cambridge University Press.

Strom, R. D. (1980) Keynote address to the Conference of the Australian Association of Special Education, Canberra, July 1980.

Van Uden, A. (1977) *A World of Language for Deaf Children: Part 1: Basic principles*, Amsterdam, Swets and Zeitlinger.

Wolff, J. G. (1973) *Language, Brain and Hearing*, London, Methuen.

Index

achondroplasia, 25, 32
American Association on Mental
    Deficiency, 15
amniocentesis, 32
anencephalus 29, 30, 31, 33, 36,
    37–8; in N. Ireland, 337
anoxia, 58, 65, 66–7
assessment, multi-professional,
    260–1, 263–74, 276; US
    procedural due process, 365,
    367, 373–4, 379–81, 389–91
asylums, 86, 89, 94

baby battering (child abuse), 71–2
behaviourism, 405, 413
Belfast, 338, 340–1, 345
Bernstein, Basil, 354, 358
Binet, Alfred, 97–8
Birmingham, 261–2; child
    guidance clinic, 100; ESN(M)
    assessment, 261, 264, 266, 272,
    275
blind, education of, 95–6, 99, 139
braille, 145
Bridgeland, Maurice, 102, 111, 117
Bristol, 192; Teacher Research
    Group, 406–9
British Association of Teachers of
    the Deaf, 426
Bullock Committee, 175, 177,
    183, 186
Burt, Cyril, 87, 98, 102, 110–17;
    The Backward Child, 179, 186,
    262

California, 14, 21
Carpenter, Mary, 106, 109, 114,
    118
cerebral palsy, 38, 58, 64–5, 296

certification, 271, 274
Challenges TEFL material, 442,
    444
Chazan, Maurice, 291–2, 311
child guidance, 100, 103, 112–14
Children and Young Persons Act
    1969, 187, 197
Chomsky, N., 434–5, 446
Chronically Sick and Disabled
    Persons Act *1970*, 210, 212
congenital defects, 25–6, 90, 336–
    7; dislocation of hip, 29, 39;
    heart disease (CHD), 27, 337
Conservation Society, 53–63
Court Committee, 272, 278–86
cretinism, 82–3
curriculum: for blind, 145–8;
    core policy, 316, 329; for
    hearing impaired, 434–47; for
    mentally handicapped,
    434–47; for remedial
    education, 180–4
cytomegalovirus, 35

deaf, *see* hearing impaired
Defoe, Daniel, 84, 91
delinquency, 59–60, 187, 190–1,
    204–5
Dendy, Mary, 304
Denmark, 10, 136
Department of Education and
    Science (DES), 316–17
Dewey, John, 438, 444, 446
diagnosis, 15–16, 175–6, 231,
    242–59
disruptive pupils, 104, 292, 309
'Distar', 441
Down's Syndrome, 16, 25, 26, 29,
    31–2, 33, 336–7

EMR (educable mentally retarded), 20–4
EPA (educational priority area), 162, 172, 178; indices of deprivation, 193, 195; preschooling in, 354–5
ESN(M) education, 260–77
Education Acts: *1870* (Forster's), 94; *1876*, 110; *1880*, 94; *1902*, 99; *1907* (Administrative Provisions), 286; *1914*, 272; *1918*, 98; *1944*, 99, 114, 179, 263, 310, 314; *1969*, 191; *1970* (Handicapped Children), 340, 341; *1976*, 291, 310; *1980*, 277, 316; *1981*, 277
educational psychologists, 141–2, 144, 263, 265
Egerton Commission, 95–6, 100, 101
Elementary Education (Defective and Epileptic Children) Act *1899*, 96–7, 100
encephalopathy, 41, 43, 50
epilepsy, 36, 65
ethnic minority children, 13, 22–4, 68, 192–3, 262

family, 105–6, 109, 112, 114; in N. Ireland, 345, 349; support to, 278–9, 283–5
Feversham Committee, 113, 118
Freud, Sigmund, 103, 111–12, 115, 118
further education, for PH, 209–10, 217–23, 292

Hadow Report, 179, 186, 307, 312
haemophilia, 26, 28
Halsey, A. H., 353–8
handicap, mental, 13–24, 99, 179, 262; diagnosis of mild, 260–77; diagnosis of severe, 242–59; historical background, 80–92

handicap, physical, 2–12, 25–40; incidence and prevalence, 26–8, 295–8, 336–8; provision, 153–72, 208–24
Headstart, 354, 356–7
Health Service (Northern Ireland) Act *1948*, 340
health services, 97, 143; provision for handicapped and families, 278–86
Healy, William, 112
hearing impaired, 39; education, 96, 99, 417–33, 437, 439; resource units, 138
higher education, 208–24
Home Office Report: *Children in Trouble*, 196, 206–7
Howe, S., 84–5, 91
hydrocephalus, 32
hyperactivity, 56, 58–9; and blood lead levels, 45–7

IEP (individualized education programme), 370–3
IT, *see* intermediate treatment
integration, 2–4, 7, 288–313, 320–1; costs, 326–7; after IT, 203–4; in ordinary schools, 343–4; of PH at post-school level, 210–12; of PH in secondary schools, 153–72; in US, 366, 382–4; of visually handicapped, 136–7, 138, 149–50, 152; of young children, 122–35
intelligence, 403, 414; and maladjustment, 103, 115
intelligence tests, 15, 93, 97–8, 115–16, 275; controls on use (US), 364, 369–70; and remedial education, 176–7; standardization, 51, 98
Inter-Departmental Committee on Physical Deterioration, 97, 101
intermediate treatment (IT), 187–207

Ireland, Northern, *see* Northern
    Ireland
Isaacs, Susan, 111—12, 117—18

Jensen, A., 89, 91, 353
Jewish Health Organization, 100,
    112

LEAs (local education authorities),
    281, 315—16, 319—21, 323—6
Langdon-Down, J., 87, 91
language learning, 414—15,
    434—6, 440—4
Lawther Working Party, 41—53,
    53—8, 60
Lawton, D., 182—3, 186
lead pollution, 41—63
legislation for special education,
    93, 96—7, 310—11
literacy, 183—4, 297
London Society for Teaching the
    Blind to Read, 94
Luther, Martin, 82
Lyward, George, 111—12, 114

mainstreaming (US), *see* integration
maladjustment, 102—19, 339
malnutrition, 94—5
Massachusetts, 10, 44, 84;
    Comprehensive Special
    Education Law, 378—97
medical officer's role in ESN(M)
    assessment, 265, 269, 272—4
Mental Deficiency Act *1913*, 98,
    272; *1914*, 98
mental handicap, *see* handicap,
    mental
Mental Health Act *1959*, 89, 92
mental testing, 98—9, 111, 114
Miller, Emmanuel, 112—13, 118
mixed-ability teaching, 306—8
mongolism, *see* Down's Syndrome
muscular dystrophy, 26, 28

NUT (National Union of
    Teachers), 276
National Association for Remedial
    Education, 173
National Association of Teachers
    in Further and Higher
    Education (NATFHE),
    219—22, 224
National Bureau of Handicapped
    Students, 217
National Council for Special
    Education, 217—18, 224
National Foundation for
    Educational Research (NFER),
    307
National Innovations Centre,
    213—15
National Union of Elementary
    School Teachers, 95
National Youth Bureau, 187—88,
    207
Needleman, H.L., 43, 46, 52, 55,
    58
neuroses, 103, 111—13
Northern Ireland, 335—52
Northern Ireland Council for
    Orthopaedic Development
    (NICOD), 341

Open University, 215, 217,
    222—3

palate, cleft, 36
Paracelsus, 80—1, 90
parents, 71—4; groups, 237—8,
    274, 285; involvement, 150—1,
    319, 329, (US:) 380, 387,
    389—91; and professionals,
    129, 225—86
partially sighted, *see* visual
    handicap
perinatal factors, 31—4, 65,
    67—70, 71, 337
phenylketonuria (PKU), 16, 39
physical handicap, *see* handicap,
    physical
physiotherapists, 162
Piaget, Jean, 413
Pinsent, *Dame* Ellen, 262

Plowden Committee, 178, 307, 355

polytechnics, PH provision in, 213–17

pregnancy complications, 34–8, 64–70, 74–5

prematurity, 67

Pre-School Playgroups Association, 421

preschool provision, 353–8; for hearing impaired, 420–6; in N. Ireland, 344

psychology: psychometrics, 115, 177, 179, 185; and special education, 110–11, 400–17

rate support grant, 317–19

reading disabilities, 65, 176–77

referral, 189–90, 260, 269, 276; in US, 384–5, 385–9

remedial education, 154, 162, 173–86

Royal Commission on the Care and Control of the Feeble-Minded (1904–8), 97, 101

rubella, 34–5, 38, 39

Rutter, M., 54–6, 63

St Augustine, 81, 90

Schonell, F., *Backwardness in the Basic Subjects*, 179, 186

schools, special, 96, 113–16, 292–3, 327, 328; argument for, 300–4, 326; closures, 320, 328; heads of, 274; in N. Ireland, 340–3, 348

Scotland, 154, 292, 340

Scottish Education Department, 154

Séguin, E., 85–6, 91

Simon, Victor, 97–8

Snowdon Working Party on Integration of the Disabled, 211

Spastics Society, 208–9

Special Education Bill *1981*, 314, 319–21

speech defects, 130–1, 133

Spens Report, 307, 312

spina bifida, 27–31, 33, 36, 296; in N. Ireland, 336–7

Stern, William, 98

Sweden, 327

Tansley, A.E., 262–3, 277

teachers, 95, 124–35, 161, 167–8, 268–70, 276; accountability, 309–10; of deaf, 422–6; peripatetic, 137, 141, 327; remedial, 184–5; and researchers, 419, 425, 429, 430–2; training, 109, 143, 152; US specialists and, 383–4, 393–4

team-teaching, 139, 151

Terman, Lewis, 98

Thomas Report, 209, 210, 224

toxicology, behavioural, 53

Tredgold, A., 87, 91

truancy, 191–2

Underwood Committee, 102, 103, 118

United States, 13–24; birth defects in, 64–5; Education for All Handicapped Children Act *1975*, 359–77; legislation on special education, 227, 327, 359–97; preschool programmes, 353–7; Vocational Rehabilitation Act *1973*, 375; universities, PH provision, 213–17

Vernon Committee, 137, 152

visual handicap, 2–12, 99, 137–52; Resource Area, 136–52

voluntary associations, 94, 95, 100, 208–9

Vygotsky, L. S., 414–15, 416

Warnock Committee, 212, 219,
223–4, 347; integration and,
288, 290, 292; multi-
professional assessment and,
261, 265–7, 272

Wood Committee, 88, 98–9, 101,
262

You and Your Baby Report
(DHSS, N. Ireland), 336–7